Securities Dispute Resolution in China

SANZHU ZHU
University of London, UK

LONDON AND NEW YORK

First published 2007 by Ashgate Publishing

Reissued 2018 by Routledge
2 Park Square, Milton Park, Abingdon, Oxon, OX14 4RN
711 Third Avenue, New York, NY 10017, USA

Routledge is an imprint of the Taylor & Francis Group, an informa business

First issued in paperback 2018

A Library of Congress record exists under LC control number: 2007013127

Notice:
Product or corporate names may be trademarks or registered trademarks, and are used only for identification and explanation without intent to infringe.

Publisher's Note
The publisher has gone to great lengths to ensure the quality of this reprint but points out that some imperfections in the original copies may be apparent.

Disclaimer
The publisher has made every effort to trace copyright holders and welcomes correspondence from those they have been unable to contact.

ISBN 13: 978-0-815-39693-2 (hbk)
ISBN 13: 978-1-138-62048-3 (pbk)
ISBN 13: 978-1-351-14960-0 (ebk)

SECURITIES DISPUTE RESOLUTION IN CHINA

For my wife Mei Hong
and
In loving memory of my grandmother and my parents

Contents

List of Laws and Regulations

Laws and Statutory Decisions

1979 Chinese–Foreign Equity Joint Venture Law
(adopted by the National People's Congress on, and effective from, 1 July 1979)

1979 Criminal Law
(adopted by the National People's Congress on 1 July 1979, revised on 14 March 1997)

1979 Criminal Procedure Law
(adopted by the National People's Congress on, effective as of 1 January 1980, revised on 17 March 1996, effective as of 1 January 1997)

1981 Economic Contract Law
(adopted by the National People's Congress on 13 December 1981, effective as of 1 July 1982, revised on, and effective from, 2 September 1993)

1982 Civil Procedure Law (for Trial Implementation)
(adopted by the Standing Committee of the National People's Congress on 8 March 1982, effective as of 1 October 1982)

1982 Constitution
(adopted by the National People's Congress on, and effective from, 4 December 1982, revised in 1988, 1993, 1999 and 2004)

1983 People's Court Organization Law
(adopted by the National People's Congress on 1 July 1979, revised on 2 September 1983 and on 31 October 2006, effective as 1 January 2007)

1985 Economic Contract Law Involving Foreign Parties
(adopted by the Standing Committee of the National People's Congress on 21 March 1985, effective as of 1 July 1985)

1986 Decision on China's Joining the Convention on the Recognition and Enforcement of Foreign Arbitral Awards
(adopted by the Standing Committee of the National People's Congress on 2 December 1986)

1986 General Principles of Civil Law
(adopted by the National People's Congress on 12 April 1986, effective as of 1 January 1987)

1987 Technology Contract Law
(adopted by the Standing Committee of the National People's Congress on 23 June 1987, effective as of 1 November 1987)

1989 Administrative Procedure Law
(adopted by the Standing Committee of the National People's Congress on 4 April 1989, effective as of 1 October 1990)

1991 Civil Procedure Law
(adopted by the National People's Congress on, and effective from, 9 April 1991)

1993 Company Law
(adopted by the Standing Committee of the National People's Congress on 29 December 1993, effective as of 1 July 1994, revised on 25 December 1999 and 27 October 2005, effective as of 1 June 2006)

1993 Economic Contract Law
(adopted by the National People's Congress on 13 December 1981, revised on, and effective from, 2 September 1993)

1993 Product Quality Law
(adopted by the Standing Committee of the National People's Congress on 22 February 1993, effective as of 1 September 1993, revised on 8 July 2000, effective as of 1 September 2000)

1994 Arbitration Law
(adopted by the Standing Committee of the National People's Congress on 31 August 1994, effective as of 1 September 1995)

1995 Negotiable Instrument Law
(adopted by the Standing Committee of the National People's Congress on 10 May 1995, effective as of 1 January 1996, revised on 28 August 2004)

1995 Security Law
(adopted by the Standing Committee of the National People's Congress on 30 June 1995, effective as of 1 October 1995)

1996 Administrative Penalty Law
(adopted by the National People's Congress on 17 March 1996, effective as of 1 October 1996)

1996 Criminal Procedure Law
(adopted by the National People's Congress on 17 March 1996, effective as of 1 January 1997)

1997 Criminal Law
(adopted by the National People's Congress on 14 March 1997, effective as of October 1, 1997, revised in 1999, August 2001, December 2001, 2002, 2005, and 2006)

1998 Securities Law
(adopted by the Standing Committee of the National People's Congress on 29 December 1998, effective as of 1 July 1999)

1999 Administrative Review Law
(adopted by the Standing Committee of the National People's Congress on 29 April 1999, effective as of 1 October 1999)

1999 Contract Law
(adopted by the National People's Congress on 15 March 1999, effective as of 1 October 1999)

2000 Legislation Law
(adopted by the National People's Congress on 15 March 2000, effective as of 1 January 2000)

2003 Securities Investment Fund Law
(adopted by the Standing Committee of National People's Congress on 28 October 2003, effective as of 1 June 2004)

2005 Company Law
(adopted by the Standing Committee of the National People's Congress on 27 October 2005, effective as of 1 June 2006)

2005 Securities Law
(adopted by the Standing Committee of the National People's Congress on 27 October 2005, effective as of 1 January 2006)

Administrative Regulations and Regulatory Rules

1981 Government Bond Regulations
(promulgated by the State Council on 28 January 1981)

1984 Notice on Finance Departments May Not Provide Guarantee for Economic Contracts
(issued by the Ministry of Finance on 31 December 1984)

1986 Government Bond Regulations
   (promulgated by the State Council on 23 November 1985)

1987 Provisional Regulations on the Administration of Enterprise Bonds
   (promulgated by the State Council on 27 March 1987)

1988 Implementing Plan for Trial of Opening up Government Bonds Transfer Market
   (approved by the State Council and issued jointly by the People's Bank of China and the Ministry of Finance on 28 March 1988)

1988 Notice on Reiteration of Finance Departments May Not Provide Guarantee for Economic Contracts
   (issued by the Ministry of Finance on 20 November 1988)

1990 Circular of the Ministry of Finance, the People's Bank of China, the State Bureau of Industry and Commerce, and the Ministry of Public Security on Crackdown on Illegal Government Bond Trading
   (issued on 22 May 1990)

1990 Provisional Measures for the Administration of Inter-regional Securities Trading
   (issued by a notice of the People's Bank of China on 19 October 1990)

1991 Measures on the Administration of Shanghai Special *Renminbi* Shares
   (issued by the People's Bank of China and the Shanghai Municipal People's Government on, and effective as of, 22 November 1991)

1992 Government Bond Regulations
   (promulgated by the State Council on 18 November 1992)

1992 Opinion on Standardization of Company Limited by Shares
   (issued by the State Commission for Economic Reform on 15 May 1992)

1992 Opinion on Standardization of Limited Liability Company
   (issued by the State Commission for Economic Reform on 15 May 1992)

1993 Circular of the General Office of the State Council on Strictly Prohibition of Administrative Organs from Providing Guaranty for Economic Activities
   (issued on 23 February 1993)

1993 Circular of the State Administration of Foreign Exchange on Strengthening Foreign Exchange (Futures) Trading
   (issued by the State Administration of Foreign Exchange on 21 April 1993)

1993 Circular of the State Council on Firmly Stopping Blind Development of the Futures Market
(promulgated by the State Council on 14 November 1993)

1993 Notice of the General Office of the State Council on Circulating the Report of the Ministry of Finance, the State Planning Commission and the People's Bank of China on the Work of Issuance of Government Bonds in 1993
(issued on 27 February 1993)

1993 Provisional Measures on the Administration of Registration of Futures Broker Firms
(issued by the State Administration for Industry and Commerce on 28 April 1993)

1993 Provisional Measures on the Prohibition of Securities Frauds
(approved by the State Council on 15 August 1993, issued by the State Council Securities Committee on, and effective from, 2 September 1993)

1993 Provisional Regulations on the Administration of Issuing and Trading of Shares
(promulgated by the State Council on 22 April 1993)

1993 Regulations on the Administration of Enterprise Bonds
(promulgated by the State Council on 2 August 1993)

1993 Trial Measures for the Administration of Foreign Exchange Futures Business
(issued by the State Administration of Foreign Exchange on 9 June 1993 upon an approval by the People's Bank of China)

1994 Circular of Asking for Instructions on Several Opinions of the State Council Securities Committee on Firmly Stopping Blind Development of the Futures Market
(issued by the General Office of the State Council on 16 May 1994)

1994 Circular of the China Securities Regulatory Commission on Improvement of Examination and Verification System to Prevent Shares from Being Stolen and Sold
(issued by the China Securities Regulatory Commission on 14 June 1994)

1994 Circular on Firmly Curb Acts of Selling Short Government Bonds
(issued jointly by the Ministry of Finance, the People's Bank of China and the China Securities Regulatory Commission on 20 May 1994)

1994 Circular on the Issue of Arbitration Agreement for Securities Agreement
(issued by the China Securities Regulatory Commission on 11 October 1994)

1994 Notice of the State Council General Office for Circulating the Opinion of the People's Bank of China and the State Planning Commission on Dealing With the Problem of Default of Repayment Due of Enterprise Bonds
(issued on 22 September 1994)

1994 Provisional Measures for the Administration of Credit Funds
(issued by the People's Bank of China on 15 February 1994)

1994 Provisional Measures on the Administration of Personnel Working in Futures Business Organizations
(issued by the China Securities Regulatory Commission on 7 November 1994)

1995 Circular on Further Control Risks of Futures Market and Sternly Strike Market Manipulation
(issued by the China Securities Regulatory Commission 24 October 1995)

1995 Circular on Reiteration of Relevant Issues Concerning Further Standardization of Securities Repurchase Business
(issued jointly by the People's Bank of China, the Ministry of Finance and the China Securities Regulatory Commission on 8 August 1995)

1995 Circular on Seriously Clear off Securities Repurchase Debts Becoming Due
(issued jointly by the People's Bank of China, the Ministry of Finance and the China Securities Regulatory Commission on 27 October 1995)

1995 Circular on Suspension of Government Bond Futures Trading
(issued jointly by the China Securities Regulatory Commission and Ministry of Finance on 23 February 1995)

1995 Provisional Measures on the Administration of Government Bond Futures Trading
(issued by the China Securities Regulatory Commission and the Ministry of Finance on 23 February 1995)

1995 Urgent Circular on Suspension of Trials of Government Bond Futures Trading
(issued by the China Securities Regulatory Commission on 17 May 1995)

1996 Circular on Several Issues Which Need to be Made Clear in Implementation of the Arbitration Law of the People's Republic of China
(issued by the General Office of the State Council on 8 June 1996)

1996 Circular of the State Council
(Original full title: Circular of the State Council Approving and Circulating the People's Bank of China's Request for Instruction on Further Improving the Work of Clearing off Securities Repurchase Debts)
> *(issued on 25 June 1996)*

1997 Circular of the People's Bank of China and the Ministry of Finance on Reorganization and Standardization of Finance Securities Organizations
> *(issued on 5 June 1997)*

1997 Circular of the People's Bank of China on Prohibition of Banking Funds from Flowing into Stock Market in Violation of Regulation
> *(issued by the People's Bank of China on 6 June 1997)*

1997 People's Bank of China's Circular on All Commercial Banks to Stop Trading Securities and Securities Repurchases at Securities Exchanges
> *(issued by the People's Bank of China on 5 June 1997)*

1997 Provisional Measures on the Administration of Securities Investment Funds
> *(approved by the State Council on 5 November 1997 and issued by the Securities Committee of the State Council on, and effective as of, 14 November 1997)*

1997 Provisional Regulations on Bond Repurchase Business among Banks
> *(issued by the People's Bank of China on, and effective as of, 5 June 1997)*

1997 Strict Prohibition of Speculation in Shares by State-owned Enterprises and Listed Companies
> *(issued by the State Council Securities Committee, in conjunction with other government authorities, on 21 May 1997)*

1998 Circular of the State Council on Further Consolidation and Standardization of the Futures Market
> *(issued by the State Council on 1 August 1998)*

1998 Procedures on the Administration of Issuance and Transfer of Enterprise Bonds
> *(issued by the People's Bank of China on 9 April 1998 and repealed by the People's Bank of China on 17 August 2000)*

1999 Circular on Distributing "Administrative Provisions on Fund Management Companies Entering into Inter-bank Market" and "Administrative Provisions on Securities Companies Entering into Inter-bank Market"
> *(issued by the People's Bank of China on 19 August 1999)*

1999 Circular on Relevant Issues about Application for Offshore Futures Business
> *(issued by the China Securities Regulatory Commission on 15 October 1999)*

1999 Measures on the Administration of Futures Broker Firms
(issued by the China Securities Regulatory Commission on 31 August 1999, as amended on 17 May 2002 and effective as of 1 July 2002)

1999 Measures on the Administration of Futures Exchanges
(issued by the China Securities Regulatory Commission on 31 August 1999, as amended on 17 May 2002 and effective as of 1 July 2002)

1999 Measures on the Administration of Qualifications for Appointment of Senior Management Personnel of Futures Broker Firms
(issued by the China Securities Regulatory Commission on 31 August 1999, as amended on, and effective as of, 23 January 2002)

1999 Measures on the Administration of Qualifications for Personnel Engaging in Futures Business
(issued by the China Securities Regulatory Commission on 31 August 1999, as amended on, and effective as of, 23 January 2002)

1999 Notice of the State Development and Planning Commission and the People's Bank of China on Relevant Issues Concerning Further Dealing Well with the Work of Enterprise Bonds Repayment
(issued on 24 March 1999)

1999 Provisional Regulations on the Administration of Futures Trading
(promulgated by the State Council on 2 June 1999, effective as of 1 September 1999)

2000 Measures for the Administration of Bond Trading in the National Inter-Bank Bond Market
(issued by the People's Bank of China on 30 April 2000)

2000 Provisional Measures on the Administration of the Members of the China Futures Association
(issued by China Futures Association on 29 December 2000)

2001 Administrative Measures on Offshore Futures Hedging Business by State-owned Enterprises
(issued by the China Securities Regulatory Commission jointly with other four government departments on 24 May 2001)

2001 Circular of the China Securities Regulatory Commission on the Issue of Guaranty by Securities Companies
(issued by the China Securities Regulatory Commission on 24 April 2001)

2001 Circular of Several Opinions of the China Securities Regulatory Commission on Implementation of "The Measures on the Administration of Client Transaction Clearing Funds"
  (issued on 8 October 2001)

2001 Measures on the Administration of Securities Exchanges
  (approved by the State Council on 30 November 1997 and issued by the Securities Committee of the State Council on 10 December 1997, revised by the China Securities Regulatory Commission on 12 December 2001)

2001 Measures on the Administration of Client Transaction Clearing Funds
  (issued by the China Securities Regulatory Commission on 16 May 2001, effective as 1 January 2002)

2002 Circular of the China Securities Regulatory Commission, the State Commission for Development and Planning and State Bureau of Taxation on Adjustment of Commissions Charged for Securities Trading
  (issued on April 4, 2002, and effective from May 1, 2002)

2002 Code of Corporate Governance for Listed Companies in China
The Code of Corporate Governance for Listed Companies in China
  (issued jointly by the China Securities Regulatory Commission and the State Economic and Trade Commission on, and effective as of, 7 January 2002)

2002 Measures on the Administration of Futures Broker Firms
  (issued by the China Securities Regulatory Commission on 17 May 2002 and effective as of 1 July 2002)

2002 Measures on the Administration of Futures Exchanges
  (issued by the China Securities Regulatory Commission on 17 May 2002 and effective as of 1 July 2002, replaced the 1999 Measures on the Administration of Futures Exchanges)

2004 Administrative Regulations on Bond Cut-off-purchase Repurchase Business at National Inter-bank Bond Market
  (issued by the People's Bank of China on 12 April 2004)

2004 Circular of the China Securities Regulatory Commission on Further Strengthening Supervision and Regulation of Client Transaction Clearing Funds of Securities Company
  (issued on 12 October 2004)

2004 Nine-point Opinion of the State Council
(Original full title: Several Opinions of the State Council on Promoting the Reform, Opening-up and Steady Development of China's Capital Market)
  (announced on 31 January 2004)

2004 Securities and Futures Disputes Arbitration Circular
(Original full title: Circular on To Do Well in Accordance With Law the Work of
Arbitration of Securities and Futures Contract Disputes)
>*(issued jointly by the Legal Affair Office of the State Council and the China Securities Regulatory Commission on 18 January 2004)*

2005 Administrative Measures on the Securities Investor Protection Fund
>*(issued by the China Securities Regulatory Commission on June 2005, effective as of 1 July 2005)*

2005 Circular of the Ministry of Finance and the State Bureau of Taxation on Adjustment of Securities Trading Stamp Duties
>*(issued on, and effective from, January 24, 2005)*

2005 Circular of the Securities Association of China on Implementation of "the Provisional Regulations on the Administration of Membership System Securities Consultant Business" and Strengthen Self Regulation
>*(issued by the Securities Association of China on 29 December 2005)*

2005 Provisions on the Administration of Bond Futures Trading on National Interbank Bond Market
>*(issued by People's Bank of China on 11 May, effective as of 15 June, 2005)*

2006 Implementing Rules of the Shenzhen Stock Exchange on Bond and Bond Repurchase Trading
>*(issued by the Shenzhen Stock Exchange on 20 September 2006 and effective as of 9 October 2006)*

2006 Provisional Regulations on the Administration of Membership System Securities Consultant Business
>*(issued by the China Securities Regulatory Commission on 12 December 2005 and effective as of 1 January 2006)*

Regulations and Rules by Local Authorities

1989 Detailed Rules of the Heilongjiang Province to Implement the Provisional Regulations on the Administration of Enterprise Bonds
>*(promulgated on 4 December 1989)*

1991 Provisional Measures of the Shenzhen Special Economic Zone on the Administration of Issuing and Trading of Shares
>*(promulgated by the Shenzhen special economic zone people's government on 15 June 1991)*

1994 Regulations on the Administration of Shanghai Futures Market
   (promulgated by the Shanghai government on 5 December 1994)

2000 Notice of Shanxi Province People's Government on Further Strengthening the
Work of Repayment of Enterprise Bonds
   (issued on 12 May 2000)

List of Judicial Interpretations and Provisions

1988 Opinion (for Trial Use) of the Supreme People's Court on Questions Concerning the Implementation of "the General Principles of Civil Law of the People's Republic of China"
> *(adopted by the Judicial Committee of the Supreme People's Court on 26 January 1988 and promulgated on 2 April 1988)*

1992 Opinion of the Supreme People's Court on Questions Concerning the Implementation of the Civil Procedure Law of the People's Republic of China
> *(adopted by the Judicial Committee of the Supreme People's Court on 14 July 1992)*

1994 Provisions of the Supreme People's Court on Several Issues Concerning Guaranty in Adjudicating Disputes Cases Involving Economic Contracts
> *(issued on 15 April 1994)*

1994 Reply of the Economic Division Court of the Supreme People's Court on Whether Financial Institutions Acting as Agents for Issuance of Enterprise Bonds Should bear liability for the Debt of Enterprise Bond Issuers
> *(replied on 29 April 1994)*

1995 SPC Futures Judicial Guidelines
(Original full title: The Notice of the Supreme People's Court on Circulating Minutes of the Symposium of the Supreme People's Court on Adjudication of Cases of Futures Disputes)
> *(issued on 27 October 1995)*

1996 Reply of the Supreme People's Court on the Issue of How to Determine the Place of Performance of Securities Repurchase Contracts
> *(replied on 4 July 1996)*

1996 Reply of the Supreme People's Court to the Shanghai High People's Court on Whether the People's Court Can Accept and Deal With Disputes Arising from Issuing or Trading of Shares between Securities Firms and between Securities Firms and Stock Exchanges
> *(replied on 8 December 1996)*

1996 SPC Securities Repurchase Judicial Guidelines
(Original full title: The Summary of the Symposium on Adjudication of Securities Repurchase Dispute Cases)
(issued by the Supreme People's Court on 29 November 1996)

1997 Circular of the Supreme People's Court on Freezing and Transferring Funds of Settlement Accounts of Securities or Futures Exchanges, Securities Registration and Settlement Organizations, Securities Business or Futures Brokerage Institutions
(issued on 2 December 1997)

1998 Circular of the Supreme People's Court on Stopping Hearing and Enforcing Securities Repurchase Economic Dispute Cases That Have Been Compiled into National Debt Clearance Chain among Securities Repurchase Participants
(issued on 18 December 1998)

1998 Provisions of the Supreme People's Court on Several Issues in Adjudicating Economic Dispute Cases Involving Economic Crime Suspicion
(issued on 21 April 1998, effective as of 29 April 1998)

2000 Circular of the Supreme People's Court on Resuming Accepting, Hearing and Enforcing Securities Repurchase Economic Dispute Cases That Have Been Compiled into National Debt Clearance Chain among Securities Repurchase Participants
(issued on 26 July 2000)

2000 Circular of the Supreme People's Court on Several Issues to Which Attention Should Be Given in Adjudicating and Enforcing Commercial Cases Involving Foreign Elements
(issued on 17 April 2000)

2000 Interpretations of the Supreme People's Court on Several Issues Concerning Application of the Security Law of the People's Republic of China
(issued on 8 December 2000, effective as of 13 December 2000)

2000 Provisions of the Supreme People's Court on the Issue of Scope of Civil Proceedings Attached to Criminal Proceedings
(issued on 13 December 2000)

2001 Circular of the Supreme People's Court on the Issue of Statute Limitation in Connection With Remaining Credits and Debts after National Coordinated Clearance among Securities Repurchase Participants
(issued on 20 January 2001)

2001 Notice of the Supreme People's Court on Temporary Refusal of Filings of Securities-Related Civil Compensation Cases
(issued on 21 September 2001)

2001 Provisions of the Supreme People's Court on Several Issues of Freezing, Auctioning State-owned Shares and Public Legal Person Shares of Listed Companies
(adopted by the Judicial Committee of the Supreme People's Court on 28 August 2001 and Promulgated on 21 September 2001, effective as of 30 September 2001)

2001 Several Provisions of the Supreme People's Court on Evidence in Civil Litigation
(adopted by the Judicial Committee of the Supreme People's Court on 6 December 2001 and promulgated on 21 December 2001, effective as of 1 April 2002)

2002 Notice of the Supreme People's Court on Relevant Issues of Filing of Civil Tort Dispute Cases Arising From False Statement on the Securities Market
(issued on 15 January 2002)

2002 Provisions of the Supreme People's Court on Several Issues Concerning Jurisdiction of Litigation of Civil and Commercial Cases Involving Foreign Elements
(adopted by the Judicial Committee of the Supreme People's Court on 25 December 2001 and promulgated on 25 February 2002, effective as of 1 March 2002)

2003 Rules of the SPC
(Original full title: Several Provisions of the Supreme People's Court on Hearing Civil Compensation Cases Arising from False Statement on the Securities Market)
(adopted by the Judicial Committee of the Supreme People's Court on 26 December 2002, and promulgated on 9 January 2003, effective as of 1 February 2003)

2003 SPC Futures Judicial Provisions
(Original full title: The Provisions of the Supreme People's Court on Several Issues Concerning Adjudication of Cases of Futures Disputes)
(adopted by the Judicial Committee of the Supreme People's Court on 16 May 2003, effective as of 1 July 2003)

2004 Circular of the Supreme People's Court on Relevant Issues Concerning Freeze and Transfer of Securities Transaction Clearing Funds
(issued on 9 November 2004. It superseded the Circular of the Supreme People's Court on the Issues Concerning Freeze and Transfer Clearing Account Funds of Securities or Futures Exchanges, Securities Registration and Settlement Organization, Securities Companies or Futures Firms issued on 2 December 1997)

2005 People's Court Second Five-Year Reform Outlines (2004–2008)
(announced by the Supreme People's Court on 26 October 2005)

2005 Provisions of the Supreme People's Court on the Issue of Jurisdiction Over and Acceptance of Lawsuits Related to Regulatory Function of Securities Exchanges
(adopted by the Judicial Committee of the Supreme People's Court on 11 November 2004 and promulgated on 25 January 2005, effective as of 31 January 2005)

2005 Provisions of the Supreme People's Court on the People's Court Enforcement of Property with Mortgage
(adopted by the Judicial Committee of the Supreme People's Court on 14 November 2005 and promulgated on 14 December 2005, effective as of 21 December 2005)

2006 Circular of the Supreme People's Court on the Issue of Acceptance of Joint Action Cases by the People's Court
(issued on 30 December 2005, effective as of 1 January 2006)

2006 Provisions of the Supreme People's Court on Several Time Limits in the Handling of Enforcement Cases by the People's Courts
(issued on 31 December 2006, effective as of 1 January 2007)

2006 Several Provisions of the Supreme People's Court on Service of Judicial Documents in Civil or Commercial Cases Involving Foreign Elements
(adopted by the Judicial Committee of the Supreme People's Court on 17 July 2006 and promulgated on 10 August 2006, effective as of 22 August 2006)

Mediation and Arbitration Rules by the Supreme People's Court

1985 Reply of the Supreme People's Court on Which Local Court Should an Application for Enforcement of Arbitral Awards Be Put Forward
(issued on 17 January 1985)

1987 Circular of the Supreme People's Court on the Implementation of "the Convention on the Recognition and Enforcement of Foreign Arbitral Awards" China Has Acceded To
(issued on 10 October 1987)

1993 Reply of the Supreme People's Court on Whether the People's Court Can Retry a Case in Which the Civil Mediation Agreement Definitely Has Error and the Party Has Not Applied for Retrial
(replied on 8 March 1993)

1995 Circular of the Supreme People's Court on Conscientiously Implement Arbitration Law and Enforce Arbitral Awards According to Law
(issued on 4 October 1995)

1997 Circular of the Supreme People's Court on Several Issues Concerning Implementation of "the Arbitration Law of the People's Republic of China"
(issued on 26 March 1997)

1998 Reply of the Supreme People's Court on Several Issues Concerning Determination of Validity of Arbitration Agreement
(adopted by the Judicial Committee of the Supreme People's Court on 21 October 1998, effective as of 5 November 1998)

2000 Supreme People's Court Arrangements between Inland and Hong Kong Special Administrative Region Concerning Mutual Enforcement of Arbitral Awards
(adopted by the Judicial Committee of the Supreme People's Court on 18 June 1999 and promulgated on 24 January 2000, effective as of 1 February 2000)

2004 Provisions of the Supreme People's Court on Several Issues about Civil Mediation Work of the People's Court
(adopted by the Judicial Committee of the Supreme People's Court on 18 April 2004 and promulgated on 16 September 2004, effective as of 1 November 2004)

2006 Interpretations of the Supreme People's Court on Several Issues Concerning Application of the Arbitration Law of the People's Republic of China
(adopted by the Judicial Committee of the Supreme People's Court on 26 December 2005 and promulgated on 23 August 2006, effective as of 8 September 2006)

Arbitration Rules of China International Economic and Trade Arbitration Commission

2003 Financial Dispute Arbitration Rules of China International Economic and Trade Arbitration Commission
(adopted by the China Council for the Promotion of International Trade and China Chamber of International Commerce on 4 April 2003 and effective as from 8 May 2003, revised on 17 March 2005, effective as of 1 May 2005)

2005 Arbitration Rules of China International Economic and Trade Arbitration Commission
(previously revised in 1988, 1994, 1995, 1998, 2000. The 2005 revision was adopted by the China Council for the Promotion of International Trade and China Chamber of International Commerce on 11 January 2005, effective as of 1 May 2005)

List of Cases

Anhui Securities Registration Company v Anhui Pengli Guomao Company Ltd. [1997]

> The Supreme People's Court Civil Judgment [1997] No. 214. *Selection of Financial Dispute Cases Heard by the Supreme People's Court (1996–1998)* (Zuigao Renmin Fayuan Shenli de Jinrong Jiufen Anli Xuanbian), compiled by the Economic Division Court of the Supreme People's Court (Beijing: China University of Politics and Law Press, 1999), pp. 532–540.

Business Center of Yunnan Provincial Branch of China Agriculture Bank v Shenzhen International Trust Investment Co. [2000]

> The Gazette of the Supreme People's Court of the People's Republic of China, Issue 5, 2004, pp. 8–13.

Chen Zhongyi v Tianyi Futures Brokerage Co. Ltd. [2003]

> Wu Qingbao et al. (eds), *Principles and Precedents of Futures Litigation (Qihuo Susong Yuanli Yu Panli)* (Beijing: The People's Court Publishing House, 2005), pp. 374–380.

Cheng Yonggang v Huaxia Securities Co. Ltd. [1994]

> *Selection of Analysis of Adjudicated Cases (Shenpan Anli Xuanxi)*, edited by Beijing Haidian District People's Court (Beijing: China Political and Law University Press, 1997), pp. 289–293.

Chengdu Hongguang Industrial Shareholding Company Case [1998]

> Daniel M. Anderson, Taking Stock in China: Company Disclosure and Information in China's Stock Markets, *Georgetown Law Journal*, Vol. 88, 1999–2000, pp. 1931–1933.

China Agriculture Bank Chengdu City Jingjiang Branch v Guotai Jun'an Securities Company Chengdu Renmin Zhonglu Business Center [2001]

> Zhang Jinhan (ed.), *Application of Law and Adjudication in Commercial Cases (Shangshi Anjian Falu Shiyong Yu Shenpan)* (Beijing: People's Publishing House, 2003), pp. 501–506.

China Great Wall Trust Investment Company v Beijing Hemu Jingmao Company [1999]

> *Studies of Judicial Decisions Related to Financial Disputes (Jingrong Shenpan Anli Yanjiu)* (Vol. 2001), edited by Economic Division Court of Beijing High People's Court (Beijing: Law Publishing House, 2001), pp. 386–392.

China Human Rights Development Fund v Beijing Chang'an Branch of China Construction Bank [1999]

> *Studies of Judicial Decisions Related to Financial Disputes (Jingrong Shenpan Anli Yanjiu)* (Vol. 2001), edited by Economic Division Court of Beijing High People's Court (Beijing: Law Publishing House, 2001), pp. 380–385.

China Life Insurance Company Chengdu Branch v Sichuan Hualong Investment Consultant Co. Ltd. [2004]

> The Gazette of the Supreme People's Court of the People's Republic of China, Issue 8, 2005, pp. 14–23.

China XX Bank v XX Securities Co. Ltd. [2001]

> The Arbitral Award (8 November 2001) *Selection of China International Economic and Trade Arbitration Awards (1995–2002) (Financial, Real Estate and Other Disputes Volume) (Zhongguo Guoji Jingji Maoyi Zhongcai Caijueshu Xuanbian (1995–2002) (Jinrong, Fangdichan Ji Qita Zhengyi Juan)*, compiled by the China International Economic and Trade Arbitration Commission (Beijing: Law Publishing House, 2003), pp. 404–415.

Daqing Lianyi Case [2002]

> Ma Shiling, *The First Joint Action Case Was Filed, Daqing Lian Case Compensation Over Ten Million Yuan (Gongtong Susong Diyi An Jian, Daqing Lianyi An Suopei Yu Qianwan)*, 11 February 2003, http://www.chinacourt.org.

Ding Wei v Zhengzhou Commodity Exchange [1997]

> Jiang, Bixin (ed.) *Understanding and Application of "the 2003 Provisions of the Supreme People's Court on Several Issues Concerning Adjudication of Cases of Futures Disputes" ("Zuigao Renmin Fayuan Guanyu Shenli Qihuo Jiufen Anjian Ruogan Wenti de Guiding" de Lijie Yu Shiyong)*, compiled by the Second Division Court of the Supreme People's Court (Beijing: The People's Court Publishing House, 2003), pp. 249–261.

Dongfang Dianzi Case [2003]

> *Jinan Shareholders Sue Dongfang Dianzi, Claiming Figure Reaches Over 3 Million Yuan (Jinan Gumin Zhuanggao Dongfang Dianzi, Suopei Jin E Da 300 Yu Wanyuan)*, 10 July 2003, http://www.chinacourt.org.

Feng Cuiyu v Dangyang Securities Business Center of Sanxia Securities Co. Ltd. [2000]

> *Essential Selection of Adjudicated Cases in China (Zhongguo Shenpan Anli Yaolan) (Civil Adjudicated Case Vol. 2001)*, edited by National Judges College and School of Law of the People's University of China (Beijing: China People's University Press, 2002), pp. 259–262.

Government Bond Service Center of Anhui Province v Beijing Trust Investment Company of the Construction Bank [1995]

Wu Zhipan and Tang Jiemang (eds), Explanation and Analysis of Typical Cases of Financial Law, 1st Issue (Jinrong Fa Dianxing Anli Jiexi, Diyi Ji) (Beijing: China Finance Publishing House, 2000), pp. 195–202.

Government Bond Service Department of the Finance Bureau of Sanming City of Fujian Province v Jun'an Securities Limited Company [1997]
The Supreme People's Court Civil Judgment [1997] No. 190. *Selection of Financial Dispute Cases Heard by the Supreme People's Court (1996–1998)* (*Zuigao Renmin Fayuan Shenli de Jinrong Jiufen Anli Xuanbian*), compiled by the Economic Division Court of the Supreme People's Court (Beijing: China University of Political Science and Law Press, 1999), pp. 689–692.

Gu Junhao v Shanghai Dingxi Road Securities Business Center of Shanghai International Trust Investment Co. [1994]
Essential Selection of Adjudicated Cases in China (*Zhongguo Shenpan Anli Yaolan*) (*Commercial and Administrative Cases Vol. 2001*), edited by National Judges College and School of Law of the People's University of China (Beijing: China People's University Press, 2002), pp. 315–319.

Guangxia (Yinchuan) Industrial Limited Company Case [2003]
Yinchuan City Intermediate People's Court Formally Accepted Yinguangxia Civil Tort Compensation Case (*Yinchuanshi Zhongyuan Zhengshi Shouli Yinguangxia Minshi Qinquan Peichang An*), 1 August 2002, http://www.chinacourt.org.

Ha'erbin Finance Securities Co. v Shenzhen Securities Business Center of Yunnan Securities Co. Ltd. [1997]
Selection of Financial Dispute Cases Heard by the Supreme People's Court (1996–1998) (*Zuigao Renmin Fayuan Shenli de Jinrong Jiufen Anli Xuanbian*), compiled by the Economic Division Court of the Supreme People's Court (Beijing: China University of Political Science and Law Press, 1999), pp. 497–507.

Hainan Province Trust Investment Co. v Guangdong Overseas Chinese Trust Investment Co. [2001]
Series of Adjudicated Cases of the Supreme People's Court of the People's Republic of China (*Zhonghua Renmin Gongheguo Zuigao Renmin Fayuan Pan'an Daxi*) (*Civil and Commercial Vol. 2001*), Chief Editor Xiao Yang, compiled by the Second Division Court of Civil Court of the Supreme People's Court (Beijing: The People's Court Publishing House, 2003), pp. 82–85.

Hainan Zhongqing Jiye Development Center v Sichuan Pingyuan Industrial Development Co. [2000]
The Gazette of the Supreme People's Court of the People's Republic of China, Issue 4, 2005, pp. 25–30.

Henan Province International Investment Trust Company v Wuhan Jinda Industrial Company Limited by Shares [1997]

> The Supreme People's Court Civil Mediation Agreement [1997] No. 286. *Selection of Financial Dispute Cases Heard by the Supreme People's Court (1996–1998)* (Zuigao Renmin Fayuan Shenli de Jinrong Jiufen Anli Xuanbian), compiled by the Economic Division Court of the Supreme People's Court (Beijing: China University of Politics and Law Press, 1999), pp. 700–703.

Hewei v Changchun Investment Consultancy Center of Jilin Province Jinhui International Investment and Development Co. Ltd. and Jilin Branch of Bank of China [1995]

> Cai Xin et al. (eds) *Commentary on Typical Cases and Complement to Legal Deficiency* (*Dianxing Anli Pingshu Ji Falü Loudong Buchong*) (Beijing: The People's Court Publishing House, 2002), pp. 445–455.

Huafang v Shangrao Securities Department of Trust Compnay of Jiangxi Shangrao Industrial and Commercial Bank [1997]

> *Carefully Selected Cases of the People's Courts (Renmin Fayuan Anli Xuan Jingbianben), Vol. 1, 2001*, edited by China Law Application Research Institute the Supreme People's Court (Beijing: Xinhua Publishing Press, 2001), pp. 740–744.

Jiangxi Province Securities Company v Zhongfang Group Nanchang Property Development Company [2000]

> The Supreme People's Court Civil Judgment (2000) No. 35. Chinese and English translation of the case at www.isinolaw.com, Document Ref No. 76590-3219.

Jiangxi Securities Trading Center of Hainan Saige International Trust Investment Co. v Nanchang Branch of the Transportation Bank [2001]

> The Gazette of the Supreme People's Court of the People's Republic of China, Issue 8, 2004, pp. 21–23.

Jin Yancheng v Shanghai Securities Business Center of Jilin Trust Investment Company of Bank of China [1996]

> *Carefully Selected Cases of the People's Courts (Renmin Fayuan Anli Xuan Jingbianben), Vol. 1, 2001*, edited by China Law Application Research Institute the Supreme People's Court (Beijing: Xinhua Publishing Press, 2001), pp. 744–749.

Jinggang B Gu Case [2003]

> *Shenyang Intermediate People's Court Hear Jinggang B Share Case, KPMG Branch Office Becomes defendant* (*Shenyang Zhongyuan Shenli Jinggang B Gu An, Bimawei Fenzhi Jigou Cheng Beigao*), 11 February 2003, http://www.chinacourt.org.

Li Chuanxiong case [1993]
The Gazette of the Supreme People's Court of the People's Republic of China, Issue 4, 1993, pp. 164–165.

Li Erjiao v Zhang Shihui [1991]
The Gazette of the Supreme People's Court of the People's Republic of China, Issue 1, 1993, pp. 29–30.

Li Xiaoqin v Chengdu City Investment Trust Co. [1997]
The Supreme People's Court Civil Judgment [1996] No.161. *Selection of Financial Dispute Cases Heard by the Supreme People's Court (1996–1998)* (Zuigao Renmin Fayuan Shenli de Jinrong Jiufen Anli Xuanbian), compiled by the Economic Division Court of the Supreme People's Court (Beijing: China University of Politics and Law Press, 1999), pp. 541–547.

Liang Jintao v Baishigao Futures Consultant Services Co. Ltd. [1992]
Adjudicated Cases of Guangdong (*Guangdong Shenpan Anli*), edited by the research department of the Guangdong High People's Court (Guangdong: Guangdong People's Publishing House, 1997), pp. 346–349.

Ningbo City Rongcheng Trading Co. Ltd. v Ningbo City Xinyuan Futures Brokerage Co. Ltd. [1995]
Wu Zhipan and Tang Jiemang (eds), *Explanation and Analysis of Typical Cases of Financial Law, 1ˢᵗIssue (Jinrong Fa Dianxing Anli Jiexi, Diyi Ji)* (Beijing: China Finance Publishing House, 2000), pp. 251–258.

Qixiangtai Road Securities Trading Center of Tianjin City International Trust Investment Co. v Center Directly Under Changchun City Branch of Industrial and Commercial Bank of China [1997]
The Supreme People's Court Civil Ruling [1997] No. 6. *Selection of Financial Dispute Cases Heard by the Supreme People's Court (1996–1998)* (*Zuigao Renmin Fayuan Shenli de Jinrong Jiufen Anli Xuanbian*), compiled by the Economic Division Court of the Supreme People's Court (Beijing: China University of Political Science and Law Press, 1999), pp. 716–717.

Qixiangtai Road Securities Business Center of Tianjin City International Trust Investment Co. v Huiyuan Urban Credit Cooperative Society of Ezhou City of Hubei Province [1996]
Selection of Financial Dispute Cases Heard by the Supreme People's Court (1996–1998) (Zuigao Renmin Fayuan Shenli de Jinrong Jiufen Anli Xuanbian), compiled by the Economic Division Court of the Supreme People's Court (Beijing: China University of Political Science and Law Press, 1999), pp. 517–521.

Qixiangtai Road Securities Business Center of Tianjin City International Investment Trust Co. v Shanghai Shenyin Securities Co. [1996]

The Gazette of the Supreme People's Court of the People's Republic of China, Issue 2, 1997, pp. 67–68.

Qixiangtai Road Securities Business Center of Tianjing City International Trust Investment Co. v Xingfu Urban Credit Cooperative Society of Qianjiang City of Hubei Province [1996]
> *Selection of Financial Dispute Cases Heard by the Supreme People's Court (1996–1998) (Zuigao Renmin Fayuan Shenli de Jinrong Jiufen Anli Xuanbian)*, compiled by the Economic Division Court of the Supreme People's Court (Beijing: China University of Political Science and Law Press, 1999), pp. 522–526.

Qingyuan City Overseas Chinese Commodity Company v Qingyuan City Tongye International Futures Trading Firm [1993]
> Wu Zhipan and Tang Jiemang (eds), *Explanation and Analysis of Typical Cases of Financial Law, 1ˢᵗIssue (Jinrong Fa Dianxing Anli Jiexi, Diyi Ji)* (Beijing: China Finance Publishing House, 2000), pp. 241–250.

Rongcheng Business Center of Shanghai Finance Securities Co. v Shanghai Fu'ermen Co. [1997]
> *Carefully Selected Cases of the People's Courts (Renmin Fayuan Anli Xuan Jingbianben), Vol. 1, 2001*, edited by China Law Application Research Institute of the Supreme People's Court (Beijing: Xinhua Publishing Press, 2001), pp. 760–763.

The Second Government Bond Service Department of the Finance Bureau of the North District of Qingdao City v Securities Company of Linzhou City of Hunan Province [1996]
> Shao Tingjie et al. (eds), *Securities Law (Zhengquan Fa)* (Beijing: Law Publishing House, 1999), pp. 328–333.

Shanghai Foreign Trade Company v Shanghai Chemicals Commodity Exchange [1994]
> *Carefully Selected Cases of the People's Courts (Renmin Fayuan Anli Xuan Jingbianben), Vol. 1, 2001*, edited by China Law Application Research Institute of the Supreme People's Court (Beijing: Xinhua Publishing Press, 2001), pp. 763–769.

Shanghai Jiabao Industry (Group) Ltd. Case [2002]
> The First Securities Civil Compensation Case Concluded by Settlement with 800 yuan Compensation to the Plaintiff (Zhengquan Minshi Peichang Shouqi Jiean Hejie Yuangao Huopei 800 yuan), *Xinhua News Agency*, 15 November 2002, http://www.chinacourt.org.

Shanghai Jiabao Industry (Group) Ltd. Case [2003]
 ST Jiabao False Statement Case Concluded—16 Plaintiffs Got Economic
 Compensation 61773.66 yuan (ST Jiabao Xujia Chenshu An Jiean – 16 Wei
 Yuangao Huode Jingji Peichang Renminbi 61773.66 yuan) *Zhengquan Ribao
 (Securities Daily)*, 28 January 2003, http://www.zqrb.com.cn.

*Shengyang Northern Securities Company v Dalian City Trust Investment Company
of China Agriculture Bank* [1996]
 The Supreme People's Court Civil Judgment [1996] No. 273. *Selection of
 Financial Dispute Cases Heard by the Supreme People's Court (1996–1998)
 (Zuigao Renmin Fayuan Shenli de Jinrong Jiufen Anli Xuanbian)*, compiled by
 the Economic Division Court of the Supreme People's Court (Beijing: China
 University of Political Science and Law Press, 1999), pp. 548–554.

*Sichuan Province Securities Company v Sichuan Xinchao Computer Industrial
Group* [1996]
 The case in Chinese is at www.isinolaw.com, Document Ref. No. 76588-
 12972.

ST Hongguang Case [2002]
 ST Hongguang Claim Case Successfully Mediated (ST Hongguang Suopeian
 Tiaojie Chenggong), *Zhongguo Zhengquan Bao (China Securities Daily)*, 26
 November 2002, p. 1.

*Suzhou Foreign Trade Commodity Holding Co. v Zhejiang Huanya Industrial Co.
Ltd.* [1997]
 Jiang, Bixin (ed.) *Understanding and Application of "the 2003 Provisions of
 the Supreme People's Court on Several Issues Concerning Adjudication of
 Cases of Futures Disputes" ("Zuigao Renmin Fayuan Guanyu Shenli Qihuo
 Jiufen Anjian Ruogan Wenti de Guiding" de Lijie Yu Shiyong)*, compiled by the
 Second Division Court of the Supreme People's Court (Beijing: The People's
 Court Publishing House, 2003), pp. 263–295.

Taiyuan Financial Market v Taiyuan Liyuan Company [1996]
 The Supreme People's Court Civil Judgment [1996] No. 301. *Selection of
 Financial Dispute Cases Heard by the Supreme People's Court (1996–1998)
 (Zuigao Renmin Fayuan Shenli de Jinrong Jiufen Anli Xuanbian)*, compiled by
 the Economic Division Court of the Supreme People's Court (Beijing: China
 University of Political Science and Law Press, 1999), pp. 555–562.

*Tong XX v XX Securities Trading Business Center of Investment Trust Company of
Construction Bank* [1994]
 Li Guoguang et al. (eds), *A Complete Book of the PRC of Leading Adjudicated
 Cases – Economic Volume (Zhonhua Renmin Gongheguo Dianxing Shenpan
 Anli Quanshu – Jingjijuan)* (Beijing: China Democracy and Law Publishing
 House, 1998), pp. 501–503.

Abbreviations

CFA	China Futures Association
CFFEX	China Financial Futures Exchange
CIETAC	China International Economic and Trade Arbitration Commission
CSRC	China Securities Regulatory Commission
GPCL	General Principles of Civil Law (1986)
PBOC	People's Bank of China
PRC	People's Republic of China
QFII	Qualified Foreign Institutional Investors (scheme)
SAC	Securities Association of China
SCSC	Securities Committee of the State Council
SPC	Supreme People's Court
STAQ	Securities Trading Automatic Quotation
WTO	World Trade Organization

Preface

In the book *Securities Regulation in China*,[1] I studied the emergence and development since the 1980s of China's securities market and regulatory system, including the development brought about by the enactment of the 1998 Securities Law of the People's Republic of China. Since then China's securities market and securities law have changed significantly. One area of the changes is the beginning in 2002 of civil litigation in the people's courts in relation to compensation claims arising from false statements made on China's securities market. I examined this development in the article "Civil Litigation Arising from False Statements on China's Securities Market".[2] In the meantime, the idea of writing a book on securities dispute resolution in China interested me and I started the research on this book.

This book aims to offer a comprehensive and detailed study of the approach and manner in which cases involving securities are dealt with by the people's courts. The scope of the book covers a wide range of securities disputes, including disputes in the sale and purchase of securities, disputes between securities agents and investor clients, disputes involving securities repurchase contracts, disputes in share and bond issuing and trading, disputes involving trading of commodity and financial futures, and disputes arising from false statements made on the securities market. By studying the path of securities dispute resolution experienced by the people's courts in the wake of emergence of securities market in China, this book attempts to shed some light on the understanding of the process of securities dispute resolution in China.

I would like to thank Alison Kirk, senior commissioning editor, Maureen Mansell-Ward, desk editor, and the other editing staff at Ashgate Publishing. Special appreciation is owed to my colleague Professor Michael Palmer for his inspiration in the early stages of formulating the theme of this book. I owe much to the kind help offered by Judge Xiao Hongkai and Chen Zetong, the Shenzhen Intermediate People's Court; Dr Richard Wu, the Faculty of Law of the University of Hong Kong; Professor Liu Heng and Liu Xingli, and their student Chen Yongxi and other friends, the School of Law of the Sun Yat-Sen University; Dr. Kang Ming, the former Deputy Secretary General of the China International Economic and Trade Arbitration Commission; Jarmo Kotilaine, Control Risks Group; Li Jialu, Shenyin & Wanguo Securities Co., and my colleague Dr Fareda Banda. I should also like to thank the anonymous reviewers appointed by Ashgate Publishing for reviewing the book proposal and their comments and suggestions. I acknowledge the Lui Che Woo Law Library and the Main Library of the University of Hong Kong, and Hong Kong

---

1   Zhu Sanzhu, *Securities Regulation in China* (Ardsley, NY: Transnational Publishers, 2000).

2   Zhu Sanzhu, "Civil Litigation Arising from False Statements on China's Securities Market", *North Carolina Journal of International Law and Commercial Regulation*, Vol. 31, No. 2, Winter 2005, pp. 377–429.

public libraries, where I benefit from their research facilities and excellent services. I also wish to record my gratitude for the internal research grants from the Faculty of Law and Social Science and the Research Office, SOAS. I owe a special debt of gratitude to my family for their support.

Zhu Sanzhu
London, January 2007

Introduction

The reform of the economic system in China, which started in late 1978, led to an emergence of a securities market in China.[1] In the 1980s, the government and enterprises began to issue government and enterprise bonds.[2] Beginning in 1984, joint stock companies were established and shares were issued to the public.[3] In 1990 and 1991 respectively, the Shanghai and Shenzhen stock exchanges were established, which marked an important stage in the establishment of China's securities market. Apart from share and bond markets, the securities repurchase market, commodity and financial futures markets also emerged and their developments have undergone a tortuous path.[4] Since the late 1990s, the investment fund market has had a sustainable development, which is further promoted by the promulgation of the Securities Investment Fund Law in 2003.[5] Following on its development in the past two decades, China's securities market as a whole has become an integrated and important part of the market economy in China.[6]

The emergence and development of China's securities market since 1980s have been accompanied by an emergence of securities disputes of various kinds in the share issuing and trading market, government and enterprise bond markets, the securities repurchase market, and commodity and financial futures markets. These are new types of civil disputes not dealt with before by Chinese courts, the people's courts. Many of these disputes involve millions of yuan, which may threaten the stability of the securities market and financial system in China;[7] others may involve

---

1   See generally Mei Xia et al., *The Re-emerging Securities Market in China* (Westport: Ouorum Books, 1992), Zhu Sanzhu, *Securities Regulation in China* (Ardsley, NY: Transnational Publishers, 2000), Stephen Green, *The Development of China's Stock Market, 1984–2002: Equity Politics and Market Institutions* (London: Routledge, 2004).

2   For details, *see* following Chapter 3: Government and Enterprise Bond Markets.

3   See Zhu Sanzhu, at p. 6, *supra* note 1. *See* also following Chapter 2: The Share Issuing and Trading Market.

4   See following Chapter 4: The Securities Repurchase Market and Chapter 5: Commodity and Financial Futures Markets.

5   Securities Investment Fund Law of the People's Republic of China, adopted by the Standing Committee of National People's Congress on 28 October 2003 and effective as of 1 June 2004.

6   In 2006, there were about 1,400 companies listed on the Shanghai and Shenzhen stock exchanges, which is in contrast to the situation in early 1990s when there were only a dozen listed companies in the Shanghai and Shenzhen stock exchanges.

7   For example, disputes in the government bond repurchase market often involve a large sum of money, which poses a threat to the financial stability. *See* following Chapter 4: The Securities Repurchase Market, particularly the section "Default by Defendant Seller".

a large number of shareholders and investors, which could have a significant social impact and thus affect social stability.[8] Over the past two decades, especially in the early years of the emergence of China's securities market, the people's courts have been faced, for the first time in their history since 1949, with the difficulties and challenges presented by those cases involving securities and securities transactions.

China's securities market is a new market that emerged during the process of China's transformation from the previous socialist and planned economy to a capitalist market economy. The study of China's system of securities dispute resolution in this book is in this particular context. Discussions are given to the development of legal and regulatory rules connected with securities dispute resolution, as well as the procedural, evidential and enforcement rules developed and applied by the people's courts. On a more general level, the book seeks to assess critically and analytically the development of securities dispute resolution in China in the past two decades, including the role played by securities regulators and other relevant administrative authorities, and the development of alternative dispute resolution through arbitration and mediation of the disputes involving securities and securities transactions.

The disputes covered by the book are civil and commercial in nature. It is beyond the scope of this book to deal with comprehensively administrative cases and administrative litigation involving securities regulators on one side and individual or companies on the other side, which arise from regulatory matters such as approval by the securities regulators of issuing and listing shares by companies.[9] The disputes covered by the book are arranged according to the market. Thus, for example, the disputes in share and bond issuing and trading are discussed in the chapters of share issuing and trading market and government and enterprise bond markets respectively.

The first five chapters of this book are arranged according to the divisions of the market. Chapter 1, The Legal, Regulatory and Judicial Framework, provides an outline of basic laws, regulations and judicial procedures most relevant to securities disputes and their resolution, including general principles of civil law, law of agency, contract law, security law and regulation, some aspects of regulation of securities market, civil procedures, civil evidential rules and enforcement rules. Where necessary, the application of these laws, regulations and judicial procedural rules in securities dispute resolution are illustrated by relevant cases decided by the people's courts or arbitral institutions. This chapter paves the way for the understanding of the legal, regulatory or judicial issues discussed in the following chapters.

Chapters 2 to 5 deal with the disputes in their respective markets. Chapter 2, The Share Issuing and Trading Market, deals with the disputes in the share issuing and trading market, with a focus on the disputes between investor principals and

---

8   This is often the case in the civil litigation arising from false statements made by listed companies on stock market that affect a large number of shareholders and investors. *See* following Chapter 6: Civil Litigation Arising from False Statements Made on the Securities Market.

9   For this type of securities dispute, *see*, in the first instance, Gao Xiqing and Cheng Dagang (eds), *Textbook on Cases of Securities Law* (*Zhengquan Faxue Anli Jiaocheng*) (Beijing: Intellectual Property Publishing House, 2004).

securities company agents. Chapter 3, Government and Enterprise Bond Markets, deals with the disputes in government and enterprise bond markets, with a focus on spot trading, while Chapter 4, The Securities Repurchase Market, deals mainly with the disputes arsing from government bond repurchase contracts. Chapter 5, Commodity and Financial Futures Markets, deals with the disputes in the trading of commodity futures and financial futures. Given the limited space in each chapter, discussions shall focus on certain aspects of the disputes in each market, especially those aspects where typical types of disputes are found in that particular market.

Whereas in Chapters 2 to 5 the disputes discussed are basically related to contracts in one form or another, Chapter 6, Civil Litigation Arising from False Statements Made on China's Securities Market, deals with, as the title suggests, civil tort cases connected with false statements made on China's securities market. Between September 2001 and January 2003, the Supreme People's Court (SPC) issued three circulars instructing local people's courts on how to deal with civil compensation claims arsing from securities market fraud.[10] Chapter 6 examines critically these circulars and their implications, with a focus on the procedural rules prescribed by the third circular of the SPC, "Several Provisions of the Supreme People's Court on Hearing Civil Compensation Cases Arising from False Statement on the Securities Market".[11]

On the basis of the examination and discussion in the previous chapters of the disputes and their resolution in different markets, Chapter 7, Development of Securities Dispute Resolution in China, assesses, on a general level, the development of securities dispute resolution in China. The issues to be addressed in this chapter include, among others, the development of the law and regulations and the development of procedural rules and judicial practice, such as the changes brought about by the 2005 amendments to the 1998 Securities Law of the People's Republic of China and 1993 Company Law of the People's Republic of China;[12] the development of the practice of alternative dispute resolution in the area of securities disputes; and some general issues in a more wider social, economic and financial contexts, such as the issue of social stability, which influences the process of securities dispute resolution.

This study is based primarily on research and analysis of over a hundred cases decided by the people's courts at all levels. The sources of the case include, first, the cases published in the Gazette of the Supreme People's Court;[13] second, the cases and commentaries compiled or edited by the Supreme People's Court or its affiliated

---

10   *See* footnote 1 of Chapter 6.

11   *See* footnote 3 of Chapter 6.

12   The 2005 Securities Law of the People's Republic of China is adopted by the Standing Committee of the National People's Congress on 27 October 2005 and effective as of 1 June 2006. The 2005 Company Law of the People's Republic of China is adopted by the Standing Committee of the National People's Congress on 27 October 2005 and effective as of 1 June 2006.

13   The Gazette of the Supreme People's Court of the People's Republic of China (Zhonghua Renmin Gongheguo Zuigao Renmin Fayuan Gongbao), an official publication of the Supreme People's Court since January 1985.

institutions[14] or by the judges from the Supreme People's Court;[15] third, the cases and commentaries compiled or edited by local people's courts or judges;[16] fourth, the cases and commentaries compiled or edited by scholars and practitioners;[17] and fifth, the cases and commentaries from other sources, for example, the cases published on some academic and research websites.[18] The majority of these cases are in Chinese only and no English translation is available. References will be given where an English translation of the case is available. This applies to only a small group of the cases cited in the book, such as the cases published on bilingual websites.[19]

Discussion and analysis of cases decided by the people's courts helps to illustrate the application of the law, regulations and judicial interpretations by the people's courts in the process of securities dispute resolution, the way the people's courts approach issues presented by cases involving securities and securities transactions, and the manner in which securities disputes are resolved by the people's courts. Cases decided by the people's courts are not binding and they are not precedent in the Chinese legal system, but it is important to study the decisions of the people's courts in order to better understand the laws and their application. With this in mind, the cases discussed in this book are selected according to priority. That is, the cases decided by the Supreme People's Court are selected first, followed by the cases decided by the people's courts at provincial level. Where the cases decided by the people's courts at lower levels are illustrative and representative regarding certain issues, they are also selected. Throughout the book, the majority of cases are those decided by the people's courts. A limited number of cases decided through arbitration and mediation are considered in the context of the discussion of alternative dispute resolution.

The sources are mainly in Chinese, including books, articles and commentaries on cases written by Chinese judges, scholars and practitioners. In certain passages, references have been made to news reports, newspapers and relevant websites. Literature in English is a supplementary but important source, including articles and books written by western scholars and practitioners as well as by Chinese scholars and practitioners. As this study is not intended to be a comprehensive theoretical

---

14   *Carefully Selected Cases of the People's Courts (Renmin Fayuan Anli Xuan Jingbianben)*, Vol. 1, 2001, edited by China Law Application Research Institute of the Supreme People's Court (Beijing: Xinhua Publishing Press, 2001).

15   For example, Wu Qingbao et al. (eds), *Principles and Precedents of Futures Litigation (Qihuo Susong Yuanli Yu Panli)* (Beijing: The People's Court Publishing House, 2005). Wu Qingbao is a judge from the Supreme People's Court.

16   For example, *Studies of Judicial Decisions Related to Financial Disputes (Jingrong Shenpan Anli Yanjiu)* (Vol. 2001), edited by Economic Division Court of Beijing High People's Court (Beijing: Law Publishing House, 2001).

17   For example, Wu Zhipan and Tang Jiemang (eds), *Explanation and Analysis of Typical Cases of Financial Law, 1st Issue (Jinrong Fa Dianxing Anli Jiexi, Diyi Ji)* (Beijing: China Finance Publishing House, 2000). Professor Wu Zhipan is the director of Financial Law Research Center of Beijing University.

18   For example, www.lawinfochina.com and www.isinolaw.com.

19   For example, some of the cases published on www.isinolaw.com have both Chinese and English texts.

and comparative study of the system of securities dispute resolution in China, less attention has been given to theoretical issues and debates and limited comparisons have been made with other countries.[20] While the basic focus of the book is to look at the position of laws and regulations and their application by the people's courts in adjudicating securities cases, additional discussions and critical analysis are given where there are differing approaches between the people's courts in certain types of cases and debates on certain issues among judges, scholars and practitioners.

Understanding securities dispute resolution in China has to take into account relevant social, economic, financial and legal factors. In what way do the people's courts uphold the legal rights and interests prescribed by the law and regulations, while responding to changing government policies about the development of securities market, formulated on economic, financial, social or political grounds? In what way do the people's courts uphold the legitimate demands and means of individuals, companies and organisations to raise capital while punishing illegal financing activities in the securities market? In what way do the people's courts uphold the principle of freedom of contract and respect legal agreements between parties while supporting the government policies of strict control and scale-down of the securities market during certain periods of time? In what way do the people's courts protect the lawful rights and interests of market participants while maintaining social and financial stabilities? The book addresses these and other questions and issues, attempting to offer an in-depth understanding of China's system of securities dispute resolution.

It is anticipated that more and more foreign securities investments will come into China consequent to China's opening up of securities and financial markets in the post-WTO era.[21] It is important that legal and judicial reforms are continually carried out to improve the process of securities dispute resolution in post-WTO China. In what way could the principles of impartiality and independence be truly implemented by the people's courts in their handling of securities disputes? In what way could the recognition and enforcement by the people's courts of arbitral awards be improved so that arbitration as an alternative dispute resolution could become a more effective platform for securities dispute resolution, particularly when involving foreign parties? In what way could the procedural rules of the people's courts be developed and improved to accommodate a more efficient and effective system of securities dispute resolution that could face challenging questions and issues, including issues arsing from cross-border matters? This book discusses these issues and assesses the outlook of China's system of securities dispute resolution in the unique situation that is post-WTO China.

---

20 Comparisons are drawn with other countries where such comparisons are necessary. For example, some comparisons with class action in the United States are made in the context of discussion of joint action under the 1991 Civil Procedure Law of the People's Republic of China. *See* Chapter 6, "Forms of Action Available to Investors".

21 *See* generally Zhu Sanzhu "Implementing China's WTO Commitments in Chinese Financial Services Law", *The China Review*, Vol. 6, No. 2 (Fall 2006), pp. 3–33.

Chapter 1

The Legal, Regulatory and Judicial Framework

Introduction

The legal, regulatory and judicial framework for securities dispute resolution in China is part of China's post-1978 legal system, built during the process of China's economic and legal transformation.[1] The year 1979 witnessed the first wave of legislation of seven important laws.[2] This was followed by the enactment of the Constitution of the People's Republic of China in 1982.[3] In 1986, the General Principles of Civil Law of the People's Republic of China (hereinafter the 1986 GPCL) was enacted, which laid down the fundamental principles of civil and commercial law.[4] In 1988, the 1982 Constitution was amended for the first time, which, *inter alia*, paved way for the significant rise of private sectors in later years.[5] During the 1980s, the people's courts and other judicial institutions were restored and an active legal profession re-emerged;[6] civil, administrative and criminal procedure laws were enacted one after another.[7]

Moving into the 1990s, as China's economic reform was gaining momentum, China's legal reform was stepping up and a comprehensive legal system was

---

1 For China's legal reform generally, *see* Stanley Lubman (ed.), *China's Legal Reform* (Oxford: Oxford University Press, 1996); Chen Alber Hung-yee, *An Introduction to the Legal System of the People's Republic of China* (3rd edition), (Singapore, Malaysia, Hong Kong: Butterworths Asia, 2004); Stanley Lubman, *Bird in a Cage: Legal Reform in China after Mao* (Stanford: Stanford University Press, 1999).

2 The Criminal Procedure Law and the Chinese–Foreign Equity Joint Venture Law, among others.

3 The 1982 Constitution re-established the constitutional principles of the 1954 Constitution that were destroyed by the 1975 and 1978 Constitutions enacted during and shortly after the ten-year Cultural Revolution (1966–1976).

4 For the background of the enactment, *see* Edward J. Epstein, "The Evolution of China's General Principles of Civil Law", *American Journal of Comparative Law*, Vol. 34, 1986, pp. 705–713.

5 Article 11 was amended to the effect that the state permits the private sector of the economy to exist and develop within the limits prescribed by law and recognizes that the private sector of the economy is a complement to the socialist public economy.

6 For a discussion about the development of China's legal profession, see Zhu Sanzhu, "Reforming State Institutions: Privatizing the Lawyers' System", in *Governance in China*, edited by Jude Howell, Chapter 4, pp. 58–76. (New York: Rowman & Littlefield, 2004).

7 The 1979 Criminal Procedure Law, the 1982 Civil Procedure Law (for Trial Implementation), and the 1989 Administrative Procedure Law.

gradually emerging. In 1993, 1999 and 2004, the 1982 Constitution was further amended three times respectively, coinciding with the stages of China's economic, social and legal reforms.[8] Crucially important in the area of civil and commercial law, the 1999 Contract Law has transformed the previous separate system of contract laws into a unified system of contract law.[9] Apart from contract law, a group of important civil and commercial law were promulgated during the 1990s.[10] In the area of procedural law, the 1982 Civil Procedure Law (for Trial Implementation) was replaced by the current 1991 Civil Procedure Law[11] and the 1979 Criminal Procedure Law was amended by the 1996 Criminal Procedure Law.[12] Towards the end of 1990s and early 2000s, and with China's entry into the WTO in 2001, there have been positive impacts not only on the law of foreign trade and investment but also on the general standard and quality of China's legal system.[13]

All these developments have contributed directly and indirectly to the development of the legal, regulatory and judicial framework for the resolution of disputes involving shares, bonds and other types of securities. The general principles of civil law, agency law, tort law, contract law, security law and civil procedure law form a basic and important part of the legal rules, in accordance with which the people's courts deal with securities-related cases. In the area of securities and company law, the Company Law of the People's Republic of China was enacted in 1993[14] and the Securities Law of the People's Republic of China was enacted in 1998,[15] both which were significantly amended in 2005.[16] Following the establishment of Shanghai and

---

8   Important amendments have been adopted, concerning, among others, rule-of-law state, public ownership and other forms of ownership, protection of private property, and protection of human rights, and so on. In total, thirty-one amendments have been adopted since 1988.

9   The 1999 Contract Law of the People's Republic of China was enacted by the National People's Congress on 15 March 1999, and effective as of 1 October 1999. Three contract laws promulgated during the 1980s and repealed by the 1999 Contract Law were the 1981 Economic Contract Law, as amended in 1993, the 1985 Economic Contract Law Involving Foreign Parties, and the 1987 Technology Contract Law. For the process of drafting the 1999 Contract Law, *see* Jiang Ping, "Drafting the Uniform Contract Law in China", *Columbia Journal of Asian Law*, Vol. 10, 1996, pp. 245–258.

10   Such as the 1995 Security Law of the People's Republic of China and the 1995 Negotiable Instrument Law of the People's Republic of China, as amended in 2004.

11   The Civil Procedure Law of the People's Republic of China, adopted by the National People's Congress and enacted on, and effective as of, 9 April 1991.

12   The Criminal Procedure Law of the People's Republic of China, adopted by the National People's Congress and enacted on 17 March 1996, and effective as of 1 January 1997.

13   For example, transparency in China's legal system has been improved as a result of China's entry into the WTO.

14   The 1993 Company Law was adopted by the Standing Committee of the National People's Congress on 29 December 1993, and effective as of 1 July 1994.

15   The 1998 Securities Law was adopted by the Standing Committee of the National People's Congress on 29 December 1998, and effective as of 1 July 1999.

16   *See* following Chapter 7: The Development of Securities Dispute Resolution in China for further discussion.

Shenzhen stock exchanges in 1990 and 1991, the Securities Committee of the State Council (SCSC) and the China Securities Regulatory Commission (CSRC) were established in October 1992, and the institutional development of China's securities regulatory system entered into a new stage.[17]

Over the years, the National People's Congress and its Standing Committee, the national and local governments, securities regulators have promulgated a growing number of the laws, regulations and rules relevant to securities market regulation and securities dispute resolution.[18] In the process of resolving securities-related cases, the Supreme People's Court has also issued a group of judicial interpretations and guidelines specifically concerning procedural issues arising in the resolution of securities dispute cases.[19] This chapter outlines some important basic legal, regulatory and judicial rules commonly applicable to all types of securities dispute cases while the rules, including special trading rules applicable only to cases in certain specific securities markets, will be outlined in the following relevant chapters.

General Principles of Civil Law

The 1986 GPCL[20] is, in a loose sense, a 'mini civil code' in the Chinese legal system.[21] The provisions provided for in the 1986 GPCL cover natural persons and legal persons, civil juristic acts, agency, civil rights and civil liabilities, statute of limitation and applicable law in civil relations involving foreign parties.[22] Embodied also in the 1986 GPCL are general principles of civil and commercial law, such as the

---

17   For a discussion about the role played by the SCSC and CSRC in early 1990s, *see* Zhu Sanzhu, *Securities Regulation in China*, pp. 8–14. Apart from the SCSC and the CSRC, the People's Bank of China, China's central bank, was designated as watchdog to oversee the securities market in conjunction with various bodies of the central and local government. The SCSC was later dissolved, leaving the CSRC and its local offices as a single national securities regulator.

18   *See* Zhu Sanzhu, *Securities Regulation in China*, "List of Legislation", pp. xi–xxi, in which a list of the relevant law and regulations, rules and local legislation promulgated up to 1999 are divided into groups promulgated by the National People's Congress and its Standing Committee, by the State Council and its Ministries and Commissions, by the securities regulatory authorities and by local authorities.

19   For example, the 2003 Provisions of the Supreme People's Court on Several Issues Concerning Adjudication of Cases of Futures Disputes. *See* Chapter 5, footnote 35.

20   The 1986 General Principles of Civil Law of the People's Republic of China was enacted by the National People's Congress on 12 April 1986, and effective as of 1 January 1987.

21   It is regarded as essentially a "general part of a German-style civil code for which all the other parts are missing." *See* William C. Jones (ed.), *Basic Principles of Civil Law in China*, at p. xv. (Armonk, New York; London: M.E. Sharpe, 1989).

22   Chapter Two: Citizen (Natural Person), Articles 9–35; Chapter Three: Legal Person, Articles 36–53; Chapter Four: Civil Juristic Acts and Agency, Articles 54–70; Chapter Five: Civil Rights, Articles 71–105; Chapter Six: Civil Liabilities, Article 106–134; Chapter Seven: Statute of Limitation, Articles 135–141; Chapter Eight: The Application of Law to Civil Law Relations with Foreign Aspects, Articles 142–150.

principle of fairness and the principle of honesty and good faith.[23] After the enactment of the 1986 GPCL, the Supreme People's Court issued in 1988 a set of detailed interpretations concerning the implementation of the 1986 GPCL (hereinafter the SPC Interpretations on the 1986 GPCL).[24] The 1986 GPCL and the interpretations of the Supreme People's Court provide the people's courts with important general law and principles in dealing with all kinds of civil and commercial cases, including cases involving securities disputes.

Legal Requirements for Civil Juristic Acts

Article 55 of the 1986 GPCL broadly requires that a civil juristic act (*minshi falü xingwei*) shall meet the following three conditions. First, the actor has relevant capacity for civil acts; second, the intention expressed is genuine; and third, the act does not violate the law or the public interest (*shehui gonggong liyi*).[25] According to the SPC Interpretations on the 1986 GPCL, civil acts performed by a party in the form of audio recording, video recording, or other audio or material means is deemed valid if two or more disinterested persons act as witnesses or if there is other proof that the civil acts conform to the provision of the Article 55 of the 1986 GPCL;[26] an act is deemed an act of deceit if one party wilfully misrepresents to or deliberately conceals from another party facts and thereby induces the other party to make a mistaken expression of intention;[27] a serious error is deemed to exist where a person performing an act misapprehends the nature of the act, the identity of the other party concerned, or the kind, quality, specification, and quantity of the subject matter, so that the consequences of his act are contrary to his true intention thereby resulting in significant loss.[28] These are some of the interpretations of the Supreme People's Court regarding legal requirements for civil juristic acts.[29] The SPC Interpretations on the 1986 GPCL provides no further provision regarding the requirement that a civil juristic act may not violate the public interest.

Failing to fulfill these requirements a civil juristic act shall be null and void. On the basis of Article 55, Article 58 of the 1986 GPCL further prescribes a list of

---

23   Chapter One: General Provisions, Articles 1–8. For a comparative analysis of the principles of the 1986 GPCL, *see* Edward J. Epstein, "Codification of Civil Law in the People's Republic of China: Form and Substance in the Reception of Concepts and Elements of Western Private Law", *University of British Columbia Law Review*, Vol. 32, 1998, pp. 153–198 (stating that "the story of China's codification of civil law is one wherein despite political and ideological odds, continuity outweighs change", at p. 195).

24   Opinion (for Trial Use) of the Supreme People's Court on Questions Concerning the Implementation of "the General Principles of Civil Law of the People's Republic of China", adopted by the Judicial Committee of the Supreme People's Court on 26 January 1988 and promulgated on 2 April 1988.

25   Article 55 of the 1986 GPCL.

26   Article 65 of the SPC Interpretations on the 1986 GPCL.

27   *Id.* art. 68.

28   *Id.* art. 71.

29   For other interpretations regarding legal requirements for civil juristic acts, *see* Articles 65 to 77 of the SPC Interpretations on the 1986 GPCL.

civil juristic acts and the circumstances under which a civil juristic act shall be null and void, including those performed by a person without civil capacity or a person with limited capacity who may not perform such an act independently according to law,[30] those performed by a person against his true intentions as a result of cheating, coercion or exploitation of his unfavorable position by the other party,[31] those performed through malicious collusion and detrimental to the interests of the state, a collective or a third party,[32] those that violate the law or the public interest,[33] and those performed under the guise of legitimate acts to conceal illegitimate purposes.[34]

Civil juristic acts that are determined to be null and void shall not be legally binding from the very beginning.[35] The party who has received property as a result of the act must return it to the injured party; if one party is at fault, he must pay damages to the other party who has been injured as a result of the act; if both parties are at fault each must bear his appropriate share of liability; if both parties have conspired maliciously to execute a civil juristic act that is detrimental to the interests of the state, a collective or a third party, the property acquired by them shall be recovered and turned over to the state or the collective, or returned to the third person.[36] According to the SPC Interpretations on the 1986 GPCL, "property acquired by them" includes property that both parties have already obtained as well as property that both parties have agreed to obtain.[37]

In relation to securities transactions, parties must fulfill legal requirements for civil juristic acts prescribed by the 1986 GPCL, the failure of which would render the transactions invalid. A common reason for invalidity of a securities transaction is violation of the law and regulations. For example, *Shengyang Northern Securities Company v Dalian City Trust Investment Company of China Agriculture Bank*[38] is a case in which a loan of 17 million yuan to finance a land development project was disguised by the agreements signed by the parties for an issue of enterprise bonds; *Anhui Securities Registration Company v Anhui Pengli Guomao Company Ltd*[39] is a case in which a loan was facilitated under a name of government bond transfer agreement. In both cases the Courts, in according with Article 58 (1) (v) and (vii) of the 1986 GPCL, held that the agreements violated the law and regulations and were null and void. In the securities repurchase market, particularly in the early years of the emergence of the market, there was widespread irregularities among financial institutions and trading centers. Legal and regulatory requirements, such as the requirement of a real and full amount of collateral securities for securities repurchase

---

30   Article 58 (1) and (2) of the 1986 GPCL.
31   *Id.* art. 58 (3).
32   *Id.* art. 58 (4).
33   *Id.* art. 58 (5).
34   *Id.* art. 58 (7).
35   *Id.* art. 58, paragraph 2.
36   Paragraph 1 and 2 of Article 61 of the 1986 GPCL.
37   Article 74 of the SPC Interpretations on the 1986 GPCL.
38   *See* footnotes 63 and 69 of Chapter 3 and accompanying texts.
39   *See* footnote 19 of Chapter 3 and accompanying text.

agreements, were ignored, which resulted in annulment of such agreements by the people's courts.[40]

As the securities business is a controlled area of business by the government, it is important that parties in a securities transaction must have business licenses approved by the government financial regulators which allow them to engage in securities business. In other words, they must have relevant capacity for their corresponding civil juristic acts, without which their capacity of civil juristic acts (*minshi falǔ xingwei nengli*) would have defects and their civil juristic acts carried out under the circumstances would be invalid. In dealing with securities dispute cases, the people's courts have to satisfy first whether the parties in the disputes have appropriate qualifications to engage in the securities transaction in question. For example, dealing in securities repurchase business is restricted to financial institutions who have an independent legal status and who have a financial business license issued by the People's Bank of China (PBOC) which allows the financial institution to engage in securities trading business. Lack of a proper qualification by the parties concerned to engage in securities repurchase business is one of the main reasons for which the people's courts invalidate their securities repurchase agreements.[41]

Civil Liability and Compensation

In accordance with the 1986 GPCL, civil liabilities include the civil liabilities arising from breach of contracts and the civil liabilities arising from committing torts. In addition, a strict liability may arise in accordance with provisions of law and regulation, which makes a person or a company responsible for the damage and loss caused by their acts and omissions regardless of culpability. Article 106 of the 1986 GPCL states that "citizens or legal persons who break a contract or do not perform some other duty must bear civil liability; citizens or legal persons who, as a result of their fault, infringe on state or collective property, or infringe on the person or property of another person, must bear civil liability; if there is no fault, but the law provides that one must bear civil liability, he must bear civil liability."[42]

The methods of bearing civil liability prescribed by the 1986 GPCL include ceasing the tort; removing the impediment; eliminating the danger; returning the property; restoring the original conditions; repairing, reconstructing or replacing; paying damages for the loss; paying the agreed-upon penalty; eliminating the influence of the wrong, restoring the reputation; making an apology.[43] These methods may be

---

40　*See* following Chapter 4: The Securities Repurchase Market, in particular, "Requirement of a Real and Full Amount of Collateral Securities".

41　*See* following Chapter 4, in particular, "Qualification to Engage in Securities Repurchase Agreement".

42　Article 106 of the 1986 GPCL. For civil liabilities for breach of contract, *see* further Articles 111 to 116 of the 1986 GPCL; for civil liabilities for torts, *see* further Articles 117 to 133 of the 1986 GPCL. *See* also the SPC Interpretations on the 1986 GPCL, Section V "Civil Liability", including Articles 142 to 161.

43　Article 134 of the 1986 GPCL. *See* also the SPC Interpretations on the 1986 GPCL, Section V "Civil Liability", including Articles 162 to 164.

used independently or jointly.[44] Apart from these methods, the people's courts, in hearing civil cases, may also make use of admonitions, they may confiscate property unlawfully obtained in the pursuit of unlawful acts, and they may, in accordance with the law, assess fines and impose detention.[45] In the resolution of securities disputes, paying damages for the loss and paying the agreed-upon penalty are the two methods most commonly applied by the people's courts in compensating the party who suffers a loss as a result of either a breach of contract or a tort committed by the other party.[46]

When two or more persons cause damage to another person, they shall bear joint liability.[47] This general principle of the 1986 GPCL applies in different areas of law, including securities law. Thus, in the civil action arising from false statements made on the securities market, for example, a wide range of parties may be held liable jointly or severally for making a false statement. Promoters, issuers, listed companies and their controlling shareholders or those who exercise actual controls over the company are subject to a strict liability[48] while securities underwriters, securities listing sponsors, accounting firms, law firms and asset valuation organizations are subject to a liability based on fault.[49] The same applies to responsible directors, supervisors, managers of issuers, listed companies, securities underwriters and securities listing sponsors, and directly responsible persons in accounting firms, law firms and asset valuation organizations.[50] Joint and several liability applies to promoters; securities underwriters, securities listing sponsors, accountant firms, law firms; asset valuation organizations; and directors, supervisors, managers of issuers, listed companies, securities underwriters and securities listing sponsors.[51]

Article 43 of the 1986 GPCL states that "enterprise legal persons shall bear civil liability for management activities of their legal representatives and other employees."[52] Such activities are interpreted by the Supreme People's Court as being carried out in the name of the legal person.[53] In *Business Center of Yunnan Provincial Branch of China Agriculture Bank v Shenzhen International Trust Investment*

---

44   Paragraph 2 of Article 134 of the 1986 GPCL.

45   *Id.* paragraph 3.

46   In one case discussed in the book, the Court ordered the defendant to make an apology to the plaintiff in accordance with Article 134 (10) of the 1986 GPCL. *See Wang Luhui v Sichuan Province Securities Co. Ltd.*, in Chapter 2, footnotes 11, 12 and accompanying texts.

47   Article 130 of the 1986 GPCL.

48   *See* Table 6.1 of following Chapter 6.

49   *See* Table 6.2 of following Chapter 6.

50   *Id.*

51   *See* Table 6.3 of following Chapter 6.

52   Article 43 of the 1986 GPCL. For discussion on legal person, *see* Fu Tingmei, "Legal Person in China: Essence and Limits", *the American Journal of Comparative Law*, Vol. 41, 1993, pp.261–297.

53   Article 58 of the SPC Interpretations on the 1986 GPCL states that, "where the legal representative of an enterprise legal person or its other employees cause economic loss to others while engaging in activities in the name of the legal person, the enterprise legal person must bear civil liability."

Co.,[54] for example, the Supreme People's Court held that where a staff member representing his company as a trader in the securities market carried out a trading activity with the company's official seal and his personal seal, the company shall bear civil liabilities. In this case, the defendant Shenzhen International Investment Trust Company had an international securities investment fund department who had a seat at Wuhan Securities Trading Center. The seat was represented by two authorized traders from the department. At the time when the department applied to the Wuhan Securities Trading Center for a seat, the department signed and sealed an authorization document and submitted to the Wuhan Securities Trading Center. The department authorized the seal of the department and personal seals of two traders in the application form. The traders conducted businesses using the department seal and their personal seals. The Supreme People's Court held that under the circumstances the department should be responsible for the civil acts carried out by its traders with the department's authorized seal.[55]

If the legal representative or other members of staff of an enterprise commit an economic crime and cause losses to others in the course of their employment, should the enterprise bear civil liability for such losses? Or should the enterprise by excused from bearing civil liability under such circumstances on the ground that such losses are caused by economic crimes committed by individual staff of the enterprise? According to an judicial interpretation issued by the Supreme People's Court,[56] the enterprise has to bear civil liability arising from the contract or performance of the contract signed by a legal representative of the enterprise or other responsible members of staff in the name of the enterprise and such legal representative or responsible members of staff misappropriate the money or property related to the contract for their personal gains.[57] The fact that the legal representative or other members of staff of the enterprise commits an economic crime in the course of their employment within the power delegated to them, which cause losses to others as well as to the enterprise, cannot form a ground to excuse the enterprise from bearing relevant civil liabilities.

In *China Human Rights Development Fund v Beijing Chang'an Branch of China Construction Bank*,[58] the defendant Beijing Chang'an Branch of China Construction Bank established a business center in 1994 in the campus of Beijing University. In 1996 the plaintiff purchased 1 million yuan 1996 (2) government bonds at the business center. After the plaintiff paid 1 million yuan to the business center, the head of the center misappropriated the money without the plaintiff's knowledge and used

---

54   *See* the Gazette of the Supreme People's Court of the People's Republic of China, Issue 5, 2004, pp. 8–13.

55   *Id.* at pp. 12–13.

56   The Provisions of the Supreme People's Court on Several Issues in Adjudicating Economic Dispute Cases Involving Economic Crime Suspicion (Zuigao Renmin Fayuan Guanyu Zai Shenli Jingji Jiufen Anjian Zhong Sheji Jingji Fanzui Xianyi Ruogan Wenti de Guiding), issued on 21 April 1998 and effective from 29 April 1998.

57   *Id.* art. 3.

58   *See Studies of Judicial Decisions Related to Financial Disputes* (*Jingrong Shenpan Anli Yanjiu*) (Vol. 2001), edited by Economic Division Court of Beijing High People's Court, pp. 380–385 (Beijing: Law Publishing House, 2001).

the money in the property market for personal gain. The center was closed down in 1998. In 1999 the head of the center was arrested by police for the misappropriation of the fund. The plaintiff sued the defendant for the return of the money and interests. The defendant submitted that the case should be dealt with as an economic crime case and its branch should not bear responsibility claimed by the plaintiff. The defendant's argument was that the bank had no depositary relationship with the plaintiff as the money was not paid into its branch before it had been misused by the head of the center.

The Court dismissed the submission from the defendant and held the defendant liable for the return of the money. The Court based its judgment on two grounds. First, the business center had been set up by the defendant and, as the business center was closed down the defendant should assume the liability for the business center. Second, the head of the business center took the money from the plaintiff and issued a receipt to the plaintiff, all of which was done in the name of the business center and in the course of the employment, so the defendant should bear the liability for the operational activities of its staff according to Article 43 of the 1986 GPCL.[59]

The Law of Agency

The 1986 GPCL sets out the basic principles of the law of agency.[60] A civil juristic act may be entrusted to an agent in writing or orally;[61] an agent shall perform civil juristic acts in the principal's name within the scope of the power of agency and the principal shall bear civil liability for the agent's acts of agency;[62] the principal shall bear civil liability for an act performed by an agent beyond the scope of his power of agency, only if he recognizes the act retroactively;[63] if the act is not so recognized, the agent shall bear civil liability for it;[64] an agent shall bear civil liability if he fails to perform his duties and thus causes damage to the principal.[65] The judicial interpretations provided by the Supreme People's Court give further guidance to the application of these principles by the people's courts.[66] *Li Erjiao v Zhang Shihui* is a

---

59   *Id.* at pp. 382–383.

60   *See* Chapter IV "Civil Juristic Acts and Agency", in particular, section 2 of Chapter IV "Agency", including articles 63–70.

61   Article 65 of the 1986 GPCL.

62   *Id.* art. 63.

63   *Id.* art. 66.

64   *Id.*

65   *Id.*

66   *See* Articles 78–83 of the SPC Interpretations on the 1986 GPCL. For example, Article 80 interprets the "emergency situation", as provided in Article 68 of the 1986 GPCL, to refer to the situation where, due to special reasons, such as sudden serious illness or loss of communication contact, the appoint agent cannot himself take care of the matters he has been entrusted with under the agency and cannot contact the principal, and thus the interest of the principal will be damaged or the damage will be aggravated unless the agent transfers his authority to a third person. In accordance with Article 68 of the 1986 GPCL, an agent can commission someone to act for him in order to protect the interest of the principal under an emergency situation without acquiring in advance the consent of the principal.

case that occurred in early years of China's securities market.[67] The plaintiff Li Erjiao entrusted the defendant Zhang Shihui to collect on her behalf the dividend of her 288 shares of the Shenzhen Development Bank from the securities company where she had opened her account. The defendant instead sold the shares through the securities company to his sister at a low price without telling the plaintiff. After relevant tax and transaction fee were deducted, the defendant gave the plaintiff a total sum of 890 yuan, being the dividend of the share and the proceeds of the sale. The Nanshan District People's Court of the Shenzhen city held that the defendant acted beyond the scope of his power of agency, which violated Article 66 of the 1986 GPCL. The Court conducted mediation and an agreement was consequently reached, under which the defendant purchased 288 shares of the Shenzhen Development Bank for the plaintiff who returned 890 yuan to the defendant.[68]

A typical agency relationship in securities trading is between an investor principal and an agent securities company where the investor opens a securities trading account in the securities company and instructs the securities company to carry out securities trading. The securities company carries out the securities trading for the investor and the investor bears civil liability for the trading carried out by the securities company. The agent must act in accordance with the instruction given by the investor principal. In commodity and financial futures market, disputes arise in which investor principals make claims for their losses on the grounds that futures broker firms fail to carry out their instructions; the issue whether a futures broker firm carried out a client's instructions was a genuinely decisive issue in some of the cases in the early years of China's futures market.[69] In the share issuing and trading market, disputes between investor principals and securities company agents constitute a majority of the disputes involving shares.[70]

One of the issues running through the agency relationship between investor principals and securities company agents in different markets of China's securities market is under what circumstances and to what extent securities company agents shall bear trading losses suffered by investor principals. In the resolution of disputes arising in the trading of futures, a distinction is made by the people's courts between those losses that have a direct causal link with the instructions of investor principals and those losses that are linked with the acts of futures broker firms. In general, for the former losses investor principals cannot recover from futures broker firms while for the latter losses investor principals can recover.[71] Similarly, a clear line is drawn by the people's courts between the loss occurred as a result of normal market risks

---

67   *See* the Gazette of the Supreme People's Court of the People's Republic of China, Issue 1, 1993, at pp. 29–30.

68   *Id.* at p. 30.

69   *See* Chapter 5, section "Carry out Clients' Instruction and Burden of Proof."

70   *See* Chapter 2, in which some aspects of the disputes between investor principals and securities company agents are examined, including, among others, mistakes made by securities companies, obligation of securities companies to process instructions from clients and duty of securities companies to safeguard against fraud.

71   *See* Chapter 5, for example, the case *Hewei v Changchun Investment Consultancy Center of Jilin Province Jinhui International Investment and Development Co. Ltd. and Jilin Branch of Bank of China* (footnote 137 and accompanying texts).

and the loss occurred as a consequence of fault or fraud of securities companies. If a loss is made not because of fault or fraud of defendant securities companies but because of normal market risks when the market is falling, such loss shall be borne by investor principals and not recoverable from securities company agents.[72]

The general principles of the 1986 GPCL regarding the law of agency have been applied and developed in the 1999 Contract Law,[73] which provides for two types of agency contracts, namely commission contracts (*weituo hetong*) and brokerage contracts (*hangji hetong*).[74] A commission contract is defined as a contract whereby the principal and the agent agree that the agent shall handle the matters of the principal,[75] and a brokerage contract is defined as a contract whereby a broker is, in his own name, engaged in trade activities for the benefit of the principal, and the principal pays the remuneration.[76] There are some special provisions that apply to brokerage contracts. Where a broker sells at a lower price or buys at a higher price than the price fixed by the principal, consent shall be obtained from the principal.[77] Where a contract is concluded between a broker and a third party, the broker shall directly have the rights and assume the obligations under the contract.[78]

Contract Law

The 1999 Contract Law and relevant provisions of the 1986 GPCL are two main sources of contract law in the system of Chinese civil and commercial law.[79] Before the 1999 Contract Law, the 1981 Economic Contract Law, as amended in 1993, was

---

72   *See* the case *Xineng Technology Company v Guotai Jun'an Securities Company* (Chapter 2, footnote 63 and accompanying texts).

73   *Supra* note 9.

74   Chapter 21 of the 1999 Contract Law regulates commission contract, including Articles 396–413; Chapter 22 regulates brokerage contract, including Articles 414–423. According to Article 423, matters not addressed in Chapter 22 shall apply the relevant provisions in Chapter 21 governing commission contracts. For example, Article 401 applies to both commission contracts and brokerage contracts, which provide that, "the agent shall report the handling of the entrusted matters according to the requirements of the principal; the agent shall report the result of the entrusted matters when the commission contract is terminated".

75   Article 396 of the 1999 Contract Law.

76   *Id.* art. 414.

77   *Id.* art. 418, which also provide that, the transaction, without the principal's consent, shall be effective to the principal if the broker makes up the price difference. Where the broker sells at a higher price or buys at a lower price then the price fixed by the principal, remuneration may be raised according to the terms of the contract. Where the principal has special instructions on price, the broker may not buy or sell violating their instructions.

78   *Id.* art. 421, which also provide that, if the third party fails to perform its obligations and causes losses to the principal, the broker shall be liable for damages, except as otherwise agreed upon by the parties.

79   Among other provisions, Articles 111–116 of the 1986 GPCL deal with specifically civil liabilities for breach of contract. For an introduction about the 1999 Contract Law, *see* Ling Bing, *Contract Law in China* (Hong Kong: Sweet and Maxwell Asia, 2002).

the main source of law, according to which the people's courts dealt with issues connected to domestic economic contracts, including contracts involving securities. The unified system of contract law brought about by the 1999 Contract Law has resolved some problems of the previous contract laws.[80] Under the 1999 Contract Law, fifteen specific contracts are regulated, ranging from sale contract to brokerage contract.[81] A wide range of general issues are prescribed by the general provisions of the 1999 Contract Law, including offer and acceptance, validity of contract, and so on.[82] The principle of freedom of contract, the principle of good faith and the principle of fostering transactions are highlighted as fundamental principles of China's contract law.[83]

Invalid Contract

The law prescribing the circumstances under which a contract shall be null and void is primarily Article 58 of the 1986 GPCL[84] and Article 52 of the 1999 Contract Law.[85] Before the 1999 Contract Law, provisions relating to invalidity of a contact were found in Article 7 of the 1993 Economic Contract Law.[86] Article 52 of the 1999 Contract Law prescribes that a contract shall be null and void under the following circumstances: first, a contract is concluded through the use of fraud or coercion by one party to damage the interests of the State;[87] second, malicious collusion is conducted to damage the interests of the State, a collective or a third party;[88] third, an illegitimate purpose is concealed under the guise of legitimate acts;[89] fourth, damaging the public interests;[90] and fifth, violating the mandatory provisions of a law or administrative regulation.[91] The provisions of Article 52 are an extension of the general principles of the 1986 GPCL in respect of legal requirements for valid

---

80   The main problem was the piecemeal and fragmented style of legislative framework and related separate and confusing application of different contract laws.

81   Fifteen Chapters of the 1999 Contract Law stipulate specific provisions governing the fifteen types of contracts (Chapters 9–23, including Articles 130–427).

82   *See* "General Provisions", including Chapters 1–8, Articles 1–129.

83   *See* Wang Liming and Xu Chuanxi, "Fundamental Principles of China's Contract Law", *Columbia Journal of Asian Law*, Vol. 13, 1999, pp. 1–34.

84   *See supra* section "Legal Requirements for Civil Juristic Acts".

85   Article 52 should be looked at in the context of Chapter 3 of the 1999 Contract Law, which is entitled "Validity of Contracts", including Articles 44–59.

86   Article 7 of the 1993 Economic Contract Law stipulates, *inter alia*, that "the following economic contracts are null and void: 1, a contract which violates the law and administrative regulations; 2, a contract which is concluded through the use of means of fraud, coercion etc.; 3, a contract concluded by an agent overstepping his power of agency or a contract concluded by an agent with himself in the name of the principal or with others for whom the agent performs acts of agency; 4, an economic contract which violates the interests of the state or social public interests."

87   Article 52 (1) of the 1999 Contract Law.

88   *Id.* art. 52 (2).

89   *Id.* art. 52 (3).

90   *Id.* art. 52 (4).

91   *Id.* art. 52 (5).

civil juristic acts and they are consistent in some respects with the provisions of the 1993 Economic Contract Law.

In sum, the circumstances under which a contract shall be null and void fall broadly into two categories. First, the circumstances under which the interests of the State, a collective or a third party are harmed as a result of fraud,[92] coercion by one contracting party,[93] a malicious collusion,[94] or the public interests are harmed.[95] Second, the circumstances under which law and regulations are broken by the parties either in violation of the mandatory provisions of law and administrative regulations[96] or in a disguised legitimate act for an illegitimate purpose.[97] Compared with the previous contract laws, the provision of the 1999 Contract Law that "a contract shall be null and void if it violates the mandatory provisions of a law or administrative regulation" limits the scope of invalid contracts, which is regarded by some leading Chinese scholars as being "crucially important".[98]

A contract that is null and void shall not be legally binding from the very beginning.[99] This position of the 1999 Contract Law is an echo of the principle of the 1986 GPCL.[100] The 1999 Contract Law further provides, *inter alia*, that if part of a contract is null and void without affecting the validity of the other parts, the other parts shall still be valid.[101] If a contract is null and void, revoked or terminated, it shall not affect the validity of the dispute settlement clause, which exists independently in the contract.[102] The property acquired as a result of a contract shall be retuned after the contract is determined to be null and void or has been revoked; when the property can not be returned or the return is unnecessary, it shall be reimbursed at its estimated price.[103] The party at fault shall compensate the other party for losses incurred as a

---

92   Article 58 (3) of the 1986 GPCL, Article 52 (1) of the 1999 Contract Law and Article 7 (2) of the 1993 Economic Contract Law.

93   *Id.*

94   Article 58 (4) of the 1986 GPCL, Article 52 (2) of the 1999 Contract Law.

95   Article 58 (5) of the 1986 GPCL, Article 52 (4) of the 1999 Contract Law and Article 7 (4) of the 1993 Economic Contract Law.

96   Article 58 (5, 6) of the 1986 GPCL, Article 52 (5) of the 1999 Contract Law and Article 7 (1) of the 1993 Economic Contract Law.

97   Article 58 (7) of the 1986 GPCL, Article 52 (3) of the 1999 Contract Law.

98   *See* Wang Liming, Xu Chuanxi, "Fundamental Principles of China's Contract Law", *Columbia Journal of Asian Law*, Vol. 13, No. 1, Spring 1999, pp.1–34, at p. 26 (stating that "[t]his provision is crucially important in that it signifies that not any just regulatory document (*guifanxing wenjian*) will invalidate a contract; only where a national law (*falü*) or administrative regulation (*xingzheng fagui*) is violated may a contract be declared invalid. Furthermore, it is not that any violation of any provision of a law or regulation will entail contract invalidation. Only where a mandatory, not merely an elective, provision is violated may the contract by invalidated.")

99   Article 56 of the 1999 Contract Law.

100   Article 58 of the 1986 GPCL, which states that civil juristic acts that are determined to be null and void shall not be legally binding from the very beginning.

101   Article 56 of the 1999 Contract Law.

102   *Id.* art. 57.

103   *Id.* art. 58.

result; if both parties are at fault, each party shall respectively be liable.[104]If the parties have maliciously conducted collusion to damage the interests of the State, a collective or a third party, the property thus acquired shall be turned over to the State or returned to the collective or the third party.[105]

Examination of validity of a securities contract involved in a dispute is a first and important stage by the people's courts in adjudicating the dispute. The finding on the validity of the contract forms an important ground for the people's courts to decide the responsibilities of the parties concerned. For example, when a dispute which involves a securities repurchase contract comes to the people's courts, the first thing the people's courts would do is to examine the validity of the securities repurchase contract to determine whether the contract is lawfully concluded. In *Qixiangtai Road Securities Business Center of Tianjin City International Investment Trust Co. v Shanghai Shenyin Securities Co.*, the Tianjin High People's Court annulled two government bond repurchase contracts in accordance with Article 7 of the 1993 Economic Contract Law on the finding that the defendant did not deposit at the Tianjin Securities Trading Center a full amount of the government bonds for the two repurchase contracts, which violated Article 52 of the 1994 Provisional Measures for the Administration of Credit Funds.[106]

Civil Liability for Breach of Contract

The 1986 GPCL sets out basic legal principles governing civil liabilities for breach of contract.[107] If a party fails to fulfill its contractual obligations or violates the term of a contract while fulfilling the obligations, the other party shall have the right to demand fulfillment or the taking of remedial measures and claim compensation for its losses.[108] The party that breaches a contract shall be liable for compensation equal to the losses consequently suffered by the other party.[109] If both parties breach the contract, each party shall bear its respective civil liability.[110] If one party is suffering losses owing to the other party's breach of contract, it shall take prompt measures to prevent the losses from increasing; if it does not promptly do so, it shall not have the right to claim compensation for the additional losses.[111]

These basic principles stated in the 1986 GPCL have been applied and developed in the 1999 Contract Law[112] which provides, *inter alia*, that where one party to a contract fails to perform the contract obligations or its performance fails to satisfy the terms of the contract, the party shall bear such liabilities for breach of contract as to continue to perform its obligations, to take remedial measures, or to compensate

---

104   *Id.*

105   *Id.* art. 59.

106   For full details of the case, *see* Chapter 4, footnote 76 and accompanying texts.

107   *See* Articles 111–116 of the 1986 GPCL.

108   Article 111 of the 1986 GPCL.

109   *Id.* art. 112.

110   *Id.* art. 113.

111   *Id.* art. 114.

112   *See* the 1999 Contract Law, Chapter 7: "Liability for Breach of Contract", including Articles 107–122.

for losses.[113] Where one party expresses explicitly or indicates through its acts that it will not perform the contract, the other party may demand it to bear the liability for the breach of contract before the expiry of the performance period.[114] If one party fails to pay the price or remuneration, the other party may request it to make the payment.[115] Where one party fails to perform the contract obligations or its performance fails to satisfy the terms of the contract, the party shall, after performing its obligations or taking remedial measures, compensate for the losses, if the other party suffers from other losses.[116] Where one party fails to perform the contract obligations or its performance fails to satisfy the terms of the contract and causes losses to the other party, the amount of compensation for losses shall be equal to the losses caused by the breach of contract, including the interests receivable after the performance of the contract, provided not exceeding the probable losses caused by the breach of contract which has been foreseen or ought to be foreseen when the party in breach concludes the contract.[117]

There are different views on the understanding of application in share trading cases of Article 114 of the 1986 GPCL, which requires the party to a contract who is suffering losses owing to the other party's breach of contract to take prompt measures to prevent the losses from increasing, failing of which the party shall not have the right to claim compensation for the additional losses.[118] In *Jin Yancheng v Shanghai Securities Business Center of Jilin Trust Investment Company of Bank of China*,[119] the editorial commentator argued that, as share trading has special features, the obligation to take measures to prevent further losses should not be determined in accordance with the provision of Article 114 of the 1986 GPCL.[120] The reason, it was argued, is because share prices may rise as well as fall and it is thus unpredictable whether the loss which has happened due to breach of contract by securities company agents will be increasing, and on the other hand, it is an autonomy of investor principals whether to carry out new trading; therefore such situation may not give rise to an obligation for the investor principal to prevent losses from further increasing.[121]

---

113 Article 107 of the 1999 Contract Law.

114 *Id.* art. 108.

115 *Id.* art. 109.

116 *Id.* art. 112.

117 *Id.* art. 113.

118 An equivalent article in the 1999 Contract Law is Article 119 which stipulates that after one party violates a contract, the other party shall take proper measures to prevent from the enlargement of losses; if the other party fails to take proper measures so that the losses are enlarged, it may not claim any compensation as to the enlarged losses.

119 *See* Chapter 2, footnote 50 and accompanying texts. In brief, it is a case in which the defendant securities company locked up the account of the plaintiff Jin Yancheng and the plaintiff thus lost good opportunities to sell his shares. The Court said the plaintiff could still have sold his shares through the defendant but failed to do so to reduce further losses for which the plaintiff has no right to claim compensation.

120 *See Carefully Selected Cases of the People's Courts* (*Renmin Fayuan Anli Xuan Jingbianben*), Vol. 1, 2001, edited by China Law Application Research Institute of the Supreme People's Court, pp. 744–749, at p. 748. (Beijing: Xinhua Publishing Press, 2001).

121 *Id.*

Security Law and Regulation

The main source of security law (*danbaofa*) is the 1995 Security Law of the PRC.[122] Before the promulgation of the 1995 Security Law, there were administrative regulations[123] and judicial guidelines,[124] which dealt with a range of issues concerning security and performance of debts. On a general level, the 1986 GPCL sets out a basic legal framework of security law,[125] the provisions of which are further interpreted by the Supreme People's Court in the implementation of the 1986 GPCL.[126] In December 2000, the Supreme People's Court issued the Interpretations on Several Issues Concerning Application of the Security Law of the PRC (hereinafter the SPC Interpretations on the 1995 Security Law),[127] which have consolidated judicial interpretations in this area of law.[128] In addition to the 1995 Security Law and judicial interpretations, there are a range of regulations and rules at both national and local levels concerning matters related to security regulation in different areas including the area of securities market.[129]

Forms of Security

Article 89 of the 1986 GPCL provides for four ways in which a debt may be secured, namely, guarantee, pledge, deposit and lien. First, a guarantor may guarantee to the creditor that the debtor shall perform his debt; if the debtor defaults, the guarantor shall perform the debt or bear joint liability according to agreement; after performing the debt, the guarantor shall have the right to claim repayment from the debtor.[130]

---

122   The 1995 Security Law of the PRC, promulgated by the Standing Committee of the National People's Congress on 30 June 1995 and effective from 1 October 1995.

123   For example, the Circular of the General Office of the State Council on Strictly Prohibition of Administrative Organs from Providing Guaranty for Economic Activities (Guowuyuan Bangongting Guanyu Yanjin Xingzheng Jiguan Wei Jingji Huodong Tigong Danbao de Tongzhi) issued on 23 February 1993.

124   The main one was the Provisions of the Supreme People's Court on Several Issues Concerning Guarantee in Adjudicating Disputes Cases Involving Economic Contracts (Zuigao Renmin Fayuan Guanyu Shenli Jingji Hetong Jiufen Anjian Youguan Baozheng de Ruogan Wenti de Guiding) issued on 15 April 1994.

125   Article 89 of the 1986 GPCL.

126   Articles 106–117 of the SPC Interpretations on the 1986 GPCL.

127   The Interpretations of the SPC on Several Issues Concerning Application of the Security Law of the PRC (Zuigao Renmin Fayuan Guanyu Shiyong Zhonghua Renmin Gongheguo Danbaofa Ruogan Wenti de Jieshi), issued on 8 December 2000 and effective from 13 December 2000.

128   Article 134 of the SPC Interpretations on the 1995 Security Law states that the judicial interpretations of the SPC on guaranty related matters issued before the promulgation of the 1995 Security Law shall not be applicable if they contravene with the 1995 Security Law and the SPC Interpretations on the 1995 Security Law.

129   *See*, for example, the Circular of the CSRC on the Issue of Guaranty by Securities Companies (Guanyu Zhengquan Gongsi Danbao Wenti de Tongzhi) issued by the CSRC on 24 April 2001.

130   Article 89 (1) of the 1986 GPCL.

Second, the debtor or a third party may offer a specific property as a pledge; if the debtor defaults, the creditor shall be entitled to keep the pledge to offset the debt or have priority in satisfying his claim out of the proceeds from the sale of the pledge.[131] Third, a party may leave a deposit with the other party; after the debtor has discharged his debt, the deposit shall either be retained as partial payment of the debt or be returned; if the party who leaves the deposit defaults, he shall not be entitled to demand the return of the deposit; if the party who accepts the deposit defaults, he shall repay the deposit in double.[132] Fourth, if a party has procession of the other party's property according to contract and the other party violate the contract by failing to pay a required sum of money within the specified time limit, the possessor shall have a lien on the property and may keep the property to offset the debt or have priority in satisfying his claim out of the proceeds from the sale of the property.[133]

Within the framework set out by Article 89 of the 1986 GPCL, the 1995 Security Law provides for detailed provisions on guarantee (*baozheng*),[134] mortgage (*diya*),[135] pledge (*zhiya*),[136] lien (*liuzhi*)[137] and deposit (*dingjin*).[138] "Mortgage" refers to a security whereby a debtor or a third party uses property as a security for an obligation without the transfer of the possession of such property, while "pledge" refers to a security whereby a debtor or a third party uses movables as a security for an obligation with the transfer of the possession of such movables to the creditor.[139] Apart from ordinary movables, a range of rights may be pledged, including bills of exchange, checks, promissory notes, bonds, certificates of deposits, shares and share certificates that are transferable according to law, trademarks, patents and copyrights that are transferable according to law.[140]

The SPC Interpretations on the 1995 Security Law provide a comprehensive interpretation regarding the application of the 1995 Security Law.[141] Article 103, for example, provides an interpretation that, where shares of a listed company are pledged, the pledge contract shall take effect on the day when the pledge is registered with the securities registration institution; where shares of a non-listed company are pledged, the pledge contract shall take effect on the day when the pledge is recorded on the shareholders' list.[142] The provisions of security law, as stated in the 1995 Security Law and interpreted by the Supreme People's Court, are also found in other laws, for example, in the 1999 Contract Law, which stipulates that the party may,

---

131 *Id.* art. 89 (2).
132 *Id.* art. 89 (3).
133 *Id.* art. 89 (4).
134 Chapter 2 of the 1995 Security Law, including Articles 6–32.
135 *Id.* Chapter 3, including Articles 33–62.
136 *Id.* Chapter 4, including Articles 63–81.
137 *Id.* Chapter 5, including Articles 82–88.
138 *Id.* Chapter 6, including Articles 89–91.
139 Articles 33 and 63 of the 1995 Security Law.
140 *Id.* art. 75.
141 On guarantee: Articles 13–46; on mortgage: Articles 47–83; on pledge: Articles 84–106; on lien: Articles 107–114; on deposit: Articles 115–122.
142 Paragraph 2 and 3 of Article 103 of the SPC Interpretations on the 1995 Security Law.

according to the Security Law of the PRC, agree that one party pays a deposit to the other party as the security for the creditor's rights; after the debt obligations are performed by the obligor, the deposit shall be returned or offset against price; if the party that pays the deposit fails to perform the agreed debt obligations, it shall have no right to reclaim the deposit; if the party that receives the deposit fails to perform the agreed debt obligations, it shall return twice the amount of the deposit.[143]

Security contract (*danbao hetong*) is defined as a contract ancillary (*cong hetong*) to a principal contract (*zhu hetong*); if the principal contract is invalid, the security contract shall be invalid as well.[144] Where a security contract is invalid because of an invalid principal contract, the guarantor shall not be responsible for the guaranty; but if the guarantor knew or should have known the invalidity of the principal contract but nevertheless provides guaranty for it, the guarantor and guarantee shall bear a joint liability for compensation after the principal contract is declared invalid.[145] In *Anhui Securities Registration Company v Anhui Pengli Guomao Company Ltd*, the principal contract, involving government bond financing, was declared invalid by the Court. Both the Anhui High People's Court and the Supreme People's Court held that the guarantor should bear a joint liability on the ground that the guarantor was aware of the fact that an illegal loan of 5 million yuan was transacted under the principal contract.[146]

Security Provided by State Authorities

The 1995 Security Law states that state authorities may not act as guarantors, except for on-lending with the use of a loan from a foreign government or an international economic organization upon the approval of the State Council.[147] In accordance with the SPC Interpretations on the 1995 Security Law, where a state authority provides security in violation of the law, the security contract is null and void; if losses are caused to creditors, it shall be dealt with in accordance with Article 5(2) of the 1995 Security Law, which states that where a debtor, a person providing security or a creditor is at fault after a security contract is declared invalid, he shall bear respective civil liability for his own fault.[148]

In *China Great Wall Trust Investment Company v Beijing Hemu Jingmao Company*,[149] the labor and personnel bureau of Shangqiu prefecture, Henan

---

143 Article 115 of the 1999 Contract Law.

144 Article 5 of the 1995 Security Law.

145 Article 20 of the Provisions of the SPC on Several Issues Concerning Guaranty in Adjudicating Disputes Cases Involving Economic Contracts, *supra* note 124.

146 The Supreme People's Court Civil Judgment [1997] No. 214. *See Selection of Financial Dispute Cases Heard by the Supreme People's Court (1996–1998)* (Zuigao Renmin Fayuan Shenli de Jinrong Jiufen Anli Xuanbian), compiled by the Economic Division Court of the Supreme People's Court, pp. 532–540, at pp. 535, 536, 538. (Beijing: China University of Politics and Law Press, 1999). For the details of the case, *see* Chapter 3, footnote 19 and accompanying texts.

147 Article 8 of the 1995 Security Law.

148 Article 3 of the SPC Interpretations on the 1995 Security Law.

149 *See* Chapter 3, footnotes 61 and 76 and accompanying texts.

province, agreed to stand guarantee for the defendant company to repay the plaintiff in relation to an issue of 5 million yuan enterprise bonds by the defendant. The Court held that the labor and personnel bureau of Shangqiu prefecture as a state organ should not act as the guarantor in this case and the guarantee was thus null and void; and because of its fault the bureau should bear a compensation liability. In *Taiyuan Financial Market v Taiyuan Liyuan Company*,[150] the finance department of Taiyuan city government provided guarantees for an issue of 20 million yuan enterprise bonds by the defendant. The Court held the finance department should bear a joint compensation liability. The problem created by the guarantee provided local government departments in charge of finance prompted the central government to take action to curb such practice.[151]

There are different views about whether a state organ guarantor should bear civil liability and what kind of civil liability a state organ should bear. One view is that the state organ should not bear any civil liability. This view argues that the law clearly prohibits the state organ from acting as guarantor; but if the enterprise guarantee knowingly asks the state organ to act as guarantor, the fault lies with enterprise guarantees.[152] Another view is that the state organ should bear a joint civil liability. This view argues that the state organ knowingly breaks the law to provide guarantee and the fault lies with the state organ.[153] The third view is that both the state organ as guarantor and the creditor of the main contract are at fault in that the state organ is wrong to break the law by providing guarantee, while the creditor of the main contract is at fault not checking the qualification of guarantors; the state organ and the creditor should therefore bear civil liability according to their respective faults.[154] In practice, the third view prevails, as applied in judicial reasoning and decisions of the people's courts and interpreted in the SPC Interpretations on the 1995 Security Law.[155]

Securities Law

The main source of securities law (*zhengquanfa*) is the 1998 Securities Law of the People's Republic of China.[156] Before the 1998 Securities Law, the 1993 Provisional Regulations on the Administration of Issuing and Trading of Shares played an

---

150 *See* Chapter 3, footnote 65 and 78 and accompanying texts.

151 *See* the two circulars issued by the Ministry of Finance in 1984 and 1988 respectively, Chapter 3, footnotes 80 and 81 and accompanying texts.

152 *Study of Judicial Decisions Related to Financial Disputes* (*Jingrong Shenpan Anli Yanjiu*) (Vol. 2001), edited by Economic Division Court, Beijing High People's Court, pp. 386–392, at p. 392. (Beijing: Law Publishing House, 2001).

153 *Id.*

154 *Id.*

155 Article 3 of the SPC Interpretations on the 1995 Security Law.

156 *Supra* note 15. For an introduction and discussion of the 1998 Securities Law, *see* Zhu Sanzhu, *Securities Regulation in China*, Chapter X, "Aspects of 1998 Securities Law of the People's Republic of China", pp. 207–224, together with a translation of full text of the Law.

important role in regulating share issuing and trading.[157] Furthermore, there were other regulations and normative documents concerning common issues of the securities market,[158] specific issues in government and enterprise bond market,[159] securities repurchase market,[160] commodity and financial futures market,[161] and the issues concerning foreign participation in China's securities market and overseas listing of Chinese companies.[162] On the other hand, lack of law and regulations in some areas of the securities market was a problem that the people's courts found in dealing with securities disputes.[163] The amendments made to the 1998 Securities Law in 2005 have brought about significant changes to the 1998 Securities Law, which marked a new stage of Chinese securities law and the regulation of securities market in China.[164]

General Provisions

The 1998 Securities Law primarily governs the issuing and trading of shares and corporate bonds.[165] This scope has now been widened by the 2005 amendments to the 1998 Securities Law to include government bonds and securities investment funds.[166] It is required that shares, corporate bonds and other securities that have been

---

157   The 1993 Provisional Regulations on the Administration of Issuing and Trading of Shares was promulgated by the State Council on 22 April 1993.

158   For example, the 1993 Provisional Measures on the Prohibition of Securities Frauds, approved by the State Council on 15 August 1993, promulgated by the State Council Securities Committee on, and effective from, 2 September 1993.

159   For example, the 1986 Government Bond Regulations and the 1993 Regulations on the Administration of Enterprise Bonds. *See* following Chapter 3 for these and other government and enterprise bond regulations.

160   For example, the 1994 Provisional Measures for the Administration of Credit Funds and the 1995 Circular on Reiteration of Relevant Issues Concerning Further Standardization of Securities Repurchase Business. *See* following Chapter 4 for these and other regulations concerning the securities repurchase market.

161   For example, the 1993 Provisional Measures on the Administration of Registration of Futures Broker Firms and the 1993 Circular of the State Council on Firmly Stopping Blind Development of Futures Market. *See* following Chapter 5 for these and other regulations concerning commodity and financial futures market.

162   For example, the 1991 Measures on the Administration of Shanghai Special *Renminbi* Shares, promulgated by the People's Bank of China and the Shanghai Municipal People's Government on, and effective as of, 22 November 1991; the 1994 Mandatory Provisions for the Articles of Association of Companies to be Listed Outside China, issued by the State Council Securities Commission and the State Commission for Restructuring the Economic System on 19 September 1994.

163   For example, in the area of commodity and financial futures market. *See* following Chapter 5 for further discussion.

164   One area of the changes is the improvement of civil liabilities and compensation in relation to the protection of investors. *See* following Chapter 7 for discussions about this and other changes.

165   Article 2 of the 1998 Securities Law.

166   Article 2 of the 2005 Securities Law.

lawfully approved for trading shall be quoted and traded on stock exchanges;[167] the trading shall be a public and centralized trading at competitive prices according to the principle of price precedence and time precedence.[168] Only securities companies that are qualified as members of a stock exchange may enter that stock exchange to participate in centralized trading at competing prices.[169] The transaction results of trading conducted in accordance with the trading rules formulated according to law may not be changed; traders who violate the rules during trading may not be exempted from civil liability.[170]

If an issuer or securities underwriter announces a prospectus, measures for offer of corporate bonds, finance or accounting report, listing document, annual report, interim report, or ad hoc report which contain or contains any false or misleading statement or major omission that causes investor losses during the course of securities trading, the issuer or the underwriter shall be liable for the losses. Also, the responsible director, supervisor or the manager of the issuer or the underwriter shall be jointly and severally liable for such losses.[171] This provision and other provisions[172] of the 1998 Securities Law regarding false statements made on the securities market have been extended into detailed procedural rules by the Supreme People's Court to guide the handling by the people's courts of civil litigation arising from the false statements.[173] Where a person bears civil liability for damages and is subject to a fine for violation of the securities law, and the property of the person is insufficient to pay both the damages and fine, he shall first bear the civil liability for damages.[174]

Securities Companies

The establishment of a securities company shall be subject to examination and approval by the securities regulatory authority; no one may engage in securities business without approval of the securities regulatory authority.[175] A securities company may take the form of either a limited liability company or a company limited by shares,[176] and should include the words "limited liability securities company" or "securities company limited by shares" in its name.[177] A range of matters regarding a securities company shall be subject to approval by the securities regulatory authority, including the establishment or closure of branches, change in its scope of business or registered capital or articles of association, merger, division, dissolution and change

---

167 Article 32 of the 1998 securities law.

168 *Id.* art. 33.

169 *Id.* art. 103.

170 *Id.* art. 115.

171 Article 63 of the 1998 Securities Law.

172 Articles 61, 161 and 202 of the 1998 Securities Law. *See* following Chapter 6 for further discussion of these provisions.

173 *See* following Chapter 6.

174 Article 207 of the 1998 Securities Law.

175 Article 117 of the 1998 Securities Law; Article 122 of the 2005 Securities Law.

176 Article 118 of the 1998 Securities Law; Article 123 of the 2005 Securities Law.

177 Article 120 of the 1998 Securities Law; Article 126 of the 2005 Securities Law.

in its corporate form.[178] Where an employee of a securities company, in the course of securities trading, violates trading rules under the instructions of the company or by taking advantage of his position, the securities company to which he belongs shall bear full liability.[179]

Under the 1998 Securities Law, securities companies were divided into comprehensive securities companies (*zonghelei zhengquan gongsi*) and brokerage securities companies (*jingjilei zhengquan gongsi*).[180] This division has now been cancelled by the 2005 Securities Law, under which securities companies are no longer named as comprehensive or brokerage companies and they may engage in, subject to approval by the securities regulatory authority, all or part of securities business, including brokerage business, consultation for securities investment, financial advice related to the activities of securities trading or securities investment, underwriting business and sponsorship, securities business on its own account and securities asset management.[181] No securities company may engage in securities business without a securities business permit issued by the securities regulatory authority.[182] In *Xineng Technology Company v Guotai Jun'an Securities Company*,[183] the defendant Guotai Jun'an securities company is an authorized comprehensive securities company and has capacity to engage in securities asset management business for clients. The Court held that the asset management agreement signed between the defendant and the plaintiff, under which the plaintiff entrusted 100 million yuan to the defendant for management, was a valid contract.[184]

Securities Companies and Investor Clients

It is required that an investor shall open a securities trading account with a securities company and shall purchase and sell securities through the securities company.[185] The securities company shall separately open a securities account and a funds account for a client, and shall manage the securities and funds delivered by the client under separate accounts and truthfully record transactions; the securities company may not make sham entries.[186] The securities company shall keep confidential the accounts opened for their clients.[187] Upon accepting an instruction to purchase or sell securities, the securities company shall purchase or sell securities as an agent in accordance with the trading rules and on the basis of the description of the securities,

---

178   Article 123 of the 1998 Securities Law; Article 129 of the 2005 Securities Law.
179   Article 145 of the 1998 Securities Law; Article 146 of the 2005 Securities Law.
180   Article 119 of the 1998 Securities Law. According to Articles 129 and 130, a comprehensive securities company may engage in brokerage business, securities business on its own account, and securities underwriting business while a brokerage securities company may only engage in securities brokerage business.
181   Article 181 of 2005 Securities Law.
182   *Id.* art. 128.
183   *See* following Chapter 2, footnote 63 and accompanying texts.
184   *Id.* at. p. 17.
185   Article 104 of the 1998 Securities Law.
186   *Id.* art. 138.
187   *Id.* art. 38.

the purchase or sale quantity, the method of bidding, and the price range instructed by a client; after a transaction is concluded, the securities company shall prepare a transaction report and deliver it to the client.[188] If a securities company deals with matters contrary to a client's instructions and thus causes losses to the client, the securities company shall be liable for the losses.[189]

A securities company and its employees may not purchase or sell securities on behalf of a client contrary to the client's instruction; may not purchase or sell securities in a client's account without the client's authorization, or purchase or sell securities under the name of a client; may not induce a client into making an unnecessary purchase or sale of securities in order to obtain a commission; may not misappropriate the securities entrusted by a client for purchase or sale or the funds in a client's account.[190] Under the 1998 Securities Law, a securities company may not finance its clients' transaction by providing securities or funds; securities sold by a securities company upon acceptance of an instruction shall be securities actually held in the client's securities account and securities purchased by a securities company shall be paid with funds actually deposited in the client's funds account.[191] This prohibition has now been lifted by the 2005 Securities Law.[192]

Civil Procedures

The primary source of civil procedure law in China is the 1991 Civil Procedure Law, which was developed on the basis of the 1982 Civil Procedure Law (for Trial Implementation).[193] After the enactment of the 1991 Civil Procedure Law, the Supreme People's Court promulgated in 1992 Opinion of the Supreme People's Court on Questions Concerning the Implementation of the Civil Procedure Law of the People's Republic of China.[194] Since 1991, civil procedural rules have been developed into a detailed and comprehensive body of rules in accordance with the principles set out in the 1991 Civil Procedure Law.[195] In the area of civil proceedings

---

188   *Id.* art. 140.

189   *Id.* art. 192.

190   *Id.* art. 73.

191   *Id.* art. 141.

192   Article 142 of the 2005 Securities Law states that "the service of a securities company to provide securities or funds for the purchase or sale of securities of its client shall be subject to the provisions of the State Council and be approved by the securities regulatory authority of the State Council."

193   *Supra* note 11.

194   Opinion of the Supreme People's Court on Questions Concerning the Implementation of the Civil Procedure Law of the People's Republic of China (Zuigao Renmin Fayuan Guanyu Shiyong Zhonghua Renmin Gongheguo Minshi Susong Fa Ruogan Wenti de Yijian), adopted by the Judicial Committee of the Supreme People's Court and promulgated on 14 July 1992.

195   The Supreme People's Court has issued various interpretations, provisions, explanations, replies, and opinions concerning different aspects of civil procedure law. For example, the Provisions of the Supreme People's Court on the Issue of Scope of Civil Proceedings Attached to Criminal Proceedings (Zuigao Renmin Fayuan Guanyu Xingshi Fudai Minshi Susong Fanwei Wenti de Guiding), issued on 13 December 2000.

concerning securities cases, a number of specific interpretations and guidelines have been issued by the Supreme People's Court, setting out detailed procedural rules for different types of securities disputes.[196] Apart from the civil procedural rules, provisions and procedural rules are available, according to which securities disputes can be resolved through arbitration and mediation.[197]

Statute of Limitation

Statute of limitation or periods of prescription (*susong shixiao*) are primarily governed by the 1986 GPCL.[198] In general, the statute of limitation shall be two years regarding applications to the people's courts for protection of civil rights.[199] The calculation of two years starts when the entitled person knows or should have known that his rights had been infringed upon.[200] The calculation shall be suspended during the last six months because of *force majeure* or other obstacles that make it impossible to pursue claims and shall be resumed on the day when the grounds for the suspension are eliminated;[201] the calculation shall be discontinued if suit is brought or if one party makes a claim for or agrees to fulfill obligations, and the calculation shall be restarted from the time of the discontinuance.[202]

The case *Business Center of Yunnan Provincial Branch of China Agriculture Bank v Shenzhen International Trust Investment Co.*[203] shows, as an example, the application of the provisions of statute of limitation by the people's courts. The plaintiff and defendant signed three securities repurchase contracts, under which the defendant agreed to repurchase 13 million yuan securities from the plaintiff on 30 September, 16 October and 29 October 1995 respectively. The plaintiff advanced 13 million yuan to the defendant after the agreements were signed, but the defendant did not issue securities safekeeping certificates to the plaintiff, nor did the defendant

---

196 The 1995 Supreme People's Court's guidelines on futures disputes, the 1996 Supreme People's Court's guidelines on securities repurchase disputes, and so on. *See* following chapters about these and other judicial interpretations and guidelines from the Supreme People's Court.

197 China International Economic and Trade Arbitration Commission Financial Disputes Arbitration Rules revised and adopted by the China Council for the Promotion of International Trade/China Chamber of International Commerce on 17 March 2005 and effective as of 1 May 2005. *See* following Chapter 7 for a discussion of this and other arbitration and mediation rules and provisions.

198 Chapter 7 "Periods of Prescription", including Articles 135–141.

199 Article 135 of the 1986 GPCL. Certain actions shall be one year, including claims for compensation for bodily injuries; sales of substandard goods without proper notice to that effect; delays in paying rent or refusal to pay rent; or loss of or damage to property left in the care of another person. Article 136 of the 1986 GPCL.

200 Article 137 of the 1986 GPCL, which also provides that under special circumstances, the people's court may extend the limitation of action; however, the people's court shall not protect his rights if twenty years have passed since the infringement.

201 Article 139 of the 1986 GPCL.

202 *Id.* art. 140.

203 *See* the Gazette of the Supreme People's Court of the People's Republic of China, Issue 5, 2004, pp. 8–13.

fulfill its repurchase obligation at the end of the agreements. After 29 October 1995 the plaintiff started to claim repayment of 13 million yuan from the defendant. The defendant returned 200,000 yuan on 31 July 1996; between 4 January and 28 August 1997 a third party paid the plaintiff 3.2 million yuan on behalf of the defendant. The plaintiff started a legal action on 8 November 1997. One of the defenses of the defendant was that the statute of limitation had expired. The Court rejected this argument on the ground that the statute of limitation was discontinued twice on 31 July 1996 and between 4 January and 28 August 1997 respectively.[204]

Article 141 of 1986 GPCL provides that if the law has other stipulations concerning limitation of action, those stipulations shall apply.[205] In securities law, both the 1998 Securities Law and the 2005 Securities Law provide no special stipulations concerning limitation of action in securities civil litigation. In general, securities cases follow the provisions of the 1986 GPCL with regard to statute of limitation. In certain circumstances, the Supreme People's Court has issued judicial provisions dealing with the issue of limitation of action, which has arisen in certain types of securities cases. One type of case is that of securities repurchase and the other comprises cases arising from false statements made on the securities market. In January 2001 the Supreme People's Court issued a circular[206] that dealt with the issue of recalculation of the statute of limitation in certain securities repurchase cases.[207] For cases arising from false statements, they are subject to special prerequisite rules set out by the circulars of the Supreme People's Court.[208]

Jurisdiction

The issue of jurisdiction is concerned with the question of which people's court has jurisdiction over a certain securities case. Under the 1983 People's Court Organization Law of the People's Republic of China,[209] the court in China consists of four levels, that is, the Supreme People's Court, the high people's courts, intermediate people's courts, and basic level people's courts.[210] Depending upon the circumstances of the case and in accordance with the provisions of the 1991 Civil Procedure Law and

---

204   *Id.* at p. 13.

205   For example, according to Article 45 of the 1993 Product Quality Law of the People's Republic of China, as amended in 2000, the right to claim compensation for damages caused by defect goods shall expire upon ten years starting from the time when such goods were delivered to initial consumers, except otherwise the time of claim is still within the period of safety use explicitly indicated.

206   Circular of the Supreme People's Court on the Issue of Statute Limitation in Connection With Remaining Credits and Debts after National Coordinated Clearance among Securities Repurchase Participants, *see* Chapter 4, footnote 30.

207   *Id. See* also footnotes 27, 29 of Chapter 4 and accompanying texts.

208   *See* following Chapter 6, in particular, the section "Administrative Penalty Decisions and Criminal Court Judgments"; "Statute of Limitation and Suspension of Proceedings".

209   The People's Court Organization Law of the People's Republic of China was adopted by the National People's Congress on 1 July 1979, as amended in 1983 and, most recently, in October 2006.

210   *Id.* art. 2.

the judicial guidelines of the Supreme People's Court with regard to jurisdiction, securities cases can start at the basic level people's courts, the intermediate people's courts or the high people's courts.

The basic principles governing court jurisdiction in China are so-called level jurisdiction (*jibie guanxia*) and territorial jurisdiction (*diyu guanxia*). Level jurisdiction means that different levels of the people's courts have jurisdictions over different cases according to their significance and whether foreign parties are involved in the case.[211] Among securities dispute cases, some are heard by basic level people's courts while others by higher level people's courts. Cases in which large sum of money or securities are involved, like the cases involving government bonds and securities repurchase contracts, are heard by high people's courts.

Territorial jurisdiction means that the people's court of the place where the defendant, whether an individual person, legal person, or any other organization, has his domicile.[212] In a contract dispute, the case shall be under the jurisdiction of the people's court of the place where the defendant has his domicile or where the contract is performed.[213] In a tort case, the jurisdiction shall be under the people's court of the place where the tort is committed or where the defendant has his domicile.[214] When two or more people's courts have jurisdiction over a case, the plaintiff may bring his lawsuit in one of these people's courts; if the plaintiff brings the lawsuit in two or more people's courts that have jurisdiction over the case, the people's court in which the case was first entertained shall have jurisdiction.[215]

In accordance with the 1991 Civil Procedure Law, the Supreme People's Court has power to designate the people's court of certain level or certain group of the people's court of certain level or individual people's courts to have jurisdiction over certain types of cases. Regarding the securities dispute cases, the Supreme People's Court has made such designations concerning certain types of securities disputes cases. Intermediate people's courts are designated by the Supreme People's Court as courts of first instance to hear cases arising from false statements made on the

---

211 *See* Articles 18–21 of the 1991 Civil Procedure Law, according to which the intermediate people's courts have jurisdiction as first instance courts over the cases involving foreign parties, the cases that are significant to local jurisdictions, and the cases that are designated by the Supreme People's Court; the high people's courts have jurisdiction as first instance courts over the cases that are significant to their jurisdictions; the Supreme People's Court has jurisdiction as first instance court over the cases that are significant to the whole country and the cases that the Supreme People's Court deems it should try.

212 Article 22 of the 1991 Civil Procedure Law.

213 *Id.* art. 24. In accordance with Article 25 of the 1991 Civil Procedure Law, the parties to a contract may agree to choose in their written contract the people's court of the place where the defendant has his domicile, where the contract is performed, where the contract is signed, where the plaintiff has his domicile or where the object of the action is located to exercise jurisdiction over the case, provided that the provisions of the 1991 Civil Procedure Law regarding jurisdiction are not violated.

214 *Id.* art. 29.

215 *Id.* art. 35.

securities market.[216] The intermediate people's courts, located in the Shanghai and Shenzhen stock exchanges, are designated by the Supreme People's Court as courts of first instance to hear the civil and administrative cases in which Shanghai Stock Exchange or Shenzhen Stock Exchange are defendants or third parties and the cases relate to regulatory function of stock exchanges.[217]

Third Party

Where the outcome of a case will affect a third party's legal interest, such party, though having no independent claim to the subject matter of the case, may file a request to participate in the proceedings or the people's court, shall notify the third party to participate; if the third party is to bear civil liability in accordance with the judgment of the people's court, he shall be entitled to the rights and obligations of the parties in the proceedings.[218] In *Li Erjiao v Zhang Shihui*,[219] for example, the defendant, who was entrusted by the plaintiff to collect the dividends of the plaintiff's 288 shares of the Shenzhen Development Bank, sold the 288 shares at a low price to his sister without telling the plaintiff. The Court said that the outcome of the case may affect legal interests of the defendant's sister. In accordance with Article 56 of the 1991 Civil Procedure Law, the Court notified the defendant's sister to join the proceedings.[220]

Appeal Procedures

If a party refuses to accept a judgment of first instant court, he shall have the right to file an appeal with the people's court at the next higher level within 15 days after the date on which the written judgment was served.[221] After hearing the appeal, the appeal court shall make the following decisions in accordance with Article 153 of the 1991 Civil Procedure Law. First, if the facts were clearly ascertained and the law was correctly applied in the original judgment, the appeal shall be rejected and the original judgment shall be affirmed.[222] Second, if the application of the law was

---

216   Article 3 of the 2003 Several Provisions of the Supreme People's Court on Hearing Civil Compensation Cases Arising from False Statement on the Securities Market. *See* Chapter 6, footnotes 3, 93, 94, 95, 96, 97, and accompanying texts.

217   Article 1 of the Provisions of the Supreme People's Court on the Issue of Jurisdiction Over and Acceptance of Lawsuits Related to Regulatory Function of Securities Exchanges (Zuigao Renmin Fayuan Guanyu Dui Yu Zhengquan Jiaoyisuo Jianguan Zhineng Xiangguan de Susong Anjian Guanxia Yu Shouli Wenti de Guiding), adopted by the Judicial Committee of the Supreme People's Court on 11 November 2004 and promulgated on 25 January 2005, effective as of 31 January 2005.

218   Article 56 of the 1991 Civil Procedure Law, which also stipulates that if a third party considers that he has an independent claim to the subject matter of a case, he shall have the right to bring an action.

219   *Supra* note 67.

220   *Id.* at p. 29.

221   Article 147 of the 1991 Civil Procedure Law.

222   Article 153 (1) of the 1991 Civil Procedure Law.

incorrect in the original judgment, the judgment shall be amended according to the law.[223] Third, if the facts were unclear or incorrectly ascertained or the evidence was insufficient in the original judgment, the appeal court shall make a ruling to set aside the judgment and remand the case to the original people's court for retrial, or the appeal court may amend the judgment after investigating and clarifying the facts.[224] Fourth, if there was violation of legal procedure in reaching the original judgment, which may have affected correct adjudication, the judgment shall be set aside and the case shall be remanded to the original people's court for retrial.[225] The parties concerned may appeal against the judgment or ruling rendered in a retrial of their case.[226]

Before the appeal court delivers its judgment, an appellant who has filed an appeal may apply for withdrawal of his appeal and the appeal court shall decide whether to approve the application or not.[227] For example, in *Qixiangtai Road Securities Trading Center of Tianjin City International Trust Investment Co. v Center Directly Under Changchun City Branch of Industrial and Commercial Bank of China*,[228] a case involving disputes over securities repurchase contracts, the defendant was not happy with the judgment of the Tianjin High People's Court and appealed to the Supreme People's Court. During the appeal proceedings, the appellant applied for withdrawal of the appeal on 14 October 1997. In accordance with Article 156 of the 1991 Civil Procedure Law, the Supreme People's Court examined the application and allowed the withdrawal. The Court said that the withdrawal application did not violate the law, nor harm the interests of the State and others and it should be allowed. The appellant was ordered to pay half of the court cost for appeal – 42,103.20 yuan. The ruling was final, after which the judgment of the Tianjin High People's Court became effective.[229]

The appeal system in China is so-called "two trials as final trial" (*liangshen zhongshen zhi*). That is, the judgment or ruling of a people's court of second instance shall be final.[230] However, if a party[231]considers that there is an error in a legally effective judgment or ruling, he may apply, through so-called "adjudication supervision procedure" (*shenpan jiandu chengxu*), to the people's court which

---

223   *Id.* art. 153 (2).

224   *Id.* art. 153 (3).

225   *Id.* art. 153 (4).

226   *Id.* art. 153 (second paragraph).

227   *Id.* art. 156.

228   *See Selection of Financial Dispute Cases Heard by the Supreme People's Court (1996–1998)* (*Zuigao Renmin Fayuan Shenli de Jinrong Jiufen Anli Xuanbian*), compiled by the Economic Division Court of the Supreme People's Court, pp. 716–717. (Beijing: China University of Political Science and Law Press, 1999).

229   *Id.* at p. 717.

230   Article 158 of the 1991 Civil Procedure Law.

231   Apart from the parties concerned, if the president of a people's court at any level or a people's court at a higher level or the supreme people's court finds definite error in a legally effective judgment or ruling of his court or lower level courts, such a case shall be dealt with in accordance with Article 177 of the 1991 Civil Procedure Law.

originally tried the case or to the people's court at the next higher level for a retrial,[232] during which time execution of the judgment or ruling shall not be suspended.[233] If the application meets any of the following conditions, the people's court shall retry the case; otherwise, the application shall be rejected. First, there is sufficient new evidence to set aside the original judgment or ruling.[234] Second, the main evidence on which the fact was ascertained in the original judgment or ruling, was insufficient.[235] Third, there was definite error in the application of the law in the original judgment or ruling.[236] Fourth, there was violation by the people's court of the legal procedure, which may have affected the correctness of the judgment or ruling.[237] Fifth, the judicial officers have committed embezzlement, accepted bribes, committed malpractices for personal benefits or perverted the law in the adjudication of the case.[238] Application for a retrial made by a party must be submitted within two years after the judgment or ruling becomes legally effective.[239]

In *Jiangxi Securities Trading Center of Hainan Saige International Trust Investment Co. v Nanchang Branch of the Transportation Bank*,[240] for example, the case was first tried by the Intermediate People's Court of Nanchang city, Jiangxi province, whose judgment was appealed by the defendant Nanchang branch of the transportation bank to the Jiangxi High People's Court. Now the Nanchang branch of the transportation bank refused to accept the final judgment of Jiangxi High People's Court and applied to the Supreme People's Court for a retrial. In accordance with the adjudication supervision procedure, the Supreme People's Court considered the application and ruled on 6 August 2001 for a retrial. A panel of three judges of the Supreme People's Court was subsequently formed and the case was retried by the panel. The case was closed in January 2003 with a final judgment of the panel.[241]

Special Procedures

One of the special procedures stipulated by the 1991 Civil Procedure Law[242] is so-called "procedure for publicizing public notice for assertion of claims" (*gongsshi cuigao chengxu*), according to which any holder of a bill transferable by endorsement or other negotiable instruments may, if the bill or instrument is stolen, lost or destroyed, apply to the basic level people's court of the place where the bill or instrument is to be paid or issued for publication of a public notice by the court for

---

232   Article 178 of the 1991 Civil Procedure Law.

233   *Id.*

234   *Id.* art. 179 (1).

235   *Id.* art. 179 (2).

236   *Id.* art. 179 (3).

237   *Id.* art. 179 (4).

238   *Id.* art. 179 (5).

239   *Id.* art. 182.

240   *See* the Gazette of the Supreme People's Court of the People's Republic of China, Issue 8, 2004, at pp.21–23.

241   *Id.* at p. 23.

242   Other special procedures under the 1991 Civil Procedure Law include bankruptcy procedures and procedures concerning qualification of electors, and so on.

assertion of claims.[243] The people's court, upon accepting the application, shall issue a public notice for the interested parties to assert their rights; the period of the public notice shall be decided at the discretion of the people's court; however, it shall not be less than sixty days.[244] If no claim is asserted, the people's court shall a judgment on the basis of the application to declare the bill or instrument null and void; the applicant shall be entitled to payment or other rights.[245]

Li Chuanxiong, a case involving stolen share certificates, was the first securities case of this kind which came to the people's court in 1993.[246] In April 1986, Li Chuanxiong from Shanghai purchased through a securities company 60 shares of Shanghai Vacuum Electronic Equipment Co. In September 1991, Li Chuanxiong's home was broken into by burglars and the certificates of 60 shares were among the things which were stolen. At the time when this happened, share trading in Shanghai was moving to paperless trading and securities companies started to computerize holdings of shareholders. But the securities company refused to enter Li Chuanxiong's shareholdings into the computer system because his share certificates were stolen. Li Chuanxiong applied to Shanghai Jing'an District People's Court for a public notice. After verification was made with the registration department of Shanghai Stock Exchange about the existence of these 60 shares under the name of the applicant, the Court issued a public notice in the Shanghai Securities newspaper. No one turned up to claim interests connected with these shares upon the expiration of sixty days. In accordance with Article 197 of the 1991 Civil Procedure Law,[247] the Court then invalided the 60 shares and the applicant was entitled for a re-issue by the company of the shares.[248]

Civil Evidence Rules

The primary source of civil evidence rules is the 1991 Civil Procedure Law in which Articles 63 to 74 especially deal with rules on civil evidence.[249] In addition, there are some other provisions in the 1991 Civil Procedure Law that also touch upon evidential matters one way or another.[250] The 1992 Opinion of the Supreme People's Court on Questions Concerning the Implementation of the Civil Procedure Law provides for interpretations on the evidential rules prescribed by the 1991 Civil Procedure Law.[251] In 2001, the Supreme People's Court promulgated the Several Provisions of the Supreme People's Court on Evidence in Civil Litigation, a long-

---

243   Article 193 of the 1991 Civil Procedure Law.

244   *Id.* art. 194.

245   *Id.* art. 197.

246   *See* the Gazette of the Supreme People's Court of the People's Republic of China, Issue 4, 1993, at pp. 164–165.

247   *Supra* note 245.

248   *Supra* note 244, at p. 165.

249   The 1991 Civil Procedure Law, Chapter 6 "Evidence", including Articles 63–74.

250   For example, Article 125 provides that the parties may present new evidence during a court session.

251   *Supra* note 194. In particular, Articles 70–78 deal with evidential rules.

awaited judicial guideline[252] that fills, to certain extent, the need for more detailed civil evidential rules. As in other areas of civil litigation, civil evidential rules play an important part in securities civil litigation.

Under the 1991 Civil Procedure Law, civil evidence broadly includes documentary evidence (*shuzheng*), material evidence (*wuzheng*), audio-visual material (*shiting ziliao*), testimony of witnesses (*zhengren zhengyan*), statements of the parties (*dangshiren de chenshu*), authenticate conclusions (*jianding jielun*) and records of inspection (*kanyan bilu*).[253] All these types of evidence must be verified before they can be taken as a basis for ascertaining a fact.[254] Where the evidence is in duplicate and where the provider refuses to offer the original copy or clues to the original copy, for which there is no other document to confirm and the party of the other side refuses to recognize, such evidence shall not be used as the grounds for ascertaining the facts.[255]

It is the duty of a party to an action to provide evidence in support of his claims.[256] If a party and his lawyer are unable to collect the evidence themselves or if the people's court considers the evidence necessary for the trial of the case, the people's court shall investigate and collect it.[257] In *China Life Insurance Company Chengdu Branch v Sichuan Hualong Investment Consultant Co. Ltd.*,[258] for example, the Court, upon an application from one of the appellants, investigated and collected a list of evidence from, among others, the trading information center of the Shanghai Stock Exchange.[259] In *Business Center of Yunnan Provincial Branch of China Agriculture Bank v Shenzhen International Trust Investment Co.*,[260] the Court initiated an investigation and collected evidence from the Wuhan Securities Trading Center concerning membership application records in order to establish the membership status of the defendant and other facts.[261]

A party can apply to the people's court for an extension of the time limit for adducing evidence if it is actually difficult for the party concerned to submit evidential material within the specified time limit for adducing evidence, and the time limit may

---

252   The Several Provisions of the Supreme People's Court on Evidence in Civil Litigation (Zuigao Renmin Fayuan Guanyu Minshi Susong Zhengju de Ruogan Guiding), adopted by the Judicial Committee of the Supreme People's Court on 6 December 2001 and promulgated on 21 December 2001, effective as of 1 April 2002.

253   Article 63 of the 1991 Civil Procedure Law.

254   *Id.*

255   Article 77 of the 1992 Opinion of the Supreme People's Court on Questions Concerning the Implementation of the Civil Procedure Law.

256   Article 64 of the 1991 Civil Procedure Law.

257   *Id.*

258   *See* the Gazette of the Supreme People's Court of the People's Republic of China, Issue 8, 2005, pp. 14–23.

259   *Id.* at p. 16.

260   *See* the Gazette of the Supreme People's Court of the People's Republic of China, Issue 5, 2004, pp. 8–13.

261   *Id.* at pp. 11–12.

be appropriately extended upon the permission of the people's courts.[262] In *Xineng Technology Company v Guotai Jun'an Securities Company*,[263] for example, the defendant Guotai Jun'an securities company applied to the Shanghai High People's Court, the court of first instance, for an extension of the time limit for adducing evidence, which was agreed and extended by the Court. Guaotai Jun'an submitted the evidence within the extended time limit, including a crucial piece of evidence concerned with the asset balance account of the plaintiff held by the defendant. In the appeal proceedings, the plaintiff challenged this piece of evidence on the ground that the evidence was not submitted within the time limit and thus the first instant court should not have admitted this piece of evidence. This argument was rejected by the Supreme People's Court.[264]

Under circumstances where there is a likelihood that evidence may be destroyed or lost, or difficult to obtain later, the parties in the proceedings may apply to the people's court for preservation of the evidence; the people's court may also on its own initiative take measures to preserve such evidence.[265] In *China Life Insurance Company Chengdu Branch v Sichuan Hualong Investment Consultant Co. Ltd.*, the Court made an evidence preservation order after the plaintiff applied to the Court for preservation of the evidence relating to the trading records of the plaintiff held by a third party in the trial.[266] An application for the evidence preservation shall not be later than seven days before expiration of the time limit for adducing evidence.[267] The people's court may require that the applicant provide relevant guarantees for the application.[268] The people's court may preserve evidence by means of sealing up, detention, photo taking, sound recording, video recording, reproduction, authentication, inspection and reconnaissance, making written records, and so on, as the case may be; the people's court may also require the parties concerned or their representatives in the litigation to be on the scene.[269]

Enforcement

Enforcement (*zhixing*) is an important part of proceedings of civil securities litigation. The 1991 Civil Procedure Law sets out basic principles of enforcement procedure (*zhixing chengxu*), which apply to all types of civil cases.[270] A party may apply to the people's court for enforcement if the other party refuses to comply with legally

---

262   Article 36 of the 2001 Several Provisions of the Supreme People's Court on Evidence in Civil Litigation.

263   *See* the Gazette of the Supreme People's Court of the People's Republic of China, Issue 8, 2004, pp. 16–20.

264   *Id.* at p. 19.

265   Article 74 of the 1991 Civil Procedure Law.

266   *Supra* note 258, at p. 15.

267   Article 23 the 2001 Several Provisions of the Supreme People's Court on Evidence in Civil Litigation.

268   *Id.*

269   *Id.* art. 24.

270   The 1991 Civil Procedure Law, Part Three "Enforcement Procedure", including Chapters 20–23 and Articles 207–236.

effective judgments or rulings; the judge may also initiatively refer the matter to the enforcement officer for enforcement.[271] The time limit for the submission of an application for enforcement shall be one year if both or one of the parties are citizens, and six months if both parties are legal persons or other organizations.[272] The time limit shall be calculated from the last day of the period of performance specified by the legal document; if the performance is in stages it shall be calculated from the last day of the period specified for each stage of performance.[273]

The people's courts have a wide range of powers, subject to the prescribed limitations, to enforce legally effective judgments, rulings, mediation agreement, arbitral awards and other legal documents. The people's courts can make inquiries into banks and other organizations,[274] freeze or transfer deposits,[275] withhold or withdraw part of the income of the person subject to enforcement order,[276] seal up, detain, freeze, sell by public auction, or sell off part of the property of the person subject to enforcement order,[277] issue a search warrant and search persons or the place where the property was concealed,[278] order a person, legal person or other organizations to hand over property or negotiable instruments in their possession,[279] and evict a person, legal person or other organizations from a building or a plot of land.[280]

These and other general provisions of enforcement procedure stated in the 1991 Civil Procedure Law have been interpreted by the Supreme People's Court in the 1992 Opinion of the Supreme People's Court on Questions Concerning the Implementation of the Civil Procedure Law[281] and in many other judicial interpretations and guidelines of the Supreme People's Court concerning different aspects of enforcement procedure and application of enforcement procedure in different areas of law.[282] In the area of securities law, the Supreme People's Court has issued a number of circulars, explanations or provisions, which address various

---

271 Article 216 of the 1991 Civil Procedure Law.
272 *Id.* art. 219.
273 *Id.*
274 *Id.* art. 221.
275 *Id.*
276 *Id.* art. 222.
277 *Id.* art. 223.
278 *Id.* art. 227.
279 *Id.* art. 228.
280 *Id.* art. 229.
281 *See* Articles 254–303. For example, Article 232 of the 1991 Civil Procedure Law requires the interest of a debt to be paid double for delay of performance, which refers, according to the interpretation of Article 293 of the 1992 Opinion of the Supreme People's Court on Questions Concerning the Implementation of the Civil Procedure Law, to doubling the interests on the base of debt interest calculated with the highest interest rate of the bank loan in the same period.
282 For example, the 2005 Provisions of the Supreme People's Court on the People's Court Enforcement of Property with Mortgage (Zuigao Renmin Fayuan Guanyu Renmin Fayua Zhixing Sheding Diya de Fangwu de Guiding), the 2006 Provisions of the Supreme People's Court on Several Time Limits in the Handling of Enforcement Cases by the People's Courts (Zuigao Renmin Fayuan Guanyu Renmin Fayuan Banli Zhixing Anjian Ruogan Qixian de Guiding).

enforcement issues in the securities market, including, among others, the issue of freezing and transferring funds of settlement accounts of securities exchanges, futures exchanges, securities registration and settlement organizations, securities companies or futures firms,[283] the issue of freezing and auctioning state-owned shares and legal person shares of listed companies,[284] and the issue of freezing and transferring settlement funds of securities trading.[285]

Summary

China's current legal, regulatory and judicial system has been gradually built up since 1978 in the wake of China's economic reform and transition to a market economy. The securities market, which emerged in the process of economic reform, has become an integrated part of China's economic system. Legal, regulatory and judicial rules have also been gradually developed into a relatively comprehensive framework to govern the securities market and the resolution of securities disputes. This chapter has outlined some aspects of important basic legal, regulatory and judicial rules commonly applicable to all types of securities dispute cases.

In the first stage of the development of China's current legal system, in the 1980s, a group of basic and important laws were enacted, including, among others, the 1981 Economic Contract Law, the 1982 Civil Procedure Law (for Trial Implementation) and the 1986 GPCL. These laws laid down basic civil procedural rules and general principles of civil and commercial law, such as the legal requirement for civil juristic acts, provisions on civil liability and compensation, law of agency, validity of contract and civil liability for breach of contract. In the late 1980s, disputes involving shares, bonds and other types of securities began to emerge along with the emergence of China's securities market. The basic laws that were promulgated in the 1980s, albeit general and abstract, provided necessary basic legal rules and procedural rules in the resolution of securities dispute cases when these cases started coming into the people's courts.

Moving into the 1990s, China's legal reform was stepping up and one of the areas of law on the legislative agenda was company and securities law. In 1993 the

---

283 The Circular of the Supreme People's Court on Freezing and Transferring Funds of Settlement Accounts of Securities or Futures Exchanges, Securities Registration and Settlement Organizations, Securities Business or Futures Brokerage Institutions (Zuigao Renmin Fayuan Guanyu Dongjie, Huabo Zhengquan Huo Qihuo Jiaoyisuo, Zhengquan Dengji Jieshuan Jigou, Zhengquan Jingying Huo Qihuo Jingji Jigou Qingshuan Zhanghu Zijin Deng Wenti de Tongzhi), issued by the Supreme People's Court on 2 December 1997.

284 The Provisions of the Supreme People's Court on Several Issues of Freezing, Auctioning State-owned Shares and Public Legal Person Shares of Listed Companies (Zuigao Renmin Fayuan Guanyu Dongjie, Paimai Shangshi Gongsi Guoyougu he Shehui Farengu Ruogan Wenti de Guiding), adopted by the Judicial Committee of the Supreme People's Court on 28 August 2001 and promulgated on 21 September 2001, effective as of 30 September 2001.

285 The Circular of the Supreme People's Court on Relevant Issues of Freezing, Transferring Settlement Funds of Securities Trading (Zuigao Renmin Fayuan Guanyu Dongjie, Kouhua Zhengquan Jiaoyi Jieshuan Zijin Youguan Wenti de Tongzhi), issued by the Supreme People's Court on 9 November 2004.

Company Law was promulgated and this was followed by the promulgation of the Securities Law in 1998. Together with other company and securities regulations, the 1993 Company Law and the 1998 Securities Law have established a regulatory framework for companies and the issuing and trading of shares and corporate bonds. Securities companies and their activities are defined and the relationship between securities company and investor clients is regulated. Both the 1993 Company Law and the 1998 Securities Law were significantly amended in 2005, which marked a new stage of company and securities regulation in China. Along with the establishment of the Shanghai and Shenzhen stock exchanges in 1990 and 1991 and the creation of the CSRC in 1992, trading rules and other detailed regulatory rules were gradually established, which helped the people's court in dealing with technical and specific issues involved in a securities dispute.

On a general level, the 1990s witnessed further development of civil and commercial law. The 1995 Security Law, which is relevant to securities transactions and the resolution of securities disputes, set out statutory forms of security on the bases of the framework laid down by the 1986 GPCL, and codified some regulatory practices that had existed until then, such as the ban on state authorities providing security for enterprises and their economic activities and contracts. The 1999 Contract Law, an important enactment of civil and commercial law, brought about a uniform contract law. New types of contract, such as brokerage contract, have been added in the statute; application of law has become consistent and clearer than the previous system of separate contract laws.

In parallel with the development of the legal and regulatory framework, since 1991 civil procedural rules have been developed into a detailed and comprehensive body of rules and continued after the 1991 Civil Procedure Law was enacted, replacing the 1982 Civil Procedure Law (for Trial Implementation). Crucial to the proceedings involving securities dispute cases, the 1991 Civil Procedure Law and the implementing rules established by the Supreme People's Court in accordance with the 1991 Civil Procedure Law cover every aspect of civil court procedures and, in some aspects, arbitral procedures. Rules on statute of limitation, jurisdiction, appeal procedure, civil evidence, enforcement and many other procedures are fundamentally as important to the securities dispute resolution by the people's court as to all other civil proceedings.

In 2001, the Supreme People's Court promulgated the Several Provisions of the Supreme People's Court on Evidence in Civil Litigation, an important judicial guideline, which enhanced civil evidential rules. In the area of securities law, between September 2001 and January 2003, the Supreme People's Court issued three circulars concerning civil compensation claims arising from securities market fraud, in particular, claims arising from false statements made on the securities market. In the area of enforcement the Supreme People's Court issued a number of circulars, explanations and provisions, addressing various enforcement issues in the securities market. All these and other judicial guidelines of the Supreme People's Court concerning securities market, such as guidelines on cases involving securities repurchase contracts, complement the general principles of civil procedure law and form a distinctive body of procedural rules governing the resolution of securities dispute by the people's court.

Chapter 2

The Share Issuing and Trading Market

Introduction

China started enterprise reform programs in the early 1980s. State-owned enterprises, which had been the dominant form of enterprises after 1949, began a restructuring process. In some parts of China, some of the state-owned enterprises were restructured into joint stock companies and shares were issued to their employees and the public for the first time in China since 1949.[1] Later, in the early 1990s, China started to open up the securities market to foreign investment through first, creating a domestic B-share market and, second, sending Chinese companies to overseas stock markets for listing.[2] Depending on the nature and holder, shares (*gufen/gupiao*) are classified into internal employee shares (*neibu zhigonggu*), public shares (*gongzhonggu*), state-owned shares (*guoyougu*), legal person-owned shares (*farengu*), individual-owned shares (*gerengu*) and foreign-owned shares (*waizigu*), including domestically listed foreign investment shares (*jingnei shangshi waizigu*) and internationally listed foreign investment shares (*jingwai shangshi waizigu*).[3]

Beginning in 1986, some major cities set up trading centers and trading in shares began in these cities through the trading centers.[4] Securities companies were set up all over the country, and engaged in share trading either on their own or as agents of investor principals. After the establishment of Shanghai and Shenzhen stock exchanges in 1990 and 1991 respectively, share issuing and trading came into a new stage. Over the years, China's stock market had been dominated by individual investors and speculative investments, which contributed to occurrences of disputes in share issuing and the trading market. "Share frenzy" was a phenomenon, particularly in the early years of China's stock market.[5] The introduction in the context of China's WTO (World Trade Organization) accession into what is known as the QFII (Qualified Foreign Institutional Investors) scheme in November 2002, which promotes medium- and long-term investments, is likely to help prevent

---

1   For more details, *see* Zhu Sanzhu, *Securities Regulation in China*, pp. 3–8. (Ardsley, NY: Transnational Publishers, 2000).

2   *Id.* pp. 14–17 and pp. 127–165.

3   *Id.* p. 5, p. 19 and pp. 127–128.

4   For a survey of these trading centers and their activities up to early 1990s, *see* Mei Xia et al., *The Re-emerging Securities Market in China*, pp. 104–112. (Westport: Quorum Books, 1992). *See also* Zhu Sanzhu, p. 7, *supra* note 1.

5   *See* Zhu Sanzhu, p. 8, *supra* note 1.

the market from being dominated by individual investors to being dominated by institutional investors.[6]

Before the promulgation of 1998 Securities Law, the 1993 Provisional Regulations on the Administration of Issuing and Trading of Shares was the first major piece of national legislation that provided a regulatory framework for share issuing and trading. At local level, some local governments issued local regulations on shares, for example, the 1991 Provisional Measures of the Shenzhen Special Economic Zone on the Administration of Issuing and Trading of Shares.[7] After the establishment of the Shanghai and Shenzhen stock exchanges, detailed rules were set out governing listing and trading of shares in these two national stock exchanges. A large number of regulations have been issued and implemented by the State Council Securities Committee and the China Securities Regulatory Commission covering every aspects of share issuing and trading, for example, the 1997 Strict Prohibition of Speculation in Shares by State-owned Enterprises and Listed Companies.[8] There regulations and rules provide guidance on various issues the people's courts are faced with in resolving disputes in share issuing and trading market in accordance with the 1986 GPCL and other relevant statutes.

Disputes Involving Shares

Disputes involving shares may happen at both the stage of share issuing and the stage of share trading. A range of issues may be involved in the disputes, such as ownership of shares, agency relationship between investor principals and securities company agents, sale and purchase contracts, settlement and transfer. Disputes between investor principals and securities company agents, particularly at the stage of share trading, comprise a majority of the disputes involving shares, and is regarded as one of the most noticeable features of civil disputes involving shares in China.[9] Discussions in this chapter focus on some important aspects of the disputes between investor principals and securities company agents.

Mistakes Made by Securities Companies

Securities companies may make various kinds of mistakes in the process of share issuing and trading on behalf of investor clients, such as the mistakes made when processing a sale or purchase order instructed by investor clients. These mistakes

---

6   *See* Zhu Sanzhu "Implementing China's WTO Commitments in Chinese Financial Services Law", *The China Review*, Vol. 6, No. 2, Fall 2006, pp. 14–21.

7   It was promulgated by the Shenzhen special economic zone people's government on 15 June 1991.

8   It was issued by the State Council Securities Committee, in conjunction with other government authorities, on 21 May 1997.

9   *See Studies of Judicial Decisions Related to Financial Disputes* (*Jinrong Shenpan Anli Yanjiu*) (Vol. 2001), edited by Economic Division Court of Beijing High People's Court, p. 396. (Beijing: Law Publishing House, 2001). The comment is made by Liu Wei, Beijing Haidian District People's Court.

are often referred to collectively as operational errors (*caozuo shiwu*).[10] In some cases, because of such operational errors, instructions from investor clients may be processed wrongly and disputes come to the people's courts. The case *Wang Luhui v Sichuan Province Securities Co. Ltd.*,[11] which happened in the early years of China's stock market, is an example in which the defendant securities company wrongly processed an instruction of the plaintiff Wang Luhui due to an operational error and Wang Luhui sued the defendant in the people's court. The case, which went through from first instant court to appeal court, illustrates the way in which the people's courts deal with the disputes arising from operational errors of securities companies.

Wang Luhui signed an agreement with the Yulong business center of Sichuan province securities company and designated the Yulong business center as his agent for the trading of the securities listed on the Shanghai Stock Exchange. On 11 August 1994, Wang Luhui instructed the defendant company to sell 1,000 shares of Hebei Huayao company at a price of 5 yuan per share. However, a trader of the defendant company by mistake typed in a purchase order instead of a sale order. Consequently 1,000 Hebei Huayao shares were purchased for Wang Luhui at a price of 5 yuan per share. After the mistake was discovered, the defendant paid the purchase from its own account. On 12 August, when the market was opened, the defendant sold the 1,000 shares at a price of 5.34 yuan per share. When Wang Luhui was told on 12 August that his 1,000 shares had not been sold out, he instructed the defendant to sell them and in the afternoon a sale was made, in which the 1,000 shares were sold at a price of 5.10 yuan per share.

The defendant explained what had happened to Wang Luhui but Wang Luhui insisted on claiming compensation. After his request was refused by the defendant, who would only prepare to offer an apology, Wang Luhui brought the case to the People's Court of Qingyang district, Chengdu city, claiming an economic loss of 30,000 yuan from the defendant, which was changed during the hearing to a claim of 77,383.70 yuan as direct and indirect losses. Wang Luhui submitted that, because of what had happened, his normal trading on 11 August failed; though the shares were sold out next day, the sale price was not satisfactory; the defendant should compensate the economic loss he suffered. The defendant submitted that it was a mistake for which a remedial measure had been taken soon after the mistake was discovered; moreover, no loss was caused to the plaintiff.

The Qingyang District People's Court considered whether the defendant was liable for compensation and if so, how to calculate the compensation. The Court said that, although the defendant took necessary remedial measures afterwards, it nevertheless caused the plaintiff unable to go ahead with his intended sale on 11 August. The defendant should therefore compensate the plaintiff on this ground. The opening price of Hebei Huayao shares on 11 August was 4.90 yuan and closing

---

10   See *Carefully Selected Cases of the People's Courts (Renmin Fayuan Anli Xuan Jingbianben)*, Vol. 1, 2001, edited by China Law Application Research Institute of the Supreme People's Court, p.739. (Beijing: Xinhua Publishing Press, 2001) where the phrase "operational error" is used by the commentator.

11   See the Gazette of the Supreme People's Court of the People's Republic of China, Issue 1, 1997, at pp. 28–30.

price 5.11 yuan; the highest price during the day was 5.98 yuan and the lowest 4.65 yuan. The Court held that the defendant would pay compensation of 808 yuan to the plaintiff, which was the difference between the price of 5.98 yuan, the highest price on 11 August, and the price of 5.10 yuan, at which the plaintiff sold the 1,000 shares on 12 August. The Court based its decision on broad provisions of Articles 106 (2) and 134 (1) (vii) of the 1986 GPCL.[12]

In a sense, what the Qingyang District People's Court awarded to the plaintiff was compensation for a possible chance the plaintiff could have had during share trading on 11 August but had lost because of the defendant. That is, had the defendant not made the mistake, the plaintiff would have had a chance to sell his 1,000 shares at the highest price of 5.98 yuan on 11 August. This award was criticized by commentators as a wrong decision by the Court.[13] They submitted that the plaintiff's "loss" determined by the Qingyang District People's Court was only a possible loss; whether such loss could become real loss depend on further conditions; such possible loss could not be treated as a loss giving rise to a civil compensation; and the price at which the plaintiff sold the 1,000 shares on 12 August was in fact higher than 5 yuan he had instructed the defendant on 11 August, which meant that the mistake made by the defendant resulted in not a loss but a gain for the plaintiff.[14]

Both plaintiff and defendant appealed the decision of the Qingyang District People's Court to the Intermediate People's Court of Chengdu city. The plaintiff Wang Luhui claimed that the defendant committed fraud on his account by buying and selling shares without his consent; the defendant defended that it was an error and no loss was caused to the plaintiff. The Chengdu Intermediate People's Court dismissed the plaintiff's appeal and cancelled the 808 yuan compensation award made by the Qingyang District People's Court. The Chengdu Intermediate People's Court said that the loss as awarded by the Qingyang District People's Court according to the difference between the highest price on 11 August and the price at which the plaintiff sold the share on 12 August had no legal basis and the application of the law by the Qingyang District People's Court was inappropriate. The Chengdu Intermediate People's Court instead applied Article 134 (10) of the 1986 GPCL[15] and ordered the defendant to apologize to the plaintiff in writing within three days after the judgment.

The reasoning of the Chengdu Intermediate People's Court was threefold.[16] First, the defendant should bear certain responsibilities for the fault that its staff mistakenly typed in a wrong order and thus caused the plaintiff's 1,000 shares unable to be sold out on 11 August; second, after the plaintiff knew on 12 August that his 1,000 shares

---

12   Article 106 (2) states that: "Citizens and legal persons who through their fault encroach upon state or collective property or the property or person of other people shall bear civil liability." Article 134 (1) (IV) states that: "The main methods of bearing civil liability shall be: (IV) compensation for losses."

13   *See* SHAO *Securities Law (Zhengquan Fa)*, edited by Shao Tingjie et al. (eds), *Securities Law* (Tingjie, *Zhengquan Fa*), p. 344 (Beijing: Law Publishing House, 1999).

14   *Id.*

15   Article 134 prescribes "extension of apology" as one of the methods of bearing civil liabilities which may be used on its own or concurrently with other methods.

16   *Supra* note 11, at p. 30.

had not been sold out on the previous day according to his instruction, he instructed the defendant to sell those shares on 12 August. The instructed price and the actual sale price on 12 August were both higher than the price the plaintiff instructed on 11 August, so that although the defendant had made an error it caused no economic loss to the plaintiff; third, after the defendant company discovered the mistake it treated the wrongly purchased 1,000 shares as their own purchase, which was an appropriate remedial measure taken by the defendant according to the trading rules of the Shanghai Stock Exchange.[17] The judgment of the Chengdu Intermediate People's Court was viewed as a good and correct judgment compared with the judgment of the Qingyang District People's Court.[18]

The replacement of the award of 808 yuan compensation with an extension of apology by the Chengdu Intermediate People's Court was partly based on the Court's finding that the defendant should bear certain responsibilities for the fault that its trader had mistakenly typed in a wrong order. In other words, the Court dealt with the issue of operational error in accordance with *fault* principles prescribed in the general provisions of the 1986 GPCL.[19] However, similar cases in which operational error was an issue may be dealt with by the people's courts not on the ground of fault but on the ground of *serious misunderstanding* in accordance with Article 59 of the 1986 GPCL which provides that a party shall have the right to request a people's court or an arbitration organization to alter or rescind a civil act that is performed by an actor who seriously misunderstands the contents of the act and such rescinded act shall be null and void from the very beginning.[20]

Serious or major misunderstanding (*zhongda wujie*), as stipulated by Article 59 of the 1986 GPCL, has been interpreted by the Supreme People's Court to mean that an actor performs his conducts on the basis of a false understanding of the nature of the conduct, the opposite party, the variety, quality, specification and amount of the objects and so on, which leads to a consequence of the conduct going against his own will and results in considerable damages.[21] If there is an act of major misunderstanding, the parties concerned can request a people's court to alter or rescind it within one year from the time when the act occurred.[22] In *Yi Shicheng and Fang Bingyin v Shanghai Business Center of Zhejiang Province Securities Co.*,[23]

---

17   The rules that the Chengdu Intermediate People's Court referred to was Article 108 (2) of the Shanghai Stock Exchange Trading Market Business Rules, which provides that where a purchase order or a sale order is submitted in an opposite way, it shall be corrected by securities companies themselves inside the exchange.

18   *Supra* note 10, at p. 740; *supra* note 13, at p. 344.

19   Article 106 (2), *supra* note 12.

20   Article 59 (1) (i) and (2) of the 1986 GPCL.

21   Article 71 of the Opinion (for Trial Use) of the Supreme People's Court on Questions Concerning the Implementation of "the General Principles of Civil Law of the People's Republic of China", adopted by the Judicial Committee of the Supreme People's Court on 26 January 1988 and promulgated on 2 April 1988.

22   *Id.* Article 73.

23   See WU Zhipan and TANG Jiemang (eds.), *Explanation and Analysis of Typical Cases of Financial Law, 1st Issue (Jinrong Fa Dianxing Anli Jiexi, Diyi Ji)*, pp.203-206. (Beijing: China Finance Publishing House, 2000).

a case arising initially from an operational error made by a third party securities company whose trader processed a sale order mistakenly at a price of 22 yuan instead of 222 yuan as instructed by its client, the issue of operational error was dealt with by the Court on the ground of misunderstanding in accordance with Article 59 of the 1986 GPCL.

On 3 June 1992, the plaintiffs Yi Shicheng and Fang Bingyin each instructed the defendant securities company to purchase 100 Erfangji shares at a limit price of 215 yuan and 216 yuan per share respectively. In the afternoon of the same day a trader of another securities company at the Shanghai Stock Exchange mistakenly processed into the computer system a sale of 2,000 Erfangji shares at a price of 22 yuan instead of 222 yuan. According to the trading practice at the Shanghai Stock Exchange, a deal price took the middle price of sale and purchase prices, so the two purchases of 100 shares instructed by the plaintiffs were made at a price of 118.50 yuan and 119 yuan per share respectively. Ten minutes later, the other securities company discovered the mistake and applied to the Shanghai Stock Exchange and the defendant for cancellation of the deal, which was done in the afternoon in accordance with the rules of the Shanghai Stock Exchange. However, the defendant did not destroy the receipt for the purchases and its staff over the counter thought the purchases had been completed. After the plaintiffs paid to the counter a total sum of 11,945.80 yuan and 11,996.20 yuan including taxes and commissions, they thought the two purchases had been settled. Several days later when Fang Bingyin attempted to sell the 100 shares he bought, he was told by the defendant that the purchase on 3 June had in fact been cancelled.

After their demand for compensation was refused by the defendant, they took the case to the people's court, claiming 21,945.80 yuan and 24,203.80 yuan compensation, calculated on the basis of the share price of 219 yuan and 242 yuan per share. The defendant submitted that they were willing to return the plaintiffs their original payments, but the purchase of 200 Erfangji shares at 11,945.80 yuan and 11,996.20 yuan was an act of major misunderstanding and the Court should rescind it. The trading records of the Shanghai Stock Exchange showed that the price of Erfangji share was rising after 4 June and started to fall at the end of June and early July.

A central question the Court was faced with was whether the defendant's act was a revocable act of major misunderstanding prescribed by Article 59 of the 1986 GPCL[24] or a breach of contract that the defendant had failed their duty of care as stipulated in the agreement with the plaintiffs. The Court said that the mistaken input into the computer system of 22 yuan instead of 222 yuan was essentially a misunderstanding by the trader about his operation; it followed that the acts of both defendant and the other securities company in relation to the purchases of 200 Erfangji shares were revocable acts of major misunderstanding prescribed by Article 59 of the 1986 GPCL; the cancellation by the defendant of the purchases afterwards upon an application from the other securities company and in consultation with the Shanghai Stock Exchange according to the trading rules and practice was appropriate; the defendant as an agent of the plaintiff did not act beyond its delegated power to

---

24   *Supra* note 20 and accompanying text.

harm the interests of the plaintiffs; the settlement of the purchases with the plaintiffs by the defendant's counter staff who thought mistakenly that the purchases had been completed was also a revocable act of major misunderstanding.[25]

Based on the above reasoning and in accordance with Article 59 of the 1986 GPCL, the Court accepted the submission from the defendant to rescind the purchases of 200 shares. The Court ruled that the act was null and void from the beginning; the defendant would return the payment of 11,945.80 yuan to Yi Shicheng and 11,996.20 yuan to Fang Bingyin, plus applicable interests. On the other hand, the Court recognized that whether one can make profits or not in share trading is closely linked with opportunities. This recognition led the Court to accept that, due to the defendant's oversight, the plaintiffs lost their opportunities to make money by continuous sale and purchase of the shares when the price of the share was rising; the defendant should bear certain responsibilities for their oversight and compensate the plaintiffs according to the circumstances. On this ground, the Court held that the defendant pay compensation 2,400 yuan plus applicable interest to each of the plaintiffs.[26]

Critical views about this case focus on the judgment of the Court with respect to the application of Article 59 of the 1986 GPCL in dealing with the operational errors occurring in this case.[27] Critics argued that the Court should have determined the case not as a case of major misunderstanding but as a case of fault by the defendant in their handling of the purchases.[28] They pointed out that, because of the defendant's oversight, the receipt for the cancelled purchases was not destroyed, which led to the defendant's counter staff to complete settlements with the plaintiffs. They argued that this act was not a subjective act of misunderstanding but an objective act of error; the defendant was fault party because of its careless act which was contrary to the duty of care that the defendant was expected to perform. In conclusion, the Court should have treated the defendant's act as a breach of duty of care rather than an act of major misunderstanding.[29]

Regarding the award of 2,400 yuan compensation to each of the plaintiffs on the basis of the recognition by the Court of the loss of opportunities by the plaintiffs to make money due to the defendant's oversight, some critics treat the award as a correct decision[30] while others criticize the award as being made by the judges at their

---

25   *Supra* note 23, at p. 205.

26   *Id.* at pp. 205, 206.

27   *See* Gao Yan and Yi Pingjun (eds), *Understanding and Application of Securities Law and Cases Comments and Analysis* (*Zhengquan Fa Lijie Shiyong Yu Anli Pingxi*) (Beijing: The People's Court Publishing House, 1996), p. 409; Li Guoguang et al. (eds), *A Complete Book of the PRC of Leading Adjudicated Cases – Economic Volume* (*Zhonhua Renmin Gongheguo Dianxing Shenpan Anli Quanshu – Jingjijuan*) (Beijing: China Democracy and Law Publishing House, 1998), p. 478; Wu Zhipan and Tang Jiemang, *supra* note 23, at p. 206.

28   *Id.*

29   *Id.* Gao Yan and Yi Pingjun, p. 409, Li Guoguang p. 478, Wu Zhipan and Tang Jiemang, p. 207.

30   *Id.* Gao Yan and Yi Pingjun, p. 412, Li Guoguang, p. 479.

discretion without any legal basis and failed to compensate the plaintiffs properly.[31] The critics argued that the compensation should instead have been calculated by a formula that took the highest price of Erfangji shares and minored its lowest price during the affected period, and then multiplied by the number of shares the plaintiffs instructed the defendant to purchase.[32]

Disputes involving operational errors made by securities companies happen more often at the stage of share trading than at the stage of share issuing. If a case involving operational errors by securities companies happens at the stage of share issuing, the legal principles that the people's courts apply to resolve the case would be no difference to the legal principles applied to the same kinds of cases at the stage of share trading. Primarily, the people's courts would engage in searching and determining who the party at fault is and where the fault lies, and decide the case accordingly. *Xia Yonglin v Wuxi Business Center of Haitong Securities Co. Ltd.*[33] is a case which happened at the stage of share issuing and involved an error made by the defendant securities company in relation to a subscription of shares by the plaintiff Xia Yonglin.

On 13 March 1997, Xia Yonglin appointed Wuxi business center of Haitong securities company as his agent for share trading. In March 1998, Wuliangye Company, a famous Chinese brewery company, launched a new issue of shares at the Shenzhen Stock Exchange at 14.77 yuan per share. Xia Yonglin applied for a subscription of 14,000 Wuliangye shares through the Wuxi business center and paid a deposit of 206,780 yuan. According to the method of subscription at that time, Xia Yonglin was first given 14 numbers, each of which was linked to the right of subscription of 1,000 shares. The numbers were created by the Shenzhen Stock Exchange and were passed on to Xia Yonglin by the Wuxi business center. If a number matches the winning number announced later by the Shenzhen Stock Exchange, the number holder would be entitled to purchase 1,000 shares. One of the numbers the Wuxi business center gave to Xia Yonglin matched the winning number announced by the Shenzhen Stock Exchange. But later it turned out that all the 14 numbers given by the Wuxi business center were wrong numbers. The reason was because the Wuxi business center had not updated its computer program according to an instruction by the Shenzhen Stock Exchange, which was issued to all securities companies sometime before the launch of Wuliangye shares. As a result, the computer at the Wuxi business center failed to read and produce correct numbers created by the Shenzhen Stock Exchange. What was passed on to Xia Yonglin was in fact 14 wrong numbers. Xia Yonglin was very disappointed and brought the case to the Wuxi City Chong'an District People's Court, claiming the right to purchase 1,000 Wuliangye shares and a compensation of 10,339 yuan in damages for his mental suffering, which was 5% of the price for 14,000 shares.

The Chong'an District People's Court said that the defendant had failed to follow the instructions of the Shenzhen Stock Exchange to update its computer program,

---

31   *Id.* Wu Zhipan and Tang Jiemang, p. 208.

32   *Id.*

33   *See* the Gazette of the Supreme People's Court of the People's Republic of China, Issue 6, 1999, pp. 208–209.

which resulted in passing on to the plaintiff wrong subscription numbers when acting for the plaintiff to subscribe Wuliangye shares. Because of the fault of the defendant, the plaintiff suffered some economic losses as the plaintiff had to spend time and expenses to resolve the matter. The defendant would bear responsibility for these losses. On the basis of this reasoning the Court awarded the plaintiff 2,000 yuan in damages in accordance with Article 66 (2) of the 1986 GPCL.[34] But the Court rejected the plaintiff's claim for mental sufferings. The Court said that the plaintiff may have suffered some distress, but the claim for 5% of the price for 14,000 shares was unfounded in fact and in law. The Court also rejected the plaintiff's claim for the right to subscribe 1,000 Wuliangye shares. The Court said that it was the Shenzhen Stock Exchange, not the defendant, who created the numbers, and the incorrect numbers the defendant passed on to the plaintiff because of its fault was not a valid certificate for the purchase of the shares.[35]

Securities Companies' Obligation to Process Instructions from Clients

Investor clients can instruct securities companies to sell or purchase shares at either a limit price or an open price according to the trading rules of the Shanghai and Shenzhen stock exchanges. If an open price is instructed, securities companies shall execute instructions at the best market price for their clients. Depending on the instruction of investor clients, sale or purchase orders can be valid for a different period of time. So if an open sale order is intended to be valid for a whole day, securities companies shall execute such an order continuously during the day at the best price for the client until the instructed share is sold out. Securities companies, in acting as an agent of investor clients, have a contractual duty to carry out instructions from investor clients. If securities companies fail to fulfill this contractual duty, they are liable for compensation for breach of contract.

Cheng Yonggang v Huaxia Securities Co. Ltd.[36] is a case in which the defendant securities company failed to carry out a sale order instructed by the plaintiff Chen Yonggang. On 24 May 1993 at 9:30 am when the Shanghai Stock Exchange was opened, Chen Yonggang instructed the defendant Huaxia securities company to sell 5,000 Tianqiao shares at market price. Cheng Yonggang filled in an instruction form, which was signed by him and the defendant. The instruction was intended to be valid for the whole day. On the same day at 9:35 am and 10:03 am Chen Yonggang instructed the defendant to sell another 3,000 and 2,000 Tianqiao shares separately. Later, during lunch time when the defendant published a list of the transactions completed in the morning, Chen Yonggang discovered that the first 5,000 shares he instructed the defendant to sell had not been sold out. Chen Yonggang made an

---

34 Article 66 (2) states that: "An agent shall bear civil liability if he fails to perform his duties and thus causes damage to the principal."

35 *Supra* note 33, at p. 209.

36 See *Selection of Analysis of Adjudicated Cases* (*Shenpan Anli Xuanxi*), edited by Beijing Haidian District People's Court (Beijing: China Political and Law University Press, 1997), pp. 289–293.

enquiry with the defendant and came to conclusion that the defendant had failed to process the sale order.

The records at the Shanghai Stock Exchange showed that the opening price of Tianqiao shares on 24 May was 28.50 yuan and the closing price 19.70 yuan; the highest price during the day was 28.50 and the lowest 19.40 yuan. Had the defendant sold the 5,000 shares at a price of 28.50 yuan the value of the shares would have been 142,500 yuan. Several days later Chen Yonggang sold the 5,000 Tianqiao shares for a total sum of 83,480 yuan. After a failed discussion with the defendant for compensation, Chen Yonggang brought the case to the Beijing Haidian District People's Court, claiming an economic loss of 59,010 yuan and interest of 2,680 yuan. The defendant submitted that they had processed the plaintiff's first sale order, but the defendant was unable to prove sufficient evidence about their submission to the Court.

The Beijing Haidian District Court held that the entrustment the plaintiff made with the defendant to sell 5,000 shares was in accordance with the trading rules of the Shanghai Stock Exchange, which formed a lawful contractual relationship between the plaintiff principal and the defendant agent; the parties should respect the contract and perform the obligations prescribed therein. The Court said that the defendant submitted to the Court that they had processed the plaintiff's first sale instruction, but because of changing share prices the 5,000 shares had not been sold out; however, the defendant could not provide sufficient evidence to show that they had carried out the plaintiff's first sale instruction. The Court ruled that the defendant had breached the contract and was liable for compensation. During the hearing the Court presided over a mediation process. The plaintiff and defendant willingly reached an agreement, according to which the defendant agreed to compensate the plaintiff 30,000 yuan and the plaintiff agreed to pay 2,360.70 yuan in court costs.[37]

From this simple case one can see that the Court's primary thinking was to determine, based on the evidence, whether the parties had performed their respective obligations. The sale order instructed by the plaintiff was intended for the whole day, so if the execution of the sale instruction failed to sell the 5,000 shares as the defendant submitted, the defendant should have continued to execute the sale during the day at the best price for the plaintiff until the shares were sold out. As the defendant was unable to discharge its burden of proof by providing a convincing explanation about the reason why they had executed the plaintiff's first sale instruction but the 5,000 shares had not been sold out, the Court concluded that the defendant had failed to fulfill its contractual obligation to carry out the instruction from the plaintiff. On this basis the Court held the defendant liable for breach of contract to compensate the plaintiff.[38]

The approach the Beijing Haidian District Court took in this case is also seen in other similar cases in which a primary task for the people's courts is to establish first whether the securities company in question has fulfilled its contractual obligation to

---

37   *Id.* at p. 292.

38   *See* an explanation about this case by Judge Zhang Jiahua of the Economic Court Division One of Beijing Haidian District Court, presiding judge of the panel for this case. *Id.,* at p. 293.

process sale or purchase orders from investor clients according to their instructions. In one case,[39] the defendant securities company processed the plaintiff's sale order at a price 16.80 yuan per share for 2,000 shares, but the sale was not completed because the computer system at the stock exchange was slow at the time with an overloading problem due to a sharp increase of share trading on that day. The computer problem only affected the trading of that particular share for a short period of time. The Court said that, although the sale was affected by a problem of the computer system, the defendant securities company should have continued to process the sale afterwards until the expiry time of the instruction. As the defendant failed to fully discharge its obligation it should bear responsibilities for the loss suffered by the plaintiff.[40]

In another case,[41] the plaintiff instructed the defendant securities company to sell 800 shares at a price of 39.90 yuan per share and the instruction was given for the whole day. The defendant executed the instruction in the morning, but no deal was made because the instruction price was 10% higher than the market price in the morning. The defendant did not continue to process the sale order during the day at the price instructed by the plaintiff, nor did the defendant inform the plaintiff until next day. The market price of the share went up to 42.20 yuan for a short time in the afternoon. The Court found in favor of the plaintiff, stating that the defendant, as a securities broker, should actively and properly implement the plaintiff's instruction during the valid period of the instruction. Because the defendant failed to perform its obligation actively the plaintiff's shares, which should have been sold out on the instruction day, were not sold out and thus caused losses to the plaintiff. The defendant was deemed liable for compensation.[42]

A common feature shared by most of these cases is that the investor clients eventually sold their shares at a lower price than the price they instructed the defendant securities companies and thus suffered a loss. In the case in which the plaintiff instructed the securities company to sell 2,000 shares at a price of 16.80 yuan,[43] the price of the share fell to 14 yuan next day at the time when the defendant told the plaintiff that the 2,000 shares had not been sold out. Three days later the plaintiff sold the 2,000 shares at a price of 12.48 yuan. The plaintiff claimed compensation of 8,640 yuan, which was the difference between 16.80 yuan and 12.48 yuan for the 2,000 shares. In the case in which the plaintiff instructed the defendant securities company to sell 800 shares at a price of 39.90 yuan per share,[44] the price of the share fell to 24.20 yuan next day at the time when the plaintiff was informed that the 800 shares had not been sold out. Six days later the plaintiff sold the 800 shares at a price of 17.80 yuan. The plaintiff sued the defendant for a compensation of loss

---

39   *See* Li Guoguang, *supra* note 27, at pp. 501–503. The names of the parties involved in the case were removed by the editor of the book.

40   *Id.* at p. 502.

41   *See* Li Guoguang, *supra* note 27, at pp. 440–441. The names of the parties involved in the case were removed by the editor of the book.

42   *Id.* at p. 441.

43   *Supra* note 39.

44   *Supra* note 41.

17,680 yuan, which was the difference between 39.90 yuan and 17.80 yuan for the 800 shares.

Should these plaintiffs be compensated with what they claimed, that is, the difference between the price that they instructed the defendant securities companies and the price at which they sold their shares later? The Court said that the appropriate calculation formula for the losses should not take the price at which the plaintiffs sold their shares as a basis for calculation but the price at the time when the plaintiffs were informed of the fact that their shares had not been sold out. In the case in which the plaintiff instructed the defendant to sell 800 shares, the Court awarded the plaintiff 12,560 yuan, which was the difference between 39.90 yuan and 24.20 yuan for 800 shares.[45] The 39.90 yuan was the price at which the plaintiff instructed the defendant to sell 800 shares and the 24.20 yuan was the price of the share at the time when the plaintiff was told that the 800 shares had not been sold out. The price at which the plaintiff sold the 800 shares six days later was 17.80 yuan. The reason for the Court not taking the price 17.80 yuan as a basis for calculation was that the plaintiff had not taken steps to prevent further losses after the plaintiff knew that the shares he instructed to sell had not been sold out; and for this reason the plaintiff should bear these further losses himself.[46]

In effect, the plaintiff himself should be responsible for any loss suffered after he was told that the sale had not been processed. In another words, the plaintiff should have sold the shares at that point to stop further losses. One can see that the people's courts were trying to resolve the disputes fairly in accordance with general principles of law. In the case involving 800 shares, the Court cited Articles 5 and 134 (1) (v) of the 1986 GPCL for the judgment,[47] while in the case involving 2,000 shares, the Court mediated the case with a compensation of 5,000 yuan for the plaintiff, which was 3,640 yuan short of the original claim made by the plaintiff, and the Court divided the court cost equally between the defendant and plaintiff. Article 5 of the 1986 GPCL provides for a very broad principle of law. It is arguable that the application by the Court of such a broad provision has no assistance to the Court to resolve the disputes fairly in specific contexts.

From commentators' point of view, this position of the people's courts in resolving these types of disputes is, on the whole, a right approach in balancing the interests between the plaintiff investors and defendant securities companies.[48] They submit that, on one had, the people's courts recognize that the failure of the defendants to carry out the instructions from the plaintiffs constitutes a breach of contract and the defendants should bear responsibilities for the breach of contract and for the losses suffered by the plaintiffs; on the other hand, in the absence of specific securities law and regulations that direct the people's courts to calculate

---

45   *Supra* note 41, at p. 440.

46   *Id.*

47   Article 5 states that: "The lawful civil rights and interests of citizens and legal persons shall be protected by law; no organization or individual may infringe upon them." Article 134 (1) (v) states that: "The main methods of bearing civil liability shall be: (v) restoration of original condition."

48   *Supra* note 41, at p. 441.

such losses, it is appropriate for the people's courts to apply the general principle of fairness according to the 1986 GPCL to calculate the losses.[49]

Designated Share Trading and Lost Opportunities

The designated share trading system refers to a system under which investors appoint one securities company as their sole agent for their share trading. Before 1 April 1998, investors decided by themselves whether to opt for the designated share trading. The system was not compulsory and investors could apply for the sole agent in accordance with voluntary principle. After 1 April 1998, the designated share trading system became compulsory in the Shanghai Stock Exchange. Investors have to register with a designated agent securities company before trading shares.

One of the important arrangements for the designated share trading system is that investors may change their designated securities company after they have registered. Securities companies may not lock up clients' designated trading accounts without consent from the clients when the clients wish to change their designated securities companies. Disputes arise when securities companies intentionally or unintentionally lock up clients' accounts and the clients lose good opportunities to trade shares. The case *Jin Yancheng v Shanghai Securities Business Center of Jilin Trust Investment Company of Bank of China*,[50] in which the defendant securities company locked up the account of the plaintiff Jin Yancheng and the plaintiff thus lost good opportunities to sell his shares, illustrates the approach the people's courts take in treating the defendants and plaintiffs and their responsibilities and calculating the losses suffered by the plaintiff clients.

On 29 August 1994, the plaintiff Jin Yancheng, who had been a customer of the defendant Shanghai securities business center, signed a designated trading agreement with the defendant, which designated the defendant as his sole agent for share trading. The agreement stipulated, among other things, that the plaintiff has the right to cancel the designation with the defendant and switch to other securities companies after any debt is cleared with the defendant. On 26 September 1994, the plaintiff requested the defendant to cancel the designation agreement and the defendant accepted his application. Three days later, on 29 September, the plaintiff entrusted another securities company to sell 2,000 Shuidao shares at a price of 20.60 yuan per share and 8,900 Lingqiao shares at a price of 24.50 yuan per share, but neither of the instructions went through because the plaintiff's account was still locked up by the defendant. The plaintiff requested the defendant again to cancel the designation and the defendant agreed to do so. On 30 September, the plaintiff instructed the other securities company to sell 4,000 Shuidao shares at a price of 19.28 yuan and 8,900 Lingqiao shares at a price of 22.40 yuan, but his instructions still could not go through. After an enquiry was made at the Shanghai Stock Exchange it became apparent that his account was still locked up by the defendant. The plaintiff then

49   *Id.*

50   See *Carefully Selected Cases of the People's Courts* (*Renmin Fayuan Anli Xuan Jingbianben*), Vol. 1, 2001, edited by China Law Application Research Institute of the Supreme People's Court (Beijing: Xinhua Publishing Press, 2001), pp. 744–749.

went to the defendant to request the cancellation and at the same time he instructed the defendant to sell 100 Chengxiang shares. The cancellation was finally made by the defendant on 5 October.

The plaintiff sued the defendant at the Shanghai Nanshi District People's Court, claiming a loss of 65,325 yuan and interests suffered as a result of the defendant's delay with the cancellation, and coupled by falling share prices between 29 September and 5 October. The closing price of Shuidao shares and Lingqiao shares on 5 October was 17.40 yuan and 18.90 yuan, compared with 20.60 yuan and 24.50 yuan at which the plaintiff instructed the defendant on 29 September. The defendant submitted that they had executed the cancellation but the cancellation was delayed due to a computer problem at the Shanghai Stock Exchange. The defendant argued that they had reminded the plaintiff that he could still sell shares through the defendant while the cancellation was being dealt with, but the plaintiff was expecting a rise of the share prices so he did not instruct the defendant for sales except a sale of 100 Chengxiang shares. The plaintiff himself should, the defendant argued, be responsible for the losses he suffered consequent to the falling share prices.

The Shanghai Nanshi District People's Court said that the defendant should compensate for the losses suffered by the plaintiff. The reasoning of the Court was threefold.[51] First, the designated trading agreement that the plaintiff and defendant signed was lawful; second, the defendant accepted the plaintiff's request to cancel the agreement but failed to deal with the cancellation on time, which was the defendant's fault; third, the submission by the defendant that the delay was caused by other reasons could not be established for lack of evidence. For these reasons the defendant should be liable for compensation. On the other hand, the Court said that the plaintiff himself should bear the losses suffered after 30 September. This is because, the Court said, the plaintiff still could sell shares through the defendant on 29 and 30 September after he knew the cancellation had not been made by the defendant on time, but the plaintiff did not choose to do so to reduce further losses. In accordance with Article 106 (2) of the 1986 GPCL,[52] the Court held that the defendant pay a compensation of 43,516 yuan to the plaintiff, which was the difference between the opening price of the shares on 29 September and their closing price on 30 September. This calculation was less than the claim of 65,325 yuan the plaintiff made on the basis of the share prices between 29 September and 5 October. The Court rejected the plaintiff's other claims.[53]

The defendant appealed to the Shanghai First Intermediate People's Court, arguing that although the cancellation was not dealt with on time, the plaintiff still had chances to sell shares through the defendant business center, and it was therefore not right for the plaintiff who had given up these chances to claim compensation afterwards. The Shanghai First Intermediate People's Court dismissed the argument and said that the appellant had failed to cancel the agreement as requested by the respondent, which caused the respondent twice unable to sell the shares at another securities company, and the appellant should compensate the losses the respondent

---

51   *Id.* at pp. 745–746.
52   *Supra* note 12.
53   *Supra* note 50, at p. 746.

suffered consequent to the falling of the share prices; on the other hand, the Court said that the respondent should bear some losses himself as he did not take steps to sell the shares through the appellant after he knew that his account was still locked up by the appellant.

In effect, the Shanghai First Intermediate People's Court confirmed the reasoning of the Shanghai Nanshi District People's Court. However, the Shanghai First Intermediate People's Court held that the way in which the first instance court calculated the compensation was not appropriate. Instead the Shanghai First Intermediate People's Court awarded 28,234 yuan to the respondent, which was calculated on the basis of the difference between the prices the respondent instructed the other securities company on 29 September and the average price of the shares on 30 September.[54] Compared with the calculation the first instance court applied based on the difference between the opening price on 29 September and the closing price on 30 September, the calculation applied by the Shanghai First Intermediate People's Court led to a much lower award than the claim of 65,325 yuan the respondent made initially based on the difference between the share prices on 29 September and 5 October. From commentators' point of view, the judgment of the appeal court reflects, more than the judgment of the first instance court, the principle of fairness. They submit that the judgment protects, on the one hand, the rights of investors, and on the other hand, the rights of securities companies.[55]

The position that plaintiffs should bear the losses suffered after they know a cancellation has not been made by defendant securities companies is confirmed by the Supreme People's Court in a later similar case, *Li Xiaoqin v Chengdu City Investment Trust Co.*[56] In this case, the plaintiff Li Xiaoqin had opened an account for share trading at the defendant Chengdu city trust investment company and had been a regular customer of the defendant. Although the plaintiff had not signed a designated trading agreement with the defendant in accordance with the rules of the Shanghai Stock Exchange, the defendant had made a designated trading arrangement for the plaintiff's account in June 1994. Since then the plaintiff had been trading shares exclusively through the defendant.

On 6 October 1994, the plaintiff instructed another securities company to sell a substantial holding of shares of six companies, but the intended sales could not proceeded because the plaintiff's account had been locked up by the defendant. The plaintiff asked the defendant to unlock the account and cancel the trading arrangement with the defendant, which the defendant promised to do. The plaintiff attempted the sale next day at the other securities company, but the sale could not go ahead because of the same reason. The plaintiff requested the defendant for cancellation again but the defendant did not unlock up the account until 10 October 1994. The

---

54   *Id.* at pp. 747–748.

55   *Id.* at p. 748.

56   The Supreme People's Court Civil Judgment [1996] No. 161. *See Selection of Financial Dispute Cases Heard by the Supreme People's Court (1996–1998)* (*Zuigao Renmin Fayuan Shenli de Jinrong Jiufen Anli Xuanbian*), compiled by the Economic Division Court of the Supreme People's Court (Beijing: China University of Politics and Law Press, 1999), pp. 541–547.

trading records at the Shanghai Stock Exchange showed that between 6, 7 and 10 October 1994 there was a significant fluctuation of share prices. On 7 October the share price index moved between 546.79 and 759.81, a significant scale of 213.01 points.[57] The prices at which the plaintiff sold the shares of six companies after the defendant unlocked the account were much lower than the prices at which the plaintiff instructed the other securities company to sell on 6, 7 and 10 October.

After her request for compensation was refused by the defendant, Li Xiaoqin sued the defendant at the Sichuan High People's Court, submitting that the defendant had failed to unlock the account on time as required by her, and as a result she was unable to sell the shares on time and lost good opportunities. Li Xiaoqin claimed that she had suffered a loss about 3 million yuan and she demanded a 3 million yuan compensation from the defendant for the loss.

The Sichuan High People's Court said that the defendant had promised to unlock the plaintiff's account and cancel the designated trading arrangement but it failed to do so until 10 October, which caused losses to the plaintiff as the plaintiff missed opportunities to sell her shares. The defendant should therefore be held responsible for their fault. On the other hand, the Court said, on 10 October after the plaintiff knew that her account had not yet been unlocked by the defendant, she should have sold shares through the defendant in order to stop further losses of the value of the shares, but she did not do so, so the plaintiff was also at fault in this dispute. In the calculation of the loss suffered by the plaintiff, the Court took the difference between the sale prices at which the plaintiff instructed the other securities company on 7 and 10 October and the prices at which the plaintiff sold her shares on the market the first time after the falling of the share prices, which amounted to a total of 441,900 yuan. In accordance with Article 117 of the 1986 GPCL,[58] the Court held that the defendant shall compensate the plaintiff 50% of the loss of 441,900 yuan and that the court cost 27,511 yuan be shared equally between the defendant and the plaintiff.[59]

The plaintiff appealed to the Supreme People's Court against the judgment of the Sichuan High People's Court, arguing that she had lost opportunities to make money because of several delays by the defendant in canceling the designated trading arrangement, that the calculation of the losses by the Sichuan High People's Court was wrong and that the application of law by the Court was inappropriate. She asked the Supreme People's Court to overturn the judgment of the Sichuan High People's Court and to order the defendant to pay 3 million yuan in damages.

The Supreme People's Court said that the defendant had agreed twice to the plaintiff to unlock the account and cancel the designated trading arrangement after the plaintiff had requested on 6 October, but the defendant failed to unlock the account until 10 October, which caused the plaintiff to lose opportunities for

---

57   *Id.* at p. 543.

58   Article 117 states that: "Anyone who encroaches on the property of the state, a collective or another person shall return the property; failing that, he shall reimburse its estimated price. Anyone who damages the property of the state, a collective or another person shall restore the property to its original condition or reimburse its estimated price. If the victim suffers other great losses, the infringer shall compensate for those losses as well."

59   *Supra* note 56, at p. 545.

share trading; the defendant should bear responsibilities for the delay. On the other hand, the Supreme People's Court said that the plaintiff should also bear some responsibilities for the losses because when the plaintiff knew on 10 October that the designated trading had not been cancelled the plaintiff did not take steps to sell the shares through the defendant, which contributed to the losses suffered later.[60] It is obvious that the reasoning of the Supreme People's Court is just a confirmation of the reasoning of the Sichuan High People's Court.

However, regarding the way in which the Sichuan High People's Court calculated the losses suffered by the plaintiff, the Supreme People's Court held that the calculation was appropriate, but the Supreme People's Court said that the division of responsibilities between the defendant and the plaintiff made by the Sichuan High People's Court was not appropriate. In accordance with Article 153 (1) (ii) of the 1991 Civil Procedure Law,[61] the Supreme People's Court changed the judgment of the Sichuan High People's Court and held that the defendant compensate the plaintiff 353,520 yuan, which was 80% of the loss of 441,900 yuan; the 50,022 yuan of the court costs and related fees at both first instance and appeal courts be shared by the defendant 80% at 40,017.60 yuan and the plaintiff 20% at 10,004.40 yuan.[62]

Compared with the division of responsibilities by the Sichuan High People's Court into 50% to be borne by the defendant and 50% to be borne by the plaintiff, the division by the Supreme People's Court into 80% to be borne by the defendant and 20% to be borne by the plaintiff is more reasonable, and which reflects the view of the Supreme People's Court that the defendant should not bear all the responsibilities for the loss suffered by the plaintiff but bear main responsibility. On the other hand, both the Sichuan High People's Court and the Supreme People's Court held that the delay by the defendant to cancel the designated trading arrangement had not entirely prevented the plaintiff from selling the shares, though the Supreme People's Court differs with the Sichuan High People's Court on the extent to which the plaintiff should bear responsibilities for her loss.

Xineng Technology Company v Guotai Jun'an Securities Company

Xineng Technology Company v Guotai Jun'an Securities Company,[63] a case involving 100 million yuan, is an important case which was first decided by the Shanghai High People's Court and was then appealed to the Supreme People's Court. In this case, the plaintiff Xineng technology company and the defendant Guotai Jun'an securities company signed an asset management agreement on 18 December 2000, under which the plaintiff entrusted the defendant to manage 100 million yuan

---

60　*Id.* at p. 546.

61　Article 153 (1) (ii) states that: "After trying a case on appeal, the people's court of second instance shall, in the light of the following situations, dispose of it accordingly: (ii) it the application of the law was incorrect in the original judgment, the said judgment shall be amended according to the law."

62　*Supra* note 56, at p. 546.

63　The Supreme People's Court Civil Judgment (2003) No. 182. *See* Gazette of the Supreme People's Court of the People's Republic of China, Issue 8, 2004, pp. 16–20.

for one year from 20 December 2000 to 20 December 2001 and invest the fund in the securities market. A supplementary agreement was subsequently entered in November 2001, which extended the asset management agreement for another year till 20 December 2002. By the end of two years, the total value of the shares in the plaintiff's account was 80,698,548.97 yuan at the closing price on 20 December 2002. A loss of 19,301,451.03 yuan was made. A central question was whether the loss of 19.3 million yuan was recoverable. It is interesting to see the Shanghai High People's Court and the Supreme People's Court discuss this central question and related issues in the context of this case.

The asset agreement signed by the Xineng technology company and the Guotai Jun'an securities company stipulated, among other provisions, that the Guotai Jun'an securities company would take necessary care (*jinshen*) and diligence (*qinmian*) to manage the fund and provide services with professional knowledge and skills; if the Guotai Jun'an securities company failed to fulfill the duty of diligent and care (*qinmian jinshen yiwu*) and losses occur as a consequence, it would compensate the losses; the Guotai Jun'an securities company had power to make decisions by themselves in share trading in the best interest of the Xieng technology company and could select securities products available at domestic securities market in a lawful manner; the Guotai Jun'an securities company would not use the fund to arrange any form of loans or debts; the Guotai Jun'an securities company would periodically provide the Xineng technology company with asset management reports; at the end of the management the Guotai Jun'an securities company would sell all the securities and deposit the proceeds to the Xineng technology company within five working days; a penalty payment at 0.04% of the proceeds would be charged for any delay.

In March 2003 the Xineng technology company sued the Guotai Jun'an securities company at the Shanghai High People's Court. The Xineng technology company's complaint was that, during the two years of the management, the Guotai Jun'an securities company failed its duty to provide the Xineng technology company with asset management reports periodically according to the agreement; at the end of the management the Guotai Jun'an securities company failed to sell the shares and deposit the proceeds to the Xineng technology company as agreed. The Xineng technology company demanded return of 100 million yuan capital, 5 million yuan damages for breach of contract, and 3.6 million yuan penalty payment for delayed sale of the shares at the end of the agreement and deposit of the proceeds to the plaintiff. During the proceedings, the defendant voluntarily returned 50 million yuan to the plaintiff in May 2003.

The Shanghai High People's Court first considered whether there was a breach of contract by the defendant Guotai Jun'an securities company. The Court said that the agreement stipulated that the Guotai Jun'an securities company would report monthly, annually and at the end of the management to the plaintiff about the management of the fund; as the defendant had failed provide the plaintiff periodically with such asset management reports it was a breach of reporting duty (*goazhi yiwu*) stipulated by the agreement. The Court further add that even if the plaintiff could have taken positive measures to obtain relevant information from the defendant about the management of its fund, this alone could not excuse the defendant from fulfilling its obligation. The defendant should be held liable for the breach of contract with respect to the reporting obligation stipulated in the agreement. Regarding the plaintiff's claim that the Guotai Jun'an securities company had failed to sell the shares and transfer the proceeds to the plaintiff according to the agreement at the end of the management, the Court said that the defendant had not sold the shares at the end of the agreement and transferred the proceeds to the plaintiff according to the agreement, for which the defendant should be liable.

In accordance with Articles 60,[64] 114 (1)[65] and 401[66] of the 1999 Contract Law, the Court held that the defendant would (i) return 30,698,548.97 yuan,[67] (ii) pay a penalty payment at a rate of 0.04% for the delay to sell the shares at the end of the management and deposit the proceeds to the plaintiff,[68] and (iii) pay 5 million yuan in damages for the breach of contract calculated according to the relevant provisions of the agreement. The court cost 553,010 yuan was divided between the defendant at 470,058.50 yuan and the plaintiff at 82,951.50 yuan. The Court rejected the plaintiff's claim for compensation of the loss of 19.3 million yuan. The reasoning of the Court was twofold. First, the Court said that, apart from the fact that the defendant had partially breached the contract, the plaintiff had not proved that the defendant had violated the law and regulations or committed obvious faults in the share investment on behalf of the plaintiff; second, the Court said that the loss was made when the share trading market was a bear market and it was a result of normal market risks, for which the defendant should not be held responsible.[69]

The plaintiff appealed to the Supreme People's Court. In addition to the submissions made at the Shanghai High People's Court, the plaintiff further submitted that the defendant had not fulfilled the duty of care and diligence stipulated in the contract; the defendant had twice purchased certain shares at a higher price than the price at which the share was sold, or sold certain shares at a lower price than the price at which the share was purchased, which, the plaintiff argued, was either moving the profits from the plaintiff's account or attempting with an intention to

---

64   Article 60 of the Contract Law states that: "The parties shall perform their obligations thoroughly according to the terms of the contract. The parties shall abide by the principle of good faith and perform the obligations of notice, assistance and maintaining confidentiality, etc. based on the character and purpose of the contract or the transaction practices."

65   Article 114 (1) states that: "The parties to a contract may agree that one party shall, when violating the contract, pay breach of contract damages of a certain amount in light of the breach, or may agree upon the calculating method of compensation for losses resulting from the breach of contract."

66   Article 401 of the Contract Law states that: "The agent shall report the handling of the entrusted matters according to the requirements of the principal. The agent shall report the result of the entrusted matters when the commission contract is terminated."

67   That is, the balance after the defendant returned 50 million yuan to the plaintiff in May 2003.

68   As the defendant returned 50 million yuan to the plaintiff during the proceedings, the calculation of the penalty payment was based on 80,698,548.97 yuan between 21 December 2002 and 13 May 2003 and 30,698,548.97 yuan between 14 May 2003 and the effective day of the judgment.

69   *Supra* note 63, at p. 18.

earn extra handling fees. The plaintiff demanded compensation of 19.3 million yuan from the defendant.

The Supreme People's Court found that the loss of 19.3 million yuan was made when the share trading market was falling. Apart from the evidence submitted by the plaintiff that the defendant had twice transacted at either higher or lower prices, the plaintiff adduced no further evidence to establish that the defendant had obviously been at fault in trading the shares or had acted in violation of the law and regulations. The Court said that the reliance by the plaintiff on the evidence that the defendant had twice transacted at either higher or lower prices over a period of two years was not sufficient to claim that the defendant had breached its duty to manage the fund with good faith and had committed fraud on the plaintiff. The 19.3 million yuan loss was a result of normal market risks. The Court rejected the appeal and upheld the judgment of the Shanghai People's High Court. The Xineng technology company was ordered to pay the appeal court costs of 160,010 yuan.[70]

The judgments of the Shanghai High People's Court and the Supreme People's Court show that a clear line is drawn by the people's courts between the loss occurred as a result of normal market risks and the loss occurred as a consequence of fault or fraud of the securities company. The plaintiff's loss of 19.3 million yuan is not recoverable because the loss is made not because of fault or fraud of the defendant securities company but because of normal market risks over the period of the management. The Supreme People's Court states the position clearly:

> … even if the normal investment decisions the defendant made in share trading on the basis of commercial judgments suffered from wrong investment judgments, as long as the defendant fulfilled the duty of care and diligence stipulated in the contract and had no obvious fault, the plaintiff cannot claim compensation of losses from the defendant on the ground that the commercial judgments the defendant made at one time proved to be in an opposite direction to the movement of the market at a later time.[71]

Duty of Securities Companies to Safeguard against Fraud

In accordance with securities regulations and trading rules,[72] securities companies, in their offering securities services, have a duty to check carefully the documents presented by the clients when the clients instruct the securities companies to sell or purchase shares. The documents normally include the instruction forms filled in by the clients, their identification cards and securities account cards. These documents have to be verified by the securities companies before a contract note is issued and signed by the securities companies and the clients. If the securities companies fail in their duty to carefully check the instructions and documents from the clients and losses are consequently caused to the clients or some other parties, the securities companies shall be liable for compensation.

---

70   *Id.* at p. 20.

71   *Id.* at pp. 19–20.

72   For example, Articles 5 and 6 of the Circular of the China Securities Regulatory Commission on Improvement of Examination and Verification System to Prevent Shares from Being Stolen and Sold. *Infra* note 74.

A large group of disputes have occurred, particularly in the late 1980s and 1990s in China's stock market, in which the securities companies failed to carefully check and verify the instructions and documents presented by clients and consequently shares or money in the accounts of clients was stolen by fraudsters. *Huafang v Shangrao Securities Department of Trust Company of Jiangxi Shangrao Industrial and Commercial Bank*[73] is a case in which disputes arose after the shares in the plaintiff's account with the defendant securities company were stolen as a result of failure of the defendant securities companies in fulfilling their duty to protect safety of the plaintiff's account. The case shows the approach and reasoning of the people's courts in dealing with the disputes between securities companies and their clients which are associated with the losses suffered by the client consequent to theft and other forms of fraud.

On 28 January 1997, the plaintiff Huafang opened an account at the defendant Shangrao securities department for trading shares in the Shanghai Stock Exchange. Next day Huafang instructed the Shangrao securities department to purchase 8,200 shares of Xidan Departmental Store and paid a total of 69,340.92 yuan. On 31 January when Huafang was to instruct the Shangrao securities department to sell the 8,200 shares, she discovered that there were only 200 shares left in her account. Huafang immediately made an enquiry and it transpired that on 30 January a person called Liuqi sold Huafang's 8,000 shares at another securities company, the Jinhua securities company of Zhejiang province, and on 31 January Liuqi withdrew the proceeds 66,800 yuan. Liuqi used a forged shareholder account card and Huafang's shareholder number for the sale and subsequent withdrawal. Huafang demanded compensation from the Shangrao securities department but was refused. She sued the two securities companies to the People's Court of Shangrao city, demanding compensation from the two defendants for the loss of 75,084.40 yuan, which was calculated on the basis of the price of the shares of Xidan Departmental Store at the time when the case came to the Shangrao People's Court.

The Shangrao People's Court found that, on 29 January, after the plaintiff purchased the 8,200 shares, the Shangrao securities department put a poster in its trading hall, on which all the transactions completed on that day were listed and were accompanied by the shareholder codes of the customers, including the plaintiff's transaction and shareholder code. The Court also found that the Jinhua securities company of Zhejiang province did not make copies of the identification card and shareholder account card when the company accepted Liuqi for opening an account, nor did the company check carefully authenticity of Liuqi's shareholder account card when Liuqi subsequently withdrew the money. The oversight of the Jinhua securities company enabled Liuqi to steal the shares and money from the plaintiff's account. The Shangrao securities department held that they should not be held responsible for the plaintiff's loss. They argued that, judging from the fact that the plaintiff opened an account on 28 January and the shares were stolen within 3 days, it was a case of premeditated fraud targeting the plaintiff, not a case in which someone committed

---

73   *See Carefully Selected Cases of the People's Courts* (*Renmin Fayuan Anli Xuan Jingbianben*), Vol. 1, 2001, edited by China Law Application Research Institute of the Supreme People's Court (Beijing: Xinhua Publishing Press, 2001), pp. 740–744.

stealing merely by obtaining trading information from the Shangrao securities department. No defense was lodged by the Jinhua securities company.

The Shangrao People's Court said that the defendants, as securities institutions who are making profits, have a duty to protect the clients' lawful rights and interests in an effective way and carry out the business strictly according to the law, regulations and trading rules. The Jinhua securities company, when accepting sale instructions from customers, failed to carefully check and verify the authenticity of the holder of the documents, which, the Court held, violated the provisions of Article 5 and 6 of the Circular of the China Securities Regulatory Commission on Improvement of Examination and Verification System to Prevent Shares from Being Stolen and Sold.[74] The Jinhua securities company should bear a main responsibility for the loss that the plaintiff's 8,000 shares were stolen. Regarding the Shangrao securities department, the Court said that it published shareholders' codes in a daily trading briefing and let out the shareholders' trading information, which provided an opportunity for others to use such information in stealing the plaintiff's shares; this practice was in violation of the trading rules of the Shanghai Stock Exchange; the Shangrao securities department should therefore bear certain responsibilities. In accordance with Article 106 (1) (2) of the 1986 GPCL,[75] the Court held that the plaintiff's direct loss 67,649.68 yuan which was the amount the plaintiff paid for the 8000 shares and interest loss 1,246.83 yuan which was calculated at a rate of 0.774% were to be borne by the Jinhua securities company for 90% at 62,006.86 yuan and by the Shangrao securities department for 10% at 6,889.65 yuan. No appeal was lodged by either of the defendants against the judgment.[76]

The approach and reasoning of the Shangrao People's Court is not unique in resolving these kinds of disputes. In similar cases the people's courts take the same approach to reason the case and deliver the judgment. The people's courts would normally look at the legal relationship between the plaintiff and defendant, examine the circumstances to establish on the basis of evidence whether there is a causal link between the stealing or other forms of fraud and the fault of the defendant, differentiate direct reasons and indirect reasons contributed by the defendants if there is more than one defendant involved, determine whether there is any contributing factor from the plaintiff, and decide the responsibility and compensation in accordance with basic legal principles and other relevant law and regulations. *Feng Cuiyu v Dangyang*

---

74   The Circular of the China Securities Regulatory Commission on Improvement of Examination and Verification System to Prevent Shares from Being Stolen and Sold (Zhongguo Zhengquan Jiandu Guanli Weiyuanhui Guanyu Jianquan Chayan Zhidu Fangfan Gupiao Daomai de Tongzhi), issued by the China Securities Regulatory Commission on 14 June 1994. Article 5 requires securities companies to check and make copies of identification cards and shareholder cards when customers open new accounts, while Article 6 requires securities companies to carefully check identification cards and shareholder cards when customers withdraw funds.

75   Article 106 (1) states that "Citizens and legal persons who breach a contract or fail to fulfill other obligations shall bear civil liability." For Article 106 (2), *see supra* note 12.

76   *Supra* note 73, at p. 742.

Securities Business Center of Sanxia Securities Co. Ltd., [77] a recent case in which 48,000 yuan was stolen from the plaintiff's account with the defendant, is another example that shows how the people's courts approach these types of cases.

On 9 June 1997, the plaintiff Feng Cuiyu signed an agency agreement with the defendant securities company and opened an account at the defendant business center for trading shares. When the plaintiff came to the defendant later to collect a trading card to be used for share trading, the plaintiff was asked to choose a security code of six numbers and give the security code to a member of the counter staff so that the code could be input into the computer system. After all the procedures for opening an account were completed, the plaintiff started to trade shares at the defendant's business center. In June 1999, the plaintiff discovered that a sum of 48,000 yuan had been withdrawn from her account by someone else. The plaintiff made an enquiry and the defendant refused to accept any responsibility. The plaintiff reported the case to the police who verified that the signature on the cash withdrawal note was different from the plaintiff's own signature.

In August 1999, the plaintiff sued the defendant in the People's Court of Dangyang city, Hubei province, claiming compensation of 48,000 yuan. The defendant argued that, although the handwriting on the cash withdrawal note was different from the plaintiff's own handwriting, all the required documents were presented at the time of the cash withdrawal and the procedures followed by their staff were in accordance with relevant regulations, and for these reasons the defendant should not be held responsible for the withdrawal. During the court hearing and upon a request from the defendant, the Dangyang People's Court verified again the signature on the withdrawal note and concluded that it was not the plaintiff's own signature which was recorded and kept in previous transactions. The Court further found that, from 1996 to March 2000, the way in which the defendant handled security codes of their customers was that the defendant first asked their customers to write down a six-digit security number and give it to a member of the counter staff, who then input the number into the computer system. The Court said that the plaintiff herself should have input the security code into the computer system. The defendant's practice of requiring staff to input the security code into the computer system created opportunities for the security code to be let out and known by others and therefore made the plaintiff's account unsafe which, the Court said, was in violation of operating rules and the fault is at the defendant. In accordance with Article 106 (2) of the 1986 GPCL,[78] the Court held that the defendant would be responsible for their fault and pay 48,000 yuan compensation to the plaintiff.[79]

The defendant appealed to the Intermediate People's Court of Yichang city, Hubei province. The evidence presented to the Yichang Intermediate People's Court and the facts of the case confirmed by the Yichang Intermediate People's Court were

---

77   *See Essential Selection of Adjudicated Cases in China* (*Zhongguo Shenpan Anli Yaolan*) (Civil Adjudicated Case Vol. 2001), edited by National Judges College and School of Law of the People's University of China (Beijing: China People's University Press, 2002), pp. 259–262.

78   *Supra* note 12.

79   *Supra* note 77, at p. 261.

the same as at the first instance court. The Yichang Intermediate People's Court rejected the appeal and upheld the judgment of the Dangyang People's Court in accordance with Article 153 (1) (i) of the 1991 Civil Procedure Law.[80] The Yichang Intermediate People's Court said that the defendant, in acting as an agent for its customers, has a duty to safeguard the fund deposited by its customers and to implement safety measures strictly and comprehensively according to the law, regulations and trading rules; as the defendant failed to implement safety measures strictly and comprehensively and the money deposited by its customers was left unsafe, the defendant should be responsible for their fault; moreover, the defendant had not adduced convincing evidence to prove that the money had been withdrawn by no one else other than the plaintiff herself.[81]

In commenting on the judgment of the above case, commentators argued that the defendant should be held responsible on two grounds.[82] First, the defendant as an agent securities company has a contractual duty to safely manage the fund entrusted by its customers. When the fund is withdrawn by others due to a fault of the defendant securities company, the defendant securities company should be held responsible for breach of contract. Second, the defendant should be held responsible on a ground of risk allocation. As a professional securities service provider, the defendant has advantages in terms of technology and cost to protect the fund deposited by its customers. The risk for the safety of the customers' funds should be allocated to professional securities services providers. If money is withdrawn fraudulently the defendant securities company should assume responsibility for its customers. Such responsibility should be imposed upon the defendant rather than established on the basis of fault of the defendant. To impose such a responsibility on securities companies a careful and responsible attitude should be generally promoted in the management of the customers' funds, which would thus improve the standard of the services of the securities companies.[83] Given the fact that irregularity is common and widespread among the practices of securities companies, particularly in the early years of China's stock market, this view makes a valid point.

Calculation and Compensation of Losses

In the above sections, discussions have been made about the way in which the people's courts calculate the losses suffered by plaintiffs. The discussions are in the context of individual cases that have difference circumstances. Looking at the various positions of the people's courts in these individual cases with respect to the calculation and compensation of the losses suffered by the plaintiffs, one can see that

---

80   Article 153 (1) (i) sates that: "After trying a case on appeal, the people's court of second instance shall, in the light of the following situations, dispose of it accordingly: (i) if the facts were clearly ascertained and the law was correctly applied in the original judgment, the appeal shall be rejected in the form of a judgment and the original judgment shall be affirmed."

81   *Supra* note 77, at p. 261.

82   *Id.* at p. 262.

83   *Id.*

the people's courts are guided by certain underlying general principles. In summary, these principles are, first, the principle that market risks are to be borne by investor principals; second, the principle that a criterion for compensation is whether these is any actual economic loss; and third, the principle of fairness of the 1986 GPCL.

It is recognized by the people's courts that the calculation of compensation for losses in share trading has special characteristics. Share prices change all the time; a price at which a certain share is purchased may be higher or lower than the price at which the same share is sold. Such market risks should generally be borne by investor principals.[84] In *Xineng Technology Company v Guotai Jun'an Securities Company*,[85] a clear line is drawn by the Supreme People's Court between the loss which is occurred as a result of normal market risks and the loss which is occurred as a consequence of fault or fraud of the securities company. The loss which is occurred as a result of normal market risks is not recoverable from the defendant.

In *Jin Yancheng v Shanghai Securities Business Center of Jilin Trust Investment Company of Bank of China*[86]and *Li Xiaoqin v Chengdu City Investment Trust Co.*,[87] the plaintiffs could not sell their shares at the price they instructed the defendant securities companies because of the delays by the defendants. Afterwards, the plaintiffs sold the shares at lower prices than the instruction prices. What the plaintiffs could claim from the defendants is not all the losses but the losses up to the point when they knew about the delay. The reasoning of the people's courts is that the plaintiffs still had chances to sell the shares through the defendants and to reduce further losses by doing so. It is arguable that this position of the people's courts is unfair to the innocent plaintiffs, but an underlying thinking of the people's courts is that market risks should be normally borne by investor principals.

Compensation to plaintiffs is based on actual losses the plaintiffs have suffered. Where, in dealing with the instructions entrusted by the plaintiffs, defendants have made mistakes or other forms of fault but no economic losses have been caused to the plaintiffs, the people's courts would dismiss the claim for compensation made by the plaintiffs. *Wang Luhui v Sichuan Province Securities Co., Ltd.*[88] is a typical example, in which the defendant securities company made a mistake in processing the plaintiff's sale order, but no loss was caused to the plaintiff. The Chengdu Intermediate People's Court overturned the award of 808 yuan compensation made by the first instance court. An essential factor the Chengdu Intermediate People's Court considered was that the plaintiff had suffered no actual loss as a consequence of the operational error made by the defendant securities company.

---

84   *See*, for example, the comments made by Shen Jian, Liu Hong, from the People's Court of Shangrao city, Jiangxi province, in commenting the case *Huafang v Shangrao Securities Department of Trust Compnay of Jiangxi Shangrao Industrial and Commercial Bank, supra* note 73, at p. 744.

85   *Supra* note 63.

86   *Supra* note 50.

87   *Supra* note 56.

88   *Supra* note 11.

In *Gu Junhao v Shanghai Dingxi Road Securities Business Center of Shanghai International Trust Investment Co.*,[89] the plaintiff's 300 Huangpu Estate shares in the plaintiff's account were sold and the proceeds were withdrawn by her husband. The plaintiff sued the defendant securities company for compensation of the shares. The plaintiff and her husband were separated at that time but were not formally divorced. The Court found that there was some fault by the defendant in handling the plaintiff's account and shares, but the Court said that the defendant's fault had not caused any actual damages to the plaintiff, and the defendant should therefore not be held for compensative responsibility. The sale of the shares and the withdrawal of the proceeds by the husband, the Court said, was a disposal of the property commonly owned by the wife and husband during the existence of their marriage in accordance with the 1980 Marriage Law of the PRC.[90]

Actual losses may include other forms of losses. The peoples' courts are generally reluctant to consider compensation of mental sufferings claimed by the plaintiffs. In *Xia Yonglin v Wuxi Business Center of Haitong Securities Co. Ltd,*[91] a case of unsuccessful subscription of Wuliangye shares by the plaintiff because of the wrong subscription numbers given by the defendant securities company, the Court, in acknowledging that the plaintiff had suffered some economic losses as the plaintiff had to spend time and expenses to resolve the matter caused by the defendant, awarded the plaintiff 2,000 yuan in damages, but the Court rejected the plaintiff's claim for mental sufferings on the ground that the claim for mental sufferings calculated at 5% of the price for 14,000 shares was unfounded in fact and in law. In another case, *Wang Gaowu v Yunji Road Securities Business Center of Huaxia Securities Co. Wuhan Branch,*[92] the Court awarded the plaintiff the expenses spent on traveling and the losses resulted from the plaintiff's absence of work because of the case. But the Court dismissed the compensation claim from the plaintiff for mental sufferings due to news reports on his involvement in the case. The Court said that these were two different legal relationships and the Court would not deal with the claim for mental sufferings.[93]

In several cases discussed in above sections, the people's courts decide the calculation and compensation of losses in accordance with the principle of fairness prescribed by Article 4 of the 1986 GPCL.[94] The people's courts recognize that share

---

89   *See Essential Selection of Adjudicated Cases in China* (*Zhongguo Shenpan Anli Yaolan*) (Commercial and Administrative Cases Vol. 2001), edited by National Judges College and School of Law of the People's University of China (Beijing: China People's University Press, 2002), pp. 315–319.

90   Article 13 states that: "The property incurred during the existence of marriage shall be jointly owned by both husband and wife, except where husband and wife are agreed otherwise. Both husband and wife shall have equal rights in the disposal of jointly owned property."

91   *Supra* note 33.

92   *See* the Gazette of the Supreme People's Court of the People's Republic of China, Issue 5, 2001, pp. 167–170.

93   *Id.* at p. 169.

94   Article 4 states that: "In civil activities, the principles of voluntariness, fairness, making compensation for equal value, honesty and credibility shall be observed."

trading has distinctive risks and the criteria for the calculation of compensation should take into account of the risk elements of the share trading while applying the general principle of fairness of the 1986 GPCL. Share prices may rise as well as fall. This feature of share trading market brings about a difficult question to the people's courts in resolving disputes associated with fluctuation of share prices in the stock market. Which share price should be the price upon which the people's courts should rely for the calculation of compensation? In what ways should the people's courts allocate the risks of share price fluctuation and divide fairly responsibilities among the parties concerned?

In *Cheng Yonggang v Huaxia Securities Co. Ltd.*,[95] the plaintiff claimed compensation of 59,010 yuan for unsold 5,000 Tianqiao shares due to the defendant's fault. The 59,010 yuan was calculated on the basis of 28.50 yuan per share, the highest price of Tianqiao shares on 24 May 1993, the day on which the plaintiff instructed the defendant to sell the 5,000 shares. The Court determined that the defendant should be responsible for its failure to carry out the plaintiff's instruction and compensate the plaintiff. But how to calculate the compensation was a difficult question for the Court to decide according to the circumstances of the case. The trial judge reasoned that the Tianqiao shares were traded on the market for the first time on that day and there was no previous price that the Court could look at for reference; the price of the share was falling on that day and afterwards. Taking these circumstances into consideration, the Court said the compensation should be calculated at a price below the opening price on 24 May and above the price at which the plaintiff sold the share several days later. The case was eventually mediated by the Court, as a result of which the defendant compensated the plaintiff 30,000 yuan and the plaintiff paid the court costs of 2360.70 yuan.[96] Compared with the initial claim of 59,010 yuan the plaintiff made on the basis of 28.50 yuan per share, what the plaintiff finally got was much lower, equivalent to 22.70 yuan per share, which is approximately the middle price between the opening price on 24 May and the price at which the plaintiff sold the shares. In mediating the dispute, the Court tried to balance the interests of the plaintiff and the defendant in the spirit of the fairness principle.

In another case,[97] the plaintiff purchased 3,000 shares on 25 May 1993 with a total sum of 82,454.40 yuan. On 13 September 1993 the 3,000 shares were fraudulently sold out and the proceeds, 67,406.40 yuan, were withdrawn by the fraudster. The plaintiff demanded the defendant securities company to compensate 82,454.40 yuan, but the Court disregarded this claim. The Court said that to demand the defendant securities company to compensate 82,454.40 yuan on the basis of the price at which the plaintiff had purchased the 3,000 shares would be against the principle of allocation of risk in the share trading market. Instead the Court awarded the plaintiff 67,406.40 yuan in damages.[98]

---

95   *See supra* note 36.

96   *Id.* at p. 293.

97   *See* Li Guoguang, *supra* note 27, at p. 474. The names of the parties involved in the case were removed by the editor of the book.

98   *Id.*

Those who advocate for protecting innocent parties involved in the disputes emphasize the application of the fairness principle. They submit that, where the share price at the time of occurrence of the dispute is higher than the price at the time of the dispute being dealt with by the people's courts, the party who has fault should be held to compensate on the basis of the price at the time of the occurrence of the dispute; in the same way, where the price at the time of the dispute being dealt with by the people's courts is higher than the price at the time of the occurrence of the dispute, the higher price should be the price for the calculation of compensation.[99] The underlying rational of this view is that the innocent party should not be burdened with responsibilities for the losses caused by the fault of others, and such a way of compensation could also better achieve a purpose of punishing those who violate the law and regulations.[100]

In *Huafang v Shangrao Securities Department of Trust Company of Jiangxi Shangrao Industrial and Commercial Bank*,[101] the plaintiff claimed for 75,084.40 yuan for her 8,000 stolen shares, which was calculated on the basis of the price of the share at the time when the case was brought to the Court. The Court eventually awarded 67,649.68 yuan plus applicable interest, which was calculated on the basis of the average price of the share published by the Shanghai Stock Exchange on the day the share was stolen and sold. This calculation by the Court, as regarded by the commentators, reflects an approach that takes into consideration both market risk elements and the principle of fairness.[102]

On the other hand, in the absence of detailed guidelines on the issue of calculation of losses, the people's courts may find it difficult under certain circumstance to balance the interests of defendants and plaintiffs and the decisions of the people's courts may be inconsistent and confusing. In some of the cases discussed in the above sections, the people's courts adopt different formulas to calculate the losses suffered by the plaintiffs. For example, in *Jin Yancheng v Shanghai Securities Business Center of Jilin Trust Investment Company of Bank of China*,[103] the first instance court based their calculations on the difference between the opening price of the shares on 29 September and their closing price on 30 September, while the appeal court based theirs on the difference between the prices the respondent instructed the other securities company on 29 September and the average price of the shares on 30 September.

Summary

In the past two decades, China has witnessed an extraordinary process, in which shares emerge and are traded as a result of economic reform and development of market economy. The 'share frenzy' phenomenon describes a frenetic involvement of countless individuals – and to some extent institutions – in the share issuing

---

99   *Id.* at p. 476.
100   *Id.*
101   *Supra* note 73.
102   *Supra* note 73, at p. 744.
103   *Supra* note 50.

and trading market. Accompanying this phenomenon is an emergence of disputes of various kinds involving shares, share issuing and trading. This chapter looks at some important aspects of the disputes between investor principals and securities company agents in the share issuing and trading market. As the disputes between investor principals and securities company agents take a large portion of the disputes involving shares, especially in the share trading market, it is important to examine the way in which those disputes are dealt with by the people's courts. In summary, following points can be drawn from the above discussions in this chapter.

First, the disputes between investor principals and securities company agents, being a new type of disputes not dealt with before by the people's courts, have brought about new, and in some cases difficult, issues to the people's courts. In resolving these disputes, the people's courts are guided by, on the one hand, the general principles of the 1986 GPCL, the principles of agency law and contract law, and on the other hand, the specific law, regulation and rules on share issuing and trading. Whilst the people's courts endeavor to resolve the disputes fairly and strike right balance between the interests of plaintiffs and defendants, the efforts of the people's courts are and were limited, especially in the early years of the share issuing and trading market, by a lack of the experience of the courts in dealing with this type of new disputes and a lack of a comprehensive body of securities law and regulations. Looking at the cases discussed above, one can see that some of the judgments of the court are confusing and inconsistent. For example, in *Jin Yancheng v Shanghai Securities Business Center of Jilin Trust Investment Company of Bank of China*,[104] the appeal court and the first instance court share a common ground on the issue of whether the defendant should be held liable for compensation, but they differ in their position as to which share price should be the price on which the calculation of compensation is based. With the development of securities law and regulation, the people's courts have gradually settled their positions on these new and difficult issues.

Second, the cause of disputes, as shown in the cases discussed above, is mainly from the defendant securities companies in most of the cases. These could be the mistakes the defendants have made, the fault of the defendants in various forms, and the failure of the defendants to fulfill their duties. As the relationship between investor principals and securities company agents is a contractual relationship, a primary task of the people's courts is to look at the plaintiffs' and defendants' agreements and the circumstances of the case to see whether the agreements are lawful according to the law and regulations, whether the parties have fulfilled their respective contractual obligations and whether there is any breach of contract by the parties. In *Cheng Yonggang v Huaxia Securities Co. Ltd.*,[105] for example, the Court found that the defendant securities company failed to process the sale order instructed by the plaintiff; in *Huafang v Shangrao Securities Department of Trust Compnay of Jiangxi Shangrao Industrial and Commercial Bank*,[106] it was established that the shares in the plaintiff's account with the defendant securities company had

---

104 *Supra* note 50.
105 *Supra* note 36.
106 *Supra* note 73.

been stolen as a result of failure of the defendant in fulfilling the duty to protect the safety of the plaintiff's account. In hearing these cases, the people's courts examine the evidence of the case to establish where the fault lies and who is the at-fault party. In fraud cases where the safety of clients' account and information is paramount, the people's courts emphasis that securities companies, as professional and profit-seeking service providers, should fulfill their contractual obligations and carry out business strictly in accordance with the law and regulations.

Third, a clear line is drawn by the people's courts between the loss occurred as a result of normal market risks and the loss occurred as a consequence of fault or fraud of securities companies. If a loss is made not because of fault or fraud of defendant securities companies but because of normal market risks when the market is falling, such loss shall be borne by investor principals and not recoverable from securities company agents. In *Xineng Technology Company v Guotai Jun'an Securities Company*,[107] The Supreme People's Court when dealing with the issue whether the plaintiff's loss of 19.3 million yuan, which was made by the defendant securities company when the market was falling was recoverable, made an important statement to the effect that, even if a normal investment decision the defendant securities company made in share trading on the basis of commercial judgments has suffered from wrong investment judgments, as long as the defendant securities company has fulfilled the duty of care and diligence stipulated in the contract and has no obvious fault, the investor plaintiff cannot claim compensation of the loss from the defendant on the grounds that the commercial judgments the defendant made at one time have been proved to be in an opposite direction to the movement of the market at a later time.

Fourth, shares rise as well as fall. This and other features of the share market are taken into account by the people's courts in considering the losses suffered by plaintiffs. In this connection, the people's courts recognize the compensable 'opportunity' to make profits in share trading which investor principals have lost because of defendant securities companies. But at the same time, the people's courts take the position that the investor principals should take steps to prevent further losses when the stock market is falling, and by failing to do so, the investor principals cannot claim compensation from the securities company agents. The circumstances under which the plaintiffs may lose the opportunity are various. These could be an error made by the defendant securities company, as in *Yi Shicheng and Fang Bingyin v Shanghai Business Center of Zhejiang Province Securities Co.*,[108] or a failure by the defendant to process the instruction of the plaintiff, as in *Cheng Yonggang v Huaxia Securities Co. Ltd.*,[109] or by the defendants locking up the plaintiff's account, as in *Jin Yancheng v Shanghai Securities Business Center of Jilin Trust Investment Company of Bank of China*[110] and *Li Xiaoqin v Chengdu City Investment Trust Co.*[111] On the one hand, it is appropriate for the people's courts to balance the interests of

---

107   *Supra* note 63.
108   *Supra* note 23.
109   *Supra* note 36.
110   *Supra* note 50.
111   *Supra* note 56.

plaintiffs and defendants fairly and in accordance with the principles of the 1986 GPCL, but on the other hand, a further distinction should be made by the people's courts between circumstances where defendants have made an error inadvertently and circumstances where defendants have failed in their obligations to protect innocent plaintiffs.

Chapter 3

Government and Enterprise Bond Markets

Introduction

China began to issue government bonds to the public in 1981 and, in the same year, the Government Bond Regulations of the PRC, the first government bond regulation, was promulgated by the State Council.[1] After 1981 a government bond market and a regulatory framework started to develop in accordance with the provisions set out in the 1981 Government Bond Regulations of the PRC and the regulations and government policies in the following years. In the early1950s, the Chinese government issued treasury bonds to finance the economy, but a proper government bond market and a corresponding regulatory system never existed prior to the 1979 economic reform in China.[2]

Depending on the proposed allocation and usage, the government bond (*guozhai*) can be either a general government bond (*guokuquan*) or a special kind of government bonds (*tezhong guozhai*), such as treasury bond (*caizheng zhaiquan*) or state investment bond (*guojia touzi zhaiquan*). Since April 1988, when the regulations were relaxed to allow transfer of government bonds on a trial basis, a secondary trading market for government bonds has been developed step by step. This chapter looks at the disputes involving sale and purchase of government bonds while next chapter looks at the disputes in the government bond repurchase market.

The second part of this chapter looks at the disputes involving enterprise bonds. Enterprises began to issue bonds in the mid-1980s in some parts of China, first to their own employees and later to the general public.[3] Enterprise bonds (*qiye zhaiquan*) issued by industrial and commercial enterprises and financial bonds (*jinrong zhaiquan*) issued by financial institutions became an integrated part of enterprise and corporate securities. Unlike the government bond regulations, there were no national rules on the regulation of enterprise bonds until March 1987 when the State Council promulgated the Provisional Regulations on the Administration of Enterprise Bonds.[4]With the development of market activities of enterprise bonds and

---

1   The Government Bond Regulations of the PRC (Zhonghua Renmin Gongheguo Guokuquan Tiaoli), promulgated by the State Council on 28 January 1981.

2   *See* Zhu Sanzhu, *Securities Regulation in China*, p. 4. (Ardsley, NY: Transnational Publishers, 2000).

3   *See* Zhu Sanzhu, *Id.* at p. 6.

4   The Provisional Regulations on the Administration of Enterprise Bonds (Qiye Zhaiquan Guanli Zhanxing Tiaoli), promulgated on, and effective as of, 27 March 1987.

on the basis of the 1987 Provisional Regulations on the Administration of Enterprise Bonds, the State Council promulgated the Regulations on the Administration of Enterprise Bonds in August 1993, which replaced the 1987 Provisional Regulations on the Administration of Enterprise Bonds.[5]

Disputes Involving Government Bonds

Between 1981 and 1992, the State Council promulgated the Government Bond Regulations of the PRC every year, which set out provisions for the issuance and administration of government bonds in that particular year. For example, the 1986 Government Bond Regulations of the PRC[6] set out the arrangement for the issuance of government bonds in 1986. The interest rate, for example, was set at 6% annually for institutional subscribers and 10% for individual subscribers.[7]

After 1992, the way in which government bond regulations were promulgated was changed. Instead of promulgating by the State Council the Government Bond Regulations of the PRC each year, the Ministry of Finance, the State Planning Commission or the PBOC promulgated from time to time detailed circulars or public announcements concerning the issuance and administration of government bonds in particular years in accordance with the basic provisions of the 1992 Government Bond Regulations of the PRC. For example, the arrangement and provisions concerning the issuance of government bonds in 1993 were formulated by the Ministry of Finance, the State Planning Commission and the PBOC and were approved by the State Council,[8] while the provisions concerning the issuance of government bonds in 1994 were promulgated by the Ministry of Finance and the PBOC in a joint notice.[9]

There were changes to the government bond policies from year to year, which were implemented in the regulation of the government bond market. The trend was to relax the regulatory framework gradually. The issuance of government bonds in 1981 was mainly to state owned enterprises, collectively owned enterprises and local governments; individuals were also able to subscribe voluntarily.[10] The 1981

---

5   The Regulations on the Administration of Enterprise Bonds (Qiye Zhaiquan Guanli Tiaoli), promulgated on, and effective as of, 2 August 1993.

6   The 1986 Government Bond Regulations of the PRC (Zhonghua Renmin Gongheguo Yijiubaliu Nian Guokuquan Tiaoli), promulgated by the State Council on 23 November 1985.

7   Article 5, 1986 Government Bond Regulations of the PRC.

8   The Notice of the General Office of the State Council on Circulating the Report of the Ministry of Finance, the State Planning Commission and the PBOC on the Work of Issuance of Government Bonds in 1993 (Guowuyuan Bangongting Zhuanfa Caizhengbu, Guojia Jiwei, Zhongguo Renmin Yinhang Guanyu Yijiujiusan Nian Guozhai Faxing Gongzuo Qingshi de Tongzhi), issued on 27 February 1993.

9   The Notice of the Ministry of Finance and the People's Bank of China on the Measures for the Issuance of 1994 Two-year Term Government Bonds (Caizhengbu, Zhongguo Renmin Yinhang Guanyu Yijiujiusi Nian Ernianqi Guokuquan Faxing Banfa de Tongzhi), issued on 17 March 1994.

10   Article 2, 1981 Government Bond Regulations of the PRC.

Government Bond Regulations of the PRC provided that government bonds could not be circulated as currency and may not be traded.[11] In the 1986 Government Bond Regulations of the PRC, it was allowed that government bonds could be pledged with banks for loans.[12] On 28 March 1988, the PBOC and the Ministry of Finance jointly issued a plan for the trial of transfer of government bonds,[13] which marked the beginning of a process to establish a government bond trading market. On 19 October 1990, the PBOC issued Provisional Measures for the Administration of Inter-regional Securities Trading,[14] which provided a regulatory framework for the transfer of government bonds across provinces among securities companies and financial institutions. The 1990 Provisional Measures emphasised that any securities companies or securities centers of financial institutions could not trade securities with non-securities trading institutions (*fei zhengquan jiaoyi jigou*) and individuals without approval.[15] The 1990 Provisional Measures also set out a brief list of mandatory clauses for securities agency contracts and securities trading contracts.[16] The process of this gradual relaxation of government bond regulations led to the establishment of a nationwide government bond secondary trading market in later years.

These are some of the regulations promulgated before 1998 by the government concerning government bonds. The 1998 Securities Law of the PRC provides for a legal framework for the issuing and trading of shares and corporate bonds, but expressly states that the issuing and trading of government bonds shall be separately provided for in other laws and administrative regulations.[17] Over the years the government has issued a large number of regulations, rules, circulars and announcements concerning government bonds. These regulations and regulatory documents form an important part of the provisions, by reference to which the people's courts deal with the disputes involving government bonds, in conjunction with application of general provisions of civil law, agency law, contract law, security law and other relevant laws, regulations and rules, such as civil evidential rules. The amended 2005 Securities Law now governs the matters concerning listing and

---

11   Article 9, 1981 Government Bond Regulations of the PRC.

12   Article 10, 1986 Government Bond Regulations of the PRC.

13   Implementing Plan for Trial of Opening up Government Bonds Transfer Market (Kaifang Guokuquan Zhuanrang Shichang Shidian Shishi Fang'an), approved by the State Council and issued jointly by the PBOC and the Ministry of Finance on 28 March 1988.

14   The Notice of the PBOC on Circulating "Provisional Measures for the Administration of Inter-regional Securities Trading" (Zhongguo Renmin Yinhang Guanyu Yinfa "Kua Diqu Zhengquan Jiaoyi Guanli Zhanxing Banfa" de Tongzhi), issued on 19 October 1990.

15   *Id*. art. 5.

16   *Id*. arts 6 and 7. Article 6 lists mandatory clauses for securities agency contracts, including, among others, the name, amount and price of the securities for trading, procedure for settlement, term of agency, and so on, while Article 7 lists mandatory clauses for securities trading contracts, including, among others, the name, amount and price of the securities for trading, procedure for settlement, liabilities for breach of contract, and so on.

17   Article 2, 1998 Securities Law. *See* also Zhu Sanzhu, *supra* note 2, at pp. 207–208.

trading of government bonds, provided that other laws and administrative regulations have special provisions and such special provisions shall apply.[18]

The main pattern of the disputes involving government bonds is the disputes arising from the claims made by plaintiffs in relation to various kinds of defaults by defendants. For example, when defendants fail to deliver the government bonds agreed with plaintiffs or default on repayments, plaintiffs take the case to the people's courts. Defaults of various kinds by defendants become a main cause of the disputes and quite often large sums of funds are involved, which is a serious problem for plaintiffs. Procedurally speaking, because large sums of funds are involved, most such disputes are dealt with by the people's courts at provincial levels as first instance courts, and if either plaintiffs or defendants make an appeal, the case goes up to the Supreme People's Court.

A common feature shared by many of these disputes is that the parities, in entering into the agreements of sale, purchase or borrowing of government bonds, tend to violate restrictive and compulsory regulations governing transfer of government bonds. The agreements are loan transactions under the name of government bond transfer; the parties have no proper license or qualification to enter into government bond agreements; the transfers are not carried out in the market designated by the government. These are some of the areas of violations. In dealing with the disputes, the people's courts first check whether the agreements in question are valid, examine whether the parties have license or qualification to engage in government bond trading, and determine whether the agreements are genuine transactions or sham transactions. If a case involves sham transactions or violates restrictive and compulsory regulations, such as a sale of government bonds which is not backed up by any real and actual government bonds, the agreement would be annulled by the people's courts and the parties would bear the consequences of such invalidity.

Loan Transaction under the Name of Government Bond Transfer

This is where government bonds are used by parties as a device for facilitating loan transactions. The agreements the parties enter into are for transfer of government bonds in name only, but what the parties are really engaged in are loan transactions, which is a violation of the law and regulations. *Anhui Securities Registration Company v Anhui Pengli Guomao Company Ltd.*[19] is a case which typically shows how a loan was facilitated under a name of government bond transfer agreement.

In March 1995, the plaintiff Anhui securities registration company and the defendant Anhui Pengli Guomao company signed an agreement in which the plaintiff agreed to provide the defendant with 1994 (2) government bonds worth

---

18   Article 2, 2005 Securities Law, adopted by the Standing Committee of the National People's Congress on 27 October 2005 and effective as of 1 January 2006.

19   The Supreme People's Court Civil Judgment [1997] No. 214. *See Selection of Financial Dispute Cases Heard by the Supreme People's Court (1996–1998)* (*Zuigao Renmin Fayuan Shenli de Jinrong Jiufen Anli Xuanbian*), compiled by the Economic Division Court of the Supreme People's Court (Beijing: China University of Politics and Law Press, 1999), pp. 532–540.

5 million yuan for six months for the defendant to sell the bonds to resolve a cash flow problem of the defendant company. The defendant agreed to return 5.39 million yuan government bonds to the plaintiff at the end of six months. A guarantor agreed and signed the agreement to provide guarantee for the defendant. Before the parties entered into the agreement, the defendant had discussed with the plaintiff about a loan facility of 5 million yuan to resolve the cash flow problem. After the agreement was signed, the plaintiff advanced 5 million yuan to the defendant. At the end of six months, the defendant failed to repay the plaintiff who took the case to the Anhui High People's Court, claiming repayment of capital and interest of 6.17 million yuan and 1.84 million yuan damages for breach of contract.

The Court found that the plaintiff had been approved by the Anhui branch of the PBOC in August 1993 to engage in financial business, including securities financing, consultation and information services, but not to engage in loan business. The Court further found that the agreement was named as a securities financing agreement stipulating that the plaintiff would provide the defendant with 5 million yuan 1994 (2) government bonds, but what the parties discussed before they entered into the agreement was a 5 million loan facility and what the plaintiff transferred in fact to the defendant was not government bonds but 5 million yuan cash. On the basis of the finding, the Court determined that the agreement was an agreement for securities financing in name only but a loan transaction in fact, which violated the law and regulations.

In accordance with Article 58 (1) (vii) of the 1986 GPCL (hereinafter, the 1986 GPCL) and Articles 7 (1) (i) and 16 (1) of the 1993 Economic Contract Law,[20] the Court held that as the plaintiff did not have a license to engage in loan business, the agreement with the defendant was null and void. The Court ruled that the defendant return 5 million yuan to the plaintiff. The Court rejected the plaintiff's other claims. As the agreement was null and void, the guarantee provided by the guarantor for the performance of the defendant was also null and void. But because the guarantor was aware of the fact that what was really transacted was an illegal loan of 5 million yuan, not the government bonds as agreed in the agreement, the Court held that the guarantor should bear a joint liability for the repayment.[21]

The plaintiff Anhui securities registration company appealed to the Supreme People's Court, arguing that the Anhui High People's Court was wrong in application of the law and determination of the facts of the case. But both of these grounds of appeal were rejected by the Supreme People's Court, who confirmed the finding of the Anhui High People's Court that the agreement was a securities financing agreement

---

20   Article 58 (1) (vii) of the 1986 GPCL states that: "Civil acts in the following categories shall be null and void: … (vii) those that are performed under the guise of legitimate acts conceal illegitimate purposes." Article 7 (1) (i) of the 1993 Economic Contract Law states that: "The following economic contracts are null and void: (i) those that are in violation of law and regulations"; Article 16 (1) states that: "After an economic contract has been determined to be null and void, the property the parties have acquired according to the contract shall be returned to the other party. The party who has fault shall compensate the loss the other party has suffered as result; if both parties have fault, each shall bear their proper share of the responsibility."

21   *Supra* note 19, at p. 536.

in name but a loan transaction in fact. The Supreme People's Court held that Anhui securities registration company should bear a responsibility for the invalidity of the agreement as it had no license to engage in loan business. On the other hand, the Supreme People's Court held that Anhui Pengli Guomao company should bear a responsibility to return the 5 million yuan it had used. In accordance with Articles 153 (1) (i) and 158 of the 1991 Civil Procedure Law,[22] the Supreme People's Court upheld the judgment of the Anhui High People's Court and rejected the appeal.[23]

Sale and Purchase of Government Bonds

Sale and purchase of government bonds in the government bond secondary trading market are subject to various regulations and rules which set out provisions stipulating who can engage in trading government bonds, what qualifications the market participants have to have, and where the transactions should be carried out, and so on. Government bonds may be transferred but have to be transferred at the securities exchanges established upon an approval of the government;[24] transfer of government bonds must be executed through a financial institution intermediary who was approved by local branches of the PBOC and who had an independent legal person status with sufficient funds and necessary technical expertise;[25] any transfer not through an intermediary authorized by the regulator is illegal.[26] These are some of the requirements the sale and purchase of government bonds have to comply with.

In late 1980s and early 1990s, one of the common problems contributing to invalid agreements in government bond transfers was caused by those who had no qualifications to engage in sale and purchase in the government bond trading market. In *The Second Government Bond Service Department of the Finance Bureau of the North District of Qingdao City v Securities Company of Linzhou City of Hunan Province*,[27] one of the key issues considered by the Court was whether the plaintiff had a qualification to engage in the government bond deal the plaintiff made with

---

22   Article 153 (1) (i) states that: "After trying a case on appeal, the people's court of second instance shall, in the light of the following situations, dispose of it accordingly: (i) if the facts were clearly ascertained and the law was correctly applied in the original judgement, the appeal shall be rejected in the form of a judgement and the original judgement shall be affirmed." Article 158 states that: "The judgement and the written order of a people's court of second instance shall be final."

23   *Supra* note 19, at p. 538.

24   Article 9, 1992 Government Bond Regulations of the PRC.

25   1988 Implementing Plan for Trial of Opening up Government Bonds Transfer Market. *Supra* note 13.

26   The Circular of the Ministry of Finance, the PBOC, the State Bureau of Industry and Commerce, and the Ministry of Public Security on Crackdown on Illegal Government Bond Trading (Caizhengbu, Zhongguo Renmin Yinhang, Guojia Gongshang Xingzheng Guanliju, Gong'anbu Guanyu Daji Guozhaiquan Feifa Jiaoyi Huodong de Tongzhi), issued on 22 May 1990.

27   *See* Shao Tingjie et al. (eds), *Securities Law* (*Zhengquan Fa*) (Beijing: Law Publishing House, 1999), pp. 328–333.

the defendant. The plaintiff was a government bond service center of the Finance Bureau of the North District of Qingdao city, who was providing government bond-related services to the public.

Between January and June 1994 the plaintiff signed four agreements with the defendant, a securities company in Linzhou city, Hunan province. Three of the four agreements were about a purchase of 1992 (3) government bonds, under which the plaintiff agreed to pay the defendant a total of 14,217,500 yuan and the defendant agreed to deliver the corresponding government bonds at a later agreed time. The fourth agreement was a repurchase agreement for 1992 (3) government bonds, under which the plaintiff agreed to pay the defendant 5 million yuan and the defendant agreed to repurchase the corresponding government bonds three months later at a price of 6,425,000 yuan. In total, the plaintiff paid the defendant 19,217,500 yuan. In default of delivery of the government bonds by the defendant, the plaintiff sued the defendant to the Wuhan Intermediate People's Court for breach of contract, claiming damages 1,562,610 yuan. In the meantime the plaintiff managed to have taken back the 19,217,500 yuan paid to the defendant.

The Wuhan Intermediate People's Court found that the plaintiff was neither an independent enterprise legal person nor a financial institution. This finding led the Court to hold that the plaintiff had no qualification to engage in trading securities in the securities secondary market and the agreements signed by the plaintiff and defendant were null and void, as they had violated Article 5 of the 1990 Provisional Measures for Administration of Inter-regional Securities Trading.[28] The Court dismissed the plaintiff's claim for damages but ordered the defendant to pay 3,203,684 yuan interest payable for the use of the plaintiff's fund, calculated according to the lending rates set by the central bank.[29]

The plaintiff appealed to the Hubei High People's Court, arguing that the finding of the Wuhan Intermediate People's Court that it had not qualified to trade in the securities secondary market was wrong. After hearing the case, the Hubei High People's Court said that although the appellant was not an independent legal person nor had a financial institution license, it nevertheless acted as a securities organization affiliated to the government finance department and played an important service role in the issuance, repayment and transfer of government bonds. Furthermore, taking into consideration the fact that all the securities organizations affiliated to the government finance authorities at that time were undergoing a process of reorganization and identification change, the Hubei High People's Court held that the appellant should be recognized as having qualification to engage in trading government bonds in the secondary market. The appeal was, however, rejected by the Court on a different ground that the transactions were in fact a selling short of government bonds by the respondent.[30]

This case is a special case in a sense that the plaintiff was a government bond service provider affiliated to the local government finance department. The finding

---

28   *Supra* notes 14, 15.

29   *See* Shao Tingjie, *supra* note 27, at p. 330. The Court delivered the judgment on 2 April 1996.

30   *Id.*

of the Hubei High People's Court was regarded by commentators as a right decision, which took into consideration appropriately of the background about the creation, operation and transformation of the securities organizations affiliated to the government at that time.[31] In other cases, however, where if it is found that the parties had no qualifications to engage in trading government bonds, the people's courts would annul the agreement entered into by the parties. For example, in *China Pacific Insurance Branch Company*,[32] the plaintiff, an insurance branch of the China Pacific insurance company, signed a contract in November 1996 with the defendant, a trust investment company, for purchase of 40 million yuan 1996 (6) government bonds. The Court found that the plaintiff was an insurance branch with no independent legal person status. The Court held that the contract was null and void.[33]

After April 1988, when the regulations were relaxed to allow transfer of government bonds, there were widespread irregular and illegal activities in sales and purchases in the government market. Short selling (*maikong*) government bonds, for example, became a serious problem, which prompted the government to issue a circular in 1994[34] to stop such activities. In *the Second Government Bond Service Department of the Finance Bureau of the North District of Qingdao City v Securities Company of Linzhou City of Hunan Province*,[35] the four agreements signed by the plaintiff and defendant for purchases by the plaintiff of a total of 19,217,500 yuan 1992 (3) government bonds were in fact a short selling by the defendant, who did not possess the government bonds agreed for sale. The Hubei High People's Court found that the appellant, the plaintiff in the first instant court, advanced the money to the respondent but no government bonds were actually delivered; the deal was in fact not backed up by any actual government bonds. The Hubei High People's Court established that the respondent was selling short the government bonds that they did not have, which violated the regulations. The Court annulled the agreements and held the respondent should bear main responsibilities.[36]

---

31   *Id.* at p. 332. (It was commented that it was right that the people's court, in examining the qualifications of the plaintiff, took into consideration as background that government bond service providers like the plaintiff were undergoing a transitional process at that time.)

32   *Studies of Judicial Decisions Related to Financial Disputes* (*Jingrong Shenpan Anli Yanjiu*) (Vol. 2001), edited by Economic Division Court of Beijing High People's Court (Beijing: Law Publishing House, 2001), pp. 374–379.

33   *Id.* at p. 376.

34   The Circular of the Ministry of Finance, the PBOC and the CSRC on Firmly Stop Activity of Government Bond Short Selling (Caizhengbu, Zhongguo Renmin Yinhang, Zhongguo Zhengjianhui Guanyu Jianjue Zhizhi Guozhaiquan Maikong Xingwei de Tongzhi), issued on 20 May 1994.

35   *See* Shao Tingjie, *supra* note 27.

36   *Id.* at p. 330.

China Life Insurance Company Chengdu Branch v Sichuan Hualong Investment Consultant Co. Ltd

China Life Insurance Company Chengdu Branch v Sichuan Hualong Investment Consultant Co. Ltd.[37] is a complicated case involving a purchase of 40 million yuan government bonds by the plaintiff, China Life Insurance Chengdu branch in 1999. However, the real transactions in the case revealed that it was not merely a case of government bond purchase, but a case in which 40 million yuan funds were channelled through the purchase of 40 million yuan government bonds to some individuals affiliated to the defendant Hualong Investment Consultant and the funds were then speculated by those individuals in the stock market. The ultimate purpose of the transactions was for China Life Chengdu branch to get from Hualong Investment Consultant a higher return than normal fixed government bond interest for the 40 million yuan government bonds.

This case, which started at the Sichuan High People's Court and went up to the Supreme People's Court, illustrates the way in which the Sichuan High People's Court and the Supreme People's Court resolved the issues of the case in accordance with the general principles of the 1986 GPCL and other relevant laws and regulations. The Court was faced with three main issues, namely, the true intention of the parties concerned in the transactions, the responsibilities of the securities agent and investor principal, and the relationship between civil liability and administrative liability.

In March 1999 China Life Chengdu branch signed an agency agreement with Chengdu Dapeng Securities Co. Ltd., a third party in the first instance court and a claimant in the appeal court, entrusting Chengdu Dapeng Securities as its agent for a purchase 40 million yuan government bonds. China Life Chengdu branch opened a deposit account 791293 with Chengdu Dapeng Securities. Hualong Investment Consultant at that time had a securities account at Chengdu Dapeng Securities, known as the account 617. China Life Chengdu branch instructed Chengdu Dapeng Securities to attach the securities account 617 of Hualong Investment Consultant to its own deposit account 791293. To attach such a securities account, a practice for lending and asset management, means that the account holder allows the securities account thus attached to access the fund of his account.

Between 29 July and 2 August 1999, China Life Chengdu branch purchased 40 million yuan government bonds at Chengdu Dapeng Securities through the account 617. On 10 August 1999 Chengdu Dapeng Securities cancelled the account 617 in accordance with an instruction of China Life Chengdu branch. On the same day Hualong Investment Consultant designated the account 617 to another securities company, Xiamen Securities in Fujian pronvice. Later the 40 million yuan government bonds in the account 617 were all disposed of at Xiamen Securities and the fund was invested in speculative share trading. During the three years between 1999 and 2001, China Life Chengdu branch received regular returns amounting to several million yuan from Hualong Investment Consultant. In 2002, having received no returns from Hualong Investment Consultant and discovered that Chengdu Dapeng Securities had

---

37 The Supreme People's Court Civil Judgment (2004) No.137. *See* Gazette of the Supreme People's Court of the People's Republic of China, Issue 8, 2005, pp. 14–23.

bought the 40 million yuan government bonds not into its own securities account B880217601 but the account 617, China Life Chengdu branch took the case to Sichuan High People's Court, claiming 40 million yuan and associated losses from Hualong Investment Consultant, and requesting the Court to hold Chengdu Dapeng Securities liable jointly with Hualong Investment Consultant.

A key issue of the case was whether it was the true intention of China Life Chengdu branch to purchase the 40 million yuan government bonds with the account 617 and then cancel the account 617, and thus handing over the control of the 40 million yuan government bonds to the holders of the account of 617. China Life Chengdu branch submitted that they had not consented to Chengdu Dapeng Securities to purchase the 40 million yuan government bonds with their funds and deposit them in the account 617; the reason that this could have happened was because Chengdu Dapeng Securities violated business operational rules and deceived China Life Chengdu branch.

On the basis of the evidence of the case and by applying relevant evidential rules,[38] the Supreme People's Court established that it was the true intention of China Life Chengdu branch to attach Hualong Investment Consultant's account 617 to its own deposit account 791293; it was also the true intention of China Life Chengdu branch to cancel the account 617 later with Chengdu Dapeng Securities, which enabled the account 617 to be switched to Xiamen Securities; Chengdu Dapeng Securities followed the instructions of China Life Chengdu branch and committed no fraud on China Life Chengdu branch. The Supreme People's Court said that China Life Chengdu branch should bear the losses it suffered, which had no causal link with the cancellation of the account 617 Chengdu Dapeng Securities made in accordance with the instruction of China Life Chengdu branch. Based on the finding and in accordance with Article 63 of the 1986 GPCL,[39] the Supreme People's Court held that China Life Chengdu branch as the principal should bear civil liabilities for the acts of the agent Chengdu Dapeng Securities which were carried out according to the instructions of China Life Chengdu branch.[40]

Regarding the attachment by China Life Chengdu branch to its deposit account 791293 of the securities account 617 of Hualong Investment Consultant in order to purchase the 40 million yuan government bonds and facilitate a handover of the control of the 40 million yuan government bonds to the holders of the account 617 for the speculation of the funds in the stock market, the Supreme People's Court said that whether the practice of attaching securities accounts of others is lawful or not does not affect the determination of the civil liabilities according to the agreement between the parities concerned; it is an administrative and regulatory matter for the

---

38   Several Provisions of the Supreme People's Court on Civil Litigation Evidence (Zuigao Renmin Fayuan Guanyu Minshi Susong Zhengju de Ruogan Guiding), adopted by the Judicial Committee of the Supreme People's Court on 6 December 2001, and effective as of 1 April 2002.

39   Article 63 states that: "Citizens and legal persons may perform civil juristic acts through agents. An agent shall perform civil juristic acts in the principal's name within the scope of the power of agency. The principal shall bear civil liability for the agent's acts of agency."

40   *Supra* note 37, at p. 22.

securities regulatory authority to decide, which falls into the administrative law and regulation and is not a relevant issue for the Court to consider in this case.[41]

Borrowing Government Bonds

Borrowing government bonds is where one party borrows government bonds from another party for a certain period of time. The borrower pays a fee and returns the borrowed government bonds at the end of the period. Disputes came to the people's courts when borrowers failed to return the borrowed government bonds or repay an equivalent sum of money. The regulations issued by the government at different times concerning government bonds have no clear provisions about whether government bonds may be borrowed through agreements between parties and whether such borrowing is prohibited. In practice, parties enter into such borrowing agreements to facilitate their financing needs.

The validity of borrowing government bonds was recognised by the Supreme People's Court in the case *the Government Bond Service Department of the Finance Bureau of Sanming City of Fujian Province v Jun'an Securities Limited Company*.[42] In this case the government bond service department of the finance bureau of Sanming city of Fujian province signed an agreement in April 1995 with Nanchang securities center of Jun'an securities company, which stipulated, among other things, that the Nanchang securities center agreed to borrow from the Sanming government bond service department 5 million yuan 1995 (3) government bonds for a period between 25 April 1995 and 25 April 1996; the Nanchang securities center would pay the Sanming government bond service department a lump sum of fee at a rate of 0.5% of total face value of the government bonds; the Nanchang securities center would return the government bonds to the Sanming government bond service department on 25 April 1996. After the agreement was signed, the Sanming government bond service department handed over the agreed government bonds to the Nanchang securities center, who paid the 250,000 yuan fee. Upon expire of the term, the Nanchang securities center failed to return the government bonds to the Sanming government bond service department, who brought the case to the Fujian High People's Court.

The Court found that both the plaintiff and defendant had qualifications to engage in government bonds business and the agreement was their true intention. The cause of the dispute was that the defendant defaulted on the return of the government bond in accordance with the provisions of the agreement. On the basis of this finding, the Court upheld the agreement was a valid contract and held that the defendant bore responsibility for the breach of the agreement. The Court ruled that the defendant return the government bonds and their interest for the borrowing period of one year at a monthly rate of 0.1386%, the upper limit of the inter-bank borrowing rate for the same period, and pay penalty interest at a daily rate of 0.05% covering the time from when the government bond was due for return to the judgment day.

---

41   *Id.*
42   The Supreme People's Court Civil Judgment [1997] No. 190. *Selection of Financial Dispute Cases Heard by the Supreme People's Court (1996–1998)*, at pp. 689–692, *supra* note 19.

The defendant appealed the judgment to the Supreme People's Court, arguing that the Fujian High People's Court was wrong to order the defendant to pay interest and penalty interest because government bonds, unlike loans, carry interest and, moreover, those three-year-term government bonds of 1995 borrowed by the defendant had not expired yet, even though the defendant failed to return them to the plaintiff at the agreed time. This argument was accepted by the Supreme People's Court, who upheld the judgment of the Fujian High People's Court that the appellant return the government bond to the respondent but cancelled the ruling of the Fujian High People's Court on the interest and penalty interest.

The Supreme People's Court instead required the appellant to pay the respondent a usage fee covering the period from the time when the return of the government bond was due until the actual return of the government bond, calculated on the basis of the rate for the fee stipulated in the agreement.[43] In confirming the validity of the agreement between the appellant and the respondent on the borrowing government bonds, the Supreme People's Court said that there is no provision in current law and regulations that prohibit borrowing government bonds and require an approval by relevant government authorities for such borrowing; the validity of the agreement in this case should therefore be recognized.[44]

In another similar case, an agreement for borrowing government bonds was annulled by the people's court but on a different ground. In *Henan Province International Investment Trust Company v Wuhan Jinda Industrial Company Limited by Shares*,[45] the international trust investment company of Henan province signed an agreement in July 1995 with the Wuhan Henda company, a shareholder of the defendant Wuhan Jinda industrial company limited by shares. The agreement stipulated, among other things, that the Wuhan Henda borrow 10 million yuan 1995 (2) government bonds from the Henan international trust investment company for one year from 14 July 1995 to 14 July 1996 at an annual borrowing rate of 7.5%; at the end of the term the Wuhan Henda was to return the bonds to the Henan international trust investment company or pay a sum of money equivalent to the face value of the bonds. The Henan international trust investment company handed over 10 million yuan 1995 (2) government bonds to the Wuhan Henda on the day the agreement was signed. At the end of term the government bonds were not returned nor was an equivalent sum of money repaid to the Henan international trust investment company, who sued for breach of agreement at the Hubei High People's Court, claiming return of the government bonds plus interest and damages for delayed repayment according to a daily rate of 0.3% stipulated in the agreement.

The Hubei High People's Court found that the agreement was not signed and performed at the trading centers designated by the government. The agreement was under a name of borrowing government bonds but it was in fact an agreement for transfer of government bonds, which should have been signed and performed at a

---

43   *Id.* at p. 692.

44   *Id.* at p. 691.

45   The Supreme People's Court Civil Mediation Agreement [1997] No. 286. *Selection of Financial Dispute Cases Heard by the Supreme People's Court (1996–1998)*, at pp. 700–703, *supra* note 19.

designated trading center. The Court held that the agreement violated Article 9 of the 1992 Government Bond Regulations of the PRC[46] and was thus null and void, for which both parties were responsible. In accordance with Articles 55 (2), 58 (1) (v) and 61 (1) of the 1986 GPCL,[47] the Court ordered the defendant to return to the plaintiff 10 million yuan worth of government bonds and, should the defendant have no actual government bonds to return, a sum of money be paid to the plaintiff, calculated on the average trading prices of the same government bonds at Shenzhen and Shanghai Stock Exchanges on the fifteenth day after the judgment became effective. The Court dismissed the plaintiff's claim for damages.[48]

Disputes Involving Enterprise Bonds

The 1987 Provisional Regulations on the Administration of Enterprise Bonds, the first piece of national regulation concerning issuance and transfer of enterprise bonds, was a preliminary set of regulatory rules, many gaps of which were filled in by the 1993 Regulations on the Administration of Enterprise Bonds. Between 1987 and 1993, drafting company law and securities law was stepping up. In May 1992, the State Commission for Economic Reform issued two opinions on the regulation of limited companies and companies limited by shares, which served at that time as provisional company regulations.[49] This was followed by the 1993 Provisional Regulations on the Administration of Issuing and Trading of Shares, and the 1993 Company Law of the PRC. The promulgation of the 1987 Provisional Regulations on the Administration of Enterprise Bonds and the 1993 Regulations on the Administration of Enterprise Bonds was part of this drafting drive of company and securities law and regulations in response to active enterprise reform at that time. After the promulgation in 1987 and 1993 of the national enterprise bond regulations by the central government, some local governments promulgated local regulations on enterprise bonds to implement the national regulations in their local regions.[50]

---

46   *Supra* note 24.

47   Article 55 (2) states that: "A civil juristic act shall meet the following requirements: ... (2) The intention expressed is genuine." Article 58 (1) (v) states that: "Civil acts in the following categories shall be null and void: ... (v) Those that violate the law or the public interest." Article 61 (1) states that: "After a civil act has been determined to be null and void or has been rescinded, the party who has acquired as a result of the act shall return it to the party who has suffered a loss. The fault party shall compensate the other party for the losses it suffered as result of the act; if both parties have fault, they shall each bear their proper share of the responsibility."

48   *Supra* note 45, at p. 702.

49   Opinion on Standardization of Limited Liability Company (Youxian Zeren Gongsi Guifan Yijian) and Opinion on Standardization of Company Limited by Shares (Gufen Youxian Gongsi Guifan Yijian), both issued by the State Commission for Economic Reform on 15 May 1992.

50   *See*, for example, the Detailed Rules of the Heilongjiang Province to Implement the Provisional Regulations on the Administration of Enterprise Bonds (Heilongjiang Sheng Shishi Qiye Zhaiquan Guanli Zhanxing Tiaoli Xize), issued on 4 December 1989.

The 1993 Regulations on the Administration of Enterprise Bonds set out a regulatory framework for the issuance and transfer of enterprise bonds. Article 12 provides that enterprises who apply for an issue of enterprise bonds must satisfy five conditions including, first, that the scale of the enterprise has reached the requirements stipulated by the government; second, that the finance and accounting of the enterprise comply with the state regulations; third, that the enterprise has the ability to repay debts; fourth, that the enterprise has a good economic record and has profits for three consecutive years prior to the issue of enterprise bonds; and fifth, that the usage of the fund raised comply with the state industrial policies.[51] Article 20 emphasises that the funds raised by the issue of enterprise bonds should be used for the business of the enterprise and should not be used in risk investments which are not related to the business of the enterprise, such as buying and selling property and dealing in share and futures.[52]

While implementing the government policies on enterprise bonds, the 1993 Regulations on the Administration of Enterprise Bonds was a direct response to the problems in the early years of enterprise bond activities, such as the problem that the funds raised from issues were used for purposes other than those stated in prospectus and issue documents approved by the regulators. On one hand, the 1993 Regulations on the Administration of Enterprise Bonds has strengthened administrative and criminal responsibilities for violation of enterprise bond regulations, and on the other hand, it noticeably included a provision concerning civil compensation responsibility which was absent from the 1987 Provisional Regulations on the Administration of Enterprise Bonds. Thus, if an enterprise violated the provisions of the 1993 Regulations on the Administration of Enterprise Bonds and caused losses to others, the enterprise would be held responsible for civil compensation.[53]

Compared with the 1987 Provisional Regulations on the Administration of Enterprise Bonds, the enhanced 1993 Regulations on the Administration of Enterprise Bonds provide a set of more comprehensive and detailed regulatory rules, which help the people's courts in dealing with specific issues in the resolution of disputes involving enterprise bonds in accordance with general provisions of civil law, contract law, company law, securities law and other relevant statutes. Without these regulatory rules the people's courts would be in a difficult and uncertain position in making appropriate judgments on specific issues, as the people's courts would only apply general principles of civil law, contract law and other general statutes.

The 1993 Company Law provides for a statutory framework for regulating corporate bonds, such as the requirement for issuing corporate bonds, the approval procedure and documentation, and so on, which applies to companies incorporated under the 1993 Company Law.[54] This framework has been updated by the amendments

---

51   Article 21, 1993 Regulations on the Administration of Enterprise Bonds.
52   *Id.* art. 20.
53   *Id.* art. 36.
54   Chapter 5, "Corporate Bonds", the 1993 Company Law, including Articles 159–173.

of the 2005 Company Law.[55] The issuing and trading of corporate bonds are also subject to the 1998 Securities Law, which complements the 1993 Company Law. For example, the 1998 Securities Law requires that an application for listing and trading of corporate bonds shall be subject to verification by the CSRC,[56] and the CSRC may authorize a stock exchange to verify an application for listing of corporate bonds pursuant to the statutory conditions and procedures.[57] Like the 2005 Company Law, the 2005 Securities Law has updated the provisions for issuing and trading of corporate bonds.[58]

Approval Requirement for the Issue of Enterprise Bonds

Any issue of enterprise bonds must be approved by the PBOC or its designated local branches in conjunction with central or local government authorities. This position is emphasised by the government in a series of enterprise bond regulations.[59] If an enterprise issues bonds without such an approval or the bond issued is in an amount that exceeds the scope that has been approved, the enterprise shall be ordered to stop the issuance, return the funds raised, and pay a fine equivalent to 5% or less of the fund raised or the amount exceeded.[60] If a case comes to the people's court and the agreement in connection with an enterprise bond issued without government approval, the agreement shall be treated as a null and void agreement on the ground that the issue and the agreement violate the compulsory provisions of enterprise bond regulations.

In *China Great Wall Trust Investment Company v Beijing Hemu Jingmao Company*,[61] the plaintiff, China Great Wall Trust Investment Company, entered into an agreement in April 1993 with the Shangqiu branch of the Henan province international trust investment company for a subscription by the plaintiff of 5 million yuan enterprise bonds to be issued by the defendant, Beijing Hemu Jingmao company, for whom the Shangqiu branch acted as an agent for the issue of the bonds. Because the issue application was not submitted and approved by the Henan branch of the

---

55   Chapter 7, "Corporate Bonds", the 2005 Company Law, including Articles 154–163.

56   Article 50 (1), the 1998 Securities Law.

57   *Id.* art. 50 (2).

58   Article 16 concerns about the requirements for issuing corporate bonds, Article 17 about the documents to be submitted for an application, and Article 57 about the requirements for listing, to name only a few provisions.

59   Article 4, 1987 Provisional Regulations on the Administration of Enterprise Bonds; Article 11, 1993 Regulations on the Administration of Enterprise Bonds; Article 8, 1998 Procedures on the Administration of Issuance and Transfer of Enterprise Bonds (Qiye Zhaiquan Faxing Yu Zhuanrang Guanli Banfa), promulgated by the PBOC on 9 April 1998 and repealed by the PBOC on 17 August 2000.

60   Articles 26, 27, 1993 Regulations on the Administration of Enterprise Bonds.

61   *Study of Judicial Decisions Related to Financial Disputes* (*Jingrong Shenpan Anli Yanjiu*) (Vol. 2001), at pp. 386–392, *supra* note 32.

PBOC and the Henan provincial government, the Court held that the agreement was null and void. The defendant was ordered to return the money to the plaintiff.[62]

In *Shengyang Northern Securities Company v Dalian City Trust Investment Company of China Agriculture Bank*,[63] the second defendant was a property developer. In order to pay for a 300 *mu* of state-owned land located in the Dalian economic and technology development zone, the property developer had to raise a substantial sum. In September 1992, the property developer signed two agreements with the Dalian City Trust Investment Company of China Agriculture Bank, the first defendant of the case, to issue 17 million yuan bonds through a private placement. The Court found that there was no approval from government financial authorities at any level which permitted the property developer to issue bonds. This violation of enterprise bond regulations constituted one of the grounds on which the Court annulled the agreement.[64]

In cases where the proposed issue of enterprise bonds was approved by the regulator but what was approved was not properly implemented, the people's courts would examine the case to decide whether the agreement related to the issue was valid or not. In *Taiyuan Financial Market v Taiyuan Liyuan Company*,[65] the defendant, Taiyuan Liyuan Company, submitted two applications to the PBOC's Taiyuan city branch between November 1992 and January 1993 for a proposed issue of 20 million short-term enterprise bonds. Three guarantors agreed to provide guarantees for the proposed issue and they signed the applications. The applications were approved by the PBOC's Taiyuan city branch in accordance with the 1987 Provisional Regulations on the Administration of Enterprise Bonds. It was also approved that the proposed issue was to be carried out by the plaintiff, Taiyuan Financial Market. Subsequently the Taiyuan Liyuan Company and the Taiyuan Financial Market signed three underwriting agreements, under which the Taiyuan Financial Market agreed to underwrite and issue 20 million yuan worth of bonds with terms of six months to one year at various monthly interest rates ranging from 0.84% to 1.41%. After the underwriting agreements were signed, the Taiyuan Financial Market advanced a total of 20 million yuan to an account designated by the Taiyuan Liyuan Company. But no bond was actually issued by the Taiyuan Financial Market according to the approval. The Taiyuan Liyuan Company invested the fund in a property development project. The Taiyuan Liyuan Company defaulted repayments to the Taiyuan Financial Market, having only repaid 9.9 million yuan principal and 1,153,040 interest. The Taiyuan Financial Market sued the Taiyuan Liyuan Company for the balance and interest at the Shanxi High People's Court.

---

62   *Id.* at pp. 388–389.

63   The Supreme People's Court Civil Judgment [1996] No. 273. *Selection of Financial Dispute Cases Heard by the Supreme People's Court (1996–1998)*, at pp. 548–554, *supra* note 19.

64   *Id.* at pp. 551–553.

65   The Supreme People's Court Civil Judgment [1996] No. 301. *Selection of Financial Dispute Cases Heard by the Supreme People's Court (1996–1998)*, at pp. 555–562, *supra* note 19.

The Shanxi High People's Court held that the underwriting agreements between the plaintiff and defendant were lawful and valid as they were in accordance with Article 4 of the 1987 Provisional Regulations on the Administration of Enterprise Bonds,[66] and were approved by the PBOC Taiyuan city branch. The defendant was in breach of the underwriting agreement and should be held liable to the plaintiff for the balance and interest according to the underwriting agreement. The Court also held three guarantors liable jointly with the defendant. The Court said that the intention of providing guarantees expressed by the first two guarantors as independent enterprise legal persons was clear and the guarantees were lawful and valid; the third guarantor provided the guarantee with a full knowledge that it, as the finance department of Taiyuan city government, should not provide such guarantee, and therefore it should be held for a joint liability.

However, the judgment of the Shanxi High People's Court was overturned by the Supreme People's Court. The Supreme People's Court said that the Taiyuan Financial Market advanced a total of 20 million yuan to the Taiyuan Liyuan Company but did not issue any enterprise bonds in accordance with the underwriting agreement; it was in fact a loan transaction in the name of issuance of enterprise bonds; the Taiyuan Financial Market had no license to engage in loan business. On these grounds, the Supreme People's Court held that the transaction between the Taiyuan Liyuan Company and the Taiyuan Financial Market was null and void; as the Taiyuan Liyuan Company used the 20 million yuan from the Taiyuan Financial Market, the Taiyuan Liyuan Company should return the balance plus interest payable based on the interest rate published by the PBOC for the relevant periods. In connection with this finding, the Supreme People's Court ruled that three guarantors should not be held liable jointly with the defendant. The Court said that what the guarantors agreed and signed was for an issue of 20 million yuan bonds, but the proposed issue for which the guarantors agreed to provide guarantees had not happened, so the guarantors should not be held liable for their guarantees.[67]

Loan Transaction in the Name of Enterprise Bond Issue

A loan transaction happens when a proposed issuance of enterprise bonds is signed by the parties in their agreements but the real transaction followed is a loan transaction in which no bond is actually issued but a sum of money is lent from bond "subscribers", "underwriters" or "issuing agents" to the enterprise "issuers". The case *Taiyuan Financial Market v Taiyuan Liyuan Company*,[68] discussed above, is an example in which the real transaction was a 20 million yuan loan facilitated to the defendant under the name of an issuance of enterprise bonds. A loan transaction under the name of an enterprise bond issue would be annulled by the people's courts on the ground that it violates the law and regulations.

---

66 Article 4 of the 1987 Provisional Regulations on the Administration of Enterprise Bonds states: "the People's Bank of China is the competent authority for enterprise bond, and the issuance of enterprise bond must be approved by the People's Bank of China."

67 *Supra* note 65, at p. 560.

68 *Id.*

Shengyang Northern Securities Company v Dalian City Investment Trust Company of China Agriculture Bank[69] is a typical case in which a loan of 17 million yuan to finance a land development project was disguised by the agreements signed by the parties for an issue of enterprise bonds. The plaintiff, Shengyang Northern Securities Company, signed two agreements with the first defendant, Dalian City Trust Investment Company of China Agriculture Bank, through whom the plaintiff agreed to purchase 17 million yuan bond to be issued by the second defendant. The plaintiff advanced 17 million yuan to the first defendant, who then advanced the funds to the second defendant. The term was one year and interest charge was 0.15% monthly. The fund was used for a purchase of land but the land was not developed pending a government planning permission. As the second defendant was unable to repay the plaintiff, supplementary agreements were signed and the repayment was extended for another year with an increase of monthly interest charge to 0.2175%. When the second defendant failed to repay the plaintiff at the end of the extended period, the plaintiff brought the case to the Liaoning High People's Court.

The Liaoning High People's Court found that the plaintiff had no license to engage in loan business and the agreements between the plaintiff and the first defendant and between the first defendant and the second defendant were sham. The deal was in fact a loan transaction in the name of a private placement of enterprise bonds. In accordance with Articles 58 (1) (v), 61 and 89 (1) (i) of the 1986 GPCL,[70] the Court held that the agreements violated the law and regulations and were null and void. The case was appealed to the Supreme People's Court who upheld the decision of the Liaoning High People's Court. The Supreme People's Court reiterated that the agreements signed by the parties were a loan transaction in the name of a private placement of bonds and the parties violated relevant financial law and regulations. Having invalidated the agreements, the Court ordered the two defendants to return 17 million yuan and interest to the plaintiff and upheld the decision of the Liaoning High People's Court that the plaintiff pay one-third of the court costs.[71]

In cases where a loan is facilitated in the name of an issue of enterprise bonds and the party who has advanced the fund has license to engage in loan business, the people's courts would take this factor into consideration when deciding the case. In *China Great Wall Trust Investment Company v Beijing Hemu Jingmao Company*,[72] the agreement signed by the plaintiff was for a subscription by the plaintiff of 5 million yuan enterprise bonds to be issued by the defendant company, but no actual bonds were issued by the defendant. The Court held that the agreement was null and void and the transaction was not an issue of enterprise bonds but a loan transaction. However, as the plaintiff was licensed to engage in loan business, the Court said that

---

69   *Id.*

70   For Article 58(1) (v) and Article 61, *see supra* note 47; Article 89 (1) (i) states that: "In accordance with legal provisions the agreement between the parties on the performance of a debt may be guaranteed using the methods below: (i) a guarantor may guarantee to the creditor that the debtor shall perform his debt. If the debtor defaults, the guarantor shall perform the debt or bear joint liability according to agreement. After performing the debt, the guarantor shall have the right to claim repayment from the debtor."

71   *Supra* note 63, at pp. 551–552.

72   *Supra* note 61.

the 4.83 million yuan plus interest the plaintiff advanced to the defendant should be protected. The Court ordered the defendant to return the plaintiff's 4.83 million yuan and interest.[73]

Guarantee Provided for Enterprise Bonds

The 1995 Security Law and relevant general provisions of the 1986 GPCL[74] are the primary sources of the security law the people's courts apply to deal with guarantee issues in the disputes involving enterprise bonds. At the regulatory level, the 1987 Provisional Regulations on the Administration of Enterprise Bonds and 1993 Regulations on the Administration of Enterprise Bonds have no mandatory requirements for enterprise bond issuers to provide guarantees for the issuance and repayment of enterprise bonds. There are some detailed provisions in the 1998 Procedures for the Administration of Issuance and Transfer of Enterprise Bonds,[75] which require that guarantees are provided by issuers and are approved by the PBOC before the proposed issue starts. These provisions also require that guarantees are made in accordance with the 1995 Security Law and relevant requirements of the PBOC.

One of the recurring problems the people's courts were often faced with in the late 1980s and early 1990s was the guarantee provided by government departments for the issuance of enterprise bonds despite the fact that the law and regulations prohibit state organs from acting as a guarantor for economic contracts between enterprises. In *China Great Wall Investment Company v Beijing Hemu Jingmao Company*,[76] Shangqiu prefecture labour and personnel bureau, Henan province, agreed to provide guarantees for repayment of the enterprise bonds to be issued by the defendant. The Bureau was later split into two bureaux in charge of personnel and labour respectively. The Court held that the Bureau was at fault to have provided this guarantee because it should not as a state organ act as a guarantor. The Court invalidated the guarantee and held the Bureau liable jointly with the defendant for compensation. As the Bureau was split into two bureaux and a clear division of the liability could not be arranged the Court held two bureaux jointly liable.[77]

Amongst the government departments, the department in charge of finance is more likely to act as guarantors for economic activities between enterprises. In *Taiyuan Financial Market v Taiyuan Liyuan Company*,[78] one of the three guarantors involved was the finance department of Taiyuan city government, who provided guarantees for an issue of 20 million yuan enterprise bonds by the defendant. The Shanxi High People's Court held that the guarantee provided by the finance department of Taiyuan city government, acting in the capacity of a government department, had no legal effect. The Court found that the finance department knew

---

73   *Id.* at pp. 388–389.
74   The general provisions provided for by Article 89 of the 1986 GPCL.
75   Chapter 4, "Guarantee", including Articles 36–43, *supra* note 59.
76   *Supra* note 61.
77   *Id.* at p. 389
78   *Supra* note 65.

that as a government finance department it should not provide the guarantee for the issue but it nevertheless went ahead with the guarantee for the issue. On the basis of this finding, the Court held that the finance department should bear a joint compensation liability.[79]

In 1984 the Ministry of Finance issued a notice which made it clear that no government finance department could provide guarantees in the name of the government finance department for economic contracts between enterprises.[80] However, this notice was ignored, particularly by local government finance departments who continued to provide guarantees to enterprises. This prompted the Ministry of Finance to issue the second notice in 1988, which reiterated that government finance departments must not provide guarantees to enterprises for their economic contracts; local government finance departments should be responsible for those guarantees that had already been provided; any such guarantees in the future would be null and void.[81]

Repayment Obligation

Enterprise bond issuers are required to repay bondholders at the end of term according to the 1993 Regulations on the Administration of Enterprise Bonds.[82] But many issuers defaulted repayments, which became a serious problem and a main cause of disputes of enterprise bonds. In September 1994, the State Council issued a notice to deal with this problem.[83] While highlighting the default as a potential problem which may affect social stability, the 1994 Notice set out a series of detailed measures in order to resolve the problem.[84] In March 1999, faced with a situation that this default problem continued to cause disputes, the State Development and Planning Commission[85] and the PBOC issued another notice with a set of detailed measures

---

79   *Id.* at p. 558. This decision of the Shanxi High People's Court on the liability of the finance department was overturned by the Supreme People's Court on a different ground. *Supra* note 67.

80   Notice on Finance Departments May Not Provide Guarantee for Economic Contracts (Guoyu Caizheng Bumeng Bude Wei Jingji Hetong Tigong Danbao de Tongzhi), issued by the Ministry of Finance on 31 December 1984.

81   Notice on Reiteration of Finance Departments may not Provide Guarantee for Economic Contracts (Guanyu Chongshen Caizheng Bumen Bude Wei Jingji Hetong Tigong Danbao de Tongzhi), issued by the Ministry of Finance on 20 November 1988.

82   Article 5, the 1993 Regulations on the Administration of Enterprise Bonds.

83   Notice of the State Council General Office for Circulating the Opinion of the People's Bank of China and the State Planning Commission on Dealing with the Problem of Default of Repayment Due of Enterprise Bonds (Guowuyuan Bangongting Zhuanfa Zhongguo Renmin Yinhang, Guojia Jiwei Guanyu Qiye Zhaiquan Daoqi Buneng Duifu Wenti Chuli Yijian de Tongzhi), issued on 22 September 1994.

84   For example, the Point 6 of the Notice asked local government to report to the State Planning Commission and the PBOC by the end of October 1994 on the measures taken to deal with the problem arising from possible default of repayments due in 1994 in their regions and related problems which may cause social unrest.

85   Before 1998 the State Development and Planning Commission was called the State Planning Commission; after a restructure in 2003 the State Development and Planning Commission has become known as the State Development and Reform Commission.

to further tackle the problem.[86] Like the 1994 Notice of the State Council, the 1999 Notice emphasised the importance of dealing with the problem, treating it as an issue that may directly affect stable development of enterprise bond market as well as social stability.[87] In the meantime, some local governments also issued notices to deal with the problem in their local regions. The Shangxi provincial government, for example, issued a notice in May 2000 which set out measures to ensure the repayments due in 2000 to be paid in due time by local enterprises involved.[88]

In resolving the disputes caused by the default of repayment by enterprise issuers, a question was raised by local people's courts to the Supreme People's Court, concerning the position of a financial institution who acted for the issuance of enterprise bonds as an agent of enterprise bond issuers and who used his own funds to have repaid bondholders on behalf of the issuer. In April 1994 the Supreme People's Court issued a reply that provides a judicial clarification about this question.[89] The Supreme People's Court states in the reply:

> An enterprise bond is a negotiable security issued according to the legal procedures by an enterprise which has agreed to repay the principal plus interest within the stipulated time limit. The issuer of enterprise bonds has an obligation to repay bondholders principal and interest in accordance with agreed time limit. Where a financial institution accepts an entrustment of agency to act for the issuer as an agent in the issuance of enterprise bonds, the issuer shall bear civil liability for the financial institution's acts of agency in accordance with the provisions of second paragraph of Article 63 of the 1986 GPCL. Thus, when the issuer fails to repay principal and interest in accordance with agreed time limit, bondholders should claim civil rights from the issuer and (or) guarantor. If a financial institution, acting as a bond sales agent, uses his funds to repay bondholders for the issuer, the financial institution becomes a bondholder who should also claim civil rights from the issuer and (or) guarantor.

Thus, where a financial institution accepts an entrustment of agency from a principal enterprise bond issuer to issue enterprise bonds, the principal shall bear civil liabilities for the financial institution's acts of agency in accordance with Article 63 (2) of the 1986 GPCL;[90] when the issuer fails to repay bondholders in accordance

---

86   Notice of the State Development and Planning Commission and the PBOC on Relevant Issues Concerning Further Dealing Well with the Work of Enterprise Bonds Repayment (Guojia Jiwei, Zhongguo Renmin Yinhang Guanyu Jinyibu Zuohao Qiye Zhaiquan Duifu Gongzuo Youguan Wenti de Tongzhi), issued on 24 March 1999.

87   It states: "… whether enterprise bonds can be repaid on due time relates directly to a sustainable development of enterprise bond market and social stability." *Id.*

88   Notice of Shanxi Province People's Government on Further Strengthening the Work of Repayment of Enterprise Bonds (Shanxi Sheng Renmin Zhengfu Guanyu Jinyibu Jiaqiang Qiye Zhaiquan Duifu Gongzuo de Tongzhi), issued on 12 May 2000.

89   The Reply of the Economic Division Court of the Supreme People's Court on Whether Financial Institutions Acting as Agents for Issuance of Enterprise Bonds Should Bear Liability for the Debt of Enterprise Bond Issuers (Zuigao Renmin Fayuan Jingji Shenpanting Guanyu Daili Faxing Qiye Zhaiquan de Jingrong Jigou Yingfou Chengdan Qiye Zhaiquan Faxingren Zhaiwu Zeren Wenti de Fuhan), replied on 29 April 1994.

90   *See supra* note 39.

with the term of agreement, bondholders shall make claims to the issuer or the issuer's guarantor. If the financial institution has repaid bondholders, it becomes a bondholder and should make claims to the issuer or the issuer's guarantor.

In *Sichuan Province Securities Company v Sichuan Xinchao Computer Industrial Group*,[91] the plaintiff, Sichuan Province Securities Company, acted as an agent of the defendant for an issuance of 5 million yuan enterprise bonds by the defendant. When the defendant was unable to fulfil its repayment obligation at the end of term, the plaintiff repaid bondholders for the defendant a total of 3,425,000 yuan. The Intermediate People's Court of Chengdu City of Sichuan Province held that the agency agreement between the plaintiff and the defendant was lawful and valid in accordance with the 1993 Regulations on the Administration of Enterprise Bonds. The defendant failed to fulfil its repayment obligation when the repayment was due, which constituted a breach of the agreement. In accordance with the 1994 Reply of the Supreme People's Court, the Court held that the plaintiff, who had repaid the bondholders on behalf of the defendant, become the holder of 3,425,000 yuan bonds and was entitled to claim from the defendant and its guarantor.[92]

China Agriculture Bank Chengdu City Jingjiang Branch v Guotai Jun'an Securities Company Chengdu Renmin Zhonglu Business Center,[93] is a complicated case which involved five parties in a dispute related to an enterprise bond of 10 million yuan. In April 1997, after an approval was granted by Sichuan Province Planning Commission and the PBOC's Sichuan branch, Sichuan Kangda company signed an agreement with Neijiang city branch of Sichuan province trust investment company who agreed to act as an agent for the issue of Sichuan Kangda company's 10 million bonds in Neijiang city, Sichuan province, guaranteed by Baita company. The agreement stipulated, among other things, that Sichuan Kangda company should credit a lump sum of principal and interest to the Neijiang city branch's account one week before the expiration of the term for the repayment to bondholders. The Neijiang city branch then signed an agreement with Guotai Jun'an securities company Chengdu business center for the Guotai Jun'an business center to sell 4 million yuan bonds. The Neijiang city branch agreed to credit the principal and interest of 4 million bonds to the Guotai Jun'an business center's account one week before the expire of the term. A similar agreement was then signed between the Guotai Jun'an business center and the plaintiff, China Agriculture Bank Chengdu city Jingjiang branch, under which the plaintiff agreed to sell 3 million yuan bonds for a fee of 45,000 yuan and the Guotai Jun'an business center agreed to credit to the plaintiff's account a lump sum of 3.66 million yuan for the repayment to bondholders before the expire of the bonds.

The plaintiff sold the bonds and at the end of the two-year term repaid bondholders a total of 3.66 million yuan. The Guotai Jun'an business center only credited 750,000 yuan to the plaintiff's account. In July 2000, the plaintiff sued the Guotai Jun'an

---

91   *See* the case at www.isinolaw.com, Document Ref. No. 76588–12972.

92   *Id.*

93   *See* Zhang Jinhan (ed.), *Application of Law and Adjudication in Commercial Cases* (Shangshi Anjian Falu Shiyong Yu Shenpan) (Beijing: People's Publishing House, 2003), pp. 501–506.

business center for the balance of 2.91 million yuan. In a related litigation in 1999, the Guotai Jun'an business center sued the Neijiang city branch, the Kangda company and the Baita company for the repayment balances. The Court held that the balance of 2.91 million yuan should be paid by the issuer, the Sichuan Kangda company, and the issuer's guarantor, the Baita company, not the Guotai Jun'an business center. The Court reasoned that the plaintiff had obtained a status of bondholder after it repaid the bondholders and thus the issuer should bear the liability to refund the plaintiff. The Court further found that the bonds sold by the plaintiff had seals of the issuer and the issuer's agent in addition to the plaintiff's own seal. The Court said that this showed that the issuer had acknowledged the plaintiff acting as an agent for the sale of the bonds. The judgment was upheld by the appeal court Sichuan High People's Court.[94]

These cases show that whatever the agency relationship and sub-agency relationship might be, the basic position regarding repayment obligation is clear. That is, the issuer of enterprise bonds has an obligation to repay bondholders principal and interest; where an agent uses his own funds to repay bondholders for the issuer the agent has a claim to make to the issuers as other bondholders. This point is further illustrated in *Jiangxi Province Securities Company v Zhongfang Group Nanchang Property Development Company*.[95]

The plaintiff, Jiangxi province securities company, signed an agreement with the defendant, a property developer, to undertake an issue to the public of a two-year enterprise bonds on behalf of the defendant for a property development project. At the end of the term, the defendant was unable to repay the bondholders. A supplementary agreement was then signed between the plaintiff and the defendant in which the plaintiff agreed to borrow 20 million yuan to repay the bondholders and the defendant would later repay the plaintiff 20 million yuan and interest and related taxes. The plaintiff agreed to waive the commission fee payable and the defendant agreed that the profit from the project when it was sold out would be divided between the defendant and plaintiff at a ratio of 6:4. After the plaintiff borrowed 20 million yuan and repaid the bondholders a further agreement was signed between the plaintiff and defendant stipulating that the defendant would repay the plaintiff a total sum of 69,749,232 yuan, which included 20 million yuan borrowed by the plaintiff.

The defendant failed to repay 20 million yuan and interest, therefore the plaintiff brought the case to the Jiangxi High People's Court. The defendant submitted that the 20 million yuan was not a debt but an investment by the plaintiff to the project, but this submission was rejected by the Court. In accordance with Article 63 and 84 (2) of the 1986 GPCL[96] and Article 21 of the 1987 Provisional Regulations

---

94   *Id.* at p. 506.

95   The Supreme People's Court Civil Judgment (2000) No. 35. *See* English translation of the case at www.isinolaw.com, Document Ref. No. 76590–3219.

96   For Article 63, *see supra* note 39; Article 84 (2) states that: "The creditor shall have the right to demand that the debtor fulfil his obligations as specified by the contract or according to legal provisions."

on Administration of Enterprise Bonds,[97] the Court ordered the defendant to pay the plaintiff 20 million yuan and interest. The defendant appealed to the Supreme People's Court, arguing that, because of the clause that the plaintiff would waive commission fee and the profit from the project would be shared by the plaintiff and defendant, the plaintiff had changed from a creditor of 20 million yuan to a partner of the project, assuming jointly the losses of the project. The Supreme People's Court, by examining the relevant provisions of the agreements in their original contexts, concluded that the clause relied upon by the defendant was not sufficient to alter the initial legal relationship between the plaintiff and defendant. The Supreme People's Court thus upheld the judgment of the Jiangxi High People's Court.[98]

Summary

Since the early 1980s government and enterprise bond activities have taken place as part of a process of economic reform and enterprise reform in China. Government and enterprise bond markets have developed gradually, together with a legal and regulatory framework. This chapter looked at some aspects of the disputes involving government and enterprise bonds and examines the way in which these disputes are dealt with by the people's courts. The disputes involving government bonds and enterprise bonds relate to different bonds in nature, but they share common features in many aspects. Some of these features are summarized as follows.

First, the cases discussed above show that a main cause of the government and enterprise bond disputes is defaults of various kinds by defendants. In the disputes involving government bonds, defendants may default on the delivery of the government bonds or default on repayments while in the disputes involving enterprise bonds; defendants may default on repayments to bondholders, which is a major problem. In relation to the default problem, another important feature of these disputes is that large sums of funds or debts are involved. This is not only a serious problem for plaintiffs, but also a serious social problem from the point of view of the government, as such problems may affect sustainable development of government and enterprise bond markets as well as social stability.[99] It is therefore not surprising to see that the government at both national and local levels have taken a series of measures to tackle the problem of the defaults on the repayment by enterprise issuers to enterprise bondholders.[100]

Second, one of the major contributors to the default problem, shown by the cases, is that the fund that is used for government bonds or raised from issues of enterprise bonds are speculated in dealings in stock market or invested in failed property projects. The case *China Life Insurance Company Chengdu Branch v Sichuan Hualong Investment Consultant Co. Ltd.*[101] shows how 40 million yuan

---

97   Article 21 states that issue of enterprise bonds by enterprises should be undertaken by securities companies.

98   *Supra* note 95.

99   *See supra* note 87.

100   *See supra* notes 83, 86 and 88.

101   *Supra* note 37.

funds were channelled through from the government bond market to the stock market and were speculated in share trading. *Shengyang Northern Securities Company v Dalian City Trust Investment Company of China Agriculture Bank*[102] and *Jiangxi Province Securities Company v Zhongfang Group Nanchang Property Development Company*[103] are two cases in which a large amount of funds are invested in property projects. From the government's point of view, speculative activities pose a threat to market stability and economic policies of the government. After the regulations were relaxed in the late 1980s to allow transfer of government bonds, short selling government bonds became a serious problem, which prompted the government to take measures to curb such activities.[104]

Third, a common feature shared by many of the cases discussed above is that there exists a widespread violation of restrictive and compulsory regulations of government and enterprise bonds, particularly in the early years of China's securities market. Parties may enter into loan transactions disguised by transfer of government bonds or issues of enterprise bonds; parties may have no proper license or qualification to enter into government bond agreements or enterprise bond agreements; agreements for enterprise bond issues may not be approved by government regulators; government organs may violate regulations to act as guarantors for enterprises. Measures have been taken by the government regulators to stop such widespread violation.[105] When the disputes come to the people's courts, as the cases discussed above show, the agreements concerning government and enterprise bonds that involve violation of the law and regulations are invalided by the people's courts.

Fourth, the people's courts play an important role in enforcing the law and regulations concerning government and enterprise bonds. In dealing with the disputes, the people's courts examine whether the agreements in question are valid, whether the parties have license or qualification to engage in the agreements, whether the agreements are genuine transactions or sham transactions, and whether the transactions are carried out in the market designated by the government. On the other hand, if there are no clear and definite regulations concerning certain specific issues, the people's courts may play a role within the jurisdiction of the court to protect the interests of the parties and to facilitate transactions. In *The Second Government Bond Service Department of the Finance Bureau of the North District of Qingdao City v Securities Company of Linzhou City of Hunan Province*,[106] the people's court takes into a due consideration of the transitional nature of the securities organizations affiliated to the government and recognizes their qualification; in *the Government Bond Service Department of the Finance Bureau of Sanming City of Fujian Province v Jun'an Securities Limited Company*,[107] the people's court recognizes the validity

---

102 *Supra* notes 63 and 69.

103 *Supra* note 95.

104 *Supra* note 34.

105 For example, the government took measures to stop government organs from acting as guarantors for enterprises in their enterprise issues. *See supra* notes 80 and 81.

106 *Supra* note 27.

107 *Supra* note 42.

of the agreement for borrowing government bonds, an issue about which there is no definite law and regulation.

Fifth, the legal framework governing government and enterprise bonds has been improved over the years, which in turn increases certainty and clarity of the law and regulations which the people's courts need in resolving the government and enterprise bond disputes. Since 1981, a large number of individual regulations, rules, circulars and announcements concerning government bonds have been issued by the State Council, the Ministry of Finance, the PBOC and some other regulators. On one hand, they have provided detailed provisions by reference to which the people's courts resolve the disputes in conjunction with application of general and basic civil law, contract law, agency law and so on, but on the other hand, they may be confusing and inconsistent to the people's courts. In some circumstances the Supreme People's Court has to clarify certain issues in accordance with basic principles of law.[108] The 1998 Securities Law provides for a legal framework for the issuing and trading of shares and corporate bonds, but expressly states that the issuing and trading of government bonds shall be separately provided for in other laws and administrative regulations.[109] The amended 2005 Securities Law goes a step further and includes the listing and trading of government bonds, which is a positive step in moving towards a clear and uniform application of law and regulations in the government bond market.

---

108 For example, the Supreme People's Court clarifies the position of financial institutions that have repaid enterprise bondholders on behalf of enterprise issuers. *See supra* note 89.

109 Article 2, 1998 Securities Law. *See* also Zhu Sanzhu, *supra* note 2, at pp. 207–208.

Chapter 4

The Securities Repurchase Market

Introduction

The securities repurchase market began in 1991 in China. Trading was first carried out in Wuhan Securities Trading Center, Tianjin Securities Trading Center and the STAQ (Securities Trading Automatic Quotation) trading network, a jointly operated market at that time covering major cities nationwide.[1] In December 1993 trading began in the Shanghai Stock Exchange, followed by the Shenzhen Stock Exchange in October 1994. The rate of government bond repurchase trading grew quickly in the first few years. It is estimated that repurchases of government bonds had reached about 30 billion yuan by the end of 1994, and by the middle of 1995 over 50% of all the government bond trading was repurchase trading.[2]

After the securities repurchase market emerged, there were widespread irregularities among financial institutions and trading centers. Interest rates were too high; terms were too long; funds were used for inappropriate purposes, such as unauthorized investments in real property and speculation in shares in the stock market; and many financial institutions were selling short government bonds. For example, in *Ha'erbin Finance Securities Co. v Shenzhen Securities Business Center of Yunnan Securities Co. Ltd,*[3] the defendant who defaulted on repayment to the plaintiff invested the fund to develop thirty-six villas in Dongguan, Guangdong province.[4] Article 52 of the 1994 Provisional Measures for the Administration of

---

1   As a nationwide trading network, the STAQ system was established in December 1990 and linked initially about eighty trading centers throughout China. For various reasons, it was closed down on 9 September 1999. For general background about the emergence of securities trading in China, *see* Zhu Sanzhu, *Securities Regulation in China*, pp. 3–8. (Ardsley, NY: Transnational Publishers, 2000).

2   *See* Bin Jiancheng, "Current Status and Development of Government Bond Repurchase Market of Our Country" (Woguo Guozhai Huigou Shichang de Xianzhuang yu Fazhan), *Study on Finance and Business (Caimao Yanjiu)*, Issue 4, 2002, pp. 81–84, at p. 81. For more about China's government bond repurchase market in the 1990s, *see* Xiao Yu, *China Government Bond Market (Zhongguo Guozhai Shichang)* (Beijing: Social Science Document Publishing House, 1999).

3   *See Selection of Financial Dispute Cases Heard by the Supreme People's Court (1996–1998) (Zuigao Renmin Fayuan Shenli de Jinrong Jiufen Anli Xuanbian)*, compiled by the Economic Division Court of the Supreme People's Court (Beijing: China University of Political Science and Law Press, 1999), pp. 497–507.

4   *Id.* at p. 503.

Credit Funds[5] provides that the repurchasing party in a security repurchase transaction shall have a real and full amount of securities, and must complete delivery of the securities to the other party or seal up for safekeeping by the other party.[6] However, this regulatory requirement was ignored and violated by financial institutions in many cases of securities repurchase agreements.[7]

Between 1994 and 1996, several important government circulars were issued to address these problems by the State Council, the Ministry of Finance, the PBOC and the CSRC, including, among others, 1994 Circular on Firmly Curb Acts of Selling Short Government Bonds,[8] 1995 Circular on Reiteration of Relevant Issues Concerning Further Standardization of Securities Repurchase Business,[9] 1995 Circular on Seriously Clear Off Securities Repurchase Debts Becoming Due,[10] and 1996 Circular of the State Council which endorsed a set of further measures proposed by the PBOC to deal with securities repurchase debts.[11] It is estimated that by the end of 1995, debts among securities repurchase participants had reached about 7 billion yuan.[12] To step up the debt clearance process was the central aim of the measures proposed by the PBOC and endorsed by the State Council, and one of the measures to achieve this aim was to set up a joint office between the PBOC, Ministry of Finance and CSRC to oversee the debt clearance process.[13]

In June 1997, in a move to prevent further banking funds from flowing into the stock market during the Asian financial crisis, the PBOC instructed all the commercial banks to stop securities repurchase trading at the Shanghai and

---

5   Provisional Measures for the Administration of Credit Funds (Xindai Zijin Guanli Zanxing Banfa), issued by the PBOC on 15 February 1994.

6   *Id*. art. 52.

7   A survey conducted by the PBOC on the securities repurchase trading at two securities exchanges before 1996 shows that 82% and 92% of all the securities trading in those two securities exchanges respectively were short selling activities. Quoted in Ouyang Mingcheng and Zhang Min, "Improving Legal Mechanism for Securities Repurchase Trading" (Zhengquan Huigou Jiaoyi de Falü Guizhi Zhi Wanshan), *Modern Legal Science* (*Xiandai Faxue*), Issue 1, 1996, pp. 63–64, at p. 63.

8   Circular on Firmly Curb Acts of Selling Short Government Bonds (Guanyu Jianjue Zhizhi Guozhaiquan Maikong Xingwei de Tongzhi), issued jointly by the Ministry of Finance, the PBOC and the CSRC on 20 May 1994.

9   Circular on Reiteration of Relevant Issues Concerning Further Standardization of Securities Repurchase Business (Guanyu Chongshen dui Jinyibu Guifan Zhengquan Huigou Yewu Youguan Wenti de Tongzhi), issued jointly by the PBOC, the Ministry of Finance and the CSRC on 8 August 1995.

10   Circular on Seriously Clear off Securities Repurchase Debts Becoming Due (Guanyu Renzhen Qingchang Zhengquan Huigou Daoqi Zhaiwu de Tongzhi), issued jointly by the PBOC, the Ministry of Finance and the CSRC on 27 October 1995.

11   Circular of the State Council Approving and Circulating the PBOC's Request for Instruction on Further Improving the Work of Clearing off Securities Repurchase Debts (Guowuyuan Pizhuan Zhongguo Renmin Yinhang Guanyu Jinyibu Zuohao Zhengquan Huigou Zhaiwu Qingchang Gongzuo Qingshi de Tongzhi), issued on 25 June 1996.

12   *See* Bin Jiancheng, *supra* note 2, at p. 83.

13   Section 8, 1996 Circular of the State Council, *supra* note 11.

Shenzhen stock markets and other securities trading centers.[14] Beginning on 6 June 1997, securities repurchase business of commercial banks was moved to the national inter-bank market. At the same time, the PBOC issued the Provisional Regulations on Bond Repurchase Business among Banks,[15] which apply to the commercial bank members who have been approved by the PBOC to enter into the national inter-bank market for bond repurchase business. In August 1999, in order to open up financing channels for fund management companies and securities companies, the PBOC issued two regulations,[16] one of which allows fund management companies to apply to enter into the national inter-bank market for bond repurchase business,[17] and the other which allows securities companies to apply for the same but with a recommendation first from the CSRC.[18]

Securities repurchase market regulations and trading rules have been updated in recent years to reflect the regulatory development of securities repurchase business over the past decade. The 2000 Measures on the Administration of Bond Trading in the National Inter-Bank Bond Market[19] provides that bond repurchase contracts include a bond repurchase master agreement and individual repurchase agreements.[20] The 2006 Implementing Rules of the Shenzhen Stock Exchange on Bond and Bond Repurchase Trading has replaced a number of circulars issued in the past years by the Shenzhen Stock Exchange concerning bond repurchase rules.[21] With the introduction of a new type of government bond repurchase agreement in 2004,[22] a

---

14   *See* the PBOC's Circular on All Commercial Banks to Stop Trading Securities and Securities Repurchases at Securities Exchanges (Guanyu Ge Shangye Yinhang Tingzhi Zai Zhengquan Jiaoyisuo Zhengquan Huigou Ji Xianquan Jiaoyi de Tongzhi), issued by the PBOC on 5 June 1997.

15   Provisional Regulations on Bond Repurchase Business among Banks (Yinhang Jian Zhaiquan Huigou Yewu Xhanxing Guiding), issued by the PBOC on, and effective as of, 5 June 1997.

16   Circular on Distributing "Administrative Provisions on Fund Management Companies Entering into Inter-bank Market" and "Administrative Provisions on Securities Companies Entering into Inter-bank Market" (Guanyu Yinfa "Jijin Guanli Gongsi Jinru Yinhang Jian Tongye Shichang Guanli Guiding" he "Zhengquan Gongsi Jinru Yinhang Jian Tongye Shichang Guanli Guiding" de Tongzhi), issued by the PBOC on 19 August 1999.

17   *Id.* art. 3, Administrative Provisions on Fund Management Companies Entering into Inter-Bank Market.

18   *Id.* art. 5, Administrative Provisions on Securities Companies Entering into Inter-Bank Market.

19   Measures on the Administration of Bond Trading in the National Inter-Bank Bond Market (Quanguo Yinhang Jian Zhaiquan Shichang Zhaiquan Jiaoyi Guanli Banfa), issued by the PBOC on 30 April 2000. Article 39 provides that if there is a conflict between this regulation and the provisions issued before this regulation, this regulation shall prevail.

20   *Id.* art. 16.

21   Implementing Rules of the Shenzhen Stock Exchange on Bond and Bond Repurchase Trading (Shenzhen Zhengquan Jiaoyisuo Zhaiquan, Zhaiquan Huigou Jiaoyi Shishi Xize), issued by the Shenzhen Stock Exchange on 20 September 2006 and effective as of 9 October 2006.

22   A type of government bond repurchase agreement in which the parties agree that, at the time when the government bondholder sells the government bond to the other party, the

group of relevant regulations and market rules have been issued by the government regulators.[23] The amended 2005 Securities Law now governs the matters concerning listing and trading of government bonds in conjunction with other relevant laws and administrative regulations, which is a step forward, although there is no specific provisions in the amendments concerning government bond repurchase business.[24]

Disputes Involving Securities Repurchase Agreements

Disputes involving securities repurchase agreements started coming into the people's courts towards the end of 1995. To deal with this new type of dispute, the people's courts applied the general provisions of the 1986 GPCL and 1993 Economic Contract Law on the one hand, and the regulations promulgated by the State Council and the PBOC on the other hand. But as there was no clear law or judicial guidelines concerning many specific issues and the way in which the disputes involving securities repurchase agreements should be dealt with, the people's courts had difficulties in dealing with this new type of dispute in the early years. Uncertainties and questions arose concerning issues such as the jurisdiction of the people's courts to hear these cases, the validity of securities repurchase agreements, and the determination of civil liabilities of the parties involved in the disputes.

Faced with the situation that more and more disputes involving securities repurchase agreements were coming into the people's courts, the Supreme People's Court organized a symposium in November 1996 to discuss the relevant issues that the people's courts were faced with in adjudicating securities repurchase disputes.[25] Participants included judges from eight High People's Courts and five Intermediate People's Courts as well as government regulators from the PBOC, Ministry of Finance and the CSRC. The issues the symposium discussed included, among others, the acceptance of securities repurchase disputes, the jurisdiction of the people's courts over these disputes, the qualification to engage in securities repurchase agreements, the legality of the content of securities repurchase agreements, and the civil liability in the securities repurchase disputes.

After the conclusion of the symposium, the Supreme People's Court issued judicial guidelines that summarized what was discussed in the symposium (hereinafter the 1996 SPC Securities Repurchase Judicial Guidelines).[26] It set out detailed provisions

---

seller shall repurchase at a later time the same bond of same quantity from the buyer at an agreed price.

23   Amongst others, Administrative Regulations on Bond Cut-off-purchase Repurchase Business at National Inter-Bank Bond Market (Quanguo Yinhang Jian Zhaiquan Shichang Zhaiquan Maiduanshi Huigou Yewu Guanli Guiding), issued by the PBOC on 12 April 2004.

24   The 2005 Securities Law, adopted by the Standing Committee of the National People's Congress on 27 October 2005 and effective as of 1 January 2006.

25   The Symposium on Adjudication of Securities Repurchase Dispute Cases, held at Wuhan city, Hubei province, from 26 to 29 November 1996.

26   The Summary of the Symposium on Adjudication of Securities Repurchase Dispute Cases (Zuigao Renmin Fayuan Guanyu Zhengquan Huigou Jiufen Anjian Zuotanhui Jiyao),

concerning substantive as well as procedural matters in the adjudication of securities repurchase disputes. These provisions have drawn references from two main sources. The sources of the 1986 GPCL, the 1993 Economic Contract Law and other relevant financial legislation on one hand, and the sources of the regulatory documents issued by the State Council, the Ministry of Finance, the PBOC and the CSRC concerning securities repurchase business on the other hand. The significance of the 1996 SPC Securities Repurchase Judicial Guidelines is that they provide some detailed and practical judicial guidelines so that local people's courts may deal with this new type of dispute with clarity and certainty.

Between 1998 and 2000 there was a period of about eighteen months, during which the people's courts stopped accepting cases of securities repurchase disputes. In implementing the debt clearance measures endorsed by the 1996 Circular of the State Council, the regulators compiled a list of securities repurchase participants who owed debts to each other. This became a national chain of debt clearance. Under the circumstances, the Supreme People's Court issued a circular in December 1998,[27] instructing the local people's courts to stop accepting those disputing institutions who had been listed in the national chain; to stop hearing those cases relevant to the national chain which had already been accepted by the people's courts; to stop enforcing those relevant cases which had been heard by the people's courts; and to defrost the accounts of those relevant parties if the accounts had been frozen by the people's courts.[28] After the clearance work came to a final stage in the middle of 2000, the Supreme People's Court instructed the local people's courts in July 2000 to resume accepting, hearing and enforcing those disputes which had been listed in the national chain of debt clearance and whose debts involved had not been completely cleared off.[29] In relation to this announcement, the Supreme People's Court further clarified the issue of statute limitation in January 2001.[30]

---

issued by the Supreme People's Court on 29 November 1996.

27   The Circular of the Supreme People's Court on Stopping Hearing and Enforcing Securities Repurchase Economic Dispute Cases that Have Been Compiled into National Debt Clearance Chain among Securities Repurchase Participants (Zuigao Renmin Fayuan Guayu Zhongzhi Shenli, Zhongzhi Zhixing Yi Bianru Quanguo Zhengquan Huigou Jigou Jian Zhaiwu Qingqian Liantiao de Zhengquan Huigou Jingji Jiufen Anjian de Tongzhi), issued by the Supreme People's Court on 18 December 1998.

28   *Id.*

29   The Circular of the Supreme People's Court on Resuming Accepting, Hearing and Enforcing Securities Repurchase Economic Dispute Cases that Have Been Compiled into National Debt Clearance Chain among Securities Repurchase Participants (Zuigao Renmin Fayuan Guayu Huifu Shouli, Shenli he Zhixing Yijing Bianru Quanguo Zhengquan Huigou Jigou Jian Zhaiwu Qingqian Liantiao de Zhengquan Huigou Jingji Jiufen Anjian de Tongzhi), issued by the Supreme People's Court on 26 July 2000.

30   The Circular of the Supreme People's Court on the Issue of Statute Limitation in Connection with Remaining Credits and Debts after National Coordinated Clearance among Securities Repurchase Participants (Zuigao Renmin Fayuan Guanyu Dui Quanguo Zhengquan Huigou Jigou Jian Jing Tongyi Qingqian Hou Shangyu de Zhaiquan Zhaiwu Susong Shixiao Wenti de Tongzhi), issued by the Supreme People's Court on 20 January 2001. The statute of limitation restarts from 26 July 2000, the day on which the Supreme People's Court instructed the people's courts to resume accepting, hearing and enforcing the disputes.

Legal Nature of Securities Repurchase Agreement

Depending on what securities are involved in a securities repurchase agreement and on whether the securities are pledged or not in the agreement, different Chinese terms are used to refer to securities repurchase agreement. Securities repurchase (*zhengquan huigou*), as a generic term, includes government bond repurchase (*guozhai huigou*), financial bond repurchase (*jinrong zhaiquan huigou*) and enterprise bond repurchase (*qiye zhaiquan huigou*). Government bond repurchase can also be called *guokuquan huigou* or *tezhong guozhai huigou* if the government bond involved is a special kind of bond issued by the government.[31] Where the securities are not pledged as a collateral security but their ownerships are assigned to the other party, the repurchase is called *maiduanshi huigou*,[32] which literally means a cut-off-purchase repurchase.

Article 3 of the 2000 Measures on the Administration of Bond Trading in the National Inter-Bank Bond Market defines bond repurchase as

> a short-term financing activity in which, when the fund receiver (the obverse repurchasing party) receives the fund by pledging the bond to the fund provider (the reverse repurchasing party), and both parties agree that, on a certain date in the future, the obverse repurchasing party shall refund the fund to the reverse repurchasing party at the amount calculated on the basis of the stipulated interest for the repurchase, while the reverse repurchasing party shall refund the originally pledged bond to the reverse repurchasing party.[33]

In contrast, normal bond sale and purchase is "a transaction in which both parties to the transaction agree on the assignment of the ownership of bonds at a price agreed by the parties."[34] Similar definitions of securities repurchase agreement are also found in the early regulations and government circulars.[35]

Three essential elements are included in the above definition of securities repurchase agreement. First, the securities are pledged as a collateral security by the seller of the securities (the cash borrower) for the transaction. Second, they are short-term financing instruments. Third, the seller repurchases those securities at a later time with a payment of interest to the other party (the cash lender). These essential elements are emphasized by the regulations and government circulars. For example, it is emphasized in the 1995 Circular on Reiteration of Relevant Issues Concerning Further Standardization of Securities Repurchase Business that sellers must have one hundred percent government or financial bonds of their own for the repurchase agreements and these securities must be placed with a securities registration and

---

31   *See* introduction, Chapter 3.

32   *See supra* note 22.

33   Article 3, 2000 Measures on the Administration of Bond Trading in the National Inter-Bank Bond Market, *supra* note 19.

34   *Id.*

35   Article 3, 1997 Provisional Regulations on Bond Repurchase Business among Banks, *supra* note 15; Section 1, 1995 Circular on Reiteration of Relevant Issues Concerning Further Standardization of Securities Repurchase Business, *supra* note 9.

custodian organization designated by the regulator; the term of repurchase agreement may not exceed one year.[36]

In *Ha'erbin Finance Securities Co. v Shenzhen Securities Business Center of Yunnan Securities Co. Ltd.*,[37] the plaintiff and defendant signed six government bond repurchase agreements between December 1994 and July 1995 with a total agreement amount of 201.50 million yuan. The defendant was the party who received the funds and who agreed to repurchase the bonds at the end of the agreements, ranging from terms of three months to eleven months. The plaintiff advanced the funds to the defendant after the agreements were signed and the defendant issued "certificates for safekeeping of government bonds" to the plaintiff without having sufficient real government bonds. The defendant defaulted at the end of the agreement and the plaintiff brought the case to the Heilongjiang High People's Court. The Court annulled the agreements on the ground that the agreements had violated the regulation that sellers in a securities repurchase agreement must have a full and real amount of securities for the transaction. This finding was affirmed by the Supreme People's Court when the case was appealed by the defendant. The Supreme People's Court said that the six agreements were actually lending agreements in the name of securities repurchase agreement.[38]

Qualification to Engage in Securities Repurchase Agreement

Dealing in securities repurchase business is restricted to financial institutions who have an independent legal status and who have a financial business license issued by the PBOC, which allows the financial institution to engage in securities trading business. The 1995 Circular on Reiteration of Relevant Issues Concerning Further Standardization of Securities Repurchase Business states that non-financial organizations, individuals and those financial institutions without a legal person status may not engage directly in securities repurchase business; any securities exchange and financial centers may not accept them as members to engage in securities repurchase business.[39]

In line with this regulatory requirement, the 1996 Securities Repurchase SPC Judicial Guidelines states that a securities repurchase agreement shall be determined as a null and void agreement if the party of the agreement has not been authorized by the PBOC to engage in securities repurchase business.[40] Accordingly a first check by the people's courts when hearing a securities repurchase dispute is to determine whether a party to a securities repurchase agreement has been authorized by the PBOC and thus qualified to engage directly in securities repurchase business. If the people's courts determine that a party to a securities repurchase agreement has no

---

36   Sections 3 and 4, the 1995 Circular on Reiteration of Relevant Issues Concerning Further Standardization of Securities Repurchase Business, *supra* note 9.

37   *Supra* note 3.

38   *Id.* at p. 505.

39   Section 2, 1995 Circular on Reiteration of Relevant Issues Concerning Further Standardization of Securities Repurchase Business, *supra* note 9.

40   Section 2, 1996 SPC Securities Repurchase Judicial Guidelines, *supra* note 26.

qualification to engage directly in securities repurchase agreement, the agreement entered into by the party shall be null and void.

In *Qixiangtai Road Securities Business Center of Tianjing City International Trust Investment Co. v Huiyuan Urban Credit Cooperative Society of Ezhou City of Hubei Province*,[41] for example, the Court was satisfied that both the plaintiff and defendant had proper qualifications to carry out securities repurchase business at the Tianjing Securities Trading Center. The plaintiff had a license for financial business approved by the Tianjing city branch of the PBOC while the defendant's license was approved by the Hubei province branch of the PBOC. Both the plaintiff and defendant signed an agreement with the Tianjing Securities Trading Center in June and December 1994 respectively, by virtue of which they became government bond repurchase dealer members at the Tianjing Securities Trading Center where they opened their accounts with the Tianjing securities registration company. In general, the people's courts, in examining the validity of a securities repurchase agreement, ensure that the parties of a securities repurchase agreement have proper qualifications and have been authorized to engage in securities repurchase business.

In *Rongcheng Business Center of Shanghai Finance Securities Co. v Shanghai Fu'ermen Co.*,[42] a case in which the parties were not authorized to engage directly in securities repurchase business, the Shanghai Shongjiang County People's Court found that the defendant Shanghai Fu'ermen company was not a financial institution but nevertheless engaged in securities repurchase dealings. In November 1994, the defendant signed a government bond repurchase agreement with the plaintiff, in which the defendant agreed to sell 150,000 yuan 1994 (2) government bonds at a rate of 100:100 and repurchase them back a month later at a rate of 100:101.80. The plaintiff paid the defendant 150,000 yuan but the defendant failed to deliver the government bonds to the plaintiff. The defendant later returned only 52,700 yuan to the plaintiff. The Court said that non-financial organizations, individuals and those financial institutions without a legal person status may not engage directly in securities repurchase business according to the regulations of the PBOC, Ministry of Finance and the CSRC.[43] As the defendant was not a financial institution, it was not qualified to enter directly into the securities repurchase agreement. The Court ruled that the agreement the defendant signed with the plaintiff was null and void.

In *the Second Government Bond Service Department of the Finance Bureau of the North District of Qingdao City v Securities Company of Linzhou City of Hunan Province*,[44] one of the four government bond agreements signed between

---

41   See *Selection of Financial Dispute Cases Heard by the Supreme People's Court (1996–1998)* (*Zuigao Renmin Fayuan Shenli de Jinrong Jiufen Anli Xuanbian*), compiled by the Economic Division Court of the Supreme People's Court (Beijing: China University of Political Science and Law Press, 1999) pp. 517–521.

42   See *Carefully Selected Cases of the People's Courts (Renmin Fayuan Anli Xuan Jingbianben)*, Vol. 1, 2001, edited by China Law Application Research Institute of the Supreme People's Court (Beijing: Xinhua Publishing Press, 2001), pp.760-763.

43   Section 2, the 1995 Circular on Reiteration of Relevant Issues Concerning Further Standardization of Securities Repurchase Business, *supra* notes 9 and 39.

44   See Shao Tingjie et al. (eds), *Securities Law (Zhengquan Fa)* (Beijing: Law Publishing House, 1999), pp. 328–333.

the plaintiff and defendant was a repurchase agreement for 1992 (3) government bonds. In determining the validity of the agreement, an issue was raised about the qualification of the plaintiff to directly engage in government bond trading including repurchase trading. The plaintiff, as a government bond service department of the finance bureau of the north district of Qingdao city, was one of the finance securities organizations (*caizheng zhengquan jigou*) affiliated to the government finance departments in the early 1990s.

These finance securities organizations had no independent legal person status, nor had they been issued with financial institution licenses. They were a special kind of securities business organizations that operated in the form of government bond services departments or government bond services centers. As government bond intermediaries, they played an important service role in the issuance, repayment and transfer of government bonds. A process of reorganization and identification change started in late 1994 following a circular issued by the PBOC and the Ministry of Finance on 30 November 1994.[45] The aim was to separate these finance securities organizations from the government finance departments and to change them into independent legal entities. On 5 June 1997 the PBOC and the Ministry of Finance issued another circular,[46] which set 31 March 1998 as the deadline for the completion of the reorganization process.

The Wuhan Intermediate People's Court initially held that the plaintiff had no qualification to engage in trading securities in the securities secondary market and the agreements signed by the plaintiff were null and void. This ruling was overturned by the Hubei High People's Court who took into consideration of the background about the creation, operation and transformation of these finance securities organizations and held that the plaintiff should be recognized as having qualification to engage in trading government bonds in the secondary market.[47] This approach was later confirmed in the 1996 SPC Securities Repurchase Judicial Guidelines, which instruct the people's courts to treat these finance securities organizations as having qualification required by the regulation to engage directly in securities repurchase business.[48] The historical background and the role these government bond intermediaries played in the issuance, repayment and transfer of government bonds are recognized in the 1996 SPC Securities Repurchase Judicial Guidelines.[49]

---

45   Circular of the PBOC and the Ministry of Finance on Issuing Measures on Reorganization of Finance Securities Organizations (Zhongguo Renmin Yinhang, Caizhengbu Guanyu Xiada Caizheng Xitong Zhengquan Jigou Qingli Banfa de Tongzhi), issued on 30 November 1994.

46   Circular of the PBOC and the Ministry of Finance on Reorganization and Standardization of Finance Securities Organizations (Zhongguo Renmin Yinhang, Caizhengbu Guanyu Qingli Guifan Caizheng Xitong Zhengquan Jigou de Tongzhi), issued on 5 June 1997.

47   *Supra* note 44, at p. 330.

48   Section 2, 1996 SPC Securities Repurchase Judicial Guidelines, *supra* note 26.

49   *Id.*

Securities Repurchase Agreements Made Outside Authorized Exchanges

Securities repurchase agreements are required to be carried out in a securities exchange or a financial center that is approved by the government to provide securities repurchase business services. The 1995 Circular on Reiteration of Relevant Issues Concerning Further Standardization of Securities Repurchase Business emphasizes that any securities exchange or financial center may not open securities repurchase business without an approval from the State Council and the PBOC; any financial institution may not involve in any securities repurchase market opened by unauthorized securities exchanges or financial centers.[50] Further, this Circular prohibits any financial institution from engaging in securities repurchase business privately outside the securities exchanges authorized by the government.[51] Before the 1995 Circular on Reiteration of Relevant Issues Concerning Further Standardization of Securities Repurchase Business, the position was not clear and numbers of the agreements were carried out outside the securities exchanges or financial centers approved by the government.

In *Ha'erbin Finance Securities Co. v Shenzhen Securities Business Center of Yunnan Securities Co. Ltd.*,[52] the six government bond repurchase agreements signed by the plaintiff and defendant between December 1994 and July 1995 were carried out outside an authorized securities exchange. The defendant was a member of Wuhan City Securities Trading Center while the plaintiff was a member of Tianjin City Securities Trading Center. But the six repurchase agreements signed between them were not carried out in one of these trading centers. The Supreme People's Court said that the six agreements signed between the plaintiff and defendant had not been conducted in a securities trading center, which violated the regulation.[53]

A similar judgment is found in *The Government Bond Service Center of Anhui Province v Beijing Trust Investment Company of the Construction Bank*.[54] The plaintiff and defendant signed a securities repurchase agreement on 29 July 1994, which stipulated that the plaintiff would purchase from the defendant 5 million yuan 1992 (5) government bonds and the defendant would repurchase the bonds on 30 July 1995 with 6.2 million yuan. The agreement was signed outside the securities exchanges authorized by the government. After the agreement was signed the plaintiff advanced 5 million yuan and the defendant issued a certificate for safekeeping the bonds to the plaintiff. The defendant defaulted on the obligation to repurchase the bonds. The Court annulled the agreement on the ground that the parties conducted the deal outside the securities exchanges approved by the government, which

---

50   Section 2, 1995 Circular on Reiteration of Relevant Issues Concerning Further Standardization of Securities Repurchase Business, *supra* note 9.

51   *Id.*

52   *Supra* note 3.

53   *Id.* at p. 505.

54   *See* Wu Zhipan and Tang Jiemang (eds), *Explanation and Analysis of Typical Cases of Financial Law, 1ˢᵗ Issue (Jinrong Fa Dianxing Anli Jiexi, Diyi Ji)* (Beijing: China Finance Publishing House, 2000), pp. 195–202.

violated the 1995 Circular on Reiteration of Relevant Issues Concerning Further Standardization of Securities Repurchase Business.[55]

This judgment was criticized by commentators who argue that the Court made a farfetched decision on the point of trading by the plaintiff and defendant outside an authorized securities exchange.[56] What the Court relied upon for the decision was the 1995 Circular on Reiteration of Relevant Issues Concerning Further Standardization of Securities Repurchase Business, which was issued on 8 August 1995.[57] But the agreement was entered into on 29 July 1994 and the term was one year till 30 July 1995, during which time there was no regulation to the effect that financial institutions were prohibited from engaging in securities repurchase business privately outside the securities exchanges approved by the government. The 1995 Circular on Reiteration of Relevant Issues Concerning Further Standardization of Securities Repurchase Business requires that agreements entered into before 8 August 1995 shall make amendments if there are irregularities, but the Circular does not explicitly invalidate them. There were many agreements that had been signed outside a designated securities exchange before 8 August 1995. For these reasons and arguments, the commentator concluded that the decision the Court made to annul the agreement was a farfetched decision without solid legal and regulatory ground.[58]

In connection with the fact that securities repurchase agreements were carried out both inside and outside authorized securities exchanges, an issue was raised by the local people's courts to the Supreme People's Court on how to determine the place of performance of securities repurchase contracts. In July 1996 the Supreme People's Court issued a reply[59] that answered the local people's courts' questions. The reply made it clear that in the case where an agreement is made inside a securities exchange, the place of performance of the contract shall be the place where the securities exchange is located; in the case that an agreement is made outside a securities exchange, the place of performance of contract shall be the place where the party who is providing the cash is located.[60] By clarifying the question, the Supreme People's Court provides the local people's courts with clear guidance for the determination of the jurisdiction of the people's courts over securities repurchase agreement disputes.

The issue of jurisdiction was further discussed at the symposium[61] and summarized by the Supreme People's Court in the 1996 SPC Securities Repurchase Judicial Guidelines, which provides that the people's court that is located at the place of a securities exchange or the place of the defendant shall have jurisdiction over disputes arising from securities repurchase agreements made inside the securities exchange; the people's court that is located at the place of the reverse repurchasing

---

55   *Id.* at p. 196.

56   *Id.* at p. 199.

57   *Supra* note 9.

58   *Supra* note 54, at p. 199.

59   Reply of the Supreme People's Court on the Issue of how to Determine the Place of Performance of Securities Repurchase Contracts (Zuigao Renmin Fayuan Guanyu Ruhe Queding Zhengquan Huigou Hetong Lüxingdi Wenti de Pifu), replied on 4 July 1996.

60   *Id.*

61   *Supra* note 25.

party or the place of the defendant shall have jurisdiction over disputes arising from securities repurchase agreements made outside the securities exchange.[62] This position is actually an application of Article 24 of the 1991 Civil Procedure Law, which provides that the people's court of the place where the defendant has his domicile or where a contract is performed shall have jurisdiction over a contract dispute.[63]

There are two views among judges about the validity of securities repurchase contracts signed before 8 August 1995 where the parties concluded outside a securities exchange. One view argues that these contracts should not be determined by the people's courts as invalid because there was no law and regulation before 8 August 1995 which expressly prohibited outside trading of securities repurchase agreements.[64] The other view argues that these contracts undermined the financial market order and harmed the interests of the state and public and therefore should be treated as invalid contracts and annulled in accordance with Article 16 of the 1993 Economic Contract Law[65] even though there was no law and regulation to prohibit such contracts before 8 August 1995.[66] The argument for the first view, which is more sensible, is that the law and policy should not be applied retrospectively; furthermore, the 1995 Circular on Reiteration of Relevant Issues Concerning Further Standardization of Securities Repurchase Business does not stipulate expressly that the agreements signed outside a securities exchange before 8 August 1995 should be null and void; therefore these agreements should not be treated as invalid agreements if no other irregularities are involved except outside trading.[67]

If an agreement is annulled by the people's court on the ground of trading outside authorized securities exchanges, the repurchase interest would be recalculated according to relevant inter-bank borrowing interest rates, which means that the plaintiff would get less than the repurchase interest they originally agreed with the defendant seller. Some critics regard this as a penalty to the plaintiff for trading outside authorized securities exchanges, but on the other hand, these critics submit that this approach treats the plaintiff and defendant unfairly and is against the principle of

---

62   Section 1, 1996 SPC Securities Repurchase Judicial Guidelines, *supra* note 26.

63   Article 24, 1991 Civil Procedure Law, adopted by the 7th National People's Congress on 9 April 1991, effective the same day. The 1991 Civil Procedure Law replaced the 1982 Civil Procedure Law (for Trial Implementation).

64   *See* Chu Hongjun and Wang Zhuan, "Adjudication of Cases of Securities Repurchase Contract Disputes" (Zhengquan Huigou Hetong Jiufeng Anjian de Shenli), *People's Judicature* (*Renmin Sifa*), Issue 11, 1996, pp. 9–11, at p. 10. (The authors are from Jiangsu High People's Court.)

65   Article 16 of the 1993 Economic Contract Law provides that where an economic contract is determined to be invalid, the property the parties obtained according to the contract shall return to the other party. The party who has fault shall compensate the consequential loss suffered by the other party; where both parties have fault, each shall bear corresponding responsibilities.

66   *Supra* note 64, at p. 11.

67   *Id.*

fairness in the 1986 GPCL and the principle of investor protection.[68] They argue that the cause of the disputes arising from the agreements conducted outside securities exchanges, in most of cases, is because of the defendant seller who concealed the truth when dealing with the plaintiff and later was unable to fulfill their obligation of repurchase or repayment; therefore they should bear greater responsibilities, but the recalculation of repurchase interest according to inter-bank annual borrowing interest rates is lenient and does not penalize them properly.[69]

Requirement of a Real and Full Amount of Collateral Securities

Article 52 of the 1994 Provisional Measures for the Administration of Credit Funds[70] requires a real and full amount of collateral securities when parties enter into a securities repurchase agreement. In practice this essential regulatory requirement was ignored and violated by many financial institutions in early years of securities repurchase market.[71] Sellers in securities repurchase agreements often had no or insufficient collateral securities to back up the agreement. Selling short government bonds became a serious problem, which prompted the government to issue the 1994 Circular on Firmly Curb Acts of Selling Short Government Bonds.[72] In this Circular, it was stressed that any dealing in government bond repurchases must be guaranteed by a full amount of actual bonds and the bonds must be kept in the central custodian center of a securities exchange.[73]

Despite of the government regulation, financial institutions conducted dealings of securities repurchase agreements without a real and full amount of collateral securities. In *Xi'an Business Center of Huaxia Securities Co. Ltd. v Haikou Huinan Branch of Hainan Fazhan Development Bank*,[74] the plaintiff and defendant were both members of Xi'an Securities Trading Center and were authorized to engage in securities repurchase business. In May 1995, the plaintiff and defendant entered into a 3 million yuan repurchase agreement at Xi'an Securities Trading Center. The plaintiff paid the defendant 3 million yuan according to the agreement. The defendant agreed to repurchase the securities with 3.36 million yuan six months later. The Shaanxi High People's Court found that no security was delivered to the plaintiff nor was any security deposited at the trading center. At the end of the agreement, the defendant failed to repay 3.36 million yuan as agreed in the agreement. The Court said the repurchase agreement signed by the plaintiff and defendant was an act of

---

68   *See* Liu Ping and Yi Shuren, "Securities Repurchase: An Important Trading Tool" (Zhengquan Huigou: Juzu Qingzhong de Jiaoyi Shouduan), *China Lawyer* (*Zhongguo Lűshi*), Issue 4, 1996, pp. 27–29, at p. 28. (The authors are from the Wuhan Tianyuan law firm.)

69   *Id.*

70   *Supra* note 6.

71   *Supra* note 7.

72   *Supra* note 8.

73   *Id.* art. 2.

74   *See Selection of Financial Dispute Cases Heard by the Supreme People's Court (1996–1998)* (*Zuigao Renmin Fayuan Shenli de Jinrong Jiufen Anli Xuanbian*), compiled by the Economic Division Court of the Supreme People's Court (Beijing: China University of Political Science and Law Press, 1999), pp. 513–516.

buying long and selling short government bonds, which violated the provisions of the 1994 Circular on Firmly Curb Acts of Selling Short Government Bonds. On this ground, the Court annulled the repurchase agreement. [75]

In *Qixiangtai Road Securities Business Center of Tianjin City International Investment Trust Co. v Shanghai Shenyin Securities Co.*,[76] the plaintiff and defendant were both authorized dealers at the Tianjin Securities Trading Center. In August 1995, the plaintiff and defendant made two government bonds repurchase deals. One was a 2 million yuan deal at a price of 100:100 and 106.96:100 with a term of three months, and the other was a 4 million yuan deal at a price of 100:100 and 105.15:100 with a term of four months. The defendant was a government bonds provider who agreed to purchase the bonds back at the end of the agreement. After the agreement was signed, the plaintiff advanced the defendant a total of 6 million yuan. At the end of the agreement the defendant failed to repay the plaintiff.

The Tianjin High People's Court found that the defendant did not deposit the full amount of the government bonds for the two deals at the Tianjin Securities Trading Center. The Court said that, as the defendant did not deposit the full amount of securities at the Tianjin Securities Trading Center for the deals, nor did the defendant transfer actual government bonds to the plaintiff, the defendant violated Article 52 of the 1994 Provisional Measures for the Administration of Credit Funds. In accordance with Article 7 of the 1993 Economic Contract Law,[77] the Court annulled the agreements.[78]

In order to stop a widespread violation of the regulation, the government reiterated the regulatory requirement of a real and full amount of collateral securities in securities repurchase agreements. The 1995 Circular on Reiteration of Relevant Issues Concerning Further Standardization of Securities Repurchase Business makes it clear that the seller in a securities repurchase agreement must possess 100% of the government bonds or financial bonds which belong to the seller; the government bonds or financial bonds shall be kept in custody by a securities registration and custodian organization designated by the branches of the PBOC in relevant provinces and cities; custodian receipts can only be issued by this designated organization; during the terms of repurchase agreements, no party may use the securities; issuance of false custodian receipts shall be subject to criminal punishment.[79]

In what way should the people's courts treat securities repurchase agreements signed before the promulgation of the 1994 Provisional Measures for the Administration of Credit Funds? This became an uncertain issue in the people's courts. Some judges argue that, for those agreements which were concluded before the promulgation of the 1994 Provisional Measures for the Administration of Credit

---

75   *Id.* at p. 514.

76   *See* Gazette of the Supreme People's Court of the People's Republic of China, Issue 2, 1997, at pp. 67–68.

77   Article 7 of the 1993 Economic Contract Law provides that an economic contract that violates law and administrative regulation is null and void.

78   *Supra* note 76, at p. 68.

79   Section 4, 1995 Circular on Reiteration of Relevant Issues Concerning Further Standardization of Securities Repurchase Business, *supra* note 9.

Funds and were short of 100% collateral securities, but where the parties signed the agreements in accordance with the rules of some securities exchanges at that time, the people's courts should not treat them as invalid agreements on the ground that the agreements were short of 100% collateral securities.[80]

This view was accepted by the Supreme People's Court in the 1996 SPC Securities Repurchase Judicial Guidelines.[81] Thus, a distinction is made between those securities repurchase contracts entered into before the promulgation of the 1994 Provisional Measures for the Administration of Credit Funds[82] and those securities repurchase agreements entered into after the promulgation of this regulation. For those securities repurchase agreements which, prior to the 1994 Provisional Measures for the Administration of Credit Funds, the parties entered into in accordance with trading rules of securities exchanges, the people's court should not treat them as invalid contracts if the securities involved in the agreements fall short of 100% requirement; for those securities repurchase contracts which the parties entered into after the 1994 Provisional Measures for the Administration of Credit Funds, the people's court should treat them as invalid contracts if the securities involved in the agreements fall short of the one hundred percent requirement.[83]

A same line regarding the pledge of collateral securities in a bond repurchase agreement has been adopted by the 2000 Measures for the Administration of Bond Trading in the National Inter-Bank Bond Market.[84] Article 17 provides that where a party makes a repurchase deal and pledges relevant bonds, the bonds shall be registered and the repurchase contract shall become effective after the registration.[85] During the term of repurchase agreement, neither party may use the pledged bonds;[86] both parties to the repurchase transaction shall, pursuant to the contract, shall send in a timely manner instruction on delivery of bonds and funds, have a full amount of bonds and funds to be used for delivery on the contractual delivery date, and shall not buy long and sell short.[87]

Default by Defendant Seller

Default by defendant sellers in one respect or another is a primary source of disputes involving securities repurchase agreements. In *Business Center of Yunnan Provincial Branch of China Agriculture Bank v Shenzhen International Trust Investment Co.*,[88]

---

80   *See* Du Erli and You Jun, "On Several Issues to Which Attention Should Paid in Hearing Securities Repurchase Dispute Cases" ("Tan Shenli Zhengquan Huigou Jiufen Anjian Ying Zhuyi de Jige Wenti"), *Journal of Liaoning Administrators College of Police and Justice*, Issue 3, 1999, pp. 24–27, at p. 26.

81   *Supra* note 26.

82   *Supra* note 5.

83   Section 3 (1), 1996 SPC Securities Repurchase Judicial Guidelines, *supra* note 26.

84   *Supra* note 19.

85   *Id.* art. 17.

86   *Id.* art. 21.

87   *Id.* art. 31.

88   *See* Gazette of the Supreme People's Court of the People's Republic of China, Issue 5, 2004, pp. 8–13.

for example, the plaintiff and defendant signed three securities repurchase contracts in June 1995 involving a total sum of 13 million yuan. The plaintiff advanced 13 million yuan to the defendant after the agreements were signed, but the defendant did not issue securities safekeeping certificates to the plaintiff, nor did the defendant fulfill its repurchase obligation at the end of the agreements. The defendant later returned only 3.8 million yuan to the plaintiff who sued the defendant in the Yunnan High People's Court.[89] In *Ha'erbin Finance Securities Co. v Shenzhen Securities Business Center of Yunnan Securities Co. Ltd.*, the Supreme People's Court said the fundamental reason for this dispute is that the defendant failed to repay the plaintiff for a long time. [90]

On a more general level, the default by the defendants and subsequent disputes pose a threat to an orderly operation of the money market and financial stability. Less than three months following the promulgation on 8 August 1995 of the Circular on Reiteration of Relevant Issues Concerning Further Standardization of Securities Repurchase Business,[91] the PBOC, the Ministry of Finance and the CSRC jointly issued the 1995 Circular on Seriously Clear Off Securities Repurchase Debts Becoming Due,[92] which set out measures for dealing with debt problems in securities repurchase business. 8 August 1995 was set out as a cut-off date by the 1995 Circular on Seriously Clear Off Securities Repurchase Debts Becoming Due. For those securities repurchase agreements which were signed before 8 August 1995 and which the seller could not make up for the securities in full before 31 October 1995, the Circular allows the parties to clear off the debts according to the term they originally agreed; for any new securities repurchase agreements after 8 August 1995, the Circular emphasizes that the parties must abide by the one hundred percent actual securities rule and deposit the securities in custody during the term of agreements.[93]

Qixiangtai Road Securities Business Center of Tianjing City International Investment Trust Co. v Huiyuan Urban Credit Cooperative Society of Ezhou City of Hubei Province,[94] a case involving a securities repurchase agreement signed before 8 August 1995 in which the defendant defaulted repayments, illustrates how the people's courts interpret and apply the regulatory provision that the parties who entered into a securities repurchase agreement before 8 August 1995 are allowed to clear off their debts according to the term they originally agreed. On 1 June 1995, the defendant and plaintiff signed an agreement at the Tianjin Securities Trading Center, which stipulated that the plaintiff purchase 5.3 million yuan government bonds at a rate of 100:100 and the defendant repurchase the bonds at a rate 111.40:100 six months later on 2 December 1995 with a total sum of 5.9042 million yuan. The plaintiff advanced 5.3 million yuan according to the agreement. The defendant neither delivered the government bonds, nor deposited a full amount of the bonds at the Tianjin Securities Trading Center. At the end of the agreement, the defendant

89   *Id*. pp. 8–9.
90   *Supra* note 3, at p. 505.
91   *Supra* note 9.
92   *Supra* note 10.
93   *Id*. art. 1.
94   *Supra* note 41.

failed to repay the plaintiff. The plaintiff sued the defendant at the Tianjin High People's Court, claiming a repayment of 5.9042 million yuan plus 580,544 yuan interest charge for delayed repayments and 65,000 yuan compensation for economic loss.

The Tianjin High People's Court found that the defendant as the seller did not deposit the full amount of bonds for the agreement, which violated the provisions of the 1994 Provisional Measures for the Administration of Credit Funds. In accordance with Articles 84 and 108 of the 1986 GPCL[95] and by reference to the provision of the 1995 Circular on Seriously Clear Off Securities Repurchase Debts Becoming Due that the parities are allowed to clear off the debts according to the term they originally agreed, the Court ruled that the defendant repay the plaintiff 5.9042 million yuan according to the agreement, and pay a penalty interest charge for the delayed repayment of 5.9042 million yuan, which was calculated at 0.005% daily from 2 December 1995 to the effective day of the judgment. The Court rejected the plaintiff's other claims.[96]

The defendant appealed the decision of the Tianjin High People's Court to the Supreme People's Court, arguing that the decision of the Court to order the defendant to pay 5.9042 million yuan was wrong. The reason was, the defendant argued, first, the 600,420 yuan repurchase interest included in the 5.9042 million yuan was too high, which was awarded not in accordance with the provisions of the 1995 Circular on Seriously Clear Off Securities Repurchase Debts Becoming Due; second, the repurchase interest should instead be calculated at inter-bank borrowing interest rates; and, third, any exceeding interest beyond the inter-bank borrowing interest rates should not be protected.

The Supreme People's Court accepted the argument by the defendant that the repurchase interest should be calculated at inter-bank borrowing interest rates. Thus, the Supreme People's Court upheld the principal part of the judgment of the Tianjin High People's Court and corrected the ruling on the repurchase interest. The Supreme People's Court said that the agreement signed by the defendant and plaintiff was invalid agreement since the seller did not deposit a full amount of securities according to the regulation of the PBOC. The defendant should repay the plaintiff repurchase interest according to the inter-bank borrowing interest rates. In accordance with Article 153 (1) (i) and (ii) of the Civil Procedure Law,[97] the Supreme

---

95   Article 84 states that "A debt represents a special relationship of rights and obligations established between the parties concerned, either according to the agreed terms of a contract or legal provisions. The party entitled to the rights shall be the creditor, and the party assuming the obligations shall be the debtor. The creditor shall have the right to demand that the debtor fulfill his obligations as specified by the contract or according to legal provisions." Article 108 states that "Debts shall be cleared. If a debtor is unable to repay his debt immediately, he may repay by installments with the consent of the creditor or a ruling by a people's court. If a debtor is capable of repaying his debt but refuses to do so, repayment shall be compelled by the decision of a people's court."

96   *Supra* note 41, at p. 519.

97   Article 153 (1) (i) and (ii) sates that: "After trying a case on appeal, the people's court of second instance shall, in the light of the following situations, dispose of it accordingly: (i) if the facts were clearly ascertained and the law was correctly applied in the original judgment,

People's Court ruled that the defendant would return the principal 5.3 million yuan and pay a penalty interest charge for the 5.3 million yuan for breach of contract, to be calculated at a daily rate of 0.005% from 2 December 1995 to the day of the repayment of 5.3 million yuan; the 600,420 yuan repurchase interest were to be recalculated at the relevant upper limit of annual inter-bank borrowing rate set by the PBOC, which was 13.59%.

In effect, the intent of the regulatory provision that the parties who entered into a securities repurchase agreement before 8 August 1995 are allowed to clear off their debts according to the term they originally agreed is inferred by the Supreme People's Court to mean that the parties are allowed to clear off the debts according to the maturity date they originally agreed but not according to the original agreement the parties agreed with regard to the repurchase interest.[98] Looking at the wording of the regulatory provision in the context of the 1995 Circular on Seriously Clear Off Securities Repurchase Debts Becoming Due,[99] it seems that the reference by the Supreme People's Court is a literal application of the provision while the reference by the Tianjin High People's Court is an application of the provision in a more wider sense.

Qixiangtai Road Securities Business Center of Tianjing City International Trust Investment Co. v Xingfu Urban Credit Cooperative Society of Qianjiang City of Hubei Province [100] is another case which was decided by the Supreme People's Court in a same way. The plaintiff and defendant signed two government bond agreements involving a total sum of 10 million yuan in March 1995. The plaintiff advanced 10 million yuan to the defendant according to the agreement but the defendant defaulted on the obligation of repurchase. The Tianjin High People's Court found that no government bond had been deposited for the two deals at the Tianjin Securities Trading Center. By reference to the 1995 Circular on Seriously Clear Off Securities Repurchase Debts Becoming Due, the Court ruled that the defendant would repay 11.827 million yuan to the plaintiff, which included the repurchase interest as agreed by the parties. This ruling was overturned by the Supreme People's Court who held that the repurchase interest for the 10 million yuan bonds would be calculated at the relevant upper limit of annual inter-bank borrowing rate, which was 13.176%.[101]

By calculating the repurchase interest at inter-bank borrowing rate, what the defendant would repay is less than the amount the parties originally agreed. Thus, the burden of defendants is reduced, which could facilitate and speed up the process of debt clearance. But on the other hand, the plaintiffs are unable to get what they

---

the appeal shall be rejected in the form of a judgment and the original judgment shall be affirmed; (ii) if the application of the law was incorrect in the original judgment, the said judgment shall be amended according to the law."

98   *Supra* note 41, at p. 521.

99   The wording is 'qixian daoqi qingchang', which literally means 'clear at the end of term', *supra* note 10, art. 1.

100   *See Selection of Financial Dispute Cases Heard by the Supreme People's Court (1996–1998)* (*Zuigao Renmin Fayuan Shenli de Jinrong Jiufen Anli Xuanbian*), compiled by the Economic Division Court of the Supreme People's Court (Beijing: China University of Political Science and Law Press, 1999), pp. 522–526.

101   *Id.* at p. 525.

originally bargained for in the agreements. In both of the above cases, the plaintiffs were found to have entered into the agreements with knowledge that the defendants had not deposited relevant government bonds at the Tianjin Securities Trading Center, for which, the Supreme People's Court said, they should bear consequential responsibilities.[102] Under the circumstances, it seems not unfair for the plaintiffs in the above two cases to get less repurchase interest than they initially agreed with the defendants. But in cases where the plaintiff is an innocent party who has no fault and no knowledge of violation of regulation by the defendant, and who has performed the contract faithfully, the application by the people's courts of the 1995 Circular on Seriously Clear Off Securities Repurchase Debts Becoming Due would lead to unfairness to the plaintiff.

In this context, some judges hold a different view on the position of the 1995 Circular on Seriously Clear Off Securities Repurchase Debts Becoming Due.[103] The submit that, by allowing the parties to clear off the debts according to the term they originally agreed if the seller could not make up for the securities in full before 31 October 1995, the 1995 Circular implicitly recognizes the legality of the activities of selling short government bonds under this special circumstances; it follows that for the securities repurchase agreements signed before 8 August 1995 and the seller could not make up for the securities in full before 31 October 1995, the people's court can choose not to annul these agreements.[104]

Validity of Securities Repurchase Contract

Before the announcement of the 1995 Circular on Reiteration of Relevant Issues Concerning Further Standardization of Securities Repurchase Business,[105] there were no national regulation or central government circulars that had comprehensively addressed problems or issues concerning the securities repurchase market. The 1994 Provisional Measures for the Administration of Credit Funds provides very limited provisions concerning the securities repurchase market, excepting Article 52, which directly addresses the securities repurchase market.[106] The 1994 Circular on Firmly Curb Acts of Selling Short Government Bonds[107] was issued with an aim to stop widespread short selling of government bonds and it did not cover other aspects of the securities repurchase market. The position of a number of important issues, such as trading outside securities exchanges, was therefore not clear. Many securities repurchase agreements were concluded outside securities exchanges and by parties who were not financial institutions. A lack of clear regulatory rules and effective regulation also led to a situation where funds were used in speculation in the stock market and investment in real property market and other unauthorized investments, which caused an inflation of fixed asset investments.

---

102   *Id*. at pp. 519 and 524.
103   *See* Chu Hongjun and Wang Zhuan, *supra* note 64, at p. 10.
104   *Id.*
105   *Supra* note 9.
106   *Supra* notes 5 and 6.
107   *Supra* note 8.

The announcement jointly by the PBOC, the Ministry of Finance and the CSRC on 8 August 1995 of the Circular on Reiteration of Relevant Issues Concerning Further Standardization of Securities Repurchase Business marked an important stage in the regulation of securities repurchase market. Compared with previous government regulations and circulars, the 1995 Circular provides a relatively comprehensive set of provisions concerning important aspects of securities repurchase market. The securities repurchase agreements that were concluded after 8 August 1995 would be subject to the 1995 Circular.

But questions remain about the position of the agreements concluded before the 1995 Circular. In general, judges, scholars and practitioners express their views on the basis of the fact that the securities repurchase agreement is a contractual relationship. They submit that securities repurchase business should apply principles of the 1986 GPCL and contract law;[108] division and undertaking of responsibilities between the parties in a dispute should be based on the examination of validity of a securities repurchase contract.[109]

In judicial practice, a combination of the application of the principles of the 1986 GPCL and contract law and the reference to those limited government regulation and circulars helped the people's courts to deal with the disputes, but in some cases and on some issues the people's courts had difficulties in determining the validity of securities repurchase contracts and to balance the interests of plaintiffs and defendants. The judgment in *The Government Bond Service Center of Anhui Province v Beijing Trust Investment Company of the Construction Bank* is regarded by critics as a farfetched judgment;[110] different views are expressed by judges about the validity of securities repurchase agreements signed before 8 August 1995 outside a securities exchange;[111] the way in which the repurchase interest in the invalid contracts concluded outside a securities exchange were calculated is criticized as being unfair to the plaintiff and thus against the principle of fairness in the 1986 GPCL and the principle of investor protection.[112]

After the 1995 Circular on Reiteration of Relevant Issues Concerning Further Standardization of Securities Repurchase Business, the 1995 Circular on Seriously Clear Off Securities Repurchase Debts Becoming Due was announced.[113] This was

---

108   *See* Li Shiping et al., *A Study on Cases Involving Cutting-edge Issues of Securities Law* (*Zhengquanfa Qianyan Wenti Anli Yanjiu*) (Beijing: China Economic Publishing House, 2001), p. 234.

109   *See* Du Erli and You Jun, *supra* note 80, at p. 27 (stating that where it is determined that a contract is valid, the defendant should pay repurchase interests according to the contract and bear responsibility for breach of contract; where a contract is invalid, a distinction should be further made to see whether the contract is wholly invalid or partially invalid; if it is wholly invalid, the defendant should return the capital, pay repurchase interests according to relevant inter-bank borrowing interest rates and pay a penalty interest charge for late repayment; if it is partial invalid, the invalid provisions should be corrected and the rights and obligations of both parties be determined according to the facts).

110   *Supra* note 54.

111   *Supra* notes 64, 66 and 67.

112   *Supra* note 68.

113   *Supra* note 10.

followed by the 1996 Circular of the State Council,[114] which came out against a background that debts in securities repurchase business had become a serious problem and a threat to financial stability as well as social stability. The fact that these three circulars were issued one after another by the PBOC, the Ministry of Finance, the CSRC, and finally the State Council showed that this debt problem was taken seriously by the government as an urgent matter. The announcement of the 1996 Circular of the State Council and the endorsement by the State Council of a set of further measures proposed by the PBOC was a further and urgent step taken by the government to speed up the process of resolving the debt problem in securities repurchase business.

From the government's point of view, the seriousness of the debt problem in securities repurchase business was twofold. First, it undermined an effective and correct implementation of the government's financial as well as economic policies. Financial institutions used securities repurchase agreements as a means to engage in unauthorized lending activities and speculative activities of buying long and selling short government securities, which posed a threat to financial stability. Second, it may affect social stability. Some financial institutions issued government bond receipts to the public individuals to raise funds for the trading of securities repurchase agreements.[115] The funds were then tied into a debt chain and the financial institutions were unable to repay those individual investors when the repayment became due. This raised a possibility of massive defaults to individual investors, which may develop into a real threat to social stability.

Underlying the measures stipulated in the 1996 Circular of the State Council, a distinction is made between individual investors and institutional investors in relation to interest repayment.[116] The interest that is agreed between financial institutions in their securities repurchase agreements shall be paid by reference to inter-bank borrowing rates; any interest in excess of the inter-bank borrowing rates shall not be protected by law.[117] As far as individual investors are concerned, the financial institutions that have raised funds from the public individuals by selling government bond receipts must guarantee to repay the individuals in accordance with the interest rates and terms the financial institutions originally promised.[118]

These measures effectively invalidate securities repurchase agreements institutional parties themselves have negotiated and signed concerning repurchase interest. The reason that the 1996 Circular of the State Council provides for such treatment of the agreements made between institutional parties is because those securities repurchase agreements had actually evolved into a means by which financial institutions carried out lending activities.[119] The purpose of these measures

---

114   *Supra* note 11.

115   *See* Ouyang Mingcheng and Zhang Min, *supra* note 7, at p. 64 (stating that some financial institutions who had no government bonds issued government bond safekeeping receipts to the public individuals to raise funds).

116   Section 4, 1996 Circular of the State Council, *supra* note 11.

117   *Id.*

118   *Id.*

119   *Id.*

is to protect creditors' rights and reduce debtors' burdens to repay interest.[120] But the 1996 Circular of the State Council fails to distinguish between those agreements that financial institutions made lawfully in accordance with government regulation and those agreements that financial institutions made in violation of the government regulation. On the one hand, intervention by the government in securities repurchase agreements made between institutional parties is necessary, to a certain extent, to stabilize financial market and resolve debt chain problem quickly and effectively. But on the other hand, it is arguable that this intervention penalizes not only those who violate government regulation but also those who abide by government regulation.

Apart from the aim of stabilizing the money market and financial stability, more importantly from the government point of view is the fact that the debt problem may pose a real threat to the social stability. The phrase "maintain social stability" appears several times in the 1996 Circular of the State Council.[121] Where it has happened that public individuals jostle for repayment of interest as a result of lack of an active organizational work and social stability is consequently affected, those who are in charge and those who have direct responsibility shall be held accountable.[122]One can see that one of the underlying reasons for the provision that individual investors are guaranteed to receive the interest originally promised by financial institutions is to prevent possible social unrest as a result of massive defaults by financial institutions.

After the promulgation of the 1996 Circular of the State Council, the Supreme People's Court in the 1996 SPC Securities Repurchase Judicial Guidelines clarifies the situation of repurchase price in securities repurchase agreements in light of the 1996 Circular of the State Council. A distinction is made between valid and invalid securities repurchase agreements. Where the people's courts have determined that a securities repurchase agreement is valid, the repurchase price agreed by the parties in the agreement shall be protected and, additionally, the defaulting seller shall pay damages by reference to relevant banking regulations on interest charges for late repayments; where the people's courts have determined that a securities repurchase agreement is invalid, the defaulting seller shall return the capital advanced by the plaintiffs, pay repurchase interest according to relevant annual inter-bank borrowing interest rates, and pay a penalty interest charge for the default.[123] Compared with the 1996 Circular of the State Council, where no distinction is made between valid and invalid securities repurchase agreements, the 1996 SPC Securities Repurchase Judicial Guidelines offers a sensible position in this respect as it protects lawful interest of the parties who abide by the law and regulations, and it also maintains integrity of contract.

---

120   *Id.*

121   In Section 1, Section 2, and the reply of the State Council at the beginning of the document, 1996 Circular of the State Council, *supra* note 11.

122   *Id.* Section 2.

123   Section 4 (1) and (2), 1996 SPC Securities Repurchase Judicial Guidelines, *supra* note 26.

In the case *Qixiangtai Road Securities Business Center of Tianjin City International Investment Trust Co. v Shanghai Shenyin Securities Co.*,[124] for example, the Tianjin High People's Court determined that the two government bond repurchase agreements signed by the plaintiff and defendant were invalid on the grounds that the agreements had not had a full amount of relevant government bonds and thus violated Article 52 of the 1994 Provisional Measures for the Administration of Credit Funds. The Court annulled the agreements in accordance with Article 7 (1) (ii) of the 1993 Economic Contract Law. By reference to the 1996 Circular of the State Council and by applying Article 108 of the 1986 GPCL,[125] the Court then ruled that the defendant (i) return the money the plaintiff had paid, (ii) pay the plaintiff interest based on an inter-bank annual borrowing interest rate of 13.86%, and (iii) pay the plaintiff a penalty interest charge for late repayment, calculated at a daily rate of 0.005%.[126] The judgment is reviewed as being made in line with the 1996 SPC Securities Repurchase Judicial Guidelines.[127]

Summary

Since its emergence in 1991, the securities repurchase market in China has undergone a tortuous process. A fast-growing rate was witnessed in the first few years of the market, accompanied by widespread irregularities and violation of regulations. This was followed by a crackdown by the government, and a series of regulatory documents was issued to address these problems. Disputes involving securities repurchase agreements arose one after another and the people's courts were faced with these new types of cases. This chapter looks at some key aspects of securities repurchase agreement disputes and examines the way in which the disputes are dealt with by the people's courts.

First, securities repurchase agreement in China has the following features. First, the party of an agreement must be a financial institution with legal person status; any non-financial institutions, individuals and financial institutions without legal person status may not engage in securities repurchase business. Second, since August 1995 after the announcement of the 1995 Circular on Reiteration of Further Standardization of Securities Repurchase Business, securities repurchase agreements are required to be carried out in a securities exchange or a financial center which is approved by the government to provide securities repurchase business services; dealing in securities repurchase agreements privately outside an authorized securities exchange is prohibited. Third, the securities available for securities repurchase agreements are

---

124 *Supra* note 76.

125 Article 108 of the 1986 GPCL, *supra* note 95.

126 *Supra* note 76, at p. 68.

127 *See* Liang Tingting et al., *Securities Law Cases and Commentary* (*Zhengquanfa Anli Yu Pingxi*), p. 251. (Guangzhou: Sun Yet-Sen University Press, 2005) (stating that the judgment is in line with the guideline Section 4 (2) of the 1996 SPC Securities Repurchase Judicial Guidelines that sellers should compensate for interest loss suffered during relevant period according to inter-bank borrowing interest rates, and pay a penalty interest charge for delayed repayment).

government bonds, the financial bonds approved by the PBOC and the securities approved for repurchases by the stock exchanges. Fourth, the content of securities repurchase agreements and the rights and obligations of the parties are restricted by the government regulation. A full amount of collateral securities is required; the securities pledged may not be used during the term of agreements; the term of agreements may not exceed over one year, and so on. Fifth, since 2004, a new type of securities repurchase agreement, *maiduanshi huigou* agreement, has been introduced in the market.[128]

Second, a main cause of securities repurchase disputes is the default by sellers on their contractual obligation to repurchase securities and repay the plaintiffs at the end of securities repurchase agreements. This is shown in most of the cases discussed in this chapter. This cause of disputes is not isolated on its own but is closely associated with what had happened in the early years of China's securities repurchase market. As shown in the above discussion, there were widespread irregularities and violation of regulations among securities repurchase participants. Short selling of government bonds and false issuance of securities safekeeping receipts were common in many securities repurchase agreements; parties engaged in securities repurchase business without having qualification to do so; funds of securities repurchase agreements were misused in speculative activities, which consequently made it impossible for sellers to fulfill their repurchase and repayment obligation on time as agreed. From lawyers' perspectives, almost all the securities repurchase disputes they surveyed were caused by the default of sellers associated with one or more of the above reasons.[129] A lack of proper regulation in the early years of the securities repurchase market has contributed to the occurrence of these problems.

Third, examination of the validity of securities repurchase contracts is a first and important stage by the people's courts in the resolution of securities repurchase agreement disputes. The people's courts examine whether securities repurchase contracts are lawfully concluded, whether the parties have necessary qualifications and authorization for engaging in securities repurchase business, whether a real and full amount of collateral securities are pledged, and whether the term of the contract is within the limit set out by the regulation. On the basis of the examination, the people's courts determine the validity of securities repurchase contracts, which form an important basis for deciding the responsibility of the parities and protecting their lawful rights. In some cases and on some issues the people's courts have had difficulties in determining the validity of securities repurchase contracts and in balancing the interest of plaintiffs and defendants. Some judgments are criticized;[130] different views are expressed by judges.[131] The 1996 SPC Securities Repurchase Judicial Guidelines helped clarify uncertain issues and minimized uncertainty in the process of resolution of securities repurchase disputes.

Fourth, in resolving securities repurchase disputes, the people's courts apply relevant principles of the 1986 GPCL and the contract law, the judicial guidelines

---

128   *See supra* notes 22, 23 and 32.
129   *See* Liu Ping and Yi Shuren, *supra* note 68, at p. 28.
130   *Supra* notes 54, 56.
131   *Supra* note 64.

of the Supreme People's Court, and more directly, refer to the administrative regulations and financial policies of the government. The role of the people's courts in this respect is to implement the administrative regulation and financial policies of the government on the one hand, and to decide cases fairly in accordance with the principles of the 1986 GPCL and the contract law on the other hand. A paramount concern of the government is the impact of securities repurchase disputes on financial market stability and social stability. This concern is reflected in the thinking of the people's courts and judges and their handling of securities repurchase disputes.[132] Given the fact that the provisions of the 1986 GPCL and the contract law are general in nature, and the fact that there was no judicial guideline until late 1996, some cases were not fairly decided.[133]

Fifth, the autonomy of the parties in exercising their contractual rights in a securities repurchase contract is rather limited in terms of qualification of the parties, the content, formality and performance of the contract. There are good reasons for securities repurchase contracts to be subject to tight control and regulation by the government. Without proper control and regulation, securities repurchase contracts could be abused, and in turn could become a source of many securities repurchase contract disputes. As shown in the above discussion, financial institutions and other securities repurchase participants used securities repurchase contracts as a means to engage in unauthorized lending activities and speculative activities of buying long and selling short government bonds. Such activities created a serious debt problem and many disputes subsequently arose. From the government's point of view, these problems and disputes posed a threat to the financial stability and social stability. Aiming to eliminate this threat, heavy regulatory measures were adopted by the government. To build a healthy and sustainable securities repurchase market a right balance needs to be struck between the autonomy of the parities in exercising their contractual rights in the securities repurchase contract and proper control and regulation of the securities repurchase market.

---

132 *See* Du Erli and You Jun, *supra* note 80, at p. 27 (stating that in dealing with securities repurchase disputes judges should associate their views with political and economic context and should bear in mind the task of maintaining financial as well as social stability). The authors are from the Intermediate People's Court of Anshan city, Liaoning province.

133 For example, the judgment in the case *Government Bond Service Center of Anhui Province v Beijing Trust Investment Company of the Construction Bank* was criticized as a farfetched judgment, *supra* notes 54, 56; the calculation of repurchase interests under certain circumstances were criticized as being against the principle of fairness in the 1986 GPCL, *supra* note 112.

Chapter 5

Commodity and Financial Futures Markets

Introduction

The establishment of the first futures exchange in Zhengzhou city of Henan province in October 1990 marked the emergence of a futures market in China in the wake of economic reform and development.[1] This was followed by the rapid establishment of many other futures exchanges. At the height of the expansion, there were over fifty futures exchanges established in major cities throughout the country.[2] Problems of excessive speculative trading and illegal activities of various kinds prompted the government in 1993 to impose a tight control over the expansion and activities of the futures market.[3] A consolidation process started thereafter, as a result of which the number of futures exchanges was reduced and the work of drafting the Futures Law was also suspended.[4] This consolidation process continued into the late 1990s and the remaining fourteen futures exchanges were further consolidated to current three exchanges after 1998,[5] namely, Zhengzhou Commodity Exchange,[6] Shanghai Futures Exchange,[7] and Dalian Commodity Exchange.[8] At the height of the expansion of the

---

1   Zhengzhou Commodity Exchange was established on 12 October 1990. Futures products currently include wheat, cotton, sugar and green bean futures contracts. *See* www. czce.com.cn. Before the establishment of Zhengzhou Commodity Exchange, beginning in 1988, some futures trading activities were introduced on a trial basis in a few commodity wholesale markets.

2   *See* Wu Qingbao and Jiang Xiangyang (eds), *Civil Liabilities of Futures Trading (Qihuo Jiaoyi Minshi Zeren)*, Preface, p. 1. (Beijing: China Legal System Publishing House, 2003).

3   *See* Circular of the State Council on Firmly Stopping Blind Development of the Futures Market (Guowuyuan Guanyu Jianjue Zhizhi Qihuo Shichang Mangmu Fazhan de Tongzhi), issued by the State Council on 14 November 1993.

4   *Supra* note 2.

5   *See* Circular of the State Council on Further Consolidation and Standardization of the Futures Market (Guowuyuan Guanyu Jinyibu Zhengdun He Guifan Qihuo Shichang de Tongzhi), issued by the State Council on 1 August 1998, in which a plan was put forward for consolidation of the fourteen futures exchanges into three.

6   *Supra* note 1.

7   Shanghai Futures Exchange was established by merging Shanghai Commodity Exchange, Shanghai Metal Exchange and Shanghai Grain and Oil Exchange in 1998 and business started in December 1999. Futures products currently include copper, aluminum, natural rubber and fuel oil futures contracts. *See* www.shfe.com.cn.

8   Located in Dalian city, Liaoning province, Dalian Commodity Exchange was established on 28 February 1993. Futures products currently include corn, soybeans, soybean

futures market, over a thousand futures firms were established, but and this number was reduced to fewer than two hundred in the same period.[9]

Between 1993 and 1998 various pieces of regulations and regulatory documents were issued by central and local government regulators, including, among others, the 1993 Provisional Measures on the Administration of Registration of Futures brokerage firms,[10] the 1993 Circular of the State Council on Firmly Stopping Blind Development of Futures Market,[11] the 1994 Opinion of the State Council Securities Committee on Firmly Stopping Blind Development of the Futures Market,[12] the 1994 Provisional Measures on the Administration of Personnel Working in Futures Business Organizations,[13] the 1994 Regulations on the Administration of Shanghai Futures Market[14] and the 1998 Circular of the State Council on Further Consolidation and Standardization of the Futures Market.[15] A central theme running through these government documents was great caution in the development of a futures market in China. On the one hand, the futures market was allowed to continue to exist and develop in order to play its proper role, but on the other hand, such existence and development had to be tightly controlled and regulated. Some commodity futures contracts were taken off the product list of commodity exchanges;[16] trading of foreign exchange futures and government bond futures were suspended;[17] offshoretrading

---

meal and soybean oil futures contracts. See www.dce.com.cn.

9   *Supra* note 2.

10   Provisional Measures on the Administration of Registration of Futures brokerage firms (Qihuo Jingji Gongsi Dengji Guanli Zhanxing Banfa) issued by the State Administration for Industry and Commerce on 28 April 1993.

11   *Supra* note 3.

12   Circular of Asking for Instructions on Several Opinions on Firmly Stopping Blind Development of the Futures Market (Guanyu Jianjue Zhizhi Qihuo Shichang Mangmu Fazhan Ruogan Yijian Qingshi de Tongzhi), issued by the General Office of the State Council on 16 May 1994.

13   Provisional Measures on the Administration of Personnel Working in Futures Business Organizations (Qihuo Jingying Jigou Congye Renyuan Guanli Zhanxing Banfa), issued by the CSRC on 7 November 1994.

14   Regulations on the Administration of Shanghai Futures Market (Shanghai Shi Qihuo Shichang Guanli Guiding), promulgated by the Shanghai government on 5 December 1994.

15   *Supra* note 5.

16   *See* Circular of the State Council Securities Committee Asking for Instructions on Stopping Trading Futures of Steel, Sugar and Coal (Guowuyuan Zhengquan Weiyuanhui Guanyu Tingzhi Gangcai, Shitang, Meitan Qihuo Jiaoyi Qingshi de Tongzhi), issued by the General Office of the State Council on 6 April 1994.

17   *See* Circular on the Summary of the Meeting of Implementing the Circular on Sternly Investigating and Dealing with Illegal Trading Activities in Foreign Exchange Futures and Foreign Exchange Deposit Trading (Guanyu Guanche "Guanyu Yanli Chachu Feifa Waihui Qihuo He Waihui Anjin Jiaoyi Huodong de Tongzhi" de Huiyi Jiyao de Tongzhi), issued jointly by the CSRC, the State Administration of Foreign Exchange, the State Administration for Industry and Commerce and the Ministry of Public Security on 14 December 1994; Circular on Suspension of Government Bond Futures Trading (Zhanting Guozhai Qihuo Jiaoyi de Tongzhi), issued jointly by the CSRC and Ministry of Finance on 23 February 1995.

of commodity futures products were cancelled.[18] As a result of crackdown by the government, the scale of the futures market was reduced substantially.

In June 1999, the State Council promulgated the Provisional Regulations on the Administration of Futures Trading,[19] which marked an important step in the regulation of futures market. Soon after the promulgation of the 1999 Provisional Regulations on the Administration of Futures Trading, the CSRC issued four implementing rules covering the regulation of the futures exchange,[20] the futures brokerage firm,[21] the qualification requirements for senior managers in a futures brokerage firm[22] and the qualification requirements for entering into futures business.[23] The 1999 Provisional Regulations on the Administration of Futures Trading and the four implementing rules from the CSRC, as a whole, gives an impetus to the process of standardization of China's new futures market and at the same time helps the people's courts in dealing with futures disputes. The four implementing rules have all been amended in 2002 by the CSRC.[24]

Article 70 (2) of the 1999 Provisional Regulations on the Administration of Futures Trading defines the futures contract (*qihuo heyue*) as a standard contract formulated by futures exchanges, which stipulates the delivery of commodities of

---

18   *See* Circular on Relevant Issues about Cancellation by Futures Brokerage Firms of Offshore Futures Business (Guanyu Qihuo Jingji Gongsi Zhuxiao Jingwai Qihuo Yewu Youguan Wenti de Tongzhi), issued by the CSRC on 12 September 1994. Starting from late 1999, a limited number of state-owned enterprises were allowed to engage in offshore trading of commodities futures products for hedging purposes upon an approval by the government regulators. *See* Circular on Relevant Issues about Application for Offshore Futures Business (Guanyu Shenqing Jingwai Qihuo Yewu Youguan Wenti de Tongzhi), issued by the CSRC on 15 October 1999; Administrative Measures on Offshore Futures Hedging Business by State-Owned Enterprises (Guoyou Qiye Jingwai Qihuo Taoqi Baozhi Yewu Guanli Banfa), issued by the CSRC jointly with other four government departments on 24 May 2001.

19   Provisional Regulations on the Administration of Futures Trading (Qihuo Jiaoyi Guanli Zanxing Tiaoli), promulgated by the State Council on 2 June 1999, effective as of 1 September 1999.

20   The Measures on the Administration of Futures Exchanges (Qihuo Jiaoyisuo Guanli Banfa), issued by the CSRC on 31 August 1999.

21   The Measures on the Administration of Futures Brokerage Firms (Qihuo Jingji Gongsi Guanli Banfa), issued by the CSRC on 31 August 1999.

22   The Measures on the Administration of Qualifications for Appointment of Senior Management Personnel of Futures Brokerage Firms (Qihuo Jingji Gongsi Gaoji Guanli Renyuan Renzhi Zige Guanli Banfa), issued by the CSRC on 31 August 1999.

23   The Measures on the Administration of Qualifications for Personnel Engaging in Futures Business (Qihuoye Congye Renyuan Zige Guanli Banfa), issued by the CSRC on 31 August 1999.

24   The Measures on the Administration of Qualifications for Appointment of Senior Management Personnel of Futures Brokerage Firms and the Measures on the Administration of Qualifications for Personnel Engaging in Futures Business were both amended on, and effective as of, 23 January 2002. The Measures on the Administration of Futures Exchanges and the Measures on the Administration of Futures Brokerage Firms were both amended on 17 May 2002 and effective as of 1 July 2002.

a certain quantity and quality at a certain time and place in the future.[25] In general, futures (*qihuo*) in China can be divided into commodity futures (*shangpin qihuo*) and financial futures (*jinrong qihuo*). In early years of China's futures market when many futures exchanges existed, there were general type of commodity futures exchanges (*shangpin qihuo jiaoyisuo*) and special type of futures exchanges, such as metal exchange (*jinshu jiaoyisuo*) and grain and oil exchange (*liangyou shangpin jiaoyisuo*). Before the government suspended trading of financial futures, there were government bond futures (*guozhai qihuo*), foreign exchange futures (*waihui qihuo*), and foreign exchange deposit trading (*waihui anjin jiaoyi*). In cases where a Chinese futures brokerage firm operated jointly with a foreign futures broker outside China, share index futures (*guzhi qihuo*) and other financial futures products were available to investors. The trading of government bond futures and financial bond futures has been resumed on 15 June 2005 on inter-bank bond market and a group of related regulations and trading rules have been promulgated.[26]

Disputes Arising from Futures Trading

After the emergence of the futures market, disputes arising from futures trading increased sharply in the first few years and began to flood into the people's courts. In the words of the deputy president of the Supreme People's Court, the futures market had become a "big litigation family" (*susong dahu*) generating a high rate of disputes and litigation.[27] These disputes involved new and difficult issues that the people's courts had not dealt with before. Furthermore, these disputes often involved large sums of money, and in some cases involved multi-party litigation. In *Xiamen Guomao Group Company Limited by Shares and Others v Hainan Zhongqing Jiye Development Center*,[28] for example, eighteen corporate plaintiffs were involved.

This situation prompted the Supreme People's Court to work out some guidelines to direct the local courts in dealing with futures dispute cases. In April 1995 the Supreme People's Court held a symposium to discuss the issues arising in the adjudication of futures disputes in the people's courts.[29] Judges from fourteen High People's Courts and six Intermediate People's Courts attended the symposium. A

---

25   Article 70 (2), 1999 Provisional Regulations on the Administration of Futures Trading, *supra* note 19.

26   *See*, among others, Provisions on the Administration of Bond Futures Trading on National Inter-Bank Bond Market (Quanguo Yinhang Jian Zhaiquan Shichang Zhaiquan Yuanqi Jiaoyi Guanli Guiding), issued by the PBOC on 11 May, effective as of 15 June 2005.

27   *See* Jiang Bixin (ed.), *Understanding and Application of "the 2003 Provisions of the Supreme People's Court on Several Issues Concerning Adjudication of Cases of Futures Disputes"* (*"Zuigao Renmin Fayuan Guanyu Shenli Qihuo Jiufen Anjian Ruogan Wenti de Guiding" de Lijie Yu Shiyong*), compiled by the Second Division Court of the Supreme People's Court (Beijing: The People's Court Publishing House, 2003), Preface, p. 1.

28   *Id*. at pp. 296–312.

29   The Symposium of the Supreme People's Court on Adjudication of Cases of Futures Disputes (Zuigao Renmin Fayuan Guanyu Shenli Qihuo Jiufen Anjian Zoutanhui), held at Chengdu city, Sichuan province, on 18–21 April 1995.

wide range of issues were discussed at the symposium, including the principles to be observed in the handling of futures cases, the jurisdiction of the people's courts over futures cases, the qualification to engage in futures business, the legal status of a broker and his civil liability, the disputes arising from breach of contract and the disputes arising from tort, the invalid civil acts relating to futures transactions and their civil liabilities, the trading of foreign exchange deposits, and the rules of burden of proof applicable to futures cases. The significance of the symposium was shown from the fact that judges from fourteen High People's Courts and six Intermediate People's Courts attended the symposium.

After the symposium, the Supreme People's Court issued in October 1995 a judicial guideline (hereinafter the 1995 SPC Futures Judicial Guidelines) setting out the positions reached in the symposium.[30] It is a comprehensive response from the Supreme People's Court to the problem of an increasing number of futures disputes coming into the people's courts. It emphases that it is an important task of the people's courts to deal with these cases fairly and expediently to protect lawful rights and interests of the parties, to punish illegal trading activities and to maintain futures market order.[31] Welcomed by the people's courts, the 1995 SPC Futures Judicial Guidelines became the first comprehensive but provisional guidelines for the substantial issues in the adjudication of futures disputes and the procedural rules according to which the people's courts should deal with this new type of case.

Apart from the symposium organized by the Supreme People's Court, similar seminars and discussions were held at local levels. For example, in Shanghai, where several futures exchanges were located and the trading of futures was active, the Shanghai Securities Regulatory Office, in conjunction with the Shanghai Commodity Exchange, the Metal Exchange and the Grain and Oil Exchange, organized a seminar on 11–12 June 1998 to discuss how to deal with futures disputes arising particularly in the futures market of Shanghai.[32] The seminar was a response to an increasing number of futures disputes in Shanghai and a forum to address new issues and problems which had not been addressed or not fully addressed by the 1995 SPC Futures Judicial Guidelines. Participants included judges from the Shanghai High People's Court and several intermediate and district courts in Shanghai.[33]

The Supreme People's Court started working on a new guideline in July 1999 on the basis of the 1995 SPC Futures Judicial Guidelines and the experiences of the people's courts in dealing with futures cases. After four stages of drafting and

---

30   The Notice of the Supreme People's Court on Circulating "Minutes of the Symposium of the Supreme People's Court on Adjudication of Cases of Futures Disputes" (Zuigao Renmin Fayuan Yinfa Guanyu Shenli Qihuo Jiufen Anjian Zuotanhui Jiyao de Tongzhi), issued by the Supreme People's Court on 27 October 1995.

31   Section 1, 1995 SPC Futures Judicial Guidelines, *Id.*

32   The Summary of Shanghai Seminar on Handling Futures Trading Disputes (Shanghai Qihuo Jiaoyi Jiufen Chuli Yantaohui Jiyao), 20 July 1998. *See* Zhong Futang et al. (eds), *Commentary and Analysis on Futures Trading Dispute Cases (Qihuo Jiaoyi Jiufen Anli Pingxi)* (Shanghai: Xuelin Publishing House, 1998), pp. 226–233.

33   *Id.*

twenty-eight drafts,[34] a new guideline came out in May 2003. The 2003 Provisions of the Supreme People's Court on Several Issues Concerning Adjudication of Cases of Futures Disputes (hereinafter the 2003 SPC Futures Judicial Provisions)[35] is a product of a long and careful work of the Supreme People's Court in consultation with futures business sector and market regulators. It represents a unified understanding and approach among the people's courts, the regulators and the futures business on major civil law issues concerning futures market and disputes.[36] Compared with the 1995 SPC Futures Judicial Guidelines, the 2003 SPC Futures Judicial Provisions provide the people's courts with a more mature and settled guideline in the handling of futures disputes.

Futures disputes are generally classified into two groups: the disputes arising in connection with the trading of futures contracts (*heyue jiaoyi jiufen*) and the disputes arising in connection with the settlement of commodities (*shiwu jiaoge jiufen*)[37] The following discussion focuses on some aspects of trading and settlement of futures contracts, where the majority of futures disputes have occurred, particularly in the early years of China's futures market. It is pointed out in the 1995 SPC Futures Judicial Guidelines that futures disputes, compared with other types of economic disputes, have distinctive features and the people's courts should handle them in accordance with the principles set out in the 1995 SPC Futures Judicial Guidelines.[38] The principles include the correct application of law,[39] balance between risks and

---

34   The drafting began on 21 July 1999. The first stage was to work on the new issues and questions that had emerged since 1995 and to incorporate them into the drafts; beginning in May 2001, the second stage was to focus on the structure; starting from early 2002, the third stage was to consult with the CSRC, futures exchanges and the Association of Futures Business; during February and May 2003, the fourth stage was to go through several rounds of discussions by the Judicial Committee of the Supreme People's Court. *See* Jiang Bixin (ed.), *supra* note 27 at pp. 18–19.

35   The 2003 Provisions of the Supreme People's Court on Several Issues Concerning Adjudication of Cases of Futures Disputes (Zuigao Renmin Fayuan Guanyu Shenli Qihuo Jiufen Anjian Ruogan Wenti de Guiding), adopted by the Judicial Committee of the Supreme People's Court on 16 May 2003, effective as of 1 July 2003.

36   *See* an interview by news reporter with Jiang Bixin, deputy president of the Supreme People's Court, on the application of the 2003 Provisions of the Supreme People's Court on Several Issues Concerning Adjudication of Cases of Futures Disputes, *supra* note 27, Jiang Bixin (ed.), at p. 19.

37   *See* Jiang Bixin (ed.), *supra* note 27, at p. 321.

38   Section 1, 1995 SPC Futures Judicial Guidelines, *supra* note 30.

39   Section 1 (1) states that the people's courts should apply the 1986 GPCL as a primary source of law and also act in light of central and local administrative regulations and normative documents; where the disputes involve foreign, Hong Kong and Macao element, the people's courts should also refer to international practice, *supra* note 30.

interests,[40] balance between fault and responsibilities[41] and respect for the agreement of parties.[42]

Qualification to Engage in Futures Trading

The futures regulation requires that futures trading must be conducted in a futures exchange; the establishment of a futures exchange must be approved by the CSRC, without which no futures exchange may be established.[43] In early years of the futures market, some futures exchanges were established upon approval from local government. A futures exchange could be involved in a dispute either as a plaintiff or a defendant. The status of the futures exchange involved in the dispute would be examined first by the people's court to see whether the futures exchange is established and functioned according to the regulation and the approval of regulators. In *Shanghai Foreign Trade Company v Shanghai Chemicals Commodity Exchange*,[44] the Shanghai Changning District People's Court was satisfied that the defendant Shanghai Chemical Commodity Exchange was a state-owned enterprise established upon an approval of the Administrative Bureau of Industry and Commerce of Shanghai Municipality, whose services were to provide for a chemical commodity trading place and facilities, to deal with clearance and transfers, and to provide other services relating to chemical commodity trading.[45]

In *Hainan Zhongqing Jiye Development Center v Sichuan Pingyuan Industrial Development Co.*,[46] the Sichuan High People's Court was satisfied that the Hainan Zhongshang Futures Exchange, where the dispute occurred, was established upon an approval of the CSRC and had an enterprise legal person business license issued by the Administration for Industry and Commerce. Its approved business was to provide members with a trading place for natural rubber and other futures contracts.[47] The examination by the people's court of the status of a futures exchange in a futures

---

40   Section 1 (2) states that, given the fact that futures trading involve speculation and high risks, the people's courts should protect lawful interests of trading parties on the one hand, and determine correctly the risks the parities should undertake, *supra* note 30.

41   Section 1 (3) states that the people's court should analysis carefully whether arties in a dispute are at fault, what is the nature of the fault, how serious is the fault, and whether there is a causal link between the fault and losses, and on the basis of these finding determine their corresponding responsibilities, *supra* note 30.

42   Section 1 (4) states that the agreement of the parties should be treated as the basis for dealing with the disputes between the parties as long as the agreement has no violation of law, regulations and custom of futures trading, *supra* note 30.

43   Articles 4, 6, 1999 Provisional Regulations on the Administration of Futures Trading, *supra* note 19.

44   *See Carefully Selected Cases of the People's Courts (Renmin Fayuan Anli Xuan Jingbianben)*, Vol. 1, 2001, edited by China Law Application Research Institute of the Supreme People's Court (Beijing: Xinhua Publishing Press, 2001), pp.763-769.

45   *Id.* at p. 765

46   *See* Gazette of the Supreme People's Court of the People's Republic of China, Issue 4, 2005, pp. 25–30.

47   *Id.* at p. 27.

dispute becomes less relevant and important after 1998 when only three futures exchanges remained nationwide, in sharp contrast to the situation in early 1990s where there were about fifty futures exchanges at the height of expansion of China's futures market.

More importantly is that the people's courts examine the status of futures brokerage firms to determine whether they are authorized dealers, established according to the regulation and by the approval of regulators. It is required that futures brokerage firms must become a member of futures exchanges to trade futures contracts on behalf of their clients;[48] the establishment of futures brokerage firms must be approved by the CSRC and registered with the Administration for Industry and Commerce;[49] financial institutions, state organs and some other institutions and individuals are not allowed to trade futures contracts and futures brokerage firms may not accept and act for them.[50]

In *Zhongyuan Grain & Oil Trading Co. v Zhumadian Region Yinfeng Co. and Zhumadian Region Vegetable Oil Co.*,[51] the Zhumadian Intermediate People's Court found that two defendants who acted as brokers for futures trading were not members of the Zhengzhou City Grain Commodity Exchange, nor had they been approved by the CSRC and registered with the Administration for Industry and Commerce to engage in futures business. The Court also found that the plaintiff was a loss-making enterprise at the time when it entrusted the defendants to trade futures contracts. On the basis of the finding, the Court annulled the brokerage agreement signed between the plaintiff and the defendants.[52] In *Suzhou Foreign Trade Commodity Holding Co. v Zhejiang Huanya Industrial Co. Ltd.*,[53] the Supreme People's Court and the first instance court Jiangsu High People's Court both found the two contracts signed between the plaintiff and defendant relating to futures trading at the Suzhou Commodity Exchange were invalid on the basis that the plaintiff had no authorization to engage in futures brokerage business. The plaintiff was a member of the Suzhou Commodity Exchange and was approved to engage in futures trading only on its own account but not as a broker who could trade on behalf of others. Furthermore, the contracts were entered into with the illegal aim of joint manipulation of market prices.[54]

An important question in the context of these cases for the people's courts to decide is who should bear losses. Should the brokerage firm bear losses for its clients because it violated the regulation for which its acts were rendered invalid? The position was not clear and consistent before the 1995 SPC Futures Judicial

---

48   Article 28, 1999 Provisional Regulations on the Administration of Futures Trading, *supra* note 19.

49   *Id*. art. 22.

50   *Id*. art. 30. A loss-making enterprise, for instance, is not allowed to be involved in futures trading.

51   *See Carefully Selected Cases of the People's Courts (Renmin Fayuan Anli Xuan Jingbianben)*, Vol. 1, 2001, edited by China Law Application Research Institute of the Supreme People's Court (Beijing: Xinhua Publishing Press, 2001), pp.769-777.

52   *Id*. p. 771.

53   *See* Jiang Bixin (ed.), *supra* note 27 at pp. 263–295.

54   *Id*. p. 273, p. 288.

Guidelines. In most cases, the people's courts ruled in favor of the clients, requesting the brokerage firms to return the lost deposits to clients. This was criticized by commentators as a wrong approach resulting from a lack of correct understanding by some people's courts of the legal relationship between brokerage, clients and futures trading.[55]

The 1995 SPC Futures Judicial Guidelines has made the position clear, according to which the people's court should first establish whether there is a causal link between the losses suffered by the clients and the invalid acts of brokerage firms. Where a brokerage firm has no qualification to engage in futures trading but has acted for its clients, the brokerage firm should not be held liable for the losses if there is evidence to prove that the brokerage firm carried out the trading according to the instructions of the client; the loss suffered by the client under these circumstances is a loss due to normal market risks.[56] In effect, although the brokerage firm has carried out invalid trading activities, it should not bear the loss for the client if there is no direct link between the invalid trading and the loss. This principle has been reiterated in the 2003 SPC Futures Judicial Provisions.[57]

Zhongyuan Grain & Oil Trading Co. v Zhumadian Region Yinfeng Co. and Zhumadian Region Vegetable Oil Co.[58] is a case which illustrates the position that a futures brokerage firm should not be held liable for the loss suffered by a client if there is no direct link between the invalid trading and the loss. In this case, as mentioned above, the Court annulled the brokerage agreement signed between the plaintiff and the defendants on the ground that the two defendants had no qualifications to engage in futures business and the plaintiff was a loss-making enterprise that should not have entrusted the defendants to trade commodity futures contracts.[59] On the issue of the liability for the loss suffered by the plaintiff in the trading, the Court made a distinction, on the basis of evidence, between those losses suffered as a result of the trading carried out by the defendant in accordance with the plaintiff's instructions and those losses suffered as a result of the trading carried out by the defendant without the plaintiff's instructions. Regarding the former losses the Court rejected the plaintiff's claim; regarding the latter losses the Court held that defendant would

---

55   *See* Wu Zhipan and Tang Jiemang (eds), *Explanation and Analysis of Typical Cases of Financial Law, 1st Issue* (*Jinrong Fa Dianxing Anli Jiexi, Diyi Ji*), pp. 247–248. (Beijing: China Finance Publishing House, 2000) (stating that the basic obligation of a futures brokerage firm is to execute truthfully trading instructions of clients and should not bear legal responsibilities for the consequences of normal trading; where acts of a futures brokerage firm are invalid because the firm lacks necessary qualification, what is affected is only commissions charged by the firm).

56   Section 7, 1995 SPC Futures Judicial Guidelines, *supra* note 19.

57   Article 14 states that "where a client's economic loss is caused by invalid futures contracts, the responsibilities should be determined and borne according to the causal link between the invalid acts and the loss. One party's loss is caused by the act of the other party, the other party should compensate the loss; if both parties are at fault each of them should bear corresponding civil responsibility according to the portion of the fault." *supra* note 35.

58   *Supra* note 51.

59   *Supra* note 52.

compensate the plaintiff.[60] This ruling was upheld by the appeal court when the defendant appealed the case to the Henan High People's Court.[61]

In the case where a futures brokerage firm oversteps its business scope (*jingying fanwei*) approved by the government authorities, the contracts related to the case shall be null and void. In *Liang Jintao v Baishigao Futures Consultant Services Co. Ltd.*, [62] the defendant Baishigao Futures Consultant Services Company was a joint venture set up by a Chinese company and a Hong Kong company in August 1991. The registered business scope of the joint venture included consultancy, training and services relating to commodity futures trading. In January 1992 the Baishigao company signed an agreement with the plaintiff Liang Jintao, which stipulates that Liang Jintao open an account at the Baishigao company and the Baishigao company act as Liang Jintao's broker for trading commodity futures. Liang Jintao deposited 250,000 yuan in the account. After a loss occurred Liang Jintao became aware that the Baishigao company had used the funds from his account for futures trading without his instructions. In the meantime, the Administration for Industry and Commerce of Shenzhen City issued a notice to the Baishigao company requiring it to stop trading commodity futures as such trading was not included in its business scope registered with the Shenzhen Administration for Industry and Commerce.

Liang Jintao demanded that the Baishigao company return all his money deposit 250,000 yuan, and a little bit of profit initially made before the loss occurred). Liang Jintao sued the Baishigao company at the Luohu District Court of Shenzhen City. The Court held that the agreement the defendant signed with the plaintiff was null and void on the ground that the defendant had overstepped its business scope. As the defendant used the plaintiff's account to trade commodity futures without the plaintiff's instructions, the Court, in accordance with Article 7 (1) (2) and Article 16 of Economic Contract Law,[63] held that the defendant shall return 200,000 yuan to the plaintiff.[64] From commentator's point of view, the defendant in this case should be held liable for returning the lost deposit to the plaintiff because the defendant traded with the plaintiff's account without his instructions and thus caused losses to him.[65] The decision of the Shenzhen Luohu District Court was upheld by the Shenzhen Intermediate People's Court.

---

60   *Supra* note 51, at p. 772.

61   *Id.* at p. 774.

62   *See Adjudicated Cases of Guangdong* (*Guangdong Shenpan Anli*), edited by the research department of the Guangdong High People's Court (Guangdong: Guangdong People's Publishing House, 1997), pp. 346–349.

63   Article 7 (1) and (2) of the 1993 Economic Contract Law stipulate that the contract that violates law and administrative regulations and the contract that is signed by means of fraud or duress shall be null and void. Article 16 stipulates that, after an economic contract is determined invalid, the property that the party has obtained in accordance with the contract shall be returned to the other party. The party who is at fault shall compensate for the loss the other party has suffered as a result; if both parties are at fault, each of them shall bear corresponding responsibilities.

64   *Supra* note 62, at p. 347.

65   *Id.* p. 349.

Forced Liquidation by Futures Exchanges or Futures Brokerage Firms

Forced liquidation (*qiangzhi pingcang*) refers to a forced measure taken by a futures exchange or a futures brokerage firm to close out the positions held by a futures brokerage firm or a client of a futures brokerage firm when the amount of margin required is falling and the futures brokerage firm or the client fails to make an additional margin on time.[66] Disputes often arise when a forced liquidation measure is taken by a futures exchange or a futures brokerage firm and losses occur subsequently. Is the forced liquidation measure a right or an obligation of futures exchanges or futures brokerage firms? Who should bear the losses occurred as a consequence of the forced liquidation taken or not taken? These are the key issues that arise from the forced liquidation measure. Three views have emerged from debates about whether forced liquidation is a right or an obligation of futures exchanges or futures brokerage firms.[67]

The first view regards the forced liquidation as a right exercisable by futures exchanges or futures brokerage firms. An underlying reference of this view is to the fact that there is no provision in current Chinese law or regulation that conceptualizes definitely whether the forced liquidation is a right or an obligation for futures exchanges or futures brokerage firms. The characterization should therefore be based on the provision of trading rules of futures exchanges and the brokerage agreements between futures brokerage firms and their clients. Futures exchanges regard forced liquidation as a right in the provisions of their trading rules while the agreements between futures brokerage firms and their clients generally stipulate that the futures brokerage firm has the right to close out the positions of a client if the client fails to make the additional margin as required.

The second view regards forced liquidation as both a right and an obligation. This view submits that, as far as futures brokerage firms are concerned, forced liquidation is both a right and an obligation of futures brokerage firms and fulfillment of such an obligation is more important. They argue that, as forced liquidation is a protective measure taken by a futures brokerage firm under circumstances where the market is not favorable to the positions of their clients, and the purpose of taking such a measure is to prevent the situation worsening for their clients, futures brokerage firms have an obligation to protect their clients.

The third view regards forced liquidation as a right in initial stages and which is transformed to an obligation afterwards. The argument here is that futures exchanges or futures brokerage firms generally set out in their trading rules or agreements two points of time, one is a time at which an additional margin has to be made and the

---

66   *See* the Summary of Shanghai Seminar on Handling Futures Trading Disputes, *supra* note 32, at p. 229.

67   *See* Wu Zhipan and Tang Jiemang (eds), *supra* note 55, at pp. 253–254. *See* also Wu Qingbao et al. (eds), *Principles and Precedents of Futures Litigation* (*Qihuo Susong Yuanli Yu Panli*) (Beijing: The People's Court Publishing House, 2005), pp. 277–281, *Studies of Judicial Decisions Related to Financial Disputes* (*Jingrong Shenpan Anli Yanjiu*) (Vol. 2001), edited by the Economic Division Court of Beijing High People's Court, p. 439. (Beijing: Law Publishing House, 2001); the Summary of Shanghai Seminar on Handling Futures Trading Disputes, *supra* note 32, at p. 229.

other is a time at which the futures exchange or futures brokerage firm must close out positions if the additional margin has not been made and further losses reach a certain point. At the time when the additional margin is not made as required, the futures exchange or futures brokerage firm acquires the right to close out the positions, but they may or may not exercise such a right at this stage. When further losses reach a certain point, the futures exchange or futures brokerage firm must fulfill its obligation of forced liquidation, failure of which would render them liable for the losses.

Some authors held the view that forced liquidation has a dual nature. In the legal relationship between a futures exchange and a futures brokerage firm and between a futures brokerage firm and its clients, forced liquidation is a contractual right exercisable by the futures exchange or the futures brokerage firm. On the other hand, the futures exchange and futures brokerage firm is required by relevant regulations and the provisions of trading rules to take the measure of forced liquidation when the amount of margin in question falls below required level. Forced liquidation is thus an obligation from a market regulation point of view. If a futures exchange or a futures brokerage firm fails this obligation, it shall bear responsibilities and consequences for allowing trading with overdraft.[68]

The 1995 SPC Futures Judicial Guidelines, the 1999 Provisional Regulations on the Administration of Futures Trading and the 2003 SPC Futures Judicial Provisions all have provisions regarding forced liquidation. Looking at the wording of these provisions, one can notice that different words are used in prescribing the exercise of forced liquidation by futures exchanges or futures brokerage firms. In the 1995 SPC Futures Judicial Guidelines the word "may" (*keyi*) is used,[69] while in the 1999 Provisional Regulations on the Administration of Futures Trading the word "shall" (*yingdang*) is used;[70] in the 2003 SPC Futures Judicial Provisions on the

---

68   *See* Wu Zhipan and Tang Jiemang (eds), *id.* at p. 254.

69   Section 5 (6) states that "In futures trading broker firms or clients shall deposit additional margin as required. If, having received a notice for depositing an additional margin, the broker firm or the client fail to make the additional margin within the time limit stipulated, the exchange or the broker firm *may* make a forced liquidation their futures contracts and the consequent losses are to be borne by the broker firm or the client. Where the exchange or the broker firm make a forced liquidation without fulfilling notification obligation and cause losses to the broker firm or the client, the exchange or the broker firm shall bear compensatory responsibilities." *Supra* note 30.

70   Article 41 states that "Where the amount of margin of a member of a futures exchange falls below required level, the member must make an additional margin. Where the member fails to make the additional margin within the time limit set out by the futures exchange in a unified way, the futures exchange *shall* make a forced liquidation of the futures contracts of the member, and the expenses connected with the forced liquidation and the losses incurred are to be borne by the member. Where the amount of margin of a client of a futures broker firm falls below required level and the client fails to make an additional margin promptly within the time limit set out by the futures broker firm in a unified way, the futures broker firm *shall* make a forced liquidation of the futures contracts of the client and the expenses connected with the forced liquidation and the losses incurred are to be borne by the client." *Supra* note 19.

other hand, the phrase used is "have the right" (*youquan*).[71] Some authors argue that forced liquidation is an obligation of futures exchanges or futures brokerage firms on the basis that the word "shall" used in the 1999 Provisional Regulations on the Administration of Futures Trading indicates that forced liquidation is an obligation rather than a right.[72] But one can equally argue that forced liquidation is a right rather than an obligation because the phrase "have the right" is used in the 2003 SPC Futures Judicial Provisions.

In judicial practice, the most common forced liquidation is liquidation taken by futures brokerage firms to close out positions of the account of a client.[73] The case *Ningbo City Rongcheng Trading Co. Ltd. v Ningbo City Xinyuan Futures Brokerage Co. Ltd.*[74] is an example. In April 1995 the plaintiff Rongcheng company signed an entrustment agreement with the defendant Xinyuan futures firm for trading commodity futures at the Shanghai Commodity Exchange. The Rongcheng company signed the agreement with a full understanding of and in agreement with the clauses of the Xinyuan futures firm on closing out positions under certain circumstances. The clauses were set out in the firm's manual, the Measures for Risk Management, and several other documents of the firm, which stipulated, among other provisions, that the firm would notify clients to increase their margins when the client had used up to 130% of their funds; the firm would notify the client before 11 am and the client must deposit the shortfall before 9 am the next day; when the client used up to 300% of their funds the firm had the right to close out all the positions without notifying the client.

By 24 July 1995, the plaintiff company had purchased through the Xinyuan firm 2,100 lots of 9,509 glue board contracts at the Shanghai Commodity Exchange. On 25 July 1995, the funds of the Rongcheng company were used up to 132% with a shortfall of margin 299,660 yuan. The Xinyuan firm prepared a notice in the afternoon requiring the Rongcheng company to make up for the shortfall. The notice was not given to the Rongcheng company until 8:45 am the next day. On 26 July 1995, after receiving the notice, the Rongcheng company prepared the money and delivered it to the Xinyuan firm at 9:25 am. But the Xinyuan firm had already closed

---

71 Article 36 states that "Where the amount of margin of a futures firm falls below required level and the futures firm fails to make an additional margin according to the time limit set out by a futures exchange, it is to be dealt with in accordance with trading rules; if the trading rules are not clear and definite, the futures exchange *has the right* to make a forced liquidation of the futures contracts of the firm, and the losses caused by the forced liquidation are to be borne by the futures firm. Where the amount of margin of a client falls below required level and the client fails to make an additional margin according to the time limit set out by a futures brokerage contract, it is to be dealt with in accordance with the provisions of the futures brokerage contract; if the provisions are not clear and definite, the futures firm *has the right* to make a forced liquidation of the futures contracts of the client, and the losses caused by the forced liquidation are to be borne by the client." *Supra* note 31.

72 *See* Wu Qingbao, *Essential Explanation of Difficult Issues in the Practice of Commercial Adjudication (Shangshi Shenpan Shiwu Nandian Jingjie)* (Beijing: The People's Court Publishing House, 2003), p. 278.

73 *Id.* at p. 285.

74 *See* Wu Zhipan and Tang Jiemang (eds), *supra* note 55, at pp. 251–258.

out all the positions of the Rongcheng company at 9:22 am, resulting in a loss of 2,145,800 yuan, including a commission charge of 37,800 yuan. The Rongcheng company sued the Xinyuan firm at the Intermediate People's Court of Ningbo City, claiming that the forced sale by the Xinyuan firm was invalid. The Xinyuan firm defended that the fund of the Rongcheng company was below required level and the forced sale was in accordance with the provisions of the futures trading.

The Ningbo Intermediate People's Court said that the entrustment agreement signed by the plaintiff and the defendant and the clauses agreed by the parties regarding futures trading were lawful and valid, and should be fulfilled according to the agreements; the defendant notified the plaintiff to deposit additional margin but failed to issue the notice according to the agreed time and gave the plaintiff necessary time for depositing the funds; under the circumstances the forced sale by the defendant constituted a breach of contract; there was a causal link between the forced sale and the losses suffered by the plaintiff; the defendant should bear compensatory responsibilities. On these grounds and in accordance with Articles 4, 106 and 134 (1) (vii) of the 1986 GPCL,[75] the Court ruled that the defendant would compensate the plaintiff 2,145,000 yuan.[76]

Cases similar to the above *Ningbo Rongcheng* case are one of the common sources of disputes, in which defendants fail to perform notification obligation one way or another before taking a forced liquidation measure to close out positions of their clients.[77] In other cases the plaintiffs generally argue that it is a duty of futures brokerage firms to take forced liquidation measures under certain circumstances to protect their clients; because of a failure of futures brokerage firms to take such measures on time, they should be liable for the losses suffered by the plaintiffs.[78] Apart from the notification obligation, discussions by judges and academics also look at other conditions a forced liquidation measure has to meet including, among others, the condition that forced liquidation should be moderate, which means that the positions to be closed out should be limited to an appropriate amount.[79] In

---

75   Article 4 of the 1986 GPCL states that civil juristic acts must respect the principles of voluntariness, fairness, compensation of equal value and good faith. Article 106 states citizens or legal person who break a contract or do not perform some other duty must bear civil liability. Citizens or legal person who, as a result of their fault, infringe on state or collective property, or infringe on the person or property of another person, must bear civil liability. Article 134 (1) (vii) prescribes "paying damages for the injuries" as one of the forms of bearing civil liability.

76   *Supra* note 74, at p. 253.

77   *See*, for example, Zhong Futang et al. (eds), *supra* note 32, at pp. 33–34 (a case in which the defendant closed out the positions of the plaintiff without first notifying the plaintiff and caused the plaintiff a loss of 125,000 yuan).

78   *See*, for example, Wu Qingbao et al. (eds), *supra* note 67, at pp. 446–447 (a case in which six plaintiffs sued the defendant Pufa futures brokerage firm and claimed that the defendant failed to perform its duty to take a forced liquidation on time).

79   *See* WU Qingbao, *Essential Explanation of Difficult Issues in the Practice of Commercial Adjudication* (*Shangshi Shenpan Shiwu Nandian Jingjie*) (Beijing: The People's Court Publishing House, 2003), pp. 285–288.; Wu Zhipan and Tang Jiemang (eds), *supra* note 55, at pp. 256–258.

this respect, Article 41 of the 1999 Provisional Regulations on the Administration of Futures Trading has been criticized for not having included a provision to the effect that forced liquidation should be moderate.[80] The 2003 SPC Futures Judicial Provisions has now addressed this issue.[81]

Where a case involves offshore futures transactions, the rules and practice of the international relevant futures market are referred to by the people's courts in their adjudication of such cases. *Zhaoxiaomei v Nanjing Jinzhongfu International Futures Trading Co. Ltd.*[82] is a case that occurred in the early years of China's futures market involving trading of American coffee futures. On 22 December 1992, the plaintiff Zhao Xiaomei and the defendant futures firm Jinzhongfu signed an agreement, according to which Zhao Xiaomei opened an account at the Jinzhongfu and deposited 20,000 US dollars for trading American coffee futures. In the early morning of 6 January 1993, Jinzhongfu closed out some of the positions in Zhao Xiaomei's account because the margin of Zhao Xiaomei's account fell below 100% mandatory margin. But according to the rules for the trading of American coffee futures at that time, Zhao Xiaomei's account could be allowed to go overnight if the amount of margin was above 50% of the mandatory margin. At the time the margin of Zhao Xiaomei's account was below 100% but above 50% of the mandatory margin. Zhao Xiaomei sued Jinzhongfu at the Intermediate People's Court of Nanjing City for the losses she suffered.

The Nanjing Intermediate People's Court established that Jinzhongfu had closed out some of the positions in Zhao Xiaomei's account without first having agreed with Zhao Xiaomei; the forced liquidation was taken when the amount of margin in Zhao Xiaomen's account was above 50% of the mandatory margin and therefore could be allowed to go overnight according to the international practice for the trading of American coffee. The Court said that the plaintiff and defendant formed a contractual relationship; the defendant acting for its clients in international futures trading must comply with relevant international trading rules; the defendant should be held responsible for the forced liquidation taken in violation of the American coffee futures trading rules. On these grounds and in accordance with Article 111 of the 1986 GPCL,[83] the Court ruled that the defendant would compensate the plaintiff 23,142 US dollars. The ruling was upheld by the Jiangsu High People's Court with the same reasoning after the defendant made an appeal.[84]

---

80 *See* Wu Qingbao, *Id.*, at p. 288.

81 Article 39 states that "the amount of positions that a futures exchange or a futures broker firm close out should be basically equal to the amount of margin that a futures broker firm or a client has to add up. The loss caused by an excessive liquidation shall be borne by those who take the forced liquidation measure." *Supra* note 35.

82 *See* Gazette of the Supreme People's Court of the People's Republic of China, Issue 3, 1994, pp. 117–119.

83 Article 111 of the 1986 GPCL states that when one of the parties does not perform his contractual obligations, or performs in a way that does not conform with the conditions set by the contract, the other party has the right to demand performance, or to select some remedial measure. Moreover, he has the right to demand damages.

84 *Supra* note 82, at pp. 118–119.

Carry Out Clients' Instruction and Burden of Proof

The issue here is whether a futures brokerage firm genuinely carries out the instructions of a client. Disputes have arisen, particularly in the early years of China's futures market, in which clients make claims for their losses on the ground that the futures brokerage firm did not carry out their instructions genuinely. *Wang Huiwen v Zhuhai City Xinguang Futures Brokerage Co. Ltd.*[85] is a 1995 case in which the plaintiff Wang Huiwen claimed that the defendant Xinguang futures brokerage firm had not carried out his instructions genuinely on to the market.

Wang Huiwen and Xinguang company signed an agreement on 13 September 1995, which stipulated that Wang Huiwen open an account and deposit 500,000 yuan and Xinguang company act as his agent in trading domestic and international commodity and financial futures, options and spot trading products. Between 16 and 24 October 1995 Wang Huiwen instructed the Xinguang company to sell 1,800 lots of Shanghai 95.11 glue board futures at the Shanghai Commodity Exchange. After a loss of 1,186,800 yuan was made, Wang Huiwen sued the Xinguang company at the Intermediate People's Court of Zhuhai City, claiming that the defendant had not executed his instructions.

After examining the evidence from the defendant, the Court said the evidence given by the defendant could not prove that the company had executed the instructions from the plaintiff, as the evidence had various problems, such as that the evidence relating to the price of the deals carried out by the defendant was in conflict with the records of the Shanghai Commodity Exchange. The Court then inferred that the defendant had not executed the trading on the market in accordance with the instructions from the plaintiff. In accordance with Article 61 of the 1986 GPCL,[86] the Court held that the defendant would return 1,186,000 yuan and 54,000 yuan commission charges and applicable interest to the plaintiff.

The defendant appealed the judgment to the Guangdong High People's Court, arguing that the problems with the evidence they gave were caused by the business practices – "first in, first out" (*xianru, xianchu*) and "mixed position operation" (*huncang caozuo*) – a common and normal practice followed by many of futures companies for the sake of convenient and expeditious trading and saving margins. The Guangdong High People's Court dismissed the argument. The Court said that the ultimate trading place in this case was at the Shanghai Commodity Exchange and the rules of the Shanghai Commodity Exchange should be the standard to judge whether a practice breached the trading rules. As the practice of "first in, first out" and "mixed position operation" was a breach of the rules of the Shanghai Commodity Exchange, the defendant, the Court said, could not justify its practice by arguing that these

---

85   *See* Gazette of the Supreme People's Court of the People's Republic of China, Issue 1, 1999, at pp. 29–30.

86   Article 61 of the 1986 GPCL states that after a civil juristic act has been determined as being without effect or has been annulled, the party who has received property as a result of the act must return it to the other party. If one party is at fault, he must pay damages to the other party who has been injured in consequence. If both parties are at fault each must bear his appropriate share of liability.

practices were common and normal practices in futures business. The Court rejected the appeal and upheld the judgment of the Zhuhai Intermediate People's Court.[87]

It is apparent from the above *Wang Huiwen* case that evidence plays a central role in this type of dispute. As an exception to the general evidential rule that those who claim shall discharge the burden of proof (*shui zhuzhang, shui juzheng*),[88] defendants, rather than plaintiffs, in this type of dispute bear the burden of proof. The 1995 SPC Futures Judicial Guidelines instructs the people's courts that where a client claims that a brokerage firm has not conducted trading in the market and the brokerage firm denies, the brokerage firm shall bear the burden of proof; if the brokerage firm adduces no relevant evidence, it shall be inferred that no trading is conducted in the market.[89] The above *Wang Huiwen* case was decided in line with this guideline of the Supreme People's Court. The Court said that when clients suspect that their brokerage firm has carried out trading in the market according to their instructions, the brokerage firm shall bear the burden of proof and the general rule that those who claim shall discharge the burden of proof is not applicable under these circumstances.[90]

The 2003 SPC Futures Judicial Provisions has now refined the position of the 1995 SPC Futures Judicial Guidelines regarding the burden of proof under circumstances where there is a suspicion or claim regarding whether a futures brokerage firm has carried out a client's trading instruction on to the market. According to Article 56 of the 2003 SPC Futures Judicial Provisions, futures brokerage firms shall discharge the burden of proof on whether a client's trading instruction has been executed on the market.[91] Article 56 also provides that, except where a client has contrary evidence to prove that his trading instruction has not been executed on the market, the people's court shall determine the issue on the basis of trading records of futures exchanges and trading settlement notification of the futures brokerage firm to see whether they match the records of the client's instruction concerning the product, direction of trading, price of trading and trading time; the quantity of the trading instructed may be treated as a reference.[92]

In general, the 2003 SPC Futures Judicial Provisions apply to cases occurring after 1 July 2003, but, in accordance with Article 63 of the 2003 SPC Futures Judicial Provisions,[93] a case which occurred before 1 July 2003 may be dealt with by reference to the 2003 SPC Futures Judicial Provisions if there was then no clear and definite provisions regarding the issue of the case. But once a case is closed and takes legal effect, it may not be retried by reference to the 2003 SPC Futures

---

87   *Supra* note 85, at p. 30.

88   Article 64, the 1991 Civil Procedure Law, adopted by the 7th National People's Congress on 9 April 1991, effective the same day.

89   Section 9, 1995 SPC Futures Judicial Guidelines, *supra* note 30.

90   *Supra* note 85, at p. 30.

91   Article 56 (1), 2003 SPC Futures Judicial Provisions, *supra* note 35.

92   *Id.* art. 56 (2).

93   Article 63 states that the conduct of futures trading or tort that happened before 1 July 2003 shall apply relevant provisions of that time; if those provisions are not clear and definite, they may be dealt with by reference to this Provision.

Judicial Provisions. *Chen Zhongyi v Tianyi Futures Brokerage Co. Ltd.,*[94] a case which occurred in June 2000, is an example of the application of Article 63 of the 2003 SPC Futures Judicial Provisions by the people's court.

The plaintiff Chen Zhongyi and the defendant Tianyi futures company signed a futures brokerage contract on 2 June 2000, which stipulated that Chen Zhongyi entrusted the Tianyi futures company to carry out futures trading and Chen Zhongyi bore the risks of the trading. Afterwards, Chen Zhongyi opened an account at the Tianyi futures company and was assigned a client code 00014959. On 9 June 2000 Chen Zhongyi instructed the Tianyi futures company to purchase twenty lots of November soybean at a total price of 441,800 yuan. When a loss of 41,800 yuan was made later, Chen Zhongyi sued the Tanyi futures company at the Intermediate People's Court of Chengdu city, Sichuan province, claiming 41,800 yuan in damages and 600 yuan commission charged by the defendant for the transactions.

At issue was whether the defendant had carried out the purchase order the plaintiff instructed on 9 June 2000. The plaintiff argued that the defendant had not carried out her purchase order on 9 June 2000. The defendant submitted it had carried out the instruction. The records of the Dalian Commodity Exchange show that there were five deals made with a client code 00001260 on 9 June 2000. Three of the deals were the same as instructed by the plaintiff in terms of product, quantity, price and time of the deal. The plaintiff instructed only one purchase on that day. The Court thus established that the defendant had practiced "mixed code trading" (*hunma jiaoyi*), that is, trading by which a common code is shared by several clients. Under such mixed code trading, it was inevitable that a client's own code and the code used in the trading may not be the same.

The issue then was whether one of the three deals carried out by the defendant was the deal instructed by the plaintiff. Since the provision in the 1995 SPC Futures Judicial Guidelines was not detailed and definite about the criterion according to which the people's court could determine whether a futures brokerage firm carried out a client's trading instruction on the market, the Court, in accordance with Article 63 of the 2003 SPC Futures Judicial Provisions, dealt with the issue by reference to Article 56 of the 2003 SPC Futures Judicial Provisions.[95] Considering that although the plaintiff submitted that her instruction had not been executed on the market on 9 June 2000, no definite evidence was adduced by the plaintiff to prove this submission, the Court thus rejected the claim of the plaintiff. This ruling of the Court on the evidential issue of the case decided by reference to the burden of proof rule of the 2003 SPC Futures Judicial Provisions was viewed as a correct ruling.[96]

Responsibility of the Futures Exchange

The 1995 SPC Futures Judicial Guidelines provide that, in the course of futures trading, futures exchanges shall undertake a responsibility to guarantee the performance of futures contracts. If any party is unable to perform timely and

---

94   *See* Wu Qingbao et al. (eds), *supra* note 67, at pp. 374–380.
95   *Supra* notes 91 and 92.
96   *Supra* note 94, at p. 380.

wholly the obligation stipulated in a futures contract, the exchange shall perform the obligation on their behalf, failure of which the exchange shall be liable for compensation. After such performance, the exchange shall have the right to pursue repayment from the defaulting party.[97] This position is further elaborated by the 1999 Provisional Regulations on the Administration of Futures Trading, which provides that, where there is a breach of contract by a member of the futures exchange in the course of futures trading, the member's deposit shall be first used to satisfy the liabilities; if the deposit of the member is insufficient, the futures exchange shall use the risk reserve fund and its own fund to satisfy the liabilities on behalf of the member, and thus acquire the right to pursue repayment from the member.[98]

There is no further definition in the 1995 SPC Futures Judicial Guidelines and the 1999 Provisional Regulations on the Administration of Futures Trading about the nature of the guarantee undertaken by the futures exchange. One view regards the "guarantee" (*baozheng*) undertaken by the futures exchange as falling into the scope of civil law guarantee, that is, a guarantee undertaken by the futures exchange with all of its own funds and trustworthiness to guarantee the trading conducted by all the members of the exchange.[99] This view also submits that there is a difference between the guarantee undertaken by the futures exchange under these circumstances and an ordinary civil law guarantee in that the futures exchange can use its regulatory means to take first the funds from the default party or the risk reserve funds to satisfy the liabilities for the breach of contract while there is no such right existing in an ordinary civil law guarantee. In this sense, the guarantee of the futures exchange is a "mixed type guarantee" (*hunhexing danbao*), combining the features of a civil law guarantee and a right of self-regulation.[100]

On the basis of the 1995 SPC Futures Judicial Guidelines and the 1999 Provisional Regulations on the Administration of Futures Trading, the 2003 SPC Futures Judicial Provisions provides further related procedural rules. Thus, where a futures exchange does not perform futures contracts on behalf of a futures brokerage firm, the futures brokerage firm shall make claims to the futures exchange according to requests of its clients;[101] if the futures brokerage firm refuses to make the claims to the futures exchange on behalf of the clients, the clients may sue the futures exchange directly, and the futures brokerage firm may join the proceedings as a third party.[102] The 2003 SPC Futures Judicial Provisions also define clearly the right and obligation of the futures exchange in the context of the guarantee undertaken by the futures exchange. If a futures brokerage firm fails to perform pecuniary obligations according to the requirements of daily settlement system of the futures exchange and nor does the futures exchange perform the obligation on behalf of the futures brokerage firm, the futures exchange shall be liable for compensation for the loss caused to the

---

97   Section 5 (1), 1995 SPC Futures Judicial Guidelines, *supra* note 30.

98   Article 44 (1), 1999 Provisional Regulations on the Administration of Futures Trading, *supra* note 19.

99   See Wu Qingbao, *supra* note 72, at p. 298.

100   *Id.*

101   Article 49 (1) 2003 SPC Futures Judicial Provisions, *supra* note 35.

102   *Id.* art. 49 (2).

other trading party;[103] the futures exchange has the right to pursue repayment from a defaulting party after the futures exchange performs an obligation on behalf of a futures brokerage firm or undertakes compensatory responsibilities.[104]

Hainan Zhongqing Jiye Development Center v Sichuan Pingyuan Industrial Development Co.,[105] a complicated and important case which involved trading of natural rubber futures R708 contracts in 1997, illustrates the application of the rule that a futures exchange has the right to pursue repayment from a default party after the futures exchange performs an obligation on behalf of a futures brokerage firm. The case was first tried by the Sichuan High People's Court, whose judgment was overturned by the Supreme People's Court after the plaintiff Hainan Zhongqing Jiye Development Center appealed the judgment to the Supreme People's Court. Hainan Zhongqing Jiye Development Center used to be Hainan Zhongshang Futures Exchange located in Haikou city, Hainan province, whose name was changed in 2000 during the proceedings.

On 5 April 1997, the defendant Sichuan Pingyuan company privately signed a "seat transfer agreement" with Sichuan Hezheng futures brokerage firm, a third party in the case. Both Pingyuan company and Hezheng firm were members of the Zhongshang Futures Exchange. According to the agreement the Pingyaun company transfer its seat (No. 165) to the Hezheng firm for a transfer fee of 300,000 yuan. The transfer agreement was not reported to the Zhongshang Futures Exchange and was a violation of the trading rule that trading seats may not be transferred. The Supreme People's Court, who found that the real nature and purpose of the agreement was to rent the seat privately,[106] rejected the argument of the Pingyuan company that it had transferred its seat to the Hezheng company and therefore should not be held liable for any consequences of the trading connected with the seat 165.

On 29 July 1997, seat 165 held 4,250 lots of R708 contracts. On 30 July the Zhongshang Futures Exchange issued a notice informing seat 165 that its deposit was insufficient and should be topped up before the opening of next trading day. From 1 August to 13 August seat 165 closed out 917 lots and 3,333 lots remained. On 18 August the Zhongshang Futures Exchange notified the seat 165 that since no sufficient deposit had been topped up the 3,333 lots constituted a breach of contract, for which 37,196,280 yuan, being 20% of total price of the commodity, was payable in accordance with the settlement rules of the Zhongshang Futures Exchange. 7,692,280 yuan was taken from the account of the Pingyuan company, and as the Pingyuan company failed to pay the balance the Zhongshang Futures Exchange paid 29,503,999.14 yuan from its own funds to the other trading parties of the Pingyuan company. In December 1998, the Zhongshang Futures Exchange sued the Pingyuan

---

103　*Id.* art. 48 (1).

104　*Id.* art. 48 (2).

105　*Supra* note 46.

106　The CSRC investigated into the irregularities and market manipulation connected with the trading of R708 rubber futures contracts in the Zhongshang Futures Exchange in 1997 and concluded that the Pingyuan company had rented out its seat and violated the regulation. *See Hainan Zhongqing Jiye Development Center v Sichuan Pingyuan Industrial Development Co.*, *supra* note 46, at pp. 26–27.

company at the Sichuan High People's Court, claiming refund of 29,503,999.14 yuan from the Pingyuan company.

The Sichuan High People's Court said that, in the course of futures trading, a futures exchange should undertake to guarantee the performance of futures contracts; if any party is unable to perform timely and wholly the obligation stipulated in the futures contracts, the futures exchange shall perform them on their behalf and thus acquire the right to pursue a refund. The Court accepted the lawfulness of the action that the Zhongshang Futures Exchange paid 29,503,999.14 yuan for seat 165 when seat 165 breached the contract. The Court said that the fact was clear with sufficient supporting evidence and the action was in compliance with the regulations. But on the other hand, the Court said that the Zhongshang Futures Exchange had contributed to the breach and should bear the responsibilities jointly with the Pingyuan company. The Court reached this judgment on the finding that on 28 and 29 July the Zhongshang Futures Exchange allowed seat 165 to open new positions of 1,000 lots and 3,150 lots respectively, which, the Court said, violated the stipulations of the CSRC on strictly control of overall amount of positions and prohibition of T+O settlement.[107] In accordance with Articles 84, 106(1) and 130 of the 1986 GPCL,[108] the Court ruled that the Zhongshang Futures Exchange and the Pingyuan company would each bear costs of 18,598,140 yuan for the breach.[109] The Zhongshang Futures Exchange appealed to the Supreme People's Court.

The Supreme People's Court overturned the judgment of the Sichuan High People's Court, citing Article 44 (1) of the 1999 Provisional Regulations on the Administration of Futures Trading,[110] section 5 (1) of the 1995 SPC Futures Judicial Guidelines[111] and Articles 153 (1) (ii) (iii) and 158 of the 1991 Civil Procedure Law.[112] Instead, the Supreme People's Court ruled that the Pingyuan company would repay

---

107　In 1995 the CSRC issued the Circular on Further Control Risks of Futures Market and Sternly Strike Market Manipulation (Guanyu Jinyibu Kongzhi Qihuo Shichang Fengxian, Yanli Daji Caozong Shichang Xingwei de Tongzhi), which stipulated that all the all the futures exchanges must strictly control the total amount of outstanding positions of the market; T+O settlement was prohibited, that is, all the futures exchanges may not allow members to use the margins returned and the profits gained by closing out positions to open new positions on the same day.

108　Article 84 of the 1986 GPCL states that an obligation is a special rights–obligation relationship created between the parties in accordance with the provisions agreed upon in a contract or according to the provision of the law. The person having the right is the oblige. The person bearing the obligation is the obligor. The oblige has the right to demand that the obligor perform his obligation according to the agreement in the contract or according to the provisions of the law. Article 106 (1) states that citizens or legal persons who break a contract or do not perform some other duty must bear civil liability. Article 130 states that when two or more trespassers cause injury to another person, they must bear joint liability.

109　*Supra* note 46, at pp. 27–28.

110　*Supra* note 98.

111　*Supra* note 97.

112　Article 153 (1) (ii) (iii) of the 1991 Civil Procedure Law provides that the appeal court, after trying a case on appeal, shall amend the original judgment according to the law if the application of the law was incorrect in the original judgment; if the facts were incorrectly or not clearly ascertained and the evidence was insufficient in the original judgment, the

the Zhongshang Futures Exchange 29,503,999.14 yuan and applicable interest; all the court costs at both first instance court and appeal court would be borne by the Pingyuan company.[113]

The Supreme People's Court's reasoning was threefold. First, the Court said that, as long as it could be established that the Zhongshang Futures Exchange paid on behalf of the Pingyuan company for the breach of contract, the Pingyuan company should repay the Zhongshang Futures Exchange. This is the only issue the Court should focus on in this case. The issue of division of responsibilities among the parties involved in the trading by seat 165 is a different legal relationship from the issue of claiming repayment by the Zhongshang Futures Exchange, which should not be tried in this proceedings; second, there is no inevitable and causal link between the fact that the Zhongshang Futures Exchange violated relevant regulations and rules and the causes of breach of contract by the Pingyuan company; and third, what the Zhongshang Futures Exchange should bear for the violation of the stipulation of the CSRC on T+0 settlement is an administrative responsibility and the Zhongshang Futures Exchange should not be held liable for the breach of contract jointly with the Pingyuan company.[114] One of the points made in an analysis of this case is that the judgment of the first instance court Sichuan High People's Court was wrong because it confused the liability of the Zhongshang Futures Exchange; what Zhongshang Futures Exchange should bear is an administrative liability not a liability for breach of contract by the Pingyuan company.[115]

Futures exchanges play an important role in futures trading. Smooth and efficient futures trading depends upon a well-regulated futures market and the role played by the futures exchange. In *Ding Wei v Zhengzhou Commodity Exchange*,[116] the Zhengzhou Commodity Exchange was blamed for lacking an appropriate supervision and control mechanism, which created conditions for a serious violation of the rules by some members of the exchange and contributed to the occurrence of the disputes of the case.[117] This was not an isolated case, and one which was particularly common in the early years of China's futures market. The 1999 Provisional Regulations on the Administration of Futures Trading set out a series of regulatory standards for the operation of futures exchanges, such as the requirement for the establishment of a risk reserve fund and other risk management systems[118] and the establishment of a set of comprehensive rules and codes of conduct to supervise and manage trading activities, risk control and working staff of futures exchanges.[119] The 2003 SPC Futures Judicial Provisions, on the other hand, clearly define the compensatory liabilities of futures exchanges in different aspects of futures trading, covering among

---

appeal court shall set aside the judgment and remand the case to the original people's court for retrial or the appeal court may amend the judgment after investing and ascertaining the facts.

113 *Supra* note 46, at p. 30.

114 *Id.* at pp. 28–29.

115 *See* Jiang Bixin (ed.), *supra* note 27, at p. 333.

116 *Id.* at pp. 249–261.

117 *Id.* at p. 260.

118 Article 35, 1999 Provisional Regulations on the Administration of Futures Trading, *supra* note 19.

119 *Id.* art. 55.

others the liabilities in relation to the notification duty of futures exchanges,[120] the trading with overdraft for which a futures exchange is responsible,[121] the forced liquidation measure taken by a futures exchange[122] and the liabilities arising in the process of settlement of physical commodities.[123]

The Financial Futures Market

The financial futures market developed in parallel with the commodity futures market in early years of China's futures market. In June 1993, the State Administration of Foreign Exchange issued the Trial Measures for the Administration of Foreign Exchange Futures Business,[124] which set out basic regulatory rules concerning foreign exchange futures and foreign exchange deposit trading. Two types of business institutions were allowed to engage in foreign exchange futures and deposit trading, that was, those financial institutions which had license to engage in spot foreign exchange dealings as an agent for clients or those joint ventures set up by such financial institutions as a special foreign exchange futures brokerage firm.[125] In both cases, they must have been able to meet certain conditions and be approved by the State Administration of Foreign Exchange.[126] Six currencies were included in the list as applicable currencies.[127] The trading would be done through a foreign futures broker, with whom the Chinese financial institutions or joint ventures were required to sign an agreement and the foreign futures broker would provide market information and other services.[128]

Like the situation in the commodity futures market, illegal activities and excessive speculation became a serious problem in the foreign exchange futures market. Many illegal trading institutions emerged and engaged in foreign exchange futures and deposit trading without authorization from government regulators; the losses suffered by enterprise and individual clients became more and more serious; the stability of financial order was affected.[129] The situation prompted the government to embark on a campaign to crack down on illegal activities in the foreign exchange futures

---

120   Article 25 (1), 2003 SPC Futures Judicial Provisions, *supra* note 35.

121   *Id.* arts 31 (1), 32 (1), 33 (1), 34 (1), 35 (1).

122   *Id.* arts 39, 40.

123   *Id.* arts 45, 47.

124   The Trial Measures for the Administration of Foreign Exchange Futures Business (Waihui Qihuo Yewu Guanli Shixing Banfa), issued by the State Administration of Foreign Exchange on 9 June 1993 upon an approval by the PBOC.

125   Article 3, 1993 Trial Measures for the Administration of Foreign Exchange Futures Business, *Id.*

126   *Id.* arts 9, 10. One of the conditions, for example, was that the applicant had no less than 7 million US dollars in paid-up capital or an equivalent amount of other foreign currencies.

127   They were sterling pound, deutsche mar, Japanese yen, Swiss franc, US dollar, and HK dollar. Article 6, *Id.*

128   *See* Articles 15, 16, *Id.*

129   *See* Circular of the State Administration of Foreign Exchange on Strengthening Foreign Exchange (Futures) Trading (Guojia Waihui Guanliju Guanyu Jiaqiang Waihui

market. Between October 1994 and June 1997, a series of circulars were issued by the government including, among others, the Circular on Sternly Investigating and Dealing with Illegal Trading Activities in Foreign Exchange Futures and Foreign Exchange Deposit Trading.[130] The policy of the government was to suspend the trial of foreign exchange futures and deposit trading for an indefinite time.[131]

The main pattern of disputes arising from the trading of foreign exchange futures or deposits was the disputes between enterprise or individual clients and agent financial institutions or joint ventures, in which the clients lost money in the trading and the agents conducted the trading with various irregularities and violation of regulations. In *Hewei v Changchun Investment Consultancy Center of Jilin Province Jinhui International Investment and Development Co. Ltd. and Jilin Branch of Bank of China*,[132] the plaintiff Hewei lost 84,500 yuan in the trading of foreign exchange deposits; two defendants did not have authorization to engage in foreign exchange futures business.[133] In *Yang Limin v Xinjiang Olympic Development General Company*,[134] the plaintiff Yang Limin lost 316,000 yuan in the trading of foreign exchange deposits; the defendant was not approved to engage in foreign exchange futures business as an agent acting on behalf of clients.[135] In these cases, the people's courts annulled the agreements signed between the plaintiffs and defendants on the ground that the defendants had no authorization to engage in foreign exchange futures business and act on behalf of clients.

A fundamental issue the people's courts had to address in these cases is whether the clients should be compensated for their losses by the defendants. A distinction was made by the people's courts in accordance with the guidelines of the 1995 SPC Futures Judicial Guidelines between those losses which had a direct causal link with the instructions of the clients and those losses which were linked with the acts of the defendants. For the former losses the plaintiffs could not recover from the defendants while for the latter losses the plaintiff could recover. In the case *Hewei v Changchun*

(Qihuo) Jiaoyi Guanli de Tongzhi), issued by the State Administration of Foreign Exchange on 21 April 1993.

130   The Circular on Sternly Investigating and Dealing with Illegal Trading Activities in Foreign Exchange Futures and Foreign Exchange Deposit Trading (Guanyu Yanli Chachu Feifa Waihui Qihuo He Waihui Anjin Jiaoyi Huodong de Tongzhi), issued jointly by the CSRC, the State Administration of Foreign Exchange, the State Administration for Industry and Commerce and the Ministry of Public Security on 28 October 1994.

131   *See* Circular on the Summary of the Meeting of Implementing the Circular on Sternly Investigating and Dealing with Illegal Trading Activities in Foreign Exchange Futures and Foreign Exchange Deposit Trading, *supra* note 17.

132   *See* Cai Xin et al. (eds), *Commentary on Typical Cases and Complement to Legal Deficiency (Dianxing Anli Pingshu Ji Falü Loudong Buchong)* (The People's Court Publishing House, 2002), pp. 445–455.

133   *Id.* at p. 453.

134   *See Essential Selection of Adjudicated Cases in China (Zhongguo Shenpan Anli Yaolan)* (Civil Adjudicated Case Vol. 2001), edited by National Judges College and School of Law of the People's University of China (Beijing: China People's University Press, 2002), pp. 432–435.

135   *Id.* at p. 432.

Investment Consultancy Center of Jilin Province Jinhui International Investment and Development Co. Ltd. and Jilin Branch of Bank of China,[136] the Court established that the losses suffered by the plaintiff Hewei were a result of the order instructed by the plaintiff and executed by the defendants. The plaintiff, the Court said, should bear those losses. But the Court also established that the defendants provided the plaintiff with incorrect trading receipts, which misled the plaintiff, and the defendant also had some other irregularities in the course of advising the plaintiff. On the basis of these findings, the Court ruled that the defendants should bear certain liabilities for the losses.[137]

In the case *Yang Limin v Xinjiang Olympic Development General Company,*[138] the defendant adduced the evidence and proved that it had executed the orders according to the instruction of the plaintiff while the plaintiff adduced insufficient evidence to prove that the defendant had not carried out her instruction on to the market or the defendant had any other fault in carrying out her instruction. The Court also established that the loss suffered by the plaintiff had a direct causal link with her instructions; the illegal operation by the defendant of foreign exchange futures business was not a direct reason for the loss; the defendant had no other fault in acting for the plaintiff. On the grounds of these findings, the Wulu Muqi Intermediate People's Court rejected the plaintiff's claim for compensation. The Court said that the loss suffered by the plaintiff was because of normal trading risks. This decision was upheld by the appeal court Xinjiang High People's Court with the same reasoning and in accordance with the 1995 SPC Futures Judicial Guidelines.[139]

In commenting on the above *Hewei* case, different views were discussed about the legal consequences of an invalid agreement between the plaintiff and defendant. One view argues that the loss of deposits by the plaintiff should be returned to the plaintiff. The defendant had no authorization to act for clients in foreign exchange futures business and the brokerage agreement was thus invalid; the plaintiff should be restored to the status existing before entering into the agreement. The second view argues that the defendant was responsible for the invalid agreement and the plaintiff had no fault in the process; the loss should therefore be borne by the defendant. The third view argues that the loss should be borne according to the fault of each party after the agreement was determined as being null and void. The defendant and plaintiff were both at fault and the loss should be shared by both of them. The fourth view argues that although the defendant had no authorization to act for the plaintiff in foreign exchange futures trading, the loss was directly caused by the order of the plaintiff; the defendant executed the order in accordance with the plaintiff's instruction; the plaintiff should bear the loss caused by market risks; the illegal trading by the defendant without authorization was only an indirect cause and the defendant should not be held liable for the loss.[140] The last view reflected

---

136 *Supra* note 132.
137 *Supra* note 132, at p. 453.
138 *Supra* note 134.
139 Section 7, 1995 SPC Futures Judicial Guidelines, *supra* note 30.
140 *Supra* note 132, at pp. 454–455.

the practice of the people's courts and the position of the 1995 SPC Futures Judicial Guidelines.

As a part of the government crackdown on illegal activities and excessive speculation in the futures market, offshore trading of futures contracts, including financial futures products, was stopped by the government in late 1994.[141] Clients lost their money in the trading of offshore financial futures products and some disputes were ended up in the people's courts. In *Qingyuan City Overseas Chinese Commodity Company v Qingyuan City Tongye International Futures Trading Firm*,[142] the plaintiff lost about 2 million yuan in 1993 in trading, through the defendant, in various commodity and financial futures products of the Chicago Mercantile Exchange, including S&P 500 futures. The defendant was not approved and registered to engage in the trading of offshore futures products. The Court annulled the agreement signed between the defendant and plaintiff and ruled that the defendant return the deposit of the plaintiff. On the other hand, the Court rejected the plaintiff's claim for the further losses apart from the deposit on the ground that the further losses suffered by the plaintiff should not be borne by the defendant.[143] This case, as an example, shows that where there is an invalid contract involving trading of offshore financial futures products, the people's courts decide the issue of division of liabilities between the defendant and plaintiff in accordance with the general principles of the law and regulation and the judicial guidelines applied in other types of futures disputes.

Trading of government bond futures was also a part of the financial futures market in the early 1990s. In February 1995, the CSRC and the Ministry of Finance jointly issued the Provisional Measures on the Administration of Government Bond Futures Trading,[144] which set out regulatory rules concerning the qualifications of government bond futures exchanges and member firms, the trading rules, and management of member firms. In the meantime, trading of government bond futures was dominated by activities of market manipulation. During February 1995, Shanghai Wanguo International Securities, the second largest securities firm in China at that time, wilfully violated trading rules by rigging prices and manipulating the government bond futures market when it sold government bond futures on a large scale to cover positions in excess of permitted limits.[145]

Shortly after this incident, the CSRC issued an urgent circular on 17 May 1995,[146] according to which, starting from 18 May 1995 all the futures exchanges must not

---

141   *See* Circular on Relevant Issues about Cancellation by Futures brokerage firms of Offshore Futures Business, *supra* note 18.

142   *See* Wu Zhipan and Tang Jiemang (eds), *supra* note 55, at pp. 241–250.

143   *Id.* at p. 243.

144   The Provisional Measures on the Administration of Government Bond Futures Trading (Guozhai Qihuo Jiaoyi Guanli Zanxing Banfa), issued by the CSRC and the Ministry of Finance on 23 February 1995.

145   For more details, *see* Zhu Sanzhu, *Securities Regulation in China* (Ardsley, NY: Transnational Publishers, 2000), p. 121 and accompanying footnote 69.

146   The Urgent Circular on Suspension of Trials of Government Bond Futures Trading (Guoyu Zanting Guozhai Qihuo Jiaoyi Shidian de Jinji Tongzhi), issued by the CSRC on 17 May 1995.

allow their members to open any new positions and all the existing positions must be closed out by the end of 31 May 1995. The reason given by the CSRC for the closure of the government bond futures market was threefold. First, several serious incidents of violation of regulations had occurred in the trading of government bond futures in the past few months, which brought about serious adverse effects both inside and outside China; second, basic conditions were not ready in China for development of a government futures trading market; and third, the closure measure was necessary to maintain economic and social stability and to protect healthy development of the financial market.[147] After ten years, in 2005, the trading of government bond futures and financial bond futures finally resumed on the inter-bank bond market.[148]

Summary

The establishment of the Zhengzhou Commodity Exchange in October 1990 marked the emergence of a futures market in China in the wake of economic reform and development. In the following few years, the experiment of the commodity and financial futures trading proved to be problematic and the futures market became a "big litigation family", generating a high rate of disputes and litigation. This chapter looks at the disputes in some aspects of the commodity and financial futures market and examine the way in which the disputes are dealt with by the people's courts. In conclusion, followings points summarize the above discussions in this chapter.

First, the experiment of commodity and financial futures markets in China since the late 1980s has gone through a tortuous passage. In the early years of its emergence, the market was dominated by market manipulation, unauthorized trading by numerous futures firms, irregularities of various kinds and excessive speculation. The market manipulation incident in the government bond futures market in February 1995 is just one example.[149] The crackdown campaign embarked upon by the government from 1993 to 1999 to stop chaotic situations and a blind development of futures market led to a substantial reduction of number of futures exchanges, cancellation of certain futures products, suspension of offshore futures trading and closure of government bond futures market. From the point of view of the government, the conditions in China were not ready for anything more than an experiment involving a selected number of futures products in a limited number of futures exchanges. The government's priority was to maintain social stability and public confidence and the stability of the financial market.

Second, the people's courts were faced with an increasing number of disputes arising from commodity and financial futures trading soon after the emergence of the futures market in China. These disputes involved new and difficult issues concerning every stage of futures trading, and which the people's courts had not dealt with before. Based on the general principles of civil law and contract law, the 1995 SPC Futures Judicial Guidelines was a comprehensive response from the Supreme People's Court to the problem of an increasing number of futures disputes

---

147   *Id.*
148   *Supra* note 26 and accompanying text.
149   *Supra* note 145.

coming into the people's courts. The promulgation by the Supreme People's Court of the 2003 SPC Futures Judicial Provisions represents a unified understanding and approach among the people's courts, the regulators and the futures business on major civil law issues concerning the futures market and disputes involving the futures market;[150] general principles of law and regulation and gave consideration to the special features of the futures market.

Third, the adjudication experiences of the futures disputes by the people's courts discussed in this chapter show that one of the guiding principles is to deal with these cases fairly and to correctly balance and protect lawful rights and interest of the parties. In the cases involving qualification to engage in futures trading, the people's courts try to draw a line between the losses the plaintiffs should bear themselves and the losses for which the defendants should be held liable;[151] in the cases involving forced liquidation measures taken by futures exchanges or futures brokerage firms, rules have been developed that define under what circumstances the futures exchanges or futures brokerage firms should be liable for the losses occurred in connection with a forced liquidation measure they have taken;[152] in the cases involving the responsibility of futures exchanges, the rights and obligations of futures exchanges are defined and these rules have been applied by the people's courts;[153] in the cases involving offshore trading of commodities or financial futures, applicable international rules and practices are respected by the people's courts in their adjudication in order to reach an appropriate and correct decision.[154]

Fourth, on the other hand, in the process of understanding the nature of the futures market and the new issues arising from the cases of futures disputes, wrong judgments were made by the people's courts, particularly in the early years of China's futures market when there was a lack of rules, regulations and judicial guidelines. In most of the early cases involving qualification to engage in futures trading, the people's courts ruled in favor of the clients, requesting the brokerage firms who engaged in unauthorized futures trading to return lost deposits to the clients, which was criticized by commentators as a wrong approach resulting from a lack of correct understanding by some people's courts of the legal relationship between brokerage, clients and futures trading.[155] The judgment of the first instance court in the case *Hainan Zhongqing Jiye Development Center v Sichuan Pingyuan Industrial Development Co.*[156] was viewed as a wrong judgment and one of the reasons was because the Court confused the civil liability for breach of contract

---

150   *Supra* note 36.

151   *See*, for example, *Zhongyuan Grain & Oil Trading Co. v Zhumadian Region Yinfeng Co. and Zhumadian Region Vegetable Oil Co.*, *supra* notes 58, 59, 60, 61 and accompanying text.

152   *See supra* note 81.

153   *See Hainan Zhongqing Jiye Development Center v Sichuan Pingyuan Industrial Development Co.*, *supra* notes 105 to 115 and accompanying text.

154   *See Zhaoxiaomei v Nanjing Jinzhongfu International Futures Trading Co. Ltd.*, *supra* notes 82, 83, 84 and accompanying text.

155   *Supra* note 55 and accompanying text.

156   *Supra* note 105.

with the administrative liability for which the plaintiff futures exchange should be held.[157]

Fifth, proper regulation of the futures market in China is important. The 1999 Provisional Regulations on the Administration of Futures Trading and the four implementing rules from the CSRC, as a whole, gives an impetus to the process of standardization of China's new futures market and helps the people's courts in dealing with futures disputes. But, on the other hand, the provisions of the 1999 Provisional Regulations on the Administration of Futures Trading could have been improved;[158] inconsistency between the regulations and judicial guidelines could have been eliminated.[159] Before 1999, many separate pieces of regulations and regulatory documents were issued, some of which were mentioned in this chapter. This pattern of regulation, which is prone to inconsistency, continues. Since late 1999 a limited number of state-owned enterprises were allowed to engage in trading of offshore commodities futures for hedging purposes upon an approval by the government regulators and a group of related regulatory documents was thus issued;[160] the trading of government bond futures and financial bond futures was resumed in June 2005 on the inter-bank bond market and a group of related regulations and trading rules was promulgated.[161] In this respect, a Futures Law, the drafting of which was suspended,[162] is necessary to provide for uniform principles and rules for the future development of China's futures market.

---

157   *Supra* note 115 and accompanying text.

158   For example, Article 41 has been criticized as being inadequate. *Supra* note 80 and accompanying text.

159   For example, regarding forced liquidation, different Chinese words are used, which indicate that the forced liquidation is either a right or an obligation. *Supra* notes 69, 70, 71 and accompanying text.

160   *Supra* note 18.

161   *Supra* note 26 and accompanying text.

162   *Supra* note 4.

Chapter 6

Civil Litigation Arising from False Statements on the Securities Market

Introduction

After the emergence of China's securities market in late 1980s and the establishment of Shanghai and Shenzhen stock exchanges in 1990 and 1991 respectively, China's securities regulatory authority and Chinese courts faced problems on how best to tackle various forms of securities fraud in order to protect the interests of investors and to maintain the integrity of China's securities market. Between September 2001 and January 2003, the Supreme People's Court (SPC) issued three circulars instructing local people's courts on how to deal with civil compensation claims arising from securities market fraud.[1] On 15 January 2002, intermediate people's courts designated by the SPC began to accept and hear civil compensation cases arising from false statements on China's securities market, marking the beginning of civil litigation in the people's court in relation to these claims.[2] This development, welcomed by the market and investors, makes it possible for investors to claim losses suffered as a result of false statements. However, there are problems and limitations in the circulars issued by the SPC, which raises serious concerns among judges, academics and practitioners. This chapter primarily examines the procedural rules prescribed by the third circular of the SPC, Several Provisions of the Supreme People's Court on Hearing Civil Compensation Cases Arising from False Statement on the Securities Market (hereinafter "Rules of the SPC"), with a focus on the limitations of these rules.[3]

---

1   The Notice of the Supreme People's Court on Temporary Refusal of Filings of Securities-Related Civil Compensation Cases (Zuigao remin fayuan guanyu she zhengquan minshi peichang anjian zan buyu shouli de tongzhi), 21 September 2001; The Notice of the Supreme People's Court on Relevant Issues of Filing of Civil Tort Dispute Cases Arising From False Statement on the Securities Market (Zuigao renmin fayuan guanyu shouli zhengquan shichang yin xujiachengshu yinfa de minshi qinquan jiufen anjian youguan wenti de tongzhi), 15 January 2002; Several Provisions of the Supreme People's Court on Hearing Civil Compensation Cases Arising From False Statement on the Securities Market (Zuigao renmin fayuan guanyu shenli zhengquan shichang yin xujiachengshu yinfa de minshi peichang anjian de ruogan guiding), 9 January 2003.

2   The Second Circular of the SPC designated certain intermediate people's courts to accept and hear civil compensation cases arising from false statement, starting from 15 January 2002, the effective date of the Second Circular of the SPC.

3   The Rules of the SPC were adopted by the Judicial Committee of the Supreme People's Court on 26 December 2002, and promulgated on 9 January 2003 and effective from

China's securities regulatory authority has been active in the past decade, tackling various forms of securities fraud on the market by means of administrative penalties and criminal charges, with an aim to protect investors and the integrity of the securities market.[4] The 1993 Provisional Measures on Prohibition of Securities Fraud were introduced specifically to deal with insider trading, market manipulation, false disclosure of information and other forms of securities fraud.[5] Similar provisions were promulgated in the 1993 Provisional Regulations on Share Issuing and Trading,[6] the 1993 Company Law,[7] and the 1998 Securities Law,[8] along with other securities rules and regulations issued by the CSRC and Shanghai and Shenzhen stock exchanges. For the first time, the revised 1997 Criminal Law created securities-related criminal offences that principally targeted various forms of securities fraud.[9] As a result, many firms and individuals who committed securities fraud have been investigated and punished by the CSRC, the principal regulator of the securities industry in China.[10] When criminal offences are committed, detected and tried, those offenders found guilty have been subject to punishments by criminal courts.[11]

---

1 February 2003 (Translation available at http://www.lawinfochina.com).

4   *See* Zhu Sanzhu (2000), *Securities Regulation in China* (Ardsley, NY: Transnational Publishers), pp. 117–25, 187–206.

5   Promulgated by then-Securities Committee of the State Council on 2 September 1993, and was effective immediately.

6   Promulgated by the State Council on 22 April 1993, and was effective immediately. According to Article 72, those who commit insider trading are subject to a fine between 50,000 to 500,000 yuan in addition to confiscation of illegal gain.

7   Adopted by the Standing Committee of the 8th National People's Congress on 29 December 1993, effective from 1 July 1994, and amended by the Standing Committee of the 9th NPC on 25 December 1999. Article 212 states that where companies provide shareholders and the public with false financial reports or conceal material facts, the person in charge or other directly responsible person shall be fined between 10,000 and 100,000 yuan and charged where crimes are committed.

8   Adopted by the Standing Committee of the 9th National People's Congress on 29 December 1998, and effective 1 July 1999. Article 5 states generally that securities fraud, insider trading and market manipulation are prohibited.

9   The 1979 Criminal Law was revised by the 8th National People's Congress on 14 March 1997, and became effective on 1 October 1 1997 (it was later amended in December 1999, August 2001, December 2001 and most recently December 2002). Articles 160, 161, 180, 181 and 182 are concerned with offenses of false disclosure, insider trading and market manipulation.

10   *See* China's Security Regulatory Commission's website at http://www.csrc.gov.cn. Between January 1994 to November 2003, the CSRC made over 300 administrative penalty decisions concerning securities frauds committed by listed companies, securities companies, accounting firms, law firms, individual directors, managers and other senior persons of these companies.

11   According to Li Guoguang, the deputy president of the Supreme People's Court, forty-six securities fraud cases, including cases involving false statement, insider trading and market manipulation, were charged and tried by the people's courts between 1997 and the end of 2001 in accordance with the revised 1997 Criminal Law. *See* Li Guoguang, "Gaofa Fuyuanzhang

On the other hand, these laws and regulations have not provided adequate protection for the rights and interests of investors who suffered economic losses as a result of securities fraud.[12] This remains a fundamental weakness of the system. Compared with the comprehensive administrative sanctions for securities fraud, there are very limited provisions in the 1993 Provisional Regulations on Share Issuing and Trading that involve civil liability and civil compensation when dealing with securities fraud.[13] Although the 1998 Securities Law strengthened the regulation of securities market and, as the first securities law in China, it brought the national securities market and the regulation into a new stage, though it failed to strengthen provisions concerning civil liability and civil compensation.[14] In the meantime, the number of listed companies on the Shanghai and Shenzhen stock exchanges dramatically increased from less than twenty in the early 1990s to 851 in 1998.[15] Additionally, the number of market investors expanded from about two million in 1992 to approximately forty million in 1998.[16] This rapid development was inevitably accompanied by a rise in the number of securities fraud cases and victim investors, whose losses were compounded by the indifference and apathy of courts which refused to hear the victims' claims.[17] Lawyers, academics and investors alike lobbied to the SPC, calling for the people's court to accept and hear these cases.[18]

Li Guoguang Xishuo Guojia Jinrong Anquan de Sifa Baozhang" ("Deputy President of the Supreme People's Court Li Guoguang Talks in Detail about Judicial Protection for the State Financial Safety"), *News Weekly*, 23 July 2002, http://www.ccmt.org.cn (Zhongguo Shewai Sangshi Haishi Shenpan Wang) (China Foreign-Related Commercial and Maritime Trial Website).

12 The provisions found in these laws and regulations are thin and incomplete concerning civil liabilities of securities fraud and civil compensation to the investors who suffered economic losses as a result of securities fraud, *infra* notes 13 and 14.

13 Article 77 in the 1993 Provisional Regulations on Share Issuing and Trading is the only article that touches the issue of civil liability and compensation. It simply states: "where the provision of this regulation is violated and losses are caused to others, it shall bear liabilities for civil compensation according to law".

14 Articles 67 to 71, 183 and 184 in the 1998 Securities Law deal with market manipulation and insider trading, which have no stipulations on related civil liabilities. Only Article 63 expressly mentions civil liability and compensation of losses caused by the false recording, misleading statement, and material omission made by issuers and securities companies.

15 CSRC, *Introduction to China's Securities Market*, http://www.csrc.gov.cn.

16 *Id.*

17 According to Li Guoguang, deputy president of the SPC, none of the civil claims brought and filed in the people's courts between 1991 and 2002 as a result of insider trading, market manipulation and false statement was continued to the stage of substantial hearing. *See* Li Guogang, *supra* note 11.

18 Guo Feng, a Beijing-based lawyer and academic who participated in drafting the Securities Law in early 1990s, actively took part in the campaign together with others on behalf of grieved investors calling for the people's court to accept and hear civil compensation claims arising from securities frauds. *See* Susan V. Lawrence, "Shareholder Lawsuits: Ally of the People", *Far Eastern Economic Review*, 9 May 2002, p. 27.

In response, the first circular of the SPC, issued on 21 September 2001, instructed local people's courts to continue to ignore all civil compensation claims arising from insider trading, market manipulation, and other securities frauds.[19] The reason given by the SPC for not accepting such cases was that the people's courts "do not have necessary conditions to accept and hear such cases due to current legislative and judicial limitations."[20] The second circular, issued four months later, partially reversed the position of the first circular by instructing local intermediate people's courts to accept and hear cases arising from false statement, but not those arising from insider trading or market manipulation.[21] The third circular, issued on 9 January 2003, expanded on the second circular, setting out more detailed procedural rules for dealing with false statement cases.[22] These procedural rules, in conjunction with the relevant provisions in the 1991 Civil Procedure Law,[23] the 1998 Securities Law, and other relevant laws and regulations, finally provided local intermediate people's courts with the guidelines necessary needed to address compensation claims arising from securities-related false statements.

This chapter first explores the elements of false statement and liability under the Rules of the SPC. An analysis of the details of the Rules of SPC from an investor-plaintiff's point of view follows, highlighting the procedural steps of the claim and the restrictions imposed by the Rules of the SPC. This is followed by an examination of the defendants' liabilities and the manner in which investors' losses are calculated and compensated – the central concern of the Rules of the SPC. Finally, this chapter considers the limitations of the Rules of the SPC as they pertain to investor protection, the future development of China's securities market and market regulation.

False Statements and the Defendant

The Rules of the SPC begin by defining the widely used phrase "civil compensation cases arising from false statement on the securities market" (*zhengquan shichang yin xujia chenshu yinfa de minshi peichang anjian*).[24] Because the false statement (*xujia chenshu*) is the central basis that gives rise to a cause of action for civil compensation, it is essential to understand what constitutes a false statement in China's securities

---

19 *See* the Notice of the Supreme People's Court on Temporary Refusal of Filings of Securities-Related Civil Compensation Cases, *supra* note 1.

20 *Id.*

21 *See* the Notice of the Supreme People's Court on Relevant Issues of Filing of Civil Tort Dispute Cases Arising From False Statement on the Securities Market, *supra* note 1.

22 *See* Rules of the SPC, *supra* note 3.

23 Adopted by the 7th National People's Congress on 9 April 1991, effective the same day. The 1991 Civil Procedure Law replaced the 1982 Civil Procedure Law (Trial Implementation).

24 Article 1 defines the civil compensation case arising from false statement on the securities market as "the civil compensation case brought to the people's court by the investors of securities market who have suffered losses as a result of the false statement made in violation of the law by those who have a duty to disclose information". Rules of the SPC, *supra* note 3.

market under the Rules of the SPC and who could be held liable for involvement in making such false statement.

False Statement

According to Article 17 of the Rules of the SPC, a false statement on the securities market is defined as a false recording (*xujia jizai*), misleading statement (*wudaoxing chenshu*), material omission (*zhongda yilou*) or improper disclosure (*bu zhengdang pilou*), all of which are made against the true fact of major events by those who have a duty to disclose information on the securities market.[25] Article 17 further defines these four types of false statements: (1) a false recording occurs when those who have a duty to disclose information present non-existing facts in disclosure documents; (2) the misleading statement is made by wrongdoers in disclosure documents or announcement to the media which influences investors to act, resulting in significant detriment to their investments; (3) a material omission is the failure to disclose, either wholly or partially, required information by one with the duty to have done so; (4) improper disclosure occurs when one who has a duty to disclose information, but fails to do so within an appropriate time frame or in the appropriate manner prescribed by law.[26] According to Article 17 of the Rules of the SPC, major events (*zhongda shijian*) should be determined by referring to relevant provisions of 1998 Securities Law.[27]

Both the 1998 Securities Law and the 1993 Provisional Regulations on Share Issuing and Trading identify three types of false statements, namely false recordings (*xujia jizai*), misleading statements (*wudaoxing chenshu*) and material omissions (*zhongda yilou*)[28] – these are identical to the aforementioned three types of false statement under the Rules of the SPC. Unlike the Rules of the SPC, the 1998 Securities Law does not define these three types of false statements.[29] Likewise, the case for the 1993 Provisional Regulations on Share Issuing and Trading identifies

---

25 Rules of the SPC, *supra* note 3, art. 17 (paragraph 1).

26 *Id.* at art. 17 (paragraphs 3–6).

27 Relevant provisions of the 1998 Securities Law include Articles 59, 60, 61, 62 and 72, which are expressly listed by Article 17 of the Rules of the SPC. Article 62 is directly relevant, and states: "when major events take place which may have a material affect on the trading price of shares of a listed company and investors are not aware of them, the company shall promptly report such events to the CSRC and the stock exchange". Article 62 further sets out a list of the major events including, among others: material change of business, major investment, important contract, material debt or loss incurred, and change of senior management staff. Articles 60 and 61 set out basic statutory requirements for interim and annual reports. Article 59 imposes an obligation to companies to disclose information in issuing and listing documents truthfully and completely. Article 72 prohibits relevant individuals and organizations from making false statements on securities trading market. Rules of the SPC, *supra* note 3, art. 17 (paragraph 2).

28 1998 Securities Law, arts 24, 59, 63 and 177; 1993 Provisional Regulations on Share Issuing and Trading, arts 17, 21, 73 and 74.

29 *See* 1998 Securities Law, arts 24, 59, 63 and 177.

the same three types of false statement, but without their respective definitions.[30] Therefore, it is helpful that the Rules of SPC not only reiterate the position of the 1998 Securities Law and 1993 Provisional Regulations on Share Issuing and Trading but also provide further definitions, albeit brief, for three types of false statement. Improper disclosure[31] is not prescribed by the 1998 Securities Law and 1993 Provisional Regulations on Share Issuing and Trading.[32] It is an offense unique to the Rules of the SPC, where it is included in the definition of false statement with the original three elements.[33]

As a result, the issue is whether improper disclosure alone can be treated as a "false statement," thus constituting independent ground for civil compensation action by investors. In other words, should the definition of false statement be broadly or narrowly interpreted? There is no clear indication in the Rules of the SPC that improper disclosure alone can constitute a false statement resulting in a civil compensation action by investors.[34] What remains to be determined is whether the Rules of the SPC intend improper disclosure to be an integrated element of the definition of false statement or a separate ground for civil action. There is no doubt that an essential requirement of the 1998 Securities Law is that disclosures should be timely and made in a manner prescribed by applicable law and regulations.[35] However, it is beyond the scope of the 1998 Securities Law definition of false statement[36] if an action is brought to the people's court claiming false statement based either on a defendants' failure to disclose required information within an appropriate time limit, or on a failure to disclose in newspaper designated by CSRC.[37] Looking at both cases dealt with by the CSRC and at cases brought to the people's court to date, punishable false statements normally fall into the three categories of false statement listed by the 1998 Securities Law.[38]

---

30   1993 Provisional Regulations on Share Issuing and Trading, arts 17, 21, 73 and 74.

31   More specifically, the delay or outright failure to disclose required information in a manner not prescribed by law and regulations.

32   The term "improper disclosure" is not found throughout the 1998 Securities Law and the 1993 Provisional Regulations on Share Issuing and Trading.

33   Article 61 of the 1998 Securities Law requires listed companies to submit their annual reports within four months from the end of a financial year, while Article 62 requires listed companies to make a prompt report of major events to the CSRC and the stock exchange. Article 63 of the 1993 Provisional Regulations on Share Issuing and Trading requires listed companies to disclose information to the national newspapers designated by the CSRC. Rules of the SPC, *supra* note 3, art. 17 (paragraph 6).

34   Rules of the SPC, *supra* note 3, art. 17.

35   *See* 1998 Securities Law, arts 61, 62, 110 and 177.

36   This must be in accordance with Article 17 of the Rules of the SPC.

37   1998 Securities Law prescribes only three types of false statements, namely, false recordings, misleading statements and material omissions.

38   Take the case involving Chengdu Hongguang Industrial Shareholding Company as an example. It is a typical case dealt with by the CSRC. Hongguang company specialized in the production of electron vacuum devices such as black and white and color television tubes and glass bulbs. When Hongguang made its public offering in June 1997, the company issued seventy million A shares, which raised 410.2 million yuan. Suspicion was generated by the great disparity between Hongguang's projected profits in its prospectus and actual profits after

There are different scholarly views on the definition of false statement under China's securities law, and such views depart on the nature, manner and classification of false statements.[39] One point equally emphasized by scholars is that false statements should relate to major or material events.[40] Such events should include: (1) existing material facts that may affect the price of securities; (2) material changes to existing facts or situations that may affect the price of securities and (3) material information composed of material facts and material changes that may affect the price of securities.[41] Article 17 of the Rules of the SPC indicates that false statements are related to material events.[42] The three-fold significance of this connection is as follows: (1) it clarifies the position of the 1998 Securities Law since the false recording and misleading statements are not clearly prescribed to the terms of material event; (2) it sets out criteria for plaintiffs and defendants to argue before the court when debating the existence of a causal link between false statements and losses and (3) it could have a positive effect on the securities market, because companies and investors would focus on key information and reduce other unnecessary information on the market, which could reduce the cost incurred by companies on disclosing information.[43]

Defendants

Those who make false statements directly or indirectly could be liable to investors in a civil suit. Article 7 of the Rules of the SPC, in accordance with relevant provisions

---

its IPO. In October 1998, the CSRC imposed sanctions to the company and thirteen directors after an investigation, which found that at the time of applying for listing, the company falsely reported its 1996 profits and concealed a major event when it did not disclose problems relating to a key production line. After the listing, the company defrauded investors by underreporting the company's losses in 1997 interim and annual reports and misusing capital raised from the offering. In the prospectus it was stated that all the capital raised would be used for expansion of color television tube production line. In fact, only 16.5% of the capital raised was used for this purpose, with the remaining used for paying back bank loans and making up for past losses, which the company never disclosed as a major event. The CSRC fined Hongguang one million yuan and confiscated 4.5 million yuan and banned He Xingyi, chairman of the board of directors, permanently from serving at senior management level any listed company or securities company. *See* Daniel M. Anderson, "Taking Stock in China: Company Disclosure and Information in China's Stock Markets", *Georgetown Law Journal*, Vol. 88, 1999–2000, pp. 1919–1952 at pp. 1931–33. For the CSRC's penalty decision, *see* Chufa Jueding (Penalty Decision) (promulgated by the CSRC, 26 October 1998), CSRC investigation series number (1998) 75, http://www.csrc.gov.cn.

    39 *See* Huan Xiding and Xu Qinzhong, "On False Statements in the Securities Law" ("Shilun Zhengquanfa Zhong de Xujia Chenshu"), *Zhengfa Xuekan* (*Journal of Political Science and Law*), No. 4, 2001, at pp. 22–25.

    40 *Id.* at pp. 22–23.

    41 *See* Guo Feng, "Determination of Tort of False Statement and Compensation" (Xujia Chenshu Qingquan de Rending ji Peichang), *Zhongguo Faxue* (*China Legal Science*), No. 2, 2003, at p. 96.

    42 Rules of the SPC, *supra* note 3, art. 17 (paragraphs 1 and 2).

    43 *See* Guo Feng, *supra* note 41, at p. 97.

of 1998 Securities Law and 1993 Provisional Regulations on Share Issuing and Trading,[44] provides a specific list of possible defendants. This list includes a wide range of companies, organizations and individuals.[45] It is noteworthy that promoters, controlling shareholders, and those who exercise actual control over the company are named at the top of the list; this is an important provision that would have a significant impact in practice.[46] It is significant that directors, supervisors, managers and other senior management personnel employed by issuers, listed companies, securities underwriters or securities listing sponsors could become defendants if they are responsible for make false statements.[47] The same duty to refrain from making false statements binds persons in accounting, law or asset-evaluation firms.[48] The Rules of the SPC do not specifically mention the position of those companies or organizations involving foreign parties, such as joint ventures, but they could become defendants in the same way, as per Article 7 of the Rules of the SPC.[49]

Compared with the Second Circular of the SPC, where possible defendants are not named in a specific list but only mentioned briefly in the context of courts' jurisdictions over such civil lawsuits, the current Rules of the SPC provide a more specific and a

---

44 Securities Law, *supra* note 8, at arts 24, 63, 72, 161, 202; Share Issuing and Trading, *supra* note 6, at art. 17.

45 Article 7 of the Rules of the SPC, *supra* note 3, states: "The defendants to the civil compensation claims arising from securities-related false statement should be those who make false statements, including (1) promoters, controlling shareholders and the like who exercise actual control; (2) issuers or listed companies; (3) securities underwriters; (4) securities listing sponsors; (5) professional intermediaries including accountant firms, law firms and asset valuation firms; (6) responsible directors, supervisors, managers and other senior management personnel of the issuers, listed companies, securities underwriters, or securities listing sponsors; directly responsible persons of professional intermediaries; and (7) other organizations or individual persons who make false statements."

46 Jia Wei, a judge of the Supreme People's Court who participated in the drafting of the Rules of the SPC, thinks that it has a positive and practical significance to highlight promoters and controlling shareholders on the list as defendants to be sued by investors. *See* Jia Wei, "The Commencement of Civil Liability for the Tort on the Securities Market – Explanation and Analysis of 'Several Provisions of the Supreme People's Court on Hearing Civil Compensation Cases Arising from False Statements on the Securities Market'" (Zhengquan Shichang Qinquan Minshi Zeren zhi Faren – Jiexi "Guanyu Shenli Zhengquan Shichang Yin Xujia Chenshu Yinfa de Minshi Peichang Anjian de Ruogan Guiding"), *Falü Shiyong (Application of Law)*, No. 3, 2003, at p. 9

47 *Id.* at p. 7.

48 Rules of the SPC, *supra* note 3, art. 7 (5), *supra* note 45.

49 Beijing KPMG Zhenhua, a joint venture accountant firm, and Hong Kong KPMC accountant firm become defendants in Jinggang B share case filed to the Intermediate People's Court of Shenyang city on 9 February 2003, for their role involved in the false statement made by Jingzhou Gangwu company, whose B share was listed on the Shanghai Stock Exchange in May 1998. *See Shenyang Zhongyuan Shenli Jinggang B Gu An, Bimawei Fenzhi Jigou Cheng Beigao (Shenyang Intermediate People's Court Hear Jinggang B Share Case, KPMG Branch Office Becomes Defendant)*, 11 February 2003, http://www.chinacourt.org (hereinafter *Shenyang*).

clearer list of possible defendants and the scope has been much widened.[50] Investors may, according to the Rules of the SPC, sue any one of the possible defendants on the list as individual defendant, or sue all of them as joint defendants.[51] Significantly, Article 7 of the Rules of the SPC leaves the list open by concluding with "other organizations and individual persons who make false statements."[52] In other words, whoever makes false statements should be held liable. This leaves courts with substantial leeway. Obvious cases include newspapers, television or other media who knowingly participate in making false statements to the public. Difficulty may arise in deciding less obvious cases, for example, where the role played by organizations or individuals is indirect.[53] Under such circumstances, it may not be easy for a local intermediate people's court to draw a clear line determining who should be made a defendant without further guidelines from the SPC. Nevertheless, the Rules of the SPC's provision on possible defendants, together with the provisions on defendants' liability, will certainly benefit investors.[54] In addition, it could play a preventative function by sending out a warning signal to those who are involved in securities-related disclosure of information one way or another.

Procedural Rules

Before investors go to the people's courts to claim compensation for their losses resulting from false statements, there must be an administrative penalty decision or a criminal court judgment made against the wrongdoers for their false statements.[55] On this basis, the people's court is afforded jurisdiction to hear investor's cases. After this initial procedural step, claimant investors face a series of issues addressed by the Rules of the SPC, including the following: (1) under what conditions will the people's courts can accept their cases? (2) which courts have jurisdiction to hear their claims? (3) what is the relevant statue of limitation period and how is it calculated? (4) what are the forms of action claimant investors can choose for their lawsuits? and (5) what is the role of mediation in their respective proceeding?

Administrative Penalty Decisions and Criminal Court Judgments

One of the restrictive provisions stipulated in the Second Circular of the SPC was that the people's court could not accept civil compensation lawsuits by investors arising from securities-related, false statements.[56] The only exception is if the CSRC or its regional office had already investigated the alleged false statements and imposed an administrative penalty on which investors could rely as a factual basis

---

50 *See* Second Circular of the SPC, *supra* note 1, art. 5.

51 Rules of the SPC, *supra* note 3, art. 12.

52 Rules of the SPC, *supra* note 3, art. 7 (7), *supra* note 45.

53 *See* Sheng Huanwei and Zhu Chuan, *infra* note 71, at pp. 101–102.

54 *See* the discussion under "Defendants' Liability and Compensation of Investors' Losses".

55 Rules of the SPC, *supra* note 3, art. 6.

56 Second Circular of the SPC, *supra* note 1, art. 2.

of their actions.[57] This restrictive rule has not been changed under the current Rules of the SPC, except that criminal judgments by the people's courts and administrative penalty decisions made by authorities other than the CSRC or its regional offices are now recognized.[58] Therefore, the people's court may hear such civil compensation actions in addition to the administrative penalty decisions made by the CSRC or its regional offices.[59]

In accordance with the Rules of the SPC, investors can go to the people's court if the alleged false statement has been investigated by one of these authorities and a sanction has been imposed.[60] This rule has both procedural and evidentiary effects. Procedurally, investors may commence litigation if there is an administrative or criminal sanction, regardless of the content of sanction documents.[61] Evidentially, the effect is that the facts concluded in the sanction documents are treated as evidence in civil litigation.[62] It has no conclusive effect with regard to the scope of defendants not named in sanction documents, and plaintiffs can decide who to sue as defendant in addition to the named defendants. In other words, administrative or criminal sanctions are treated only as a basis for the court to accept cases, not as a basis for determining defendants in the civil suit. This is regarded as beneficial for investors by allowing them to choose whom to sue and whom not to sue. Therefore, the investor may enlarge or limit the number of defendants beyond the sanction document.[63]

Although it is a positive step that the Rules of the SPC have expanded the reach of authorities whose penalty decisions are recognized as a prerequisite for acceptance of civil actions by the people's courts, this prerequisite rule, together with its original format stipulated in the Second Circular of the SPC, has nevertheless suffered a

---

57 *Id.*

58 Rules of the SPC, *supra* note 3, art. 5. Administrative penalty decisions made by authorities other than the CSRC and its regional offices include the decision made by the Ministry of Finance as well as decisions made by other authorities and institutions that have power to impose administrative penalties. In accordance with Articles 16, 17, 18 of the 1996 Administrative Penalty Law, whether an organization has power to impose administrative penalty, except those which limit personal freedom, is primarily a matter decided by the State Council, provincial or autonomous region governments. Further, the organization has to be one with a function to administer public affairs.

59 *Id.*

60 The majority of cases filed in the people's court so far are based upon the penalty decisions of the CSRC and its regional offices or criminal court judgments. The Jinggang B share case, which was filed in the Intermediate People's Court of Shenyang city on 9 February 2003, is the first case based upon a penalty decision made by the Ministry of Finance in September 2002 against Jingzhou Gangwu company for the false statement it made in connection with the listing of its B share in 1998. For the news report of the case, see *Shenyang, supra* note 49.

61　　　　*See* Song Yixing, "Thoughts on Several Issues of the Litigation System for Civil Compensation Arising from False Statements" (Xujia Chenshu Minshi Peichang Susong Zhidu Ruogan Wenti de Sikao), *Falü Shiyong (Application of Law)*, Vol. 4, 2003, at p. 9 (discussing more on the procedural and evidential effects of the rule).

62 *Id.*

63 *Id.*

great deal of criticism. The main criticism is that allowing angry shareholders to flood the people's court would have adverse social and political repercussions.[64] Others criticize the rule from a legal and procedural point of view. In their view this restrictive rule in fact reduces the civil litigation process based on the availability of administrative decisions or criminal court judgments, though this has no statutory basis in the 1991 Civil Procedure Law and effectively limits and thereby deprives of investors' civil litigation rights.[65] Further, critics assert that the expanded rules deprive investors of the right to bring a civil claim supplementary to a criminal proceeding in accordance with the 1996 Criminal Procedure Law.[66] In both critiques, the SPC is chastised for exceeding its judicial interpretation power.

One of the possible consequences of this rule is that it encourages makers of false statements to use either social connections or bribery to influence the administrative investigation in order to escape civil litigation and civil compensation.[67] It is true that administrative processes in China[68] are not as transparent as court proceedings where cases are tried openly. It is therefore possible that an administrative investigation process may be influenced behind the scenes by personal connections, local protections or political forces. For example, it has been noted that the timing of the investigation and the inability of the CSRC to pursue five directors involved in the case of Hainan Minyuan Modern Agricultural Company was suspect for political reasons as well as personal connections.[69] The process can even be hijacked by wrongdoers or their

---

64 *See* Lawrence, *supra* note 18 at p. 27 (stating that "so for many officials, angry shareholders organizing themselves into nationwide networks for the purpose of lawsuits spells trouble"). *See also* William I. Friedman, "One Country, Two Systems: The Inherent Conflict Between China's Communist Politics and Capitalist Securities Market", *Brooklyn Journal of International Law*, Vol. 27, 2001–2002, p. 477 (describing "stock fever" in China and citizens on several occasions have taken to the streets and rioted against police for the mere opportunity to engage in securities market).

65 *See* Guiping Lu, "Private Enforcement of Securities Fraud Law in China: A Critique of the Supreme People's Court 2003 Provisions Concerning Private Securities Litigation", *Pacific Rim Law and Policy Journal*, 2003, 781, 795–98; *see also* Yin Jie, "On the System of Civil Liability of Securities-Related False Statements" ("Zhengquan Xujia Chenshu Minshi Zheren Zhidu Lun"), *Fauxe* (*Legal Science*), Vol. 6, 2003, at pp. 110–11.

66 *See* Tu Binhua, "On the Mechanism for Civil Compensation Liabilities for Securities-related False Statements" ("Zhengquan Xujia Chenshu Minshi Peichang Zheren Jizhi Lun"), *Fauxe* (*Legal Science*), Vol. 6, 2003, at p. 96.

67 *See*, for example, Yin Jie, *supra* note 65, at p. 111.

68 This is where a case is investigated by an administrative authority and an administrative penalty decision is subsequently made.

69 Two of the largest shareholders of Hainan Minyuan Modern Agricultural Company apparently had ties to China's senior leader at that time. Hainan Minyuan Modern Agricultural Company made its public offering on 30 April 1993. The company's 1995 yearly report indicated a profit of 0.001 yuan per share and a stock price around 3.65 yuan. In January 1997, the company announced a profit in 1996 of 0.867 yuan per share, an improvement of 1290.68 times over profits in 1995. Minyuan's price rose to 26.18 yuan. The company released a mysterious "supplemental report" on 1 February 1997, which changed some of the company's financial indicators. Towards the end of February 1997, trading of the company's stock was suspended and in March 1997, five directors who approved the false reports resigned and

accomplices without being noticed by public and grieved investors.[70] The result is that the case may never come to the people's court, and the investors who suffered losses may never be compensated. The abuse of the administrative investigation process could be prevented if the civil court played an active and decisive role in deciding whether a given statement or an activity amounts to false statement and whether it is subject to civil compensation. This could only happen if the prerequisite rule is lifted by an amendment of the Rules of the SPC.

On the other hand, some authors, particularly judges, support the prerequisite procedure set out by the Rules of the SPC.[71] They argue that the procedure is necessary for the time being for the following three reasons. First, it is in line with the current limited judicial sources of the people's court; it is otherwise difficult for the people's court to cope with a situation of "securities litigation time bomb."[72] Second, it can help plaintiffs collect evidence and reduce their burden of proof; therefore, it is good for the protection of investors.[73] Third, it is in line with the current provision of the 1998 Securities Law with regard to the power of the administrative regulator and the role of administrative penalty.[74] The 1998 Securities Law gives administrative regulators a strong overall power to monitor the securities market, and the administrative penalty occupies a central place for the regulation of China's securities market. Proponents argue that it is therefore appropriate to rely upon the role of the administrative regulator and administrative penalty before making use of judicial process and the exclusive role played by civil litigation in compensating victims.[75] While arguing for the prerequisite procedure, these authors also acknowledge that there is a defect in the system.[76] Specifically, when an alleged false statement is not punished by administrative regulator or criminal court for

---

disappeared. Responding to requests from investors, an investigation into Minyuan's financial reports was launched on 5 March 1997. After a year-long investigation, the CSRC found that the company had fraudulently inflated accounts by 1.2 billion yuan from illegal real estate transactions in Beijing. Minyuan audaciously refused to help the CSRC find the five directors, and the CSRC later released a notice stating that it was searching for the five directors but that Minyuan was under "no obligation" to help. See more details in Daniel M. Anderson, *supra* note 38.

70 In the case of Hainan Minyuan Modern Agricultural Company, a question was asked whether the five fugitive directors had behind-the-scenes protectors that were able to stop the CSRC from compelling Minyuan's help in the investigation. *Id.* at p. 1935.

71 *See* Kong Lin and Ye Jun, "Conditions for Acceptance of Civil Compensation Cases Arising from False Statements on the Securities Market" ("Zhengquan Shichang Yin Xujia Chenshu Yinfa de Minshi Peichang Anjian de Shouli Tiaojian"), *Falü Shiyong (Application of Law)*, Vol. 4, 2003, at pp. 21, 22 (one of the authors is from the Supreme People's Court). Sheng Huanwei and Zhu Chuan, "On Causal Link of Civil Compensation Cases Arising from Securities-related False Statements" (Zhengquan Xujia Chenshu Minshi Peichang Yinguo Guanxi Lun) *Faxue (Legal Science)*, Vol. 6, 2003, at p. 102 (both authors are from the number one Intermediate People's Court of Shanghai).

72 *Id.* Kong Lin and Ye Jun, at p. 21.

73 *Id.*

74 *Id.*

75 *Id.*

76 *Id.* at p. 22.

one reason or another, those investors who suffered losses as a result of the false statement will not be able to get remedies through civil compensation litigation.[77]

Acceptance of Case by the Court

In accordance with Article 6 of the Rules of the SPC, the people's court should accept a suit by investors if brought under two presumptions: (1) if the losses suffered by investors themselves result from a false statement on the securities market, and (2) if the case complies with the four provisions for the initiation of a civil lawsuit set out in Article 108 of the 1991 Civil Procedure Law.[78] At the heart of Article 6 of the Rules of the SPC is the requirement that investors must have suffered losses as a result of false statements and the victims must be the investors themselves.[79] Apart from a copy of any relevant administrative penalty decisions or criminal court judgments, claimants are required to submit certified documents proving their identities, as well as any evidence of their investment loss, such as trading receipts.[80] There must be an effective administrative penalty decision or a criminal court judgment on point at the time when the civil litigation is brought to the people's court.[81]

---

77 *Id.*

78 *See* 1991 Civil Procedure Law, *supra* note 23, art. 108. These four conditions include: (1) plaintiffs are those individuals, legal persons, or other organizations whose interests are directly related to the lawsuits; (2) there are specific defendants; (3) there are specific claims, facts, and reasons; (4) it is within the scope of civil litigation matters the people's court accept and within the jurisdiction of the court concerned. In accordance with the Opinion on Questions Concerning Application of the Civil Procedure Law (Supreme People's Court, issued on 14 July 1992), arts 139, 141, 142 (PRC), if the case does not comply with these four conditions, the people's court shall make a ruling not to accept the case, or, where applicable, transfer the case to the court that has jurisdiction. If the claimant applies again and the application complies with these conditions, the people's court shall accept the case.

79 Rules of the SPC, *supra* note 3, art. 6.

80 *Id.* The purpose of the requirement for submission of certified documents showing the identity of claimants is said to make sure that plaintiffs are those genuine investors who suffered losses as a result of false statement. *But see* Tu Binhua, *supra* note 66, at p. 96 (arguing that such a requirement is an unnecessary burden for investors since their identities have already shown on original documents of accounts or settlement of securities).

81 For example, in the Jiuzhou case the claimant was rejected by the people's court because the administrative penalty decision in question had not become effective. The Jiuzhou group, a listed company from Fujian province, and its thirteen responsible staff were sanctioned by the CSRC on October 26, 2001, for the false statements it made concerning the company's profits in 1996, 1997, and 1998, respectively. Mr. Cao, a shareholder of the company who suffered a loss of 104,000 yuan, filed a case in the people's court. In examining whether his application satisfies the requirement that there must an effective administrative penalty decision, the court found that three directors of the company had never received the administrative penalty decisions from the CSRC and the CSRC and, when questioned, could not provide evidence to prove the delivery of the decision to the directors. In accordance with the Admin. Penalty Law, *supra* note 59, arts 40–41, and Second Circular, *supra* note 1, art. 2, the court ruled that since the decision was not delivered to all the parties concerned, it did not become effective. Mr Cao's application was therefore turned down by the court.

"Investor" is defined as a natural person, legal person, or other organization that subscribes and trades securities on the securities market.[82] The securities market is defined as: (1) a market where shares are issued to the public; (2) a trading market where securities are traded openly; (3) a transferring market where securities are transferred by securities companies acting as agents and (4) other securities markets established with the approval of the government.[83] If investors enter into transactions on these markets and suffer losses as a result of false statements, they can sue the makers of false statements for compensation under the Rules of the SPC.[84] Beyond this, the Rules of the SPC are not applicable. Two kinds of transactions are explicitly excluded from the application of the Rules of the SPC: (1) transactions illegally concluded outside the securities market established by the government, and (2) transactions concluded on the securities market established by the government but through an agreement of assignment – a transaction directly negotiated between the parties.[85]

Statute of Limitation and Suspension of Proceedings

The Rules of the SPC stipulate that the limitation period for such civil suits is two years from the date when an administrative penalty decision is announced, or when a criminal court judgment becomes effective.[86] The two-year period is standard for most civil actions.[87] If there are more than two administrative decisions concerning the same false statement but different false statement makers, the period is calculated from both the date when the first administrative decision is announced and – if there is both an administrative penalty decision and a criminal court judgment – from the date when the criminal court judgment becomes effective, if this comes before the administrative penalty decision.[88] Since the calculation is based on administrative penalty decisions or criminal court judgments, it is crucial that the decision or judgment in question is final. The situation may become complicated if an administrative penalty decision is subject to an administrative review or administrative litigation or

---

See Yang Limao and Chen Chaoyang, *"Discussion on Prerequisite Procedure in Securities Tort Litigation"* (*Zhengquan Qinquan Susong Qianzhi Chengxu de Tantao*), http://www. chinacourt.org (Zhongguo Fayuan Wang), 25 November 2002.

82   Rules of the SPC, *supra* note 3, art. 2.

83   *Id.*

84   *Id.* at arts 1 and 2.

85   *Id.* at art. 3.

86   *Id.* at art. 5.

87   Article 135 of the 1986 GPCL. *See also* the 1986 General Principles of the Civil Law, arts 137, 140. This further provides that under special circumstances the people's court may extend the limitation period; the limitation period shall be discontinued if a suit is brought or if one party makes a claim for or agrees to fulfillment of obligations and a new limitation period shall be counted from the time of the discontinuance. The two-year period generally starts on the day when the plaintiff knows or ought to have known that his or her rights have been infringed. *Id.*

88   Rules of the SPC, *supra* note 3, art. 5.

if the criminal court judgment is subject to a supervision procedure set out in Articles 203 to 207 of the 1996 Criminal Procedure Law.[89]

With regard to administrative penalties, Article 11 of the Rules of the SPC provides that after the civil court begins to hear a case it may suspend the hearing if the defendant applies for an administrative review or initiates administrative litigation against the administrative penalty he received and, if the penalty in question is cancelled the court should end the hearing.[90] However, Article 11 does not provide further guidance as to who will bear the cost of a cancelled proceeding if the hearing comes to an end because the administrative penalty in question is cancelled.[91]

The Rules of the SPC provide no further procedural guidance regarding criminal judgments. If a defendant appeals against the criminal judgment in accordance with the supervision procedure of Articles 203–207, this gives rise to several questions. Assuming a civil court starts to hear a case and the defendant appeals against the criminal judgment, should the civil court suspend the hearing in the same way as it suspends the cases involving administrative penalty decisions? Or should the court continue to hear the case until the judgment is overturned by the criminal appeal court, which gives the civil court a reason to end the hearing? Under such circumstances, who is going to bear the cost of failed civil proceeding? The defendant or his representative can appeal at any time against an effective and final judgment if there exists one of the circumstances prescribed by Article 204 of the 1996 Criminal Procedure Law, that is, as if new evidence emerges with an error in judgment regarding the fact of the case.[92] It is therefore necessary for the Rules of the SPC to provide further guidance regarding the situation that arises when a criminal court judgment is subject to a supervision procedure.

Jurisdiction of the Court

Intermediate people's courts are the courts designated by the Rules of the SPC as courts of first instance to hear such lawsuits.[93] They include the intermediate people's courts that are located: (1) in the cities where provincial governments or autonomous

---

89 According to art. 9 of the 1999 Administrative Review Law, a defendant can apply for an administrative review of the penalty decision made by the CSRC or other administrative authorities within sixty days from the date of the receipt of the decision. Alternatively, he can, in accordance with art. 39 of the 1989 Administrative Procedure Law, directly apply within three months to the people's court for an administrative litigation unless it is required by administrative regulation that he has to go through the administrative review process first.

90 Rules of the SPC, *supra* note 3, art. 11.

91 *Id.*

92 Other circumstances prescribed by art. 204 of the 1996 Criminal Procedure Law include where the law is found to have been no doubt wrongly applied and where the judge who tried the case is found to have accepted bribery.

93 Rules of the SPC, *supra* note 3, art. 8.

region governments are located;[94] (2) in the four metropolitan cities;[95] (3) in the cities that have a separate planning arrangement[96] and (4) in the cities of special economic zones.[97] The second level intermediate people's courts, in accordance with the 1991 Civil Procure Law, have jurisdiction as first instance courts over three categories of civil cases: (1) cases involving foreign parties; (2) the cases that are significant to local jurisdictions and (3) the cases that are designated by the SPC.[98] Cases arising from securities-related false statements are complicated and of wide significance, so it is anticipated that the SPC would, in accordance with the provisions of the 1991 Civil Procedure Law, designate intermediate people's courts as the primary court to deal with these cases.[99] This arrangement is criticized because it "may prevent defrauded investors from getting timely judicial remedies due to the limited number of intermediate level courts and the potentially large number of suits."[100]

Regarding jurisdiction of the court, the Rules of the SPC distinguish between issuer or listed company defendants and other defendants.[101] Where the defendants are issuers or listed company defendants, the intermediate people's court at the location of issuers or listed companies shall have jurisdiction over the case, as designated by the Rules of the SPC.[102] Where the defendants are an organization or individual other than issuers or listed companies, the intermediate people's court located at the residence of the defendants shall have jurisdiction over the case, as per the Rules of SPC.[103] The basic principle regarding the so-called geographical jurisdiction (*diyu guanxia*) is prescribed by Article 22 of the 1991 Civil Procedure Law.[104] Article 22 provides that the people's court that is located at the residence or domicile of defendants, whether an individual or legal person, is the court that has jurisdiction over the civil action at issue.[105] Where there are several defendants in an action with residences in multiple jurisdictions, the people's courts in these different jurisdictions shall all have jurisdictions over the action.[106] According to Article 35 of the 1991 Civil Procedure Law, the plaintiffs can start the action at any one of these

---

94   There are twenty-seven cities where provincial governments and autonomous regional governments are located, such as Guangzhou in Guangdong province and Lasha in the Tibet autonomous region.

95   These four metropolitan cities are Beijing, Tianjing, Shanghai, and Chongqing.

96   These are the cities that are separated from other cities in terms of budgetary arrangement, investment priority, appointment of administration, and so on. They are often those few big and important cities of a province or autonomous region apart from their capital cities.

97   They are Shenzhen, Zhuhai, Shantou in Guangdong province and Xiamen in Fujian province.

98   1991 Civil Procedure Law, supra note 23, art. 19.

99   See Rules of the SPC, supra note 3.

100   Guiping Lu, *supra* note 65, at p. 794.

101   Rules of the SPC, *supra* note 3, art. 9.

102   *Id.*

103   *Id.*

104   1991 Civil Procedure Law, *supra* note 23, art. 22.

105   *Id.*

106   *Id.*

courts.[107] If the plaintiffs commence the action at more than one of these courts, the court that first accepts the case shall have the jurisdiction over the action.[108]

According to the Rules of the SPC, where the defendants are not issuers or listed companies, the intermediate people's court that has jurisdiction and has accepted the case may, upon application by the parties involved or consent by all the plaintiffs, add relevant issuers or listed companies as defendants to the case.[109] However, that court must transfer the case to the intermediate people's court located at the residence of the issuer or listed company defendants.[110] On the other hand, if no application has been put forward by the parties or no consent has been obtained from the plaintiffs, and if the court regards it as necessary to add relevant issuers or listed companies as defendants, the court may then notify the issuer or listed company to join the litigation as defendants, though the court may not transfer the case thereafter.[111]

The problem with the distinction made by the Rules of the SPC between issuer and listed company defendants and other defendants and the priority given to the intermediate people's courts situated at the location of issuers or listed companies is that it may leave plaintiff shareholders and other defendants in a disadvantageous position. This is because the local intermediate people's courts in proximity to an issuer or listed company have a tendency to make rulings or judgments in favor of these large issuers or listed companies against small and distant plaintiff shareholders.[112] To protect themselves, the plaintiff shareholders may, in accordance with Article 10 of the Rules of the SPC, refuse to give consent to the court to add a relevant issuer or a listed company as an additional defendant; therefore the court may not transfer the case to the local court of issuers or listed companies. Note that the court can freely add issuers or listed companies as defendants if the court as deemed necessary.[113] In effect, this provision gives plaintiff shareholders a limited degree of procedural protection. The same is true for the defendants who prefer to have their case heard at their residence rather than to be transferred to the local court of issuer or listed company defendants.

Forms of Action Available to Investors

The Second Circular of the SPC ruled out class action suits (*jituan susong*) as an acceptable form of action for civil compensation cases arising from securities-related false statements.[114] This continues to be the position in the current Rules of

---

107   1991 Civil Procedure Law, *supra* note 23, art. 35.

108   *Id.*

109   Rules of the SPC, *supra* note 3, art. 10.

110   *Id.*

111   *Id.*

112   *See* Walter Hutchens, *infra* note 134, at p. 640 (arguing that the Rules of the SPC require that suits be brought in the defendant's home jurisdiction, where the connections among local courts, local listed companies, and local governments suggest that plaintiff cannot easily prevail).

113   Rules of the SPC, *supra* note 3, art. 10.

114   Second Circular, *supra* note 1, art. 4.

the SPC.[115] The form of action available for plaintiffs to bring compensation claims to the court is instead limited to individual action (*dandu susong*) or joint action (*gongtong susong*).[116] In accordance with the 1991 Civil Procedure Law, joint action refers to an action where one or both parties consist of two or more persons with an object of action being the same or of the same category.[117] The people's court considers that, with the consent of the parties, the action can be combined into one trial.[118] Since joint actions, particularly those with a large number of parties on either side, have representatives to manage the case on behalf of other participants, they are also commonly called a representative action (*daibiaoren susong*).[119] As the number of claimants involved in a securities-related false statement case tends to be large, it follows that the joint action should be a dominant form of action for this type of case.

This is reflected in the Rules of the SPC, which contain further detailed rules regarding joint action and when priority is given to joint rather than individual action.[120] Thus, when there are both individual and joint actions initiated by different plaintiffs suing the same defendants based on the same false statement they made, the court may order the individual action plaintiff to join the joint action.[121] Similarly, when more than one joint action involves the same defendants based on the same false statement, the court may consolidate the claims into one joint action.[122] The number of plaintiffs in a joint action should be determined before the hearing, and where the number of plaintiffs is large, two to five representatives may be elected as litigation representatives.[123] These litigation representatives, through a special power of attorney granted to them by the other plaintiffs, represent the plaintiffs in court, change or cancel claims made by the plaintiffs, and settle or reach a mediation agreement with defendants.[124] Each of the litigation representatives may entrust one or two legal representatives for the action.[125] Where the case involves a large

---

115   Rules of the SPC, *supra* note 3, art. 12.

116   *Id.*

117   The same category (tongyi zhonglei) means the rights and obligations in an action fall into a same type. For example, three different and unconnected defendants owe a plaintiff rent of various amounts. The rent and obligation to pay it fall into same category. Instead of dealing with these three suits individually, the court may combine them into one joint action. *See* Liu Jiaxing, *Minshi Susong Jiaocheng* (*Textbook on Civil Litigation*), Beijing Daxue Chubanshe (Beijing University Press, 1982).

118   1991 Civil Procedure Law *supra* note 23, art. 53.

119   *See* Tu Binhua, *supra* note 66, at p. 97. *See* also Note, *infra* note 129, at p. 1523 (footnote 2) (noting "although formally called daibiaoren susong (representative lawsuits), many Chinese commentators and press accounts use the terms jituan susong or jituanxing susong (class action), especially when referring to suits in which the number of plaintiffs is not fixed").

120   Rules of the SPC, *supra* note 3, arts 13, 14, 15 and 16.

121   *Id.* at art. 13.

122   *Id.*

123   *Id.* at art. 14.

124   *Id.* at art. 15.

125   *Id.* at art. 14.

number of plaintiffs, the court may assign a total amount of compensation in the judgment itself, with an attached appendix that lists the names of every plaintiff and the compensation awarded to each of them.[126] The Rules of the SPC came into effect on 1 February 2003, and the first joint action case involving several hundred plaintiffs was accepted in that month by the Intermediate People's Court of Ha'erbin City.[127] This has since been followed by more joint action cases coming into the people's court.[128]

Articles 54 and 55 of the 1991 Civil Procedure Law separates joint actions[129] into two categories: (1) cases in which the number of parties is fixed and (2) cases in which the number of parties is not known at the time the case is filed.[130] Since

---

126   *Id.* at art. 16.

127   On February 9, 2003, the Intermediate People's Court of Ha'erbin city formally accepted a case represented by the Guohao Law Firm's Shanghai office involving an initial group of 107 plaintiffs and another 300 or more plaintiffs to be added to the case by the middle of that month. In March 2002, the Guohao Law Firm's Shanghai and Beijing offices were entrusted respectively by five representatives on behalf of 679 investors to sue Daqing Lianyi, a listed company, for the losses caused by the false statement it made. However, the case was not accepted by the court until after the Rules of the SPC became effective. *See* Ma Shiling, *The First Joint Action Case Was Filed, Daqing Lianyi Case Compensation Over Ten Million Yuan* (*Gongtong Susong Diyi An Jian, Daqing Lianyi An Suopei Yu Qianwan*), 11 February 2003, http://www.chinacourt.org.

128   The Dongfang Dianzi case was filed to the Intermediate People's Court of Qingdao city in July 2003, which involved an initial group of 141 shareholder plaintiffs with more to join. After four individual cases suing Guangxia (Yinchuan) Industrial Limited Company were accepted by the Intermediate People's Court of Yinchuan city on July 31, 2003, the lawyers representing the case prepared more documents involving about 1,000 plaintiffs. *See* "Jinan Shareholders Sue Dongfang Dianzi, Claiming Figure Reaches Over 3 Million Yuan" ("Jinan Gumin Zhuanggao Dongfang Dianzi, Suopei Jin E Da 300 Yu Wanyuan"), *Zhongguo Fayuan Wang*, 10 July 2003, http://www.chinacourt.org; "Yinchuan City Intermediate People's Court Formally Accepted Yinguangxia Civil Tort Compensation Case" ("Yinchuanshi Zhongyuan Zhengshi Shouli Yinguangxia Minshi Qinquan Peichang An"), "), *Zhongguo Fayuan Wang*, 1 August 2002, http://www.chinacourt.org.

129   *See*, for example, Note, "Class Action Litigation in China", *Harvard Law Review*, Vol. 111, 1998, at pp. 1523–1541 (describing as "class actions" instead of joint actions).

130   Article 54 impacts cases in which the number of parties is fixed at the time the case is filed. It provides that if the number of parties on either side of the litigation is large, such parties may choose representatives to carry out the litigation. Article 55 also impacts cases in which the number of parties is not fixed at the time the case is filed. It provides that if many parties have similar claims but the actual number of parties is not known at the time the case is filed, the court may issue a notice detailing the case and the claims and notifying all persons whose rights are similarly affected to register with the court within a specified period. The parties who have registered may select representative. If the parties fail to do so, the people's court may choose representatives in consultation with the registered parties. Article 55 also provides that the court's ruling or judgment is binding on all those who have registered with the court, and is applicable to those who have not registered with the court but who have brought lawsuits within the prescribed limitation period. Both Articles 54 and 55 provide that the acts of the representatives are binding on the parties whom they represent. However, if the representatives change or abandon claims, accept the claims of the opposing party, or settle

Article 55 allows the court's rulings or judgments to be applied to those who have not registered with the court at the time the case is filed but who later bring lawsuits within the prescribed statutory limitation period, a joint action under Article 55 may accommodate a potentially large number of plaintiffs, compared with the joint action under Article 54, in which definite parties are determined and filed to the court before the case is heard.[131] Because Article 14 of the Rules of the SPC requires that the number of plaintiffs in a joint action be determined before the hearing, it effectively limits such litigation to the first category of joint action prescribed by Article 54 of 1991 Civil Procedure Law.[132] One of the negative consequences of this limitation from a point of view of investor claimants is that they have to bear a burden to make sure that they join the action before the hearing otherwise they may not be compensated or could incur unnecessary costs if they later bring individual actions. Some criticize this limitation as a substantial procedural hurdle to investors' access to judicial recourse because it could lead to judicial inefficiency and injustice to small investors.[133]

The joint action permitted under the Rules of the SPC resembles a US class action in some respects, though it differs in regards to the registration requirement, the right of plaintiffs, the power of representatives, and the binding effect of the court's rulings or judgments.[134] Some Chinese scholars advocate that the US-style class action is more economic and better for this type of litigation and the SPC should adapt it for such litigation, subject to further amendments to the 1991 Civil Procedure Law.[135] Others, particularly judges from the people's courts, argue that conditions are not ripe for such a move.[136] They posit that since China at present has no organization similar to the intermediaries in the United States who register hundreds and thousands of investors and calculate their losses, it is unrealistic to rely upon only the people's

---

the case, they must seek the consent of the parties whom they represent. According to Articles 59 and 62 of the Supreme People's Court Opinions on "Several Issues Relating to Application of the Civil Procedure Law of the PRC", "large" parties are generally meant to be more than ten parties and, two to five representatives may be elected and they may entrust one or two persons as their legal representatives. *See* 1991 Civil Procedure Law, *supra* note 23.

131   *Id.*

132   Rules of the SPC, *supra* note 3, art. 14.

133   *See* Guiping Lu, *supra* note 65, at pp. 798–801.

134   *See* Tu Binhua, *supra* note 66, at p. 97. The author explains the difference between a class action and a Chinese representative action in three respects: (1) registration, (2) the power of representatives, and (3) the application of the court's rulings or judgments. *See generally* Walter Hutchens, "Private Securities Litigation in China: Material Disclosure about China's Legal System?", *University of Pennsylvania Journal of International Economic Law*, Vol. 24, 2003, at p. 641. *See also* Note, *supra* note 129, at p. 1525 (stating that "in the case of class actions, China appears to have drawn heavily on the American experience").

135   *See* Walter Hutchens, *supra* note 134, at p. 643; Susan V. Lawrence, *supra* note 18, at p. 27; Tu Binhua, *supra* note 66, at p. 97.

136   *See* Jia Wei, *supra* note 46, at p. 8; Xi Xiaoming and Jia Wei, "Understanding and Application of 'Several Provisions of the Supreme People's Court on Hearing Civil Compensation Cases Arising from False Statements on the Securities Market'" (Guanyu Shenli Zhengquan Shichang Yin Xujia Chenshu Yinfa de Minshi Peichang Anjian de Ruogan Guiding de Lijie yu Shiyong), *Renmin Sifa* (*People's Judiciary*), No. 2, 2003, at p. 11.

courts to make announcements, register plaintiffs and undertake work in relation to application of judgments.[137] It is therefore necessary to draw a distinction between a joint action with fixed plaintiffs and a joint action with a large number of indefinite plaintiffs, which is in line with the current conditions of the people's court and the securities market.[138] To a certain extent, their arguments explain the reason why the Rules of the SPC have adopted the joint action with a fixed number of plaintiffs as the most suitable form of action for this type of litigations.[139]

But critics view the failure to adapt the US-style class action in China for private securities litigation as economic and political in nature: large class actions could expose state-owned listed companies to massive private securities litigation judgments as well as cause political unrest as the concentration of large numbers of aggrieved shareholders into an organized group has the potential to trigger anxiety and sharpen conflict between dispersed individual investors and the state.[140] A study of the development of class actions in China both before and after the enactment of the 1991 Civil Procedure Law – including suits in the area of low quality products, consumer fraud, environmental pollution, economic contracts, local government actions, and securities law violations – evince that the increasing prevalence of class actions as one aspect of the explosion in civil litigation over the past decade.[141] This increase in class action civil litigation provides an insight into fundamental tensions in the Chinese legal system: such tensions exist between the government policy of increasing the importance of the courts, in part to force local officials to obey the law, and the legal system's responsiveness to plaintiffs; between government's desire to harness a market-driven legal profession to further implementation of the law and its desire to continue to tightly regulate lawyers; and between government efforts to shape the legal system and the plurality of factors that contribute to the evolution of that system.[142] The fact that only a limited form of joint action is allowed by the Rules of the SPC as a platform for the civil litigation arising from securities-related false statements reflects yet another tension between an urgent need to accommodate efficiently a large number of such cases and the people's courts' economic and political limitations.

The Role of Judicial Mediation and Settlement by the Party

The Rules of the SPC instruct the people's courts to stress (*zhaozhong*) mediation while adjudicating cases, and to encourage parties to settle their disputes.[143] The principles and procedures as to how the people's courts conduct mediation in civil proceedings are set out in the 1991 Civil Procedure Law, which emphasizes the

---

137   *Id.*

138   *Id.*

139   *Id.* Jia Wei, author of the articles, is a judge of the Supreme People's Court and participated in the drafting of the Rules of SPC, *supra* note 46.

140   *See* Walter Hutchens, *supra* note 134, at pp. 644–645; *see also* Susan V. Lawrence, *supra* note 18, at p. 27.

141   *See* Note, *supra* note 129, at p. 1523.

142   *Id.*, at pp. 1523–1541.

143   *See* Rules of the SPC, *supra* note 3, art. 4.

consent (*ziyuan*) of the party concerned.[144] It is required that the people's courts should engage in mediation on a voluntary basis of the parties and distinguish right from wrong based on clear facts.[145] Mediation can be conducted by the court before trial or at any stage prior to judgment,[146] but if it does not result in an agreement or if one party retracts before the delivery of the written mediated agreement, the court should adjudicate promptly.[147] A mediated agreement becomes legally binding once it has been delivered to and signed by the parties.[148] However, if one party can prove that a legally effective mediated agreement was entered into in violation of the principle of voluntariness or its content has violated the law, the same case can be retried.[149] Although the Rules of the SPC do not reiterate these provisions,[150] there is no doubt that these are the procedures that must be adhered to when the people's courts conduct mediations in cases involving securities-related false statements.

Given the fact that the people's courts have limited resources, while there is a need to deal with timely and efficiently a large number of securities-related false statement cases, judicial mediation could play an important role in handling such cases since by its nature judicial mediation could speed up proceedings and thus save time and resources. It is in this context that judicial mediation should be stressed. Needless to say, it should be conducted fairly and lawfully in accordance with the procedure set out in the 1991 Civil Procedure Law. Most importantly, it must be conducted on a voluntary basis. It is reported that Chengdu Intermediate People's Court successfully mediated the S.T. Hongguang case, the first securities-related false statement civil case mediated by the people's court.[151] Before the enactment of 1991 Civil Procedure Law, which replaced the 1982 Civil Procedure Law (Trial Implementation), coercion and unlawfulness were the most noteworthy problems associated with judicial mediation.[152] Although the 1991 Civil Procedure Law emphasizes the principle of voluntary submission to mediation and compliance with the law on mediating cases, there is still widespread abuse of the judicial mediation

---

144 *See* 1991 Civil Procedure Law, *supra* note 23, arts 85–91. Apart from Chapter 8, there are few relevant articles concerning mediation in other chapters of the 1991 Civil Procedure Law.

145 *Id.* art. 85. Consequently, a mediated agreement must be produced based on the willingness of both parties and should not violate the law. *Id.* at art. 88.

146 *Id.* art. 128.

147 *Id.* art. 91.

148 *Id.* art. 89.

149 *See* 1991 Civil Procedure Law, *supra* note 23, at p. 180.

150 There is only one brief article in the Rules of the SPC that deals with the issue of judicial mediation. *See* Rules of the SPC, *supra* note 3, art. 4.

151 A court mediation agreement was reached between eleven plaintiffs and two defendants, with ninety percent of the plaintiff claims compensated. See "ST Hongguang Suopeian Tiaojie Chenggong" ("ST Hongguang Claim Case Successfully Mediated"), *Zhongguo Zhengquan Bao* (*China Securities Daily*), 26 November 2002, at p. 1.

152 *See* Michael Palmer, "The Revival of Mediation in the People's Republic of China: (2) Judicial Mediation", *Yearbook on Socialist Legal System* 145 (William. E. Butler ed. 1989); s*ee also* Weng Xiaobin, "On Reform of Judicial Mediation System" (Lun Fayuan Tiaojie Zhidu Gaige), *Xiandai Faxue* (5 *Modern Law Science*), 2000, at p. 66.

system.[153] The stress on the role of judicial mediation by the Rules of the SPC may lead to abuses of the proceedings by some local people's courts in handling this type of cases. There are cases in which the parties have settled their disputes under encouragements from the judges and the cases have been withdrawn from the people's court.[154] It is still too early to say whether this is a positive development and the future trend of private securities litigation in China. It is certain that the people's courts and judges will follow the Rules of the SPC to encourage parties to settle their disputes.[155]

Defendants' Liability and Compensation of Investors' Losses

Any company, organization or individual involved in making false statements about the securities market is liable for the loss suffered by investors as a result of those statements.[156] Different rules apply to determine the liability of different defendants; some are subject to strict liability, while others are subject to a fault-based liability.[157] Investor compensation for losses is limited to the amount of the actual losses.[158] In order to claim compensation, investors must first establish a causal link between false statements and their losses.[159] The court then sets a cut-off date, which determines a reasonable period for the calculation of losses, and applies one of two different

---

153   *See* Fu Weiwei and Zhang Xuliang, "On the Problem and Reform of Current Judicial Mediation System" (Lun Xianxing Fayuan Tiaojie Zhidu de Biduan he Gaige), *Falü Shiyong* (*Application of Law*), No. 4, 2000, at p. 12. To illustrate the point that the judicial mediation system was seriously abused, the author cited an example: a total of 34,567 administrative cases were filed in 1994 to the people's courts at all levels of first instant courts, out of which 15,317 (44%) were withdrawn as a result of judicial mediation where plaintiffs were persuaded to withdraw their cases.

154   Peng Miaoqiu, an investor from Shanghai, settled her case with Shanghai Jiabao Industry (Group) Ltd. before Shanghai's Second Intermediate People's Court in November 2002, the first such case concluded by a settlement between the parties. *See Zhengquan Minshi Peichang Shouqi Jiean Hejie Yuangao Huopei 800 yuan* (*The First Securities Civil Compensation Case Concluded by Settlement with 800 yuan Compensation to the Plaintiff*), *Xinhua News Agency*, 15 November 2002, http://www.chinacourt.org (*Zhongguo Fayuan Wang*). In January 2003, another sixteen plaintiffs settled their cases before the same people's court with the same defendant company for a total of 61,773.66 yuan. *See* "ST Jiabao Xujia Chenshu An Jiean – 16 Wei Yuangao Huode Jingji Peichang Renminbi 61773.66 yuan" ("ST Jiabao False Statement Case Concluded – 16 Plaintiffs Got Economic Compensation 61,773.66 yuan") *Zhengquan Ribao* (*Securities Daily*), 28 January 2003, http://www.zqrb.com.cn.

155   *See* Rules of the SPC, *supra* note 3, art. 4 (instructing local courts that they should stress on mediation, and encourage parties to settle).

156   Rules of the SPC, *supra* note 3, arts 7, 21, 22, 23, 24, 25, 26, 27 and 28.

157   Rules of the SPC, *supra* note 3, arts 21, 22, 23, 24 and 25. *See* Table 6.1, Parties subject to strict liability and Table 6.2, Parties subject to fault-based liability.

158   Rules of the SPC, *supra* note 3, art. 30.

159   *Id*. art. 18.

formulas to calculate actual losses suffered.[160] These formulas depend upon the time when the investors sold their affected securities.[161]

Defendants' Liability

Issuers, listed companies and their promoters (or controlling shareholders) are central targets of the Rules of the SPC. The Rules hold issuers or listed companies liable if they make false statements and cause investor losses.[162] Promoters are also liable if they make false statements and cause losses to investors.[163] When promoters provide guarantees the disclosures made by issuers, they are jointly liable with those issuers.[164] When controlling shareholders[165] manipulate issuers or listed companies to violate securities law and make false statements using the name of the issuers or listed companies, this can cause losses to investors. These losses are to be compensated by the issuers or listed companies.[166] These issuers or listed companies then make claims for compensation from the controlling shareholders or those who have actual control over the company.[167] Where controlling shareholders or those who have actual control over issuers or listed companies make false statements it constitutes a violation of Articles 4, 5, and 188 of the 1998 Securities Law.[168] Because of the loss incurred by the investors, the aforementioned responsible party shall bear responsibilities to compensate investors.[169] Responsible directors, supervisors and managers of the issuers and listed companies shall bear a joint liability for the losses caused by their companies unless they can show that there is no fault on their part.[170]

Securities underwriters and securities listing sponsors who are similarly involved in making false statements and causing losses to investors bear liability for compensation, unless they can show that it occurred through no fault on their part.[171] If they know or ought to know of the false statement made by issuers or listed companies, and neither correct them nor issued a statement of reservation, they

---

160   *Id.* art. 33.
161   *See* Rules of the SPC, *supra* note 3, arts 31 and 32. *See* Table 6.6, Formulas for the calculations of actual losses.
162   Rules of the SPC, *supra* note 3, art. 21.
163   *Id.*
164   *Id.* art. 26.
165   This also includes those who have actual control over issuers or listed companies.
166   Rules of the SPC, *supra* note 3, art. 22.
167   *Id.*
168   Article 4 of the 1998 Securities Law emphasizes on the principle of good faith in issuing and trading of securities, while Article 5 prohibits fraudulent and insider trading and manipulation of the securities market. Article 188 states that anyone who disrupts the order of the securities trading market by fabricating and disseminating false information that affects securities trading shall be fined and subject to criminal liability where applicable.
169   Rules of the SPC, *supra* note 3, art. 22.
170   *Id.* art. 21.
171   *Id.* art. 23.

are regarded as having committed a common tort (*gongtong qinquan*).[172] Therefore, the securities underwriters and securities listing sponsors bear joint liability with the issuers or listed companies.[173] Moreover, responsible directors, supervisors, and managers of securities underwriters and securities listing sponsors bear a joint liability with their companies unless they can show no fault on their part.[174]

Accountancy firms, law firms and asset valuation organizations and their directly responsible staff bear liability if they are involved in making false statements.[175] The resulting losses to investors are a violation of Article 161 and 202 of the 1998 Securities Law.[176] The absence of fault will again exculpate those charged.[177] If accountancy firms, law firms or asset valuation organizations know or ought to know the false statement made by issuers or listed companies but neither correct the statements nor issue a statement of reservation, they shall be regarded as committing a common tort.[178] Therefore, they will bear a joint liability with the issuers or listed companies.[179]

Article 28 of the Rules of the SPC explains the circumstances under which the responsible directors, supervisors and managers of issuers, listed companies, securities underwriters and securities listing sponsors are to be held liable for making false statements jointly with their companies.[180] This includes: (1) participation in making false statements; (2) knowing or ought to know about the false statement

---

172   *Id.* art. 27.

173   *Id.* Article 130 of the 1986 GPCL generally stipulates that when two or more persons jointly infringe upon another person's rights and cause him damage, all shall be jointly liable.

174   Rules of the SPC, *supra* note 3, art. 28.

175   Rules of the SPC, *supra* note 3, arts 24 and 7 (6). There is no provision in the Rules of the SPC that defines "directly responsible persons" (zhijie zeren ren) of professional intermediaries. From Article 7 (6) of the Rules of the SPC where it states: "responsible directors, supervisors, managers and other senior management personnel of the issuers, listed companies, securities underwriters, or securities listing sponsors; directly responsible persons of professional intermediaries", it could assume that "directly responsible persons" of professional intermediaries would normally include partners and senior management personnel of accountant firms, law firms, and asset valuation organizations, equivalent to directors, supervisors, managers and other senior management personnel of the issuers, listed companies, securities underwriters, or securities listing sponsors. See *supra* note 45.

176   Article 161 of the Securities Law imposes an obligation to professional institutions and individuals who produce documents such as audit reports, asset appraisal reports, and legal opinions for the issuance or listing of securities. They also impose an obligation for securities trading activities to check and verify the truthfulness, accuracy, and completeness of the contents of the reports to be produced by them. Furthermore, they bear joint and several liability for the parts of such reports for which they are responsible. Article 202 prescribes the penalties for the above professional institutions and individuals if they make false statements, including confiscation of illegal gains, fine, suspension of business, and disqualification, compensation for losses, and criminal liability.

177   *See* Rules of the SPC, *supra* note 3, art. 24.

178   *Id.* art. 27.

179   *Id.*

180   *Id.* art. 28.

but never making an objection and (3) all other circumstances under which they should bear responsibility for the false statement and its effects.[181] This last, "catch-all" provision[182] could lead the court to exercise their discretion to hold directors, supervisors and managers of issuers, listed companies, securities underwriters, and securities listing sponsors liable for the false statement made by their companies.

In total, promoters, issuers, listed companies and their controlling shareholders or those who exercise actual controls over the company are subject to a strict liability (see Table 6.1), while securities underwriters, securities listing sponsors, accounting firms, law firms, and asset valuation organizations are subject to a liability based on fault (see Table 6.2). The same applies to responsible directors, supervisors, managers of issuers, listed companies, securities underwriters and securities listing sponsors, and direct responsible persons of accounting firms, law firms, and asset valuation organizations (see Table 6.2). Joint and several liability applies to promoters; securities underwriters, securities listing sponsors, accountant firms, law firms; and asset valuation organizations, and directors, supervisors, managers of issuers, listed companies, securities underwriters, and securities listing sponsors (see Table 6.3). In addition, other organizations or individuals who made false statements in violation

Table 6.1   Parties subject to strict liability

Promoters	Liable for the losses caused to investors by their false statements (Article 21)
Issuers	Liable for the losses caused to investors by their false statements (Article 21)
Listed companies	Liable for the losses caused to investors by their false statements (Article 21)
Controlling shareholders or those who have actual control over issuers or listed companies	1. Liable if they manipulate issuers or listed companies and make false statements in violation of securities law using the name of the issuers or listed companies and cause losses to investors, which shall be compensated by the issuers or listed companies first, who then make claims from the controlling shareholders or those who have actual control over the company (Article 22) 2. Liable if they make false statements in violation of Articles 4, 5 or 188 of the 1998 Securities Law and cause losses to investors (Article 22)

---

181   *Id.* For a general discussion on liabilities of company directors to shareholders for false statements, including the theoretical basis, constitutional element, behavior, intention, and gross negligence, and so on, *see* Cui Zhennan and Ma Mingsheng, "Study on Liabilities of Directors to Shareholders for False Statements" (Xujia Chenshu Zhong Dongshi Dui Gudong Zheren Yanjiu), *Zhongguo Faxue* (*China Legal Science*), Vol. 2, 2003, at p. 96.

182   A typical provision found in other laws and regulations of the PRC.

Table 6.2   Parties subject to fault-based liability

Securities underwriters	Liable for the losses caused to investors by false statements unless they can show that there is no fault by them (Article 23)
Securities listing sponsors	Liable for the losses caused to investors by false statements unless they can show that there is no fault by them (Article 23)
Intermediaries (accountancy firms, law firms, asset valuation organizations and their directly responsible persons)	Liable for the part they are responsible for if they make false statements in violation of Article 161 and 202 of the 1998 Securities Law and cause losses to investors unless they can show that there is no fault by them (Article 24)
Responsible directors, supervisors and managers of issuers, listed companies, securities underwriters and securities listing sponsors	Bear a joint liability for the losses caused to investors by their companies unless they can show that there is no fault by them (Articles 21, 23)

of Articles 5, 72, 188 and 189 of the 1998 Securities Law[183] and cause losses to investors are liable for compensation.[184]

The Rules of the SPC clarify some of the ambiguities found in the provisions of the 1998 Securities Law pertaining to liabilities for making false and misleading statements.[185] Securities underwriters and their responsible directors, supervisors and managers are now held liable under the Rules of the Provisions, on the basis of fault liability.[186] Moreover, the same applies to responsible directors, supervisors and

---

183 *See* Sec. Law, *supra* note 8, arts 5, 72, 188, 189. Information disseminated by any mass medium is required to be truthful and objective according to the 1998 Securities Law. Any organization or individual is prohibited form fabricating and disseminating false information or misleading information to affect securities trading. This includes stock exchanges, securities companies, securities registration and clearing institutions, securities trading service organizations, intermediary organizations, securities associations and the securities regulatory authority, state functionaries, news media, and their employees or staff members thereof and other persons concerned. The penalties for violating organizations and individuals if they make false or misleading statements, including fines, and additional administrative sanctions for state functionaries and criminal liability. *See also supra* note 168.

184 *See* Rules of the SPC, *supra* note 3, art. 7, 25.

185 These are the provisions in Articles 61, 161 and 202 of the 1998 Securities Law, *supra* note 8.

186 1998 Securities Law, *supra* note 8, art. 63. If an issuer or securities underwriter announces a prospectus, measures for offer of corporate bonds, finance or accounting report, listing document, annual report, interim report, or ad hoc report which contain or contains any false or misleading statement or major omission that causes investor losses during the course of securities trading, the issuer or the underwriter shall be liable for the losses. Also, the responsible director(s), supervisor(s), and/or the manager of the issuer or the underwriter shall be jointly and severally liable for such losses.

Table 6.3   Parties subject to joint and several liability

Promoters	Liable jointly with issuers for the losses caused to investors, if they provide guarantees for the disclosure made by the issuers (Article 26)
Securities underwriters, securities listing sponsors, accountant firms, law firms, and asset valuation organizations	Liable jointly for the losses caused to investors, if they know or ought to know the false statement made by the issuer or listed company but neither correct them nor issue a statement of reservation (Article 27)
Responsible directors, supervisors and managers of issuers, listed companies, securities underwriters and securities listing sponsors	Liable jointly with their company for the losses caused to investors if they: 1. participate in making false statements; 2. know or ought to know the false statement but make no objections; and 3. other circumstances under which they should be held responsible (Article 28)

managers of issuers, and listed companies under Article 63 of the 1998 Securities Law.[187] The liability of accounting firms, law firms, asset valuation organizations, and their directly responsible persons is also interpreted as a fault liability under Articles 161 and 202 of the 1998 Securities Law.[188] The 1998 Securities Law and the 1993 Provisional Regulations on Share Issuing and Trading both contain provisions requiring companies applying for listing, to submit to the CSRC and stock exchanges recommendation letters from securities companies and members of stock exchanges.[189] However, neither of the regulations have provisions regarding the liability of securities companies for making false statements in their capacity as securities listing sponsors.[190] The Rules of the SPC now add securities listing sponsors in the list of possible defendants.[191] This details their liability when making a false statement, which covers the aforementioned omissions of the 1998 Securities Law and the 1993 Provisional Regulations on Share Issuing and Trading.[192] It is important to note that the Rules of the SPC include controlling shareholders and those who have actual control over issuers or listed companies in the list of possible defendants, holding them to the standard of strict liability.[193]

There are valid criticisms and suggestive comments about the provisions of the Rules of the SPC regarding defendants' liabilities. In contrast to the view that securities underwriters and their responsible directors, supervisors and managers should be held liable for false statements on a fault basis, some authors argue that strict liability should be applied to securities underwriters in the same way it applies

---

187   *Id.*
188   1998 Securities Law, *supra* note 8, arts 161, 202.
189   *See* 1998 Securities Law, *supra* note 8, art. 45.
190   *Id. See* arts 45, 63.
191   Rules of the SPC, *supra* note 3, arts 7 (4), 23, 27, and 28.
192   *See* Jia Wei, *supra* note 46, at p. 9.
193   *Id.* Rules of the SPC, *supra* note 3, arts 7 (1) and 22.

to issuers.[194] This is because the current Chinese securities market needs to strengthen and not weaken underwriters' liabilities, to preventing them from assisting issuers to make false statements and harm investors.[195] Regarding the application of fault liability, some authors criticize the Rules of the SPC for not providing clear criteria by which to determine fault.[196] These authors also suggest that the doctrine of duty of care should be applied when determining the defendants' fault.[197] It is also argued that joint and several liability should not be strictly applied unless plaintiffs can prove that defendants acted intentionally or conspired prior to their actions.[198]

Causal Link between False Statement and Investors' Losses

Defendants' liabilities are limited to actual losses suffered by investors.[199] For the calculation of actual losses, there first must be a causal link (*yinguo guanxi*) between the false statement and the loss suffered by investors.[200] To establish a causal link between the false statement and investors' losses, the court must find that: (1) the investments are securities directly connected with the false statement; (2) the purchase date of the securities is between the date on which the false statement is made and the date on which the false statement is exposed or corrected and (3) that investors suffer losses as a result of selling securities on or after the date on which the false statement is exposed or corrected, or as a result of continued ownership of the securities after the false statement is exposed or corrected.[201]

The date on which the false statement is exposed (*xujia chenshu jieluri*) refers to the date it is exposed for the first time by the mass media that is circulated or broadcasted nationwide, such as newspapers, radio or television.[202] The dates on which the false statement is corrected (*xujia chenshu gengzhengri*) refers to the date on which those who made the false statement voluntarily correct it to the public through the media.[203] This correction shall adhere to regulatory formalities for the suspension of trading, and it shall be broadcast through the media designated by the CSRC.[204] Although the Internet is not mentioned by the Rules of the SPC, it should presumably be treated as a platform for the purpose of the application of the Rules.[205]

---

194   *See* Bai Yan and Fu Jun, "Compensation Liability for the Tort of False Statement" (Xujia Chenshu Qinquan de Peichang Zheren), *Zhongguo Faxue* (*China Legal Science*), Vol. 2, 2003, at p. 104.
195   *Id.*
196   *See* Tu Binhua, *supra* note 66, at pp. 94–95.
197   *Id.* at p. 95.
198   *Id.* at p. 95.
199   Rules of the SPC, *supra* note 3, at art. 30.
200   *Id.* at art. 18.
201   *Id.* at art. 18 (1), (2) and (3).
202   *Id.* at art. 20.
203   *Id.*
204   *Id.*
205   National newspapers and specialist securities newspapers are now found online, for example, *Renmin Ribao* (*People's Daily*) (http://www.people.com.cn) and *Zhengquan Ribao* (*Securities Daily*) (http://www.zqrb.com.cn).

The date on which the false statement is made, exposed or corrected is crucial in determining the causal link between the false statement and investors' losses, which, in turn, determines whether an investor is entitled to compensation.[206]

Table 6.4 illustrates this causal link with an example of a listed company who has a share listed on Shanghai Stock Exchange on 1 July 2003, and whose false statement made on 1 July 2003 is exposed or corrected on 31 July 2003. Investors A, B, C and D purchased and sold the company's shares on different dates. In accordance with the Rules of the SPC, Investors A and B are entitled to claim compensation as there is a causal link between the false statement and their losses, but neither Investor C nor D could establish a causal link and are entitled to claim compensation, even though they may have suffered losses as a result of the false statement.

Academics, practitioners, and judges have criticized these causation rules as cumbersome because they require the plaintiff to have purchased shares in reliance on false statements as shown by purchasing them after the statement was made.[207] These rules also require the plaintiff to sell or continue to hold the shares until after the false statement has been publicly exposed or corrected.[208] Some criticize the rules on the grounds that false statements can be optimistic or pessimistic statements (*youduo* or *youkong*) and either may purposely defraud the market and investors. In one such example, the purpose of a false pessimistic press release issued by one listed company was to benefit the directors and senior management members by allowing them to have a low stock option exercise price.[209] Thus, arguments show that it is incorrect to presume that no causal link exists if investors sell their securities before the exposure or correction day.[210] These causation rules should be interpreted more widely in order to reach situations in which investors are misled by fraudulent pessimistic statements and suffer losses as a result.[211] Some criticize the rules from a market practice point of view. They argue that often before a false statement is exposed rumors start to appear on the market and prices start to fall; therefore, it is unfair to exclude those investors who sell their securities and suffer losses in

---

206 *See* Zhang Yongjian, "On Several Dates Concerning the Tort of False Statement" (Lun Xujia Chenshu Qinquan Xingwei de Jige Shijiandian), *Falü Shiyong* (4 *Application of Law*), 2003, at pp. 13–16 (analyzing these dates).

207 Rules of the SPC, *supra* note 3, art. 18.

208 *Id.*

209 *See* Guiping Lu, *supra* note 65, at pp. 803–804 (explaining that the author uses this hypothetical situation to argue that the provisions of the Rules of the SPC deny recovery to investors who are in the same situation as the investor in this hypothetical situation, and who also suffered losses as a result of the listed company's false pessimistic press release).

210 *See* Guo Feng, *supra* note 41, at p. 99.

211 *See* Sheng Huanwei, Zhu Chuan, *supra* note 71, at p. 102 (arguing that art. 18 of the Rules of the SPC only applies to optimistic false statements, but that there is a need for judges to interpret this rule more broadly in order to apply it to pessimistic false statements), *see also* Yin Jie, *supra* note 65, at p. 112 (arguing that at present, all of the cases brought to court are cases involving optimistic false statements made to enlarge profits and conceal losses; however, as the market develops and becomes more sophisticated, pessimistic false statements are inevitable and investors will be affected by them).

Table 6.4   Causal link between false statement (FS) and investors' losses

Investor	June 2003	1 July 2003: *FS* made	2–30 July 2003	31 July 2003: *FS* exposed or corrected	August 2003	Causal link?
A			Purchased on 2 and 30 July	Sold on 31 July and suffered loss	Sold on 15, 20, and 28 August respectively and suffered loss	√
B			Purchased on 2 and 30 July	Held until 31 July and suffered loss	Still holding and suffered loss	√
C	Purchased on 30 June		Sold on 30 July			X
D			Purchased on 2 July and sold on 30 July			X

order to stop falling prices before the exposure day.[212] These critics suggest that a flexible criterion such as "the date on which false statements are widely known by the market and investors" should replace the current rigid requirement of "the date on which false statements are exposed for the first time by national newspapers, radio, or [television]."[213]

Article 18 of the Rules of the SPC does not require investors to prove that a causal link exists between their investment and the false statement.[214] If they can show that they purchased relevant securities after the date on which the false statement is made and that they sold or held them until after the public exposure or correction of the false statement, then they have established a causal link.[215] In other words, the court assumes that all the investors who purchased relevant securities during the prescribed period have made their investment in reliance on the false statement and thus are affected. These investors are then exempted from proving a causal link.[216] The presumption of reliance can be rebutted if defendants prove one of the following: (1) the plaintiff sold the relevant securities before the date on which the false investment was exposed or corrected; (2) the plaintiff purchased the relevant securities on the date on which the false statement was exposed or corrected or thereafter; (3) the plaintiff knew the existence of the false statement but nevertheless

---

212   Jiao Jinhong, "On 'the Fraud on the Market Theory'" ("Qizha Shichang Lilun" Yanjiu) *Zhongguo Faxue* (*China Legal Science*), Vol. 2, 2003, at p. 114.

213   *Id.*

214   Rules of the SPC, *supra* note 3, art. 18.

215   *Id.* at art. 18 (1), (2) and (3).

216   Rules of the SPC *supra* note 3, at art. 18, Kong Lin, Ye Jun, *supra* note 71, at p. 23, Guiping Lu, *supra* note 65, at p. 804 (discussing fraud on the market theory in the United States and its influence on the Rules of the SPC).

made the investment; (4) all or part of the losses suffered by the plaintiff were caused by other risk elements of the securities market and (5) the plaintiff made the investment in bad faith in order to manipulate the price of the securities.[217] The defense of "other risk elements of the securities market" may be problematic because it is difficult for defendants to prove such risks to the court.[218] In other words, it is difficult for the defense to discharge their burden of proof that the losses of investors are caused by other market risk elements, specifically, proving that the loss was not caused by their false statement. It is suggested that a system should be established that enables expert witnesses to appear regularly before the court to assist judges when making this decision.[219] Given that the "other risk element" defense is often replied upon by defendants, the use of expert witnesses and quality evidence will assist in the decision-making process of the people's court.[220]

Calculation of Actual Losses of Investors

There are three aspects to actual losses (*shiji shunshi*) suffered by investors resulting from false statements: (1) the difference of their investment; (2) the commission, charge, and stamp duty connected with their lost investment and (3) the interest lost for their investment as calculated according to bank deposit rates for the relevant period.[221] To calculate the loss actually suffered by investors, the court must first determine a date (*jizhunri*) upon which the calculation is based.[222] This date is defined as a date prescribed to determine a reasonable period for the calculation of losses, thus limiting the compensation to investors for the losses caused by false statements.[223] Article 33 of the Rules of the SPC provides the following guidelines for the court to determine such a cut-off date.[224]

First, the cut-off date should be the date on which the aggregated trading volumes of the security affected by the false statement reaches one hundred percent of its tradable volumes.[225] This is after the date when the false statement is exposed or corrected, disregarding all large volume trading through agreements. Second, if the court is unable to determine the cut-off date in accordance with the above criterion before the hearing, the cut-off date should be the thirtieth trading date after the false

---

217 Rules of the SPC, *supra* note 3, art. 19.

218 *See* Jiao Jinhong, *supra* note 212, at p. 114.

219 *Id.*

220 *See* "Liaoning's first Securities False Statement Compensation Case Started Hearing Yesterday" ("Liaoning Shouli Zhengquan Xujia Chenshu Peichang An Zuori Kaishen"), *Zhongguo Fayuan Wang*, 25 July 2003, http://www.chinacourt.org; "Shareholder Sue Director of Listed Company for 90 Thousand" ("Gumin Zhuanggao Shangshi Gongsi Dongshizhang Suopei 9 Wan"), *Zhongguo Fayuan Wang*, 9 July 2003, http://www.chinacourt.org (relying upon other risk elements as a defense).

221 Rules of the *SPC, supra* note 3, at art. 30.

222 *Id.* art. 33.

223 *Id.* art. 33.

224 *Id.* art. 33 (1), (2), (3) and (4).

225 *Id.* art. 33 (1).

statement is exposed or corrected.[226] Third, where the security affected has been de-listed from the trading market, the cut-off date should be the trading day preceding the day that the security was de-listed.[227] Fourth, where the security affected has been suspended from trading, the cut-off date should be the trading day preceding the day that the trading of the security was suspended.[228] Finally, where the trading has been restored, the cut-off date should be determined in accordance with the aggregated trading volumes of the affected security as mentioned above.[229]

Table 6.5 takes the same example used in Table 6.4[230] to illustrate the cut-off date determined in accordance with the guidelines set out by Article 33 of the Rules of the SPC.[231] Depending upon the position of the defendant company,[232] there could be four cut-off dates.

As shown in Table 6.5, the primary method used by the court to determine the cut-off date is aggregation of trading volumes of the security affected by the false statement. The cut-off date is calculated by reference to when the aggregated trading volume of the security affected by the false statement reaches one hundred percent of its tradable volume, after the date on which the false statement was exposed or corrected.[233] Scholars have expressed views that this method may not necessarily reflect the true picture of market demand and supply movements when the market, as a whole, is rising.[234] Instead, it would be proper take as the basis for calculation of losses an average closing price of each trading day during a reasonable bounce back period.[235] Others argue that this method is vulnerable to abuse, because those who make the false statements may use illegal means to manipulate the trading volumes.[236] When this happens, the calculation of investors' losses would be affected.[237]

On the basis of the cut-off date, two different formulas are available to calculate actual losses suffered by the investors depending on if or when they sold their securities prior to or after the cut-off date.[238] For those investors who sold their

---

226   *Id.* art. 33 (2).

227   *Id.* art. 33 (3).

228   *Id.* art. 33 (4).

229   *Id.* art. 33 (4).

230   *See* Table 6.4, Causal link between false statement (FS) and investors' losses.

231   Compare Rules of the SPC, *supra* note 3 (showing no clear indication as to whether or not to disregard a public holiday when calculating the thirtieth trading day), with 1986 GPCL, art. 154 (providing that if the last day of a time period falls on a Sunday or an official holiday, the day after the holiday shall be taken as the last day).

232   The position of trading volumes of the defendant company's share, and whether the share is de-listed or suspended. *See* Table 6.5, Cut-off date for the calculation of investors' actual losses.

233   The Rules of the SPC, *supra* note 3, art. 33 (1).

234   *See* Guo Feng, *supra* note 41, at p. 99.

235   *Id.* at p. 99.

236   *See* Song Yixing, *supra* note 62, at p. 10.

237   *Id.* at p. 10.

238   Rules of the SPC, *supra* note 3, arts 31 and 32; *see* Wang Dan, "On the Method for the Calculation of Compensation from Securities-related False Statements" (Zhengquan Xujia Chenshu Peichang Jishuan Fangfa Lun), *Faxue* (*Legal Science*), Vol. 6, 2003, at pp. 103–108 (discussing these formulae and other calculation method in general).

Table 6.5 Cut-off date for the calculation of investors' actual losses

	31 July 2003:*False statement exposed or corrected*	20 August 2003: Cut-off date	24 August 2003: Cut-off date	30 August 2003: Cut-off date	15 September 2003: Cut-off date
Determined by aggregated trading volumes	Trading volumes of defendant company's share at 50%	Trading volumes of the defendant company's share has been aggregated to 100%			
Court unable to determine by trading volumes				The 30th trading date after the date when the false statement was exposed or corrected	
Where defendant company's share has been de-listed			Preceding the de-listing day		
Where defendant company's share has been suspended			Preceding the suspension day		
Where defendant company's share has been restored after suspension					Trading volumes of defendant company's share has been accumulated to 100%

securities on or prior to the cut-off date, actual losses are determined by multiplying the number of securities they held by the difference between the average purchase price and the actual price at which they sold their securities.[239] For those investors who sold their securities after the cut-off date or continued to hold them, actual losses are calculated by multiplying the number of securities they hold by the difference between their average purchase price and the average closing prices of every trading

---

239 Rules of the SPC, *supra* note 3, art. 31.

day from the date when the false statement was exposed or corrected, until the cut-off date.[240]

Table 6.6 illustrates an application of these two different formulas to calculate the actual losses of Investors A and B of the defendant company. Suppose the court determined the cut-off date as August 20, 2003, in accordance with an aggregated trading volume of the defendant company's share. The actual losses of Investor A who bought 400 shares with 6,000 yuan and sold them both before and after the cut-off date are 4,540 yuan in total. Investor B who bought 200 shares with 3,000 yuan and still holds them after the cut-off date has an actual loss of 2,340 yuan.

Compensation of Investors' Losses

The combined effect of these rules can be determined by carefully following the causal link between actual losses, the cut-off date, and the calculation formulas. First, only those investors who purchase affected securities after a false statement is made, and before the false statement is exposed or corrected, and who then sell the affected securities or continue to hold them after the false statement is exposed or corrected, are entitled to claim compensation for the losses they suffered. Second, investor plaintiffs would not be able to claim compensation if defendants could prove: (1) that the plaintiffs purchased or sold the securities outside, the period prescribed by the Rules of the SPC; (2) or their losses were caused by other risk elements of the market; (3) or they had knowledge of the false statement but nevertheless made an investment (4) or they made the investment in bad faith in order to manipulate of the market. Third, those plaintiffs who have satisfied the causal link test and are entitled to compensation, including the following reimbursements: (1) the difference of their investments; (2) the commission charges and stamp duties connected with their lost investments and (3) interests of their losses calculated against bank interest rates for deposit for the affected period.[241] Finally, depending upon whether the plaintiffs sell the affected securities before or after the cut-off date, their lost investment is calculated by: multiplying the number of securities they hold by either the difference between the average purchase price and the actual price at which the securities were sold, or the difference between the average purchase price and the average closing

---

240   *Id.* art. 32.

241   The Rules of the SPC do not provide further guidelines as to how the commissions, charges, and stamp duties are calculated. Presumably, in accordance with the principle of "actual loss", the calculation would be based on what investors have paid for commissions and stamp duties connected with their lost investment. Starting from January 24, 2005, the rate of stamp duty for securities trading is 0.1%. *See* Circular of the Ministry of Finance and the State Bureau of Taxation on Adjustment of Securities Trading Stamp Duties, issued on, and effective from, 24 January 2005. Starting from 1 May 2002, the commission that securities houses charge investors for the trading of A share, B share and investment funds may not be higher than 0.3% of the trading amount in question. *See* Circular of the CSRC, the State Commission for Development and Planning and State Bureau of Taxation on Adjustment of Commissions Charged for Securities Trading, issued on 4 April 2002, and effective from 1 May 2002.

Table 6.6   Formulas for the calculation of actual losses

Investors' actual losses	1 July 2003: *False statement made*	31 July 2003: *False statement exposed or corrected*		20 August 2003: *Cut-off date*	28 August 2003
Investor A: Average purchase price 15 yuan minors average selling price 4 yuan = 11 yuan x 200 = 2,200 yuan	Purchased 200 shares on July 2 at 10 yuan per share, and another 200 shares on 30 July at 20 yuan per share. *Total: 6000 yuan for 400 shares*	Sold 100 shares on 31 July at 6 yuan per share	Sold 50 shares on 15 August at 3 yuan per share	Sold 50 shares on 20 August at 1 yuan per share	
Investor A: Average purchase price 15 yuan minors average price of closing prices of each trading day 3.3 yuan = 11.7 yuan x 200 = 2,340 yuan	Same as above	Share price 7 yuan at close of trading	Share price 2 yuan at close of trading	Share price 1 yuan at close of trading	Sold 200 shares on 28 August at 2.50 yuan per share
Investor B: Average purchase price 15 yuan minors average price of closing prices of each trading day 3.3 yuan = 11.7 yuan x 200 =2,340 yuan	Purchased on 2 July 100 shares at 10 yuan per share, and on 30 July 100 shares at 20 yuan per share. *Total: 3000 yuan for 200 shares*	Price at 7 yuan per share at the close of trading	Price at 2 yuan per share at the close of trading	Price at 1 yuan per share at the close of trading	Still holding 200 shares

prices of every trading day from the date when the false statement is exposed or corrected until the cut-off date.

Some authors believe that the scope of compensation prescribed by the Rules of the SPC is too narrow and should be enlarged to include indirect losses or expenses of investors.[242] They argue that only by such an enlargement of the scope of compensation could victim investors be made whole, as if the false statement had not happened.[243]

---

242 *See* Yin Jie, *supra* note 65, at p. 112; Bai Yan, Fu Jun, *supra* note 195, at p. 101. This would include the subscription of affected securities expense, the litigation expense (including fees for lawyers and courts), all traveling expenses, and the lost salaries resulting from attendance at the litigation.

243 *Id.* Bai Yan, Fu Jun, at p. 100.

These authors assert that this complies with the general fairness principle of civil law, and prevents the occurrence of false statements by increasing the cost of making false statements.[244] For other authors, the compensation provisions of the Rules of the SPC already comply with the fairness principle of civil law since they define a scope of actual losses for investors while not imposing any extra burden on defendants.[245] They argue that this is consistent with China's current conditions on the securities market with respect of the protection of investors.[246]

In contrast to the provisions of the Rules of the SPC regarding the calculation of investors' losses on the securities trading market, the Rules of the SPC give little attention to the calculation of investors' losses on the securities issuing market, a shortcoming which some regard as a significant failure.[247] Article 29 of the Rules of the SPC simply states that where investors suffered losses as a result of false statements made on the securities issuing market, they are entitled to compensation from wrongdoers in accordance with Article 30 of the Rules of the SPC.[248] Additionally, where the false statement leads to a cancellation of the issue of securities, investors are entitled to a refund of their money plus interest calculated according to bank deposit interest rates for the same period. The calculation formula for losses occurring on the securities trading market under Article 30 may, to certain extent, apply to the calculation of the losses occurring on the issuing market. However, as the circumstances on the issuing market are different from those on the trading market, it is necessary for the Rules of the SPC to provide a set of detailed guidelines separately governing the calculation of the losses occurring on the issuing market.[249] As pointed out by one practicing lawyer, another omission in the Rules of the SPC that may cause serious problem in practice is a lack of more detailed guidelines on the practical determination of the false statement date, the exposure or correction date, and the cut-off date.[250] Every single alternation of these crucial dates may lead to a large-scale increase or decrease in compensation figures.[251]

Summary: Limitations of the Rules of the SPC

The SPC took the unprecedented step of issuing three circulars within a short period of time – between September 2001 and January 2003 – giving instructions to local people's courts on how to handle civil compensation claims arising from securities

---

244 *Id.* at p. 101.

245 *See* Guo Feng, *supra* note 41, at p. 99.

246 *Id.*

247 *See* Tu Binhua, *supra* note 66, at p. 93.

248 Rules of the SPC, *supra* note 3, art. 29.

249 *See* Tu Binhua, *supra* note 66, at p. 93 (discussing the way different situations in the securities-issue market affect false statement makers' liability and the compensation of damages).

250 *See* Song Yixing, *supra* note 62, at pp. 9–10. Song Yixing is a practicing lawyer from Shanghai Wenda Law Firm.

251 *Id.* at p. 10.

fraud in China's securities market.[252] This demonstrated that the SPC was, on one hand, under unavoidable pressure from the public to issue guidelines for the people's court to deal with such cases; while on the other hand, the SPC was reluctant to make the people's court fully open and available for such cases due to social, political, legal and other reasons. Although the current Rules of the SPC are generally welcomed by lawyers, academics and investors at large, they nevertheless fall short of expectations. Indeed, the SPC and the Rules of the SPC could not surpass the limit of the second circular on certain key issues. Under these circumstances, it is unrealistic to expect the SPC to make any radical moves. The Rules of the SPC, as discussed above, must inevitably be limited in regards to the following key issues.

First, the Rules of the SPC limit the scope of cases that will be accepted and heard by the people's court. Compared with the second circular, the Rules of the SPC are a positive step towards allowing criminal court judgments and the penalty decisions of other administrative authorities – besides the CSRC – to be used to accept cases for the people's court. However, the prerequisite rule set out effectively limits the scope of cases to be accepted and heard by the people's court. In addition, the Rules of the SPC only apply to the cases arising from false statements, which now excludes from the people's court civil actions related to insider trading or market manipulation. Social, political, legal and procedural criticisms of this prerequisite rule point to this defect and show that it is an unpopular provision of the Rules of the SPC.

Second, the Rules of the SPC limit the eligibility of shareholder investors for compensation of losses suffered as a result of false statements. The Rules of the SPC do not discriminate against any group of shareholder investors or any individual, legal person or other organization who subscribes and trades securities on the securities market established by the government. They have the right to file a case in the people's court and seek compensation if they suffer losses as a result of a false statement. However, the actual provisions of the Rules of the SPC concerning causal links actually limit the eligibility of shareholder investors for the compensation of their losses. In effect, all the shareholder investors who purchase or sell affected securities at times other than those prescribed by the Rules of the SPC are excluded from the scope of compensation regardless of whether or not they suffered losses.

Third, the Rules of the SPC fail to provide shareholder investors with a helpful and effective procedure by which they may access the court and judicial remedies. Lawyers will face unpredicted difficulties bringing their cases to the people's court in a timely and efficient manner. Many factors contribute to this difficultly: (1) the Rules of the SPC's cautiously chosen form of joint action for investors to bring their lawsuits; (2) a limited number of intermediate people's courts designated by the Rules of the SPC in contrast to a large number of potential lawsuits; (3) a priority given to the intermediate people's courts located at the places of issuer or listed company defendants and (4) the Rules of the SPC lack provisions on the determination and calculation of losses suffered on the issuing market and on the practical determination of the false statement date and other crucial dates. These factors combine to hamper lawyers' abilities to reliably obtain compensation for every shareholder investor who suffers a loss as a result of the false statement.

---

252   *See supra* note 1.

Fourth, the Rules of the SPC play only a limited role in assisting the prevention of market abuse and the regulation of China's securities market. There is no doubt that the Rules of the SPC, by prescribing a specific and wide-range list of possible defendants and their corresponding liabilities, particularly targeting issuers, listed companies, and their promoters or controlling shareholders, will have a positive impact on the corporate governance and the regulation of China's securities market as a whole. However, there are a limited number of cases tried by the people's court and a limited number of investors who are eligible for compensation. The way in which actual losses are calculated, as well as the potential consequence of the prerequisite rule that defendants may interfere with administrative investigation process in order to escape civil penalties, means that the application of the Rules of the SPC would not bring about substantial costs for defendants. Therefore, this would not effectively deter them from making false statements on the securities market.

In conclusion, the Rules of the SPC are a first and important step towards the establishment of a civil litigation and compensation system to address securities fraud cases on China's securities market by the people's court. However, it fails to surpass its predecessors and transcend their limitations. Though the SPC may find it difficult, a balance must be struck between the court, the government, the social stability,[253] the protection and development of state-owned listed companies, and the need to protect and compensate all investors who suffer losses as a result of securities frauds. In addition, the gaps and defects of the current primary legislations also contribute to the limitations of the Rules of the SPC. Further changes and improvements are still necessary in order for the system to operate effectively. Nevertheless, the system established by the Rules of the SPC has brought securities civil litigation arising from false statements in China to a new stage of evolution.

---

253   *See* Yang Wei and Pan Jing, "Li Guoguang: To Work on Adjudication and to Protect Social Stability is the First and Important Task of the People's Court" (Li Guoguang: Zhua Shenpan Bao Wending Shi Fayuan Shouyao Renwu), http://www.chinacourt.org (*Zhongguo Fayuan Wang*), 15 September 2002 (where Li Guoguang, deputy president of the Supreme People's Court, speaking at a meeting on the trial of civil compensation cases arising from false statements on the securities market on 12–14 September 2002, in Lanzhou city, Gansu province, emphasized that protecting social stability is the first and most important task of the people's court).

Chapter 7

The Development of Securities Dispute Resolution in China

Introduction

On the basis of the examination and discussion in the previous chapters of securities disputes and their resolution in different securities markets, this chapter attempts to offer an overall assessment of the development of securities dispute resolution in China. This includes the development of law and regulations, the development of judicial procedures and rules, and the development of alternative resolution of securities disputes through mediation and arbitration leading to the major and important amendments made in 2005 to the 1998 Securities Law and the 1993 Company Law.[1] The final part of this chapter examines some of the key amendments and, in this context, discusses the future prospects of securities dispute resolution in China.

China's securities market is a new and transitional market that emerged in the process of China's transformation from a socialist and planned economy to a capitalist market economy. The development of securities dispute resolution in China takes place in this particular context. Furthermore, understanding the system of securities dispute resolution that has taken place over the past two decades in China has to take into account relevant factors of China's administrative, economic, legal, social and political system. This chapter looks at the roles played by securities regulators and other relevant administrative authorities, the function of the judicial committee of the people's court in relation to securities dispute resolution, and the issues of financial security and social stability and their influence to the process of securities dispute resolution.

Development of Securities Dispute Resolution

The emergence of a securities market in China in the late 1980s, consequent to the economic reform begun in China in 1978,[2] brought about securities disputes of various kinds in different securities and futures markets. The resolution of these new types of disputes, not dealt with before by the people's courts or mediation and arbitration organizations, led to the development of legal, regulatory and judicial rules and procedures applicable to these securities disputes in China. On a general

---

1   *See* footnote 12 of Introduction. For English translation of the 2005 Securities Law of the PRC, *see China Law and Practice*, February 2006, pp. 31–84. For English translation of the 2005 Company Law of the PRC, *see China Law and Practice*, December 2005/January 2006, pp. 21–71.

2   *See* footnote 1 of Introduction.

level, the legal system in China has gone through substantial development and reform since 1978, during which time a basic legal, regulatory and judicial framework for all areas of civil and commercial dispute resolution including securities dispute resolution was laid down, as outlined in Chapter 1. Since China's accession to the World Trade Organization (WTO) in 2001, positive developments have taken place with regard to the resolution of disputes involving foreign parities and/or cross-border issues.

Development of Law, Regulations and Judicial Procedures

In 1980s, as part of the initial process of China's economic and legal transformation, the Economic Contract Law was adopted in 1981 (as amended in 1993), followed by the 1986 GPCL.[3] With the emergence of the securities market, administrative regulations and departmental rules began to emerge for the regulation of the share issuing and trading markets as well as for the government and enterprise bond market.[4] Towards the late 1980s and early 1990s, legislative work on securities law and company law was stepping up, which led to the promulgation of the Company Law in 1993 while the promulgation of the securities law was delayed until 1998. After the securities repurchase market and commodity and financial futures market emerged in early 1990s, some relevant regulations and rules were promulgated.[5] Overall, there were rather limited legal and regulatory rules available for the people's court to apply when securities disputes started coming into the people's court. What the people's court had was the general principles of civil law, law of agency and economic contract law on one hand, and limited and sometimes confusing and inconsistent administrative regulations and rules on the other hand.[6] This lack of legal and regulatory rules, coupled with inexperience of the people's court in handling new securities disputes, led to inappropriate,[7] inconsistent[8] and wrong[9] judgments. This period of time could be regarded as the first stage of the development.

---

3   *See* Chapter 1.

4   *See* Chapter 2 and Chapter 3.

5   *See* Chapter 4 and Chapter 5.

6   For example, regulations, rules, circulars and announcements concerning government bonds were issued by the State Council, the Ministry of Finance, the PBOC and some other regulators, which were, in some circumstances, confusing and inconsistent to the people's courts, and thus the Supreme People's Court had to clarify certain issues in accordance with basic principles of law. *See* footnotes 89 and 108 of Chapter 3 and accompanying text.

7   The judgment of the case *Jin Yancheng v Shanghai Securities Business Center of Jilin Trust Investment Company of Bank of China*, which occurred in 1994, for example, was viewed as being inappropriate to apply Article 114 of the 1986 GPCL to the case. *See* footnotes 119, 120, 121 of Chapter 1 and footnote 50 of Chapter 2 and accompanying text.

8   Without detailed guidelines on the issue of calculation of losses, the people's courts may adopt different formulas to calculate the losses suffered by the plaintiffs in stock market. *See*, for example, *Jin Yancheng v Shanghai Securities Business Center of Jilin Trust Investment Company of Bank of China*, footnote 103 of Chapter 2 and accompanying text.

9   The judgment of the first instance court in *Wang Luhui v Sichuan Province Securities Co. Ltd*, a case from 1994, for example, was criticized by commentators as a wrong judgment. *See* footnotes 11 and 13 of Chapter 2 and accompanying texts.

The 1990s witnessed a sharp increase in securities disputes coming into the people's courts, ranging from disputes between agent securities companies and investor clients, disputes involving government and enterprise bonds and securities repurchase contracts, and disputes in the commodity and financial futures markets.[10] Faced with the situation, the Supreme People's Court started issuing judicial guidelines to local people's courts on the resolution of certain types of securities disputes, such as the 1995 SPC Futures Judicial Guidelines[11] and the 1996 SPC Securities Repurchase Judicial Guidelines.[12] The crackdown campaign embarked upon by the government after 1993 in the securities repurchase market and the commodity and financial futures markets[13] caused uncertainty about the development of the markets and impacted as well on the resolution of the disputes involving securities repurchase and futures contracts. The process of resolving these disputes in the people's courts became predominantly a process of implementing government policy. In 1997, the Provisional Measures on the Administration of Securities Investment Funds was issued, which set out regulatory standards for securities investment funds, and helped the people's courts deal with the disputes related to investment funds.[14] The 1998 Securities Law brought the regulation of securities market to a new stage but it failed to strengthen provisions concerning civil liability and civil compensation.[15] This period of time could be regarded as the second stage of the development.

Between the end of the 1990s and towards 2004, positive developments took place. Between September 2001 and January 2003, the Supreme People's Court issued three circulars concerning civil compensation claims arising from securities market fraud.[16] Since January 2003, civil compensation cases arising from false statements made on the securities market have been accepted and heard by the people's courts in accordance with the guidelines of the Supreme People's Court.[17] In 2003, the Securities Investment Fund Law was promulgated,[18] providing statutory provisions for the regulation of the securities investment fund market. In the same year, on the basis of the 1995 SPC Futures Judicial Guidelines, the Supreme People's

---

10 *See* Chapters 2, 3, 4 and 5.

11 *See* footnote 30 of Chapter 5.

12 *See* footnote 26 of Chapter 4.

13 *See* Chapter 4 and Chapter 5.

14 The Provisional Measures on the Administration of Securities Investment Funds (Zhengquan Touzi Jijin Guanli Zanxing Banfa) approved by the State Council on 5 November 1997 and issued by the SCSC on, and effective as of, 14 November 1997. In *Zong Chenghua v Boshi Fund Management Co., Ltd.*, a case involving investment by the plaintiff in Xiangzheng Fund established before 1997 and listed on the Shanghai Stock Exchange in 1999, a key issues was whether the structure and operation of the Fund should be subject to the standards set out by the 1997 Provisional Measures on the Administration of Securities Investment Funds. *See Studies of Judicial Decisions Related to Financial Disputes (Jinrong Shenpan Anli Yanjiu)* (Vol. 2001), edited by the Economic Division Court of Beijing High People's Court, pp. 412–417. (Beijing: Law Publishing House, 2001).

15 *Infra* note 169.

16 *See* footnote 1 of Chapter 6.

17 *See* Chapter 6.

18 *See* footnote 5 of Introduction.

Court issued the 2003 SPC Futures Judicial Provisions,[19] a more mature and settled guideline compared with its predecessor, thus moving the handling of futures disputes into a new stage. Reform of the contract law system during this period led to the enactment of the 1999 Contract Law, which transformed the previous separate system of contract laws into a unified system of contract law.[20] The 2000 Legislation Law attempts to make it clear, among other things, how to interpret the law and the level of authority between law, administrative regulations, rules, national law and regulations and local law and regulations.[21] This period of time could be regarded as the third stage of the development.

In 2004, the State Council announced a blueprint, the so-called "nine-point opinion", for the future development of the capital market in China,[22] point seven of which calls for the strengthening of law and regulations for a significant and steady development of capital market, the protection of rights and interests of investors, and a clearing-up of those administrative regulations, local laws and regulations, departmental rules and policy documents that hinder the development of the market.[23] This was followed by a major and important amendment in 2005 of the 1998 Securities Law and the 1993 Company Law.[24] The new 2005 Securities Law and the 2005 Company Law, both effective as of 1 June 2006, have opened up a new stage of the development of the law and regulations for the resolution of securities disputes.[25]

It is anticipated that judicial interpretations and detailed procedures with regard to the implementation of the 2005 Securities Law and the 2005 Company Law will be formulated by the Supreme People's Court.[26] The judicial interpretations and guidelines on the resolution of securities disputes issued by the Supreme People's Court in the past years, as shown in the discussions in previous chapters, played a crucial role in formulating detailed procedures to implement the provisions of the law and regulations and facilitating the resolution of securities disputes by the people's court. But on the other hand, the judicial interpretations and guidelines, as shown in the case of civil litigation arising from false statements, could play a questionably restrictive role and the Supreme People's Court has been chastised for exceeding its

---

19   *See* footnote 35 of Chapter 5.

20   *See* footnote 9 of Chapter 1.

21   The 2000 Legislation Law of the PRC was enacted by the National People's Congress on 15 March 2000, and effective as of 1 January 2000. For a critical assessment on law-making process in China, *see* Jan Michiel Otto et al. (eds), *Law-Making in the People's Republic of China* (The Hague: Kluwer Law International, 2000).

22   Several Opinions of the State Council on Promoting the Reform, Opening-up and Steady Development of China's Capital Market (Guowuyuan Guanyu Tuijin Ziben Shichang Gaige Kaifang he Wending Fazhan de Ruogan Yijian) announced on 31 January 2004.

23   *Id.* Point 7.

24   *See infra* section "Amendments of Securities Law and Company Law and Future Prospects".

25   *Id.*

26   For example, detailed procedures and guidelines are necessary for civil litigations related to the provisions of the 2005 Securities Law on civil liability and civil compensation arising from losses caused by insider trading and market manipulation.

judicial interpretation power.[27] Further reforms on judicial procedures and judicial system generally are necessary, particularly in the areas of joint action proceeding and the role of the judicial committee of the people's court.

Reform on Joint Action Procedures and its Limitation

In December 2005, the Supreme People's Court issued a circular, instructing local people's courts on the changes made to the handling of cases of joint action.[28] Starting from January 2006, joint actions involving numerous parties either on one side or on both sides shall be dealt with by basic level people's courts; if the court who accepts such a joint action thinks that the case is not suitable for a joint action, the court may try the case individually; if a case of joint action is of major significance within the jurisdiction of a provincial high people's court, the case shall be dealt with by an intermediate people's court; if, due to special circumstances, a joint action case must be tried by a high people's court as the first instance court, the matter shall be submitted to the Supreme People's Court for approval before the court accepts the case.[29] The purpose of this change, as stated in the Circular, is to make it convenient for the parties to litigate as well as for the people's courts to mediate the cases locally, to increase efficiency of dealing with such type of cases as well as save court resources, and to strengthen the supervision and guidance by the Supreme People's Court on the adjudication work of the people's courts of lower levels.[30]

As joint action is much related to securities litigation, particularly compensation claim cases arising from false statements made on the securities market,[31] the changes made to the handling of joint action cases will affect the securities litigation in a form of joint action. In certain way, the changes would be helpful to securities litigation in that investor plaintiffs in a joint action case may find it convenient and time saving to bring their case to a local basic level people's court in terms of availability of the court. But, overall, the changes that touch only one aspect of current system of joint action have not brought about any other positive changes to lift limitations of joint action system in general and the joint action procedures in securities litigation in particular.[32] Without lifting other limitations, such as the requirement for a fixed number of plaintiffs before the hearing,[33] the joint action as an important platform for the civil litigation arising from securities-related false statements would not be able to use its full potential to accommodate efficiently the securities civil litigation.

---

27   *See* footnotes 64, 65 and 66 of Chapter 6.

28   The Circular of the Supreme People's Court on the Issue of Acceptance of Joint Action Cases by the People's Court (Zuigao Renmin Fayuan Guanyu Renmin Fayuan Shouli Gongtong Susong Anjian Wenti de Tongzhi), issued by the Supreme People's Court on 30 December 2005 and effective as of 1 January 2006.

29   *Id.* Point 7.

30   *Id.* First paragraph.

31   *See* Chapter 6, section "Forms of Action Available to Investors".

32   For discussion about limitations of joint action, *see* Chapter 6, section "Forms of Action Available to Investors".

33   *See* footnote 130 of Chapter 6.

Judicial Committees of the People's Court

Judicial committees[34] are established at all levels of the people's courts in accordance with the 1983 People's Court Organization Law.[35] The judicial committees is presided over by the president of the courts at each level and consists of senior judges who are nominated by the president of the courts and appointed by the Standing Committee of the National People's Congress or the standing committees of local people's congresses.[36] In accordance with the provisions of the 1983 People's Court Organization Law and the 1991 Civil Procedure Law, the role of the judicial committee is to summarize and refine adjudicating experiences of the people's court, to discuss major or difficult cases and other issues concerning adjudication work, and to deal with the cases submitted to the judicial committee when an effective judgment or ruling of the court is found to have been wrongly decided either on the fact of the case or the application of law.[37]

Securities disputes, particular in the areas of sell and purchase of government bonds, securities repurchase agreements and futures contracts, may involve a large sum of money or difficult issues. The judicial committees of a court, where a securities dispute involving a large sum of money or difficult issues is tried, are often involved in discussing and deciding such cases. For example, in *China Life Insurance Company Chengdu Branch v Sichuan Hualong Investment Consultant Co. Ltd.*,[38] a major and complicated case involving a purchase of 40 million yuan government bonds in 1999 by the plaintiff, China Life Insurance Company Chengdu branch, the judicial committee of the Sichuan High People's Court was involved in discussing and deciding the case in the first instance level of hearing of the case.[39] In *Henan Province International Investment Trust Company v Wuhan Jinda Industrial Company Limited by Shares*,[40] a case involving difficult issues connected to a borrowing of 10 million yuan government bonds, the judicial committee of the first instance court, the Hubei High People's Court, was involved in discussing and deciding the case.[41]

On the one hand, the judgment of such cases may benefit from the collective thoughts of senior judges of the judicial committee on difficult and uncertain issues, but on the other hand, the system of the judicial committee operates on the basis that the members of the judicial committee are briefed on the cases rather than participating fully in the hearing of the cases themselves. Criticisms and debates are raised in the

---

34   "Judicial committee" (*Shenpan Weiyuanhui*) of the people's court is also translated as "adjudication committee" of the people's court.

35   Article 11 of the People's Court Organization Law of the PRC, promulgated in July 1979, as amended in September 1983, requires that a judicial committee is established at each level of the people's court.

36   *Id.*

37   Articles 11 and 14 of the 1983 People's Court Organization Law and Article 177 of the 1991 Civil Procedure Law.

38   *See* footnote 37 of Chapter 3 and full facts of the case in Chapter 3.

39   *Id.* footnote 37 at p. 17.

40   *See* footnote 45 of Chapter 3 and full facts of the case in Chapter 3.

41   *Id.* footnote 45 at p. 702.

judicial committee system of the on their way to discuss major or difficult cases and their adverse consequential impact on the appeal system.[42] In The People's Court Second Five-Year Reform Outlines (2004–2008),[43] a set of proposals are outlined by the Supreme People's Court for the reform of the judicial committee.[44] It remains to be seen how the system of the judicial committee, which is deeply rooted as a key mechanism in the judicial system in China, is to be reformed, and how the problems associated with this system are to be eliminated – the outcome of which would have direct impact on all areas of dispute resolution by the people's courts, including securities dispute resolution. It is an important reform project because it affects the way in which the people's courts operate, and affects the judicial reform process to be guided by the principle of impartiality and independence in the post-WTO China.

Securities Dispute Resolution in China's Administrative, Economic, Legal, Social and Political Contexts

Securities civil dispute resolution in China relies to certain extent on administrative authorities and regulars. In the securities repurchase market, for example, the administrative regulars, in implementing the 1996 Circular of the State Council,[45] compiled a list of securities repurchase participants who owed debts to each other in a national chain of debt clearance. Correspondingly, the Supreme People's Court issued three circulars in 1998, 2000 and 2001 respectively, instructing local people's courts to stop accepting, hearing and enforcing the cases of securities repurchase disputes listed on the national chain of debt clearance, which lasted about eighteen months between 1998 and 2000.[46] In the futures market, the Supreme People's Court instructed local people's courts that some disputes may be resolved first by administrative authorities, and if such attempts still could not resolve the disputes, and they must be resolved through litigation, the people's courts should accept such

---

42   There are increasing debates and discussion papers in recent years on the system of judicial committee. *See*, for example, Chu Hongjun and Chen Jingyu, "Study on Several Problems of the System of Judicial Committee – Also on the Reform and Improvement of the System of Judicial Committee" ("Shenpan Weiyuanhui Zhidu Ruogan Wenti Yanjiu – Jian Lun Shenpan Weiyuanhui Zhidu de Gaige He Wanshan"), pp. 50–54, *Falü Shiyong (Application of Law)*, No. 10, 2005; Guan Shengyin, "Exploration and Improvement on Working Mechanism of the Judicial Committee" ("Shenpan Weiyuanhui Gongzuo Jizhi Tansuo Ji Wanshan"), pp. 27–30, *Renmin Sifa (People's Judiciary)*, No. 10, 2004.

43   The People's Court Second Five-Year Reform Outlines (2004–2008) (Renmin Fayuan Di'erge Wunian Gaige Gangyao), announced by the Supreme People's Court on 26 October 2005, which covers eight areas of the of work of the people's court and altogether includes fifty lists of issues, proposals and measures.

44   *Id.* Lists 23 and 24, which outline five proposals, such as the proposal to change the meeting (*huiyi*) of the judicial committee into hearing (*shenli*).

45   *See* footnote 11 of Chapter 4.

46   *See* footnotes 27, 28, 29, 30 of Chapter 4 and accompanying texts.

cases.[47] In compensation claim cases involving false statements, before investors can go to the people's courts to claim compensation for their losses resulting from false statements, there must be an administrative penalty decision made by the CSRC, the Ministry of Finance or other competent administrative authorities against the wrongdoers for their false statements.[48]

On the one hand, involvement of administrative authorities and regulators and the actions taken by them may speed up the process of dispute resolution, as in the case of securities repurchase triangle debt cases, and thus save the resources of the people's courts and reduce the adverse impact of the disputes on the respective securities market and on the economy as a whole. But on the other hand, the involvement of administrative authorities and regulators in civil proceedings, as in the case of false statement cases, may lead to a situation where an alleged false statement is not investigated or punished by administrative regulator for one reason or another and those investors who suffered losses as a result of the false statement will not be able to get remedies through civil compensation litigation.[49] Moreover, changing government policies, formulated on economic, financial, social or political grounds, may prevail in the process of dispute resolution through administrative authorities and regulators at the cost of the legal rights and interests prescribed by law and regulations, which should be upheld by the people's courts through judicial process.

Financial security (*jinrong anquan*) and social stability (*shehui wending*) were concerns of the government and the people's court in the process of securities dispute resolution. The default of repayments to bondholders by many enterprise bond issuers in the early 1990s was treated as a potential threat to social stability and a series of measures was taken by the government at both national and local levels to tackle the problem.[50] Similarly, the debt problem in the securities repurchase market was treated by the government as an urgent matter as it was becoming a threat to social stability as well as to financial stability and implementation of government economic policy.[51] In the commodity and financial futures markets, the closure of the government bond futures market in May 1995 and the crackdown campaign embarked upon by the government from 1993 to 1999 to stop chaotic situations and a blind development of the futures market, show that the priority of the government was to maintain social stability, public confidence and the stability of financial market.[52]

In line with the priority of the government policy, the people's court takes the protection of social stability also as a priority of the people's court in the

---

47   *See* Point 4 of the 1995 SPC Futures Judicial Guidelines; footnote 30 of the Chapter 5.

48   *See* Chapter 6, section "Administrative Penalty Decision and Criminal Court Judgment".

49   *Id.* generally and footnote 77.

50   *See* footnotes 83, 84, 86, 87, 88 of Chapter 3 and accompanying texts.

51   *See* footnotes 91, 92, 121 of Chapter 4 and accompanying texts.

52   *See* footnotes 146, 147 of Chapter 5 and accompanying texts.

resolution of securities disputes.[53] Some judges advocated that judges, in dealing with securities repurchase disputes, should associate their views with political and economic context and should bear in mind the task of maintaining financial as well as social stability.[54] The adoption by the Supreme People's Court of the prerequisite rule in the procedures for the hearing of compensation claims of investors arising from false statements is seen by some commentators as a rule to prevent angry shareholders from flooding the people's court and thus having adverse social and political repercussions.[55] For others, particularly judges, the prerequisite rule can help plaintiffs collect evidence and reduce their burden of proof; therefore, it is good for the protection of investors.[56] Indeed, the people's courts should protect lawful rights and interests of market participants and take this task as a priority.

Early in 1995, the Supreme People's Court instructed local people's courts that, where a case of disputes in the commodity and financial futures market had a wider social coverage or related to social stability in other ways, the people's courts need to initiatively listen to the opinion of futures regulators, and where necessary, seek instructions from the court of higher level, in order that such cases could be dealt with timely, properly and fairly.[57] In the same document, the Supreme People's Court instructed local people's courts to adhere to the principle of respecting lawful agreements made between the parties; thus, as long as the agreement reached between the parties were not in violation of the provisions of law and administrative regulations and the practice of futures trading, the agreement should be treated as the basis for resolving the disputes between the parties.[58]

This cautious attitude towards issues relating to social and financial stability, and the emphasis at the same time on the protection of lawful rights and interests of market participants and on the principle of respecting lawful contracts of the parties, continue to be found in the judicial guidelines of the Supreme People's Court. In 2004, for example, the Supreme People's Court issued procedures for freezing and transferring settlement funds in securities trading, an important procedure which touches upon interests of every shareholders and investors.[59] The aim of the procedure, as stated by the Supreme People's Court, is to ensure financial security and social stability, to protect lawful rights and interests of the parties, and to ensure lawful enforcement by the people's courts.[60] Looking at the way in which the people's courts associate the resolution of securities disputes with the issue of financial security and social stability, it is obvious that the people's courts assume a dual role of maintaining financial and social stability on one hand while protecting lawful rights and interest

---

53   Li Guoguang, deputy president of the Supreme People's Court, speaking at a meeting on the trial of civil compensation cases arising from false statements on the securities market on 12–14 September 2002, emphasized that protecting social stability is the first and most important task of the people's court. *See* note 253 of Chapter 6.

54   *See* footnote 132 of Chapter 4.

55   *See* footnote 64 of Chapter 6.

56   *Id.* footnote 73.

57   Point 4 of the 1995 SPC Futures Judicial Guidelines; footnote 30 of Chapter 5.

58   *Id.*

59   *See* footnote 285 of Chapter 1.

60   *Id.*

of market participants and upholding the principle of freedom of contract and respect to lawful agreements of the parties on the other hand. The understanding of the resolution of securities disputes by the people's courts in this respect should be within China's administrative, economic, legal, social and political contexts.

China's Accession to the WTO and Securities Disputes Involving Foreign Parties or Cross-border Issues

China's entry into the WTO in 2001 and the implementation of China's WTO commitments in Chinese financial services law have further opened up China's securities market.[61] As more foreign securities investments are coming into China and also more Chinese companies are listing abroad, it is important to have an efficient and effective legal and judicial framework in the post-WTO China for the resolution of securities disputes involving foreign parties or cross-border issues. In the early 1990s, as in other areas of foreign investments, arbitration through the China International Economic and Trade Arbitration Commission (CIETAC) was referred to as a means to resolve corporate and securities disputes involving foreign parties.[62] In December 1986, China joined the 1958 Convention on the Recognition and Enforcement of Foreign Arbitral Awards (the New York Convention),[63] and in 1987, the Supreme People's Court issued a circular instructing local people's courts on the implementation of the 1958 New York Convention.[64] The 1991 Civil Procedure Law provides that the people's courts shall recognize and enforce foreign arbitral awards in accordance with the international treaties concluded or acceded to by China or with the principle of reciprocity.[65]

In the environment of China's WTO membership, CIETAC amended its arbitration rules in 2005, and a special set of arbitration rules, the Financial Dispute Arbitration Rules, was added to the rulebook of CIETAC in 2003.[66] Disputes, including financial and securities disputes involving foreign parities, would benefit from these developments if they are arbitrated by CIETAC.[67] Another development in recent years is the arrangements made between Mainland China and Hong Kong in 2000

---

61   *See* Zhu Sanzhu "Implementing China's WTO Commitments in Chinese Financial Services Law", *The China Review*, Vol. 6, Number 2 (Fall 2006), pp. 3–33.

62   *See* Zhu Sanzhu, *Securities Regulation in China*, pp. 101–102. (Ardsley, NY: Transnational Publishers, 2000).

63   The Decision of the Standing Committee of the National People's Congress on China's Joining the Convention on the Recognition and Enforcement of Foreign Arbitral Awards, adopted on 2 December 1986.

64   Circular of the Supreme People's Court on the Implementation of "the Convention on the Recognition and Enforcement of Foreign Arbitral Awards" China has Acceded to (Zuigao Renmin Fayuan Guanyu Zhixing Woguo Jiaru de "Chengren Ji Zhixing Waiguo Zhongcai Caijue Gongyue" de Tongzhi), issued on 10 October 1987.

65   Article 269 of the 1991 Civil Procedure Law.

66   *See infra* notes 131 and 132.

67   For a brief critical assessment of the 2005 CIETAC Arbitration Rules, *see* Darren Fitzgerald, "CIETAC's New Arbitration Rules: Do the Reforms Go Far Enough? *Asian Dispute Review*, 2005, pp. 51–53. For a brief analysis of the 2003 CIETAC Financial Dispute

on the mutual enforcement of arbitral awards,[68] which creates a closer cooperative relationship between Mainland China and Hong Kong in the enforcement of arbitral awards. Given the fact that Hong Kong is, and is going to be, a place to host a majority of Chinese companies seeking listing abroad,[69] an effective and efficient enforcement of arbitral awards through the cooperation between Mainland China and Hong Kong would be a necessary part of the arbitral and judicial framework for the resolution of the securities disputes submitted for arbitration through arbitral organizations of Mainland China and Hong Kong.

The 1986 GPCL provides for basic principles governing choice of applicable laws in a civil and commercial case involving foreign parties[70] while the 1991 Civil Procedure Law provides for procedural principles concerning issues related to a civil litigation involving foreign parties, such as the issue of requesting a foreign court to assist in the service of legal documents and investigation and collection of evidence or assisting a foreign court in such matters by the people's court.[71] In dealing with securities disputes that involve foreign or international elements, the people's courts are found to apply international norms and practice if such application is appropriate for the justice of the case.[72] In recent years prior to and after China's accession to

---

Arbitration Rules, *see* James M. Zimmerman and Diarmuid O'Brien, "CIETAC Financial Dispute Arbitration Rules: Practice and Problems", *Asian Dispute Review*, 2004, pp. 69–70.

68   The Supreme People's Court Arrangements between Inland and Hong Kong Special Administrative Region Concerning Mutual Enforcement of Arbitral Awards (Zuigao Renmin Fayuan Guanyu Neidi Yu Xianggang Tebie Xingzhengqu Xianghu Zhixing Zhongcai Caijue de Anpai), adopted by the Judicial Committee of the Supreme People's Court on 18 June 1999 and issued on 24 January 2000, effective as of 1 February 2000.

69   Some authors submit that, given the litigation risk, Sarbanes-Oxley compliance costs, and the burden of initial and ongoing disclosure requirements associated with listings in the US, Chinese issuers have largely turned away from US listings and are now focusing their attention instead on listings on the HKSE. *See* John Moore and Nick-Anthony Buford, "In the Ascendancy", *International Financial Law Review*, Vol. 25, Issue 9, pp. 26–30, 2006. *See* also Jack C. Auspitz, Charles C. Comey and Paul W. Boltz, "Asian Issuers Face Rising Class Action Threat", *International Financial Law Review*, Vol. 23, Issue 7, pp. 23–25, 2004.

70   Chapter 8, "Application of Law in Civil Relations with Foreign Elements" including articles 142–150. Article 142, for example, provides that international practice may be applied to mattes for which neither the law of PRC nor any international treaty concluded or acceded to by China has any provisions.

71   Part IV, "Special Provisions on Civil Litigation Procedures Involving Foreign Elements" including Chapters 24–29 and Articles 237–269. Article 262, for example, provides that requesting a foreign court for assistance or assisting a foreign court in the service of legal documents and investigation and collection of evidence shall be conducted in accordance with the international treaty concluded or acceded to by China or the principle of reciprocity.

72   In *Zhaoxiaomei v Nanjing Jinzhongfu International Futures Trading Co. Ltd.*, for example, the Court decided the case by reference to relevant rules for the trading of American coffee futures. *See* footnotes 82 and 83 of Chapter 5 and accompanying text. The Supreme People's Court instructed the local people's courts to deal with the futures dispute cases involving foreign parties and parties from Hong Kong and Macau by reference to relevant international practice. *See* Point 1 of the 1995 SPC Futures Judicial Guidelines, note 30 of Chapter 5.

the WTO, the Supreme People's Court has issued several circulars and provisions with an aim to improve the handling of civil and commercial cases involving foreign parties.[73] But despite these developments, continuous legal and judicial reforms, to be guided by the principles of fairness, efficiency, impartiality and independence, are necessary and crucial to further improvements of judicial process and the handling of disputes involving foreign parties by the people's courts.

Alternative Resolution of Securities Disputes

Alternative dispute resolution is promoted as part of the legal and regulatory framework for civil securities dispute resolution in China, alongside civil securities litigation in the people's courts. Mediation by the people's courts, often called judicial mediation (*sifa tiaojie*), mediation by securities professional associations or securities exchanges and arbitration are all available for the resolution of securities disputes. The development of alternative resolution of securities disputes outlined below suggests that a future trend in securities dispute resolution in China is to encourage more securities disputes to be resolved through mediation and arbitration.

Mediation by the People's Courts

Mediation (*tiaojie*) by the people's court during a civil proceeding, as an alternative dispute resolution in a limited sense, is an integrated part of civil procedural rules. The 1991 Civil Procedure Law set out basic principles and procedural rules for mediation by a civil court,[74] for which the Supreme People's Court provided some implementing interpretations in 1992.[75] In 2004, on the basis of the mediation experiences of the people's courts, the Supreme People's Court issued a further

---

73   Including, among others, the Circular of the Supreme People's Court on Several Issues to which Attention Should Be Given in Adjudicating and Enforcing Commercial Cases Involving Foreign Elements (Zuigao Renmin Fayuan Guanyu Shenli he Zhixing Shewaiceng Shangshi Anjian Yingdang Zhuyi de Jige Wenti de Tongzhi), issued on 17 April 2000; the Provisions of the Supreme People's Court on Several Issues Concerning Jurisdiction of Litigation of Civil and Commercial Cases Involving Foreign Elements (Zuigao Renmin Fayuan Guanyu Shewai Minshangshi Anjian Susong Guanxia Ruogan Wenti de Guiding), adopted by the Judicial Committee of the Supreme People's Court on 25 December 2001 and issued on 25 February 2002, effective as of 1 March 2002; the Several Provisions of the Supreme People's Court on Service of Judicial Documents in Civil or Commercial Cases Involving Foreign Elements (Zuigao Renmin Fayuan Guanyu Shewai Minshi Huo Shangshi Anjian Sifa Wenshu Songda Wenti Ruogan Guiding), adopted by the Judicial Committee of the Supreme People's Court on 17 July 2006 and issued on 10 August 2006, effective as of 22 August 2006.

74   The 1991 Civil Procedure Law, Chapter Eight: Mediation, including Articles 85–91, and in addition, some other relevant articles in other sections of the 1991 Civil Procedure Law.

75   Articles 91–97 of the 1992 Opinion of the Supreme People's Court on Questions Concerning the Implementation of the Civil Procedure Law of the People's Republic of China.

guideline on the mediation work by the people's courts.[76] In general, the people's courts may conduct mediation on a voluntary basis when the facts of the case are clear and right and wrong are distinguished;[77] if one party or both parties are not willing to be mediated, the people's court should adjudicate the case without delay.[78] Where possible, mediation may be conducted at the end of the court debate;[79] upon an agreement by all the parties involved, mediation may take place prior to the court debate.[80] A mediation agreement reached by the two parties must be voluntary without compulsion and must not violate the provisions of the law.[81] Looking at these procedural rules, it is obvious that the parties' willingness and their agreement to mediation is at the heart of the mediation process by the people's courts.

As in other areas of civil litigation where mediation by court is applicable,[82] securities civil litigation is integrated with an application of mediation by the people's courts. Where possible, the people's courts mediate the dispute instead of going through a full proceeding. For example, in *Cheng Yonggang v Huaxia Securities Co. Ltd.*,[83] a case in which the defendant securities company failed to carry out a sale order instructed by the plaintiff Chen Yonggang, the Court found that the defendant had breached the contract and was liable for compensation. The Court mediated the case and the plaintiff and defendant willingly reached an agreement, according to which the defendant agreed to compensate the plaintiff 30,000 yuan and the plaintiff agreed to pay 2,360.70 yuan in court costs. In *Li Erjiao v Zhang Shihui*,[84] a case involving an agency relationship, the Court conducted mediation and an agreement was consequently reached, under which the defendant purchased 288 shares of the Shenzhen Development Bank for the plaintiff, who returned 890 yuan to the defendant.

Cases are mediated not only at the level of first instance courts but also at the level of appeal courts; and not only contract cases and but also in tort cases. In *Henan Province International Investment Trust Company v Wuhan Jinda Industrial*

---

76   The Provisions of the Supreme People's Court on Several Issues about Civil Mediation Work of the People's Court (Zuigao Renmin Fayuan Guanyu Renmin Fayuan Minshi Tiaojie Gongzuo Ruogan Wenti de Guiding) adopted by the Judicial Committee of the Supreme People's Court on 18 April 2004 and promulgated on 16 September 2004, effective as of 1 November 2004.

77   Article 85 of the 1991 Civil Procedure Law.

78   Article 92 of the 1992 Opinion of the Supreme People's Court on Questions Concerning the Implementation of the Civil Procedure Law of the People's Republic of China.

79   Article 128 of the 1991 Civil Procedure Law.

80   Article 1 of the 2004 Provisions of the Supreme People's Court on Several Issues about Civil Mediation Work of the People's Court.

81   Article 88 of the 1991 Civil Procedure Law.

82   Mediation is not applicable in some areas of civil litigation, such as bankruptcy proceedings and cases involving personal status. *See* Article 2 of the 2004 Provisions of the Supreme People's Court on Several Issues about Civil Mediation Work of the People's Court.

83   *See* footnote 36 of Chapter 2 and accompanying text.

84   *See* footnote 67 of Chapter 1 and accompanying text.

Company Limited by Shares,[85] a case involving a transaction of borrowing 10 million yuan 1995 (2) government bonds, the defendant appealed the judgment of the Hubei High People's Court to the Supreme People's Court. During the appeal proceeding, the Supreme People's Court presided over a mediation process in which the defendant (appellant) and the plaintiff (respondent) voluntarily reached an agreement, in accordance with which the appellant agreed to return 10 million yuan government bonds by 30 June 1998. On this basis, the Supreme People's Court closed the case with a mediation agreement instead of a judgment, which was signed by both parties.[86] In *S.T. Hongguang*, a securities-related false statement civil case, a court mediation agreement was reached after mediation by the Chengdu Intermediate People's Court between eleven plaintiffs and two defendants, with ninety percent of the plaintiff claims compensated.[87]

By mediating the case and thus changing a full litigation proceeding into a mediation process, the people's courts can deal with securities dispute cases in a relatively efficient and time-saving manner. Given the fact that the people's courts are facing an ever-increasing caseload, the resolution of dispute by judicial mediation is helpful as far as the people's courts and their resources are concerned. A key issue is whether the voluntary principle set out in the 1991 Civil Procedure Law could be adhered to by all the people's courts at all levels and at all times. Before the 1991 Civil Procedure Law, coercion was one of the problems associated with judicial mediation.[88] After the enactment of the 1991 Civil Procedure Law, which emphasized that judicial mediation was to be conducted on a voluntary basis, such problems continue to occur, especially among the people's courts at local levels.[89] It is therefore important that the voluntary principle is truthfully implemented while achieving the goals stated by the Supreme People's Court in 2004 in its guidelines on judicial mediation.[90]

A mediation agreement reached shall have legal effect and must be performed by the parties concerned. If one party refused to perform, the other party may apply to the people's court for enforcement.[91] Parties may apply for a retrial if they can show by evidence that a mediation agreement which takes legal effect has violated the voluntary principle or the content of the agreement are unlawful; the people's court shall retry the case if the claim is confirmed to be true by the court.[92] The

---

85   *See* footnote 45 of Chapter 3 and accompanying text.

86   *Id.* at pp. 702, 703.

87   *See* footnote 151 of Chapter 6 and accompanying text.

88   *See* footnote 152 of Chapter 6.

89   *See* footnote 153 of Chapter 6.

90   The preface of the 2004 Provisions of the Supreme People's Court on Several Issues about Civil Mediation Work of the People's Court states that the Provisions are formulated in order to ensure correct mediation of civil cases by the people's court, to resolve disputes timely, to ensure parties to exercise their litigation rights lawfully and make it convenient for them to exercise such rights, and to save judicial resources.

91   Article 216 of the 1991 Civil Procedure Law.

92   Article 180 of the 1991 Civil Procedure Law. Article 182 of the 1991 Civil Procedure Law requires that an application for a retrial made by a party must be submitted within two years after the judgment or ruling becomes effective.

people's court can initiate a retrial as well without an application from the parties concerned if it is discovered that an effective mediation agreement definitely has error and must be retried.[93] In *Hainan Province Trust Investment Co. v Guangdong Overseas Chinese Trust Investment Co.*,[94] a case of securities repurchase dispute, a mediation agreement was reached by the parties and the Court served the agreement document to both parties. During the process of enforcement of the agreement, the Court decided to retry the case after it was discovered that an office of the defendant involved in the case had been shut down by the Guangdong Branch of the People's Bank of China. The effect of the retrial was later recognized by the Supreme People's Court at the appeal stage.[95]

Cases are sometimes settled outside court (*tingwai hejie*) between the parties. In *Wulumuqi Branch of China Pacific Insurance Co. v Dalian Securities Co. Ltd.*,[96] a case concerning the purchase of securities, the defendant appealed the judgment of Xinjiang Autonomous Region High People's Court to the Supreme People's Court. During the appeal proceeding, an outside-court settlement agreement was reached between the appellant and two respondents and the appellant applied for withdrawal of the appeal. After an examination, the Court allowed the withdrawal in accordance with Article 156 of the 1991 Civil Procedure Law[97] and on the basis that the settlement agreement was lawful and was a true intention of the parties. Half of the court costs paid by the appellant were then refunded to the appellant.[98] There were cases involving compensation arising from false statements made by listed companies that were settled between plaintiffs and defendants.[99]

Settlement outside court initiated by parties themselves during a proceeding is beneficial in certain ways to both the people's court and the parties themselves. It is a way encouraged by the people's courts.[100] According to Article 4 of the 2004

93　*See* Reply of the Supreme People's Court on whether the People's Court Can Retry a Case in which the Civil Mediation Agreement Definitely Has Error and the Party Has not Applied for Retrial (Zuigao Renmin Fayuan Guanyu Minshi Tiaojieshu Queyou Cuowu Dangshiren Meiyou Shenqing Zaishen de Anjian Renmin Fayuan Kefou Zaishen de Pifu), replied by the Supreme People's Court on 8 March 1993.

94　*See Series of Adjudicated Cases of the Supreme People's Court of the People's Republic of China* (*Zhonghua Renmin Gongheguo Zuigao Renmin Fayuan Pan'an Daxi*) (*Civil and Commercial 2001 Volume*), Chief Editor Xiao Yang, compiled by the Second Division Court of Civil Court of the Supreme People's Court (Beijing: the People's Court Publishing House, 2003), at pp. 82–85.

95　*Id.* at p. 85.

96　*See Series of Adjudicated Cases of the Supreme People's Court of the People's Republic of China, supra note* 94 at pp. 41–42.

97　Article 156 of the 1991 Civil Procedure Law states that if an appellant applies for withdrawal of his appeal before a people's court of second instance delivers its judgment, the Court shall decide whether to approve the application or not.

98　*Supra* note 96 at p.41.

99　*See* footnote 154 of Chapter 6.

100　For example, Article 4 of the 2003 Several Provisions of the Supreme People's Court on Hearing Civil Compensation Cases Arising from False Statement on the Securities Market instruct the people's courts to encourage parties to settle. *See* Chapter 6, section "The Role of Judicial Mediation and Settlement by the Party".

Provisions of the Supreme People's Court on Several Issues about Civil Mediation Work of the People's Court, the people's court may, upon an application by the parties who have reached a settlement agreement, issued a mediation agreement after confirming the settlement agreement; the period the parties have applied for outside-court settlement is not taken into account in the calculation of time limits for trial.[101] Where the parties ask the people's court to coordinate the settlement process, the people's court may help them by sending out court staff or inviting or entrusting relevant units or individuals for coordination.[102] There is no doubt that these procedural arrangements could play a role in facilitating settlement by parties.

Mediation by Professional Associations and Securities Exchanges

Mediation of disputes by securities professional associations and securities exchanges is one of the functions designated by the securities law and regulations. The 1998 Securities Law stipulates that securities associations are self-regulatory organizations of the securities industry;[103] securities firms should join securities associations;[104] securities associations shall, among other functions and responsibilities, mediate disputes between members and between members and their clients.[105] In the futures market, the 2002 Measures on the Administration of Futures Broker Firms requires that futures brokerage firms join the China Futures Association;[106] disputes concerning futures business between futures brokerage firms or between futures brokerage firms and investors may be submitted to the China Futures Association for mediation.[107] The 2002 Measures on the Administration of Futures Exchanges stipulates that board of directors of a futures exchange may set up a special mediation committee depending on the need, and the committee is accountable to the board of directors.[108]

The Securities Association of China (SAC), established in August 1991, is the first national securities professional self-regulatory association established in China,

---

101   Time limits are required for trial. For example, Article 135 of the 1991 Civil Procedure Law requires that a case tried under ordinary procedure should be concluded within six months after the case is accepted for hearing by the people's court.

102   Article 4 of the 2004 Provisions of the Supreme People's Court on Several Issues about Civil Mediation Work of the People's Court.

103   Article 162 of the 1998 Securities Law.

104   *Id.*

105   *Id.* art. 164 (v).

106   Article 4 of the 2002 Measures on the Administration of Futures Broker Firms, issued by the CSRC on 17 May 2002 and effective as of 1 July 2002.

107   *Id.* art. 33.

108   Article 27 of the 2002 Measures on the Administration of Futures Exchanges, issued by the CSRC on 17 May 2002 and effective as of 1 July 2002. This provision is the same as the provision in Article 31 of the 1999 Measures on the Administration of Futures Exchanges which was replaced by the 2002 Measures.

with branches in local regions for securities firms and dealers.[109] The China Futures Association (CFA), established in December 2000, is the national futures self-regulatory association in China.[110] The Articles of Association of the SAC states that the SAC exercises its functions and responsibilities in accordance with relevant provisions of the Securities Law.[111] One of these functions and responsibilities is to mediate disputes involving securities business between members and between members and their clients.[112] The CFA has a similar role. One of the functions and responsibilities stated in the Articles of Association of the CFA is to mediate disputes involving futures business between members, between members and their clients, and between certified brokers and their clients.[113] Disputes between members or between members and their clients may be submitted to the CFA for mediation.[114]

The 2005 Securities Law has made a noticeable amendment to the 1998 Securities Law with respect to the mediation function of securities associations. The previous provision "mediate disputes between members and between members and their clients" has been changed to "mediate disputes involving securities business between members and between members and their clients."[115] This change effectively narrows the scope of disputes that could be submitted to the securities association, focusing rightly on the disputes that are relevant to securities business. One of the tasks for next few years in light of the 2005 Securities Law, highlighted by the fourth general meeting of the SAC held in January 2007 is to work on the mediation procedures of the SAC.[116]

Another recent regulatory development is in the area of securities consultancy businesses through the membership system.[117] In relation to this development,

---

109   For discussion about the SAC, *see* Zhu Sanzhu, *Securities Regulation in China*, pp. 69–70, *supra* note 62.

110   The work to establish China Futures Association started in 1995 when all the formalities and procedures for establishment had been gone through, but the work was stopped because of the crackdown on blind development of futures market by the government at that time. By the end of September 2003, the Association had 189 members located in 32 provinces and cities, including three Commodity Futures Exchanges as special members.

111   Article 5 of the Articles of Association of the SAC, adopted at the fourth general meeting of the SAC on 22 January 2007.

112   *Id.* art. 5 (v).

113   Article 10 of the Articles of Association of the CFA, adopted on 2 June 2006.

114   Article 16 of the Provisional Measures on the Administration of the Members of the China Futures Association, issued on 29 December 2000.

115   Article 176 (v) of the 2005 Securities Law has now replaced Article 164 (v) of the 1998 Securities Law.

116   *See* the Work Report presented by Huang Xiangping, Chairman of the SAC, at the fourth general meeting of the SAC on 22 January 2007.

117   Several regulatory documents have recently been issued by the CSRC including, among others, Provisional Regulations on the Administration of Membership System Securities Consultant Business (Huiyuanzhi Zhengquan Touzi Zixun Yewu Guanli Zanxing Guiding) issued by the CSRC on 12 December 2005 and effective as of 1 January 2006. Article 1 defines membership-based securities consultancy business as a kind of securities consultancy business in which securities consultancy institutions, through television, radio, internet, fax, email, telephone, and so on, solicit and take members, provide services of

establishment of an effective mediation system within securities associations becomes a part of the regulatory framework and a task of the SAC. In a circular that set out a number of tasks for the implementation of self-regulation of membership-based securities consultancy business,[118] the SAC plans to establish procedures for mediation of disputes that are unable to be resolved through consultation between securities consultancy firms and their members.[119] Such mediation would apply to the securities consultancy firms who have qualified to provide membership-based securities consultancy business.[120]This development would provide an additional platform for dispute resolution in the area of membership-based securities consultancy businesses. The securities consultancy firms and their members could resolve their disputes through consultation first and, if that fails, they may apply for mediation by the SAC as an alternative to the resolution through arbitration or the people's courts.

Arbitration

Arbitration (*zhongcai*) in China[121] is primarily governed by the 1994 Arbitration Law of the PRC.[122] In 2006, the Supreme People's Court promulgated a full interpretation on the application of the 1994 Arbitration Law.[123] Between 1995 and 2005, the Supreme People's Court issued a number of individual circulars and replies on various issues concerning the implementation of the 1994 Arbitration Law.[124]

---

information, analysis, forecast or consultancy regarding securities investment and charge consultancy fees accordingly.

118   The Circular of the SAC on Implementation of "The Provisional Regulations on the Administration of Membership System Securities Consultant Business" and Strengthen Self Regulation (Zhongguo Zhengquan Xiehui Guanyu Guance Luoshi "Huiyuanzhi Zhengquan Touzi Zixun Yewu Guanli Zanxing Guiding" Jiaqiang Zilü Guanli de Tongzhi), issued by the SAC on 29 December 2005.

119   *Id.* Point 8.

120   *Id.*

121   For a comprehensive and comparative study of commercial arbitration in China, *see* Ming Kang, *A Study of Commercial Arbitration Service* (*Shangshi Zhongcai Fuwu Yanjiu*) (Beijing: Law Publishing House, 2005).

122   The Arbitration Law of the PRC was adopted by the Standing Committee of the National People's Congress on 31 August 1994 and effective as of 1 September 1995.

123   The Interpretations of the Supreme People's Court on Several Issues Concerning Application of the Arbitration Law of the PRC (Zuigao Renmin Fayuan Guanyu Shiyong Zhonghua Renmin Gongheguo Zhongcai Fa Ruogan Wenti de Jieshi), adopted by the Judicial Committee of the Supreme People's Court on 26 December 2005 and promulgated on 23 August 2006, effective as of 8 September 2006.

124   Including, among others, the Circular of the Supreme People's Court on Conscientiously Implement Arbitration Law and Enforce Arbitral Awards According to Law (Zuigao Renmin Fayuan Guanyu Renzhen Guance Zhongcai Fa Yifa Zhixing Zhongcai Caijue de Tongzhi) issued on 4 October 1995; the Circular of the Supreme People's Court on Several Issues Concerning Implementation of "the Arbitration Law of the PRC" (Zuigao Renmin Fayuan Guanyu Shishi Zhonghua Renmin Gongheguo Zhongcai Fa Jige Wenti de Tongzhi) issued on 26 March 1997; the Reply of the Supreme People's Court on Seversl

Before the promulgation of the 1994 Arbitration Law, the 1991 Civil Procedure Law established procedural principles governing enforcement of arbitral awards in general[125] and the arbitration of disputes involving foreign parties in particular,[126] while the 1986 GPCL provided for principles concerning the way in which civil acts are altered or rescinded by arbitration organizations.[127] There were also some other judicial guidelines from the Supreme People's Court before 1994 concerning matters related to arbitration.[128]

CIETAC was established in April 1956 as an arbitration agency of the China Council for the Promotion of International Trade to deal with disputes involving foreign parties in foreign trade and investment.[129] Since its establishment CIETAC has changed its name twice to reflect its changing face and expansion of the scope of jurisdiction.[130] The arbitration rules of CIETAC have been amended throughout the years and the current rules are the 2005 Arbitration Rules of CIETAC.[131] In addition to the general rules, CIETAC adopted its Financial Dispute Arbitration Rules in 2003, which apply to financial disputes including disputes involving securities.[132]

Issues Concerning Determination of Validity of Arbitration Agreement (Zuigao Renmin Fayuan Guanyu Queren Zhongcai Xieyi Xiaoli Jige Wenti de Pifu), adopted by the Judicial Committee of the Supreme People's Court on 21 October 1998 and effective as of 5 November 1998.

125   In accordance with Article 217 of the 1991 Civil Procedure Law, a party may apply to the people's court for enforcement of an arbitral award; the people's court shall enforce it or decide, based upon the evidence adduced by the other party, not enforce it if there exists one of the circumstances listed under Article 217, such as there is an error in application of law.

126   Chapter 28 of the 1991 Civil Procedure Law deals specifically with arbitration involving foreign parties, including Articles 257–261.

127   In accordance with Article 59 of the 1986 GPCL, a party can request an arbitration organization to alter or rescind a civil act if the act is obviously unfair or is performed by an actor who seriously misunderstood the content of the act.

128   For example, the Reply of the Supreme People's Court on Which Local Court Should an Application for Enforcement of Arbitral Awards Be Put Forward (Zuigao Renmin Fayuan Guanyu Shenqing Zhixing Zhongcai Caijue Ying Xiang Hedi Fayuan Tichu de Pifu), issued on 17 January 1985.

129   *See* www.cietac.org.cn. Two sub-commissions were created in Shenzhen (1984) and Shanghai (1989) (www.cietac-sh.org). Shenzhen commission has now been renamed as CIETAC South China, effective from June 18, 2004 (www.sccietac.org).

130   Formerly known as the Foreign Trade Arbitration Commission, CIETAC changed its name to the Foreign Economic and Trade Arbitration Commission in 1980, and then change to current name in 1988. Since 2000, CIETAC is also known as the Arbitration Court of the China Chamber of International Commerce.

131   The Arbitration Rules of CIETAC was amended in 1988, 1994, 1995, 1998, 2000, and 2005. The 2005 Arbitration Rules of CIETAC was adopted by the China Council for the Promotion of International Trade and China Chamber of International Commerce on 11 January 2005 and effective as from 1 May 2005.

132   The Financial Disputes Arbitration Rules of CIETAC was adopted by the China Council for the Promotion of International Trade and China Chamber of International Commerce on 4 April 2003 and effective as from 8 May 2003, as amended 17 March and effective as from 1 May 2005.

Apart from CIETAC, arbitration organizations have been established in provinces and cities all over the country in accordance with the 1994 Arbitration Law and relevant administrative regulations, dealing primarily with disputes involving domestic parties.[133]

Arbitration was employed as a means to resolve securities disputes in the early years of China's securities market.[134] The 1993 Provisional Regulations on the Administration of Issuing and Trading of Shares, the main piece of regulation of the stock market in the early years, stipulated that parties in a dispute related to issuing and trading of shares may apply to arbitration tribunals for mediation and arbitration in accordance with provisions of their agreements.[135] Regarding the disputes between securities firms or between securities firms and stock exchanges arising from the issuing and trading of shares, the 1993 Provisional Regulations on the Administration of Issuing and Trading of Shares requires such disputes be mediated or arbitrated by the arbitration organization set up upon an approval of the State Council Securities Commission (SCSC) or designated by the SCSC.[136]

In accordance with this provision of the 1993 Provisional Regulations on the Administration of Issuing and Trading of Shares, in 1994 the SCSC designated CIETAC as the arbitration tribunal for disputes between securities firms or between securities firms and stock exchanges.[137] At the time of this designation, the Securities Law was under draft. A Securities Arbitration Commission was proposed by the 1993 Draft of the Securities Law to be set up within the Securities Association of China, dealing with disputes between securities firms and between securities firms and their clients, but this proposal was removed from the 1994 Draft of the Securities Law.[138] Both the 1998 Securities Law and the 2005 Securities Law have no provisions on the establishment of a specialist securities dispute arbitration tribunal.

Securities disputes between securities firms or between securities firms and stock exchanges that were arbitrated by CIETAC constituted a small portion of the cases

---

133　In accordance with Article 79 of the 1994 Arbitration Law, the arbitration organizations established before the implementation of the 1994 Arbitration Law were required to reorganize in accordance with the provisions of the 1994 Arbitration Law. To ensure a smooth transition, the General Office of the State Council issued in 1996 Circular on Several Issues Which Need to Be Made Clear in Implementation of the Arbitration Law of the PRC, which addressed a number of issues including transition arrangements between old arbitration organizations and reorganized arbitration organizations.

134　*See* Zhu Sanzhu, *Securities Regulation in China*, pp. 98–102, "Dispute Resolution", *supra* note 62.

135　Article 79 of the 1993 Provisional Regulations on the Administration of Issuing and Trading of Shares.

136　*Id.* art. 80.

137　The Notice of the SCSC on Designation of CIETAC as Arbitration Organization for Securities Disputes (Guowuyuan Zhengquan Weiyuanhui Guanyu Zhiding Zhongguo Guoji Jingji Maoyi Zhongcai Weiyuanhui Wei Zhengquan Zhengyi Zhongcai Jigou de Tongzhi), issued on and effective as of 26 August 1994.

138　*See* Zhu Sanzhu, *Securities Regulation in China*, pp. 69–70, *supra* note 62.

dealt with by CIETAC.[139] Like other kinds of disputes, securities disputes between securities firms or between securities firms and stock exchanges would follow the procedures set out by the Arbitration Rules of CIETAC, effective at the time when such a case came to CIETAC. In a case involving government bond repurchase dispute,[140] for example, the procedure followed was the 1998 Arbitration Rules of CIETAC. Briefly speaking, CIETAC examined the issue of jurisdiction; a panel was formed with three arbitrators who were selected from a list of arbitrators specializing in securities law; both parties presented their case by their representative; the panel then delivered their final decision, giving the facts of the case, opinions of the panel and final ruling.[141] Substantive points of law and regulations applied by the panel were no different from those applied by the people's court in a similar government bond dispute case.[142] After the application of the Financial Disputes Arbitration Rules of CIETAC in 2003, the securities disputes, together with other types of financial disputes, are subject primarily to the procedures set out in the current 2005 Financial Disputes Arbitration Rules of CIETAC.[143]

Following the enactment of the 1994 Arbitration Law, the regulatory arrangement that the disputes between securities firms or between securities firms and stock exchanges were required to be mediated or arbitrated by CIETAC was inconsistent with the provisions of the 1994 Arbitration Law. On one hand, the 1994 Arbitration Law provides that both parties should be willing to adopt the method of arbitration to resolve disputes and should reach an arbitration agreement;[144] if there was no arbitration agreement and one party applies for arbitration, the arbitration organization shall not accept the case;[145] if parties reach an arbitration agreement and one party initiates a suit in the people's court, the people's court shall not accept the

---

139   This is shown, for example, by *The Selection of China International Economic and Trade Arbitration Awards (1995–2002) (Financial, Real Estate and Other Disputes Volume) (Zhongguo Guoji Jingji Maoyi Zhongcai Caijueshu Xuanbian (1995–2002) (Jinrong, Fangdichan Ji Qita Zhengyi Juan)*, compiled by CIETAC. (Beijing: Law Publishing House, 2003). The selection includes 176 typical cases selected among the cases dealt with by CIETAC during 1995–2002, which are divided into three volumes: International Investment Disputes Volume, Sale of Goods Disputes Volume and Financial, Real Estate and Other Disputes Volume. *See* Preface of the selection.

140   Between *Applicant China XX Bank and Respondent XX Securities Co. Ltd.*, *see* the Arbitral Award (8 November 2001) in *The Selection of China International Economic and Trade Arbitration Awards (1995–2002) (Financial, Real Estate and Other Disputes Volume)*, pp. 404–415. *Id.*

141   *Id.*

142   *See* generally Chapter 4, "The Securities Repurchase Market".

143   *Supra* note 132. In accordance with Article 3 of the 2005 Financial Disputes Arbitration Rules of CIETAC, parties in a financial dispute case can agree to be subject to the Financial Disputes Arbitration Rules; if there is no agreement, the general arbitration rules of CIETAC shall apply.

144   Article 4 of the 1994 Arbitration Law.

145   *Id.*

case except if the arbitration agreement is invalid;[146] and the arbitration organization should be chosen by the agreement of the parties.[147]

On the other hand, the regulatory arrangement required that disputes between securities firms and between securities firms and stock exchanges related to the issuing and trading of shares must adopt the method of arbitration for resolution;[148] an arbitration clause for dispute resolution shall be included in contracts concluded between securities firms or between securities firms and stock exchanges in relation to share issuing and trading;[149] CIETAC shall be the arbitration tribunal for such disputes, as designated by the SCSC.[150] A question was subsequently raised whether parties may bring a suit to the people's court if there was no arbitration agreement or the arbitration agreement was invalid between securities firms or between securities firms and stock exchanges. In 1996, the Supreme People's Court clarified this question in a reply to the Shanghai High People's Court.[151] In accordance with Articles 4 and 5 of the 1994 Arbitration Law,[152] the Supreme People's Court confirmed that the people's court may accept and deal with the disputes related to the share issuing and trading between securities firms or between securities firms and stock exchanges if there was no arbitration agreement between the parties or the agreement was invalid.[153] The clarification by the Supreme People's Court effectively brought the regulatory arrangement in line with the principles of the 1994 Arbitration Law.

In 2004, the Legal Affair Office of the State Council and the CSRC jointly issued a circular on the arbitration of securities and futures contractual disputes (hereinafter the Securities and Futures Disputes Arbitration Circular).[154] The Securities and Futures Disputes Arbitration Circular, a joint statement of the two government legal and regulatory departments, is an important promotion of arbitration in securities contractual dispute resolution, with an aim to make full use of special advantages of arbitration, such as expedition, flexibility, low cost and closed hearing.[155] Two

---

146   *Id.* art. 5.

147   *Id.* art. 6.

148   Point 1 of the Circular on the Issue of Arbitration Agreement for Securities Agreement (Guanyu Zhengquan Zhengyi Zhongcai Xieyi Wenti de Tongzhi), issued by the CSRC on 11 October 1994.

149   *Id.*

150   *Id.* Point 2.

151   The Reply of the Supreme People's Court to the Shanghai High People's Court on Whether the People's Court Can Accept and Deal With Disputes Arising from Issuing or Trading of Shares between Securities Firms and between Securities Firms and Stock Exchanges (Zuigao Renmin Fayuan Guanyu Zhengquan Jingying Jigou Zhijian Yiji Zhengquan Jingying Jigou Yu Zhengquan Jiaoyichangsuo Zhijian Yin Gupiao Faxing Huozhe Jiaoyi Yingqi de Zhengyi Renmin Fayuan Nengfou Shouli Gei Shanghai Shi Gaoji Renmin Fayuan de Fuhan), issued on 8 December 1996.

152   *Supra* notes 144, 145 and 146.

153   *Supra* note 151.

154   The Circular on to Do Well in Accordance With Law the Work of Arbitration of Securities and Futures Contract Disputes (Guanyu Yifa Zuohao Zhengquan, Qihuo Hetong Jiufen Zhongcai Gongzuo de Tongzhi), issued on 18 January 2004.

155   *Id.*

issues of importance among those addressed by the Securities and Futures Disputes Arbitration Circular are the scope of arbitration of securities and futures contractual disputes and the arbitration clause in securities and futures contracts.[156] Excepting disputes between listed companies and public investors, a wide range of securities contractual disputes is listed in the Securities and Futures Disputes Arbitration Circular as falling into the scope of arbitration.[157] In accordance with the mandatory requirement as stated in the 1994 Arbitration Law that there must be an arbitration agreement before starting arbitration, the Securities and Futures Disputes Arbitration Circular set 30 June 2004 as a deadline for securities and futures model contracts to have an arbitration clause.[158] Parties have right to choose any arbitration organization for arbitration,[159] not only CIETAC as in early years.

Amendments of Securities Law and Company Law and Future Prospects

The year 2005 witnessed major and important amendments to the 1998 Securities Law and the 1993 Company Law at the same time by the legislature, which is regarded as a "legal construction year for China's securities market."[160] The proposal to amend the 1998 Securities Law was formally listed in its legislative agenda by the Standing Committee of the National People's Congress in June 2003, which was only four years after the 1998 Securities Law came into effect in July 1999.[161] The fact that

---

156   Other issues addressed include the appointment of securities and futures professionals as arbitrators, the work of securities and futures contractual dispute arbitration in accordance of law, and the guidance and supervision of the arbitration of securities and futures contractual disputes. *Id.*

157   Including (1) disputes between securities issuers and securities companies or between securities companies arising from securities issuing and underwriting, (2) disputes between securities companies, futures broker firms, securities investment consultancy organizations, futures investment consultancy organizations and their clients arising from providing of services, (3) disputes between fund promoters, fund management companies and fund custodian organizations arising from fund issuing, management and custody, (4) disputes between accountant firms, law firms, asset and credit appraisal organizations and securities issuers, listed companies arising from providing of services, (5) disputes arising from change of shareholding in listed companies, securities companies, futures broker firms and fund management companies, (6) disputes between securities companies, securities investment consultancy organizations, futures investment consultancy organizations, futures broker firms, listed companies, fund management companies, registration and clearance organization and participants of securities and futures market arising from other contracts related to securities and futures trading. *Id.* Point 1.

158   *Id.* Point 2. An arbitration clause is required by some regulations in certain types of contracts. For example, Article 52 of the 2001 Measures on the Administration of Securities Exchanges requires listing agreements to have an arbitration clause.

159   *Id.* Point 2.

160   *See* Junhai Liu, "Innovation of Securities Legal System" ("Zhengquan Falǔ de Zhidu Chuangxin"), *China Finance (Zhongguo Jinrong)*, Issue 22, 2005, pp. 48–50, at p. 50.

161   *See* Legal Department of the CSRC, "Landmark of the Development of Chinese Securities Legal System – Background, Process and Significance of Securities Law Amendments" (Zhongguo Zhengquan Fazhi Fazhan de Lichengbei – "Zhengquanfa" Xiuding

the 1998 Securities Law was subject to major amendments within such a short time shows that there were problems in the 1998 Securities Law on the one hand,[162] and on the other hand there was an urgent need to change the law in the wake of a fast changing securities market in China, referred to by the securities regulator as a "new and transitional market".[163] From the judges' point of view, the 2005 amendments to the 1998 Securities Law, covering 40 percent of the provisions of the old Law,[164] will have a positive impact on securities-related criminal, administrative and civil litigation procedures.[165]

The amendments to the 1993 Company Law complemented the legal framework of securities market under the 2005 Securities Law. Between 1993 and 2005, the 1993 Company Law was amended two times in 1999 and 2004 respectively, but they were minor amendments as compared with the 2005 amendments, which cover many important changes.[166] In relation to the securities law, one of the important 2005 amendments is that the provisions concerning issue of new shares, issue of corporate bonds and listing requirement and procedures for joint stock companies, previously stipulated in the 1993 Company Law, have been moved to the 2005 Securities Law, which is viewed by some scholars as a change which has made company law and securities law well-matched with each other.[167] Another important amendment is the introduction of provisions concerning derivative action in the 2005 Company Law. In accordance with Article 152 of the 2005 Company Law, shareholders may bring a lawsuit directly before the people's court in their own name under certain circumstances for the benefits of the company if the supervisory board or the board

---

de Beijing, Licheng He Yiyi), *China Securities Journal* (*Zhongguo Zhengquan Bao*), 17 November 2005.

162   For discussion of the 1998 Securities Law, *see* Zhu Sanzhu, *Securities Regulation in China*, pp. 207–224; English translation of the 1998 Securities Law, pp. 225–269, *supra* note 62.

163   *See* Legal Department of the CSRC, "Landmark of the Development of Chinese Securities Legal System – Background, Process and Significance of Securities Law Amendments", *supra* note 161.

164   The revised 2005 Securities Law includes 12 chapters and 240 articles, which come from the original 214 articles of the 1998 Securities Law, having added 53 articles, deleted 27 articles, and amended some existing articles. *See* Legal Department of CSRC, "Landmark of the Development of Chinese Securities Legal System – Background, Process and Significance of Securities Law Amendments", *supra* note 161.

165   *See* Shouye Cao, "Major Contents of Revision of Securities Law and Impact on Litigation" (Zhengquan Fa Xiuding de Zhuyao Neirong Yiji Dui Susong de Yingxiang), *China law* (*Zhongguo Falü*), Issue 2, 2006, pp.23–25, at p. 24. (English translation of the article at pp. 81–84). Shouye Cao is a senior judge of the Supreme People's Court.

166   Two articles (art. 67 and art. 229) were amended in 1999 and one article (art.131) in 2004. In contrast, forty-six articles or paragraphs were deleted, forty-one articles or paragraphs were added and 137 articles or paragraphs were amended in 2005; *see* an interview with Professor Zhao Xudong, who was a member of the company law revision team: "Talk by Company Law Revision Expert" (Gongsi Fa Xiugai Zhuanjia Tan), *Legal Daily* (*Fazhi Ribao*), 30 October 2005.

167   *See* Junhai Liu, "Innovation of New Company Law System" (Xin Gongsi Fa de Zhidu Chuangxin), *Legal Daily* (*Fazhi Ribao*), 1 November 2005.

of directors refuse or fail to start a lawsuit as requested by the shareholders.[168] These and other important amendments to the 1993 Company Law, together as a whole with the amendments to the 1998 Securities Law, have consolidated and improved the regulatory framework of listed companies in China's securities market.

Civil Liability and Civil Compensation

One of the weaknesses of the 1998 Securities Law was that an emphasis was given to administrative and criminal penalties while less attention was paid to civil liability and civil compensation.[169] There were far fewer provisions in the 1998 Securities Law on civil liability and civil compensation than on administrative and criminal penalties.[170] Companies or individuals who committed insider trading or market manipulation were subject only to administrative and criminal penalties.[171] Provisions were absent in some other important areas in the 1998 Securities Law concerning civil liability and civil compensation.[172]

---

168   Article 152 states that "Where any director or senior executive of a company is under the circumstances of Article 150 of this Law, in case of a limited liability company, the shareholders, or in case of a joint stock company, the shareholders separately or jointly holding one percent or more of the company's shares for 180 consecutive days may request in writing the supervisory board or the supervisor of the limited liability company having no supervisory board to bring a lawsuit before the people's court; where any supervisor of the company is under the circumstances of Article 150 of this Law, the said shareholders may request in writing the board of directors or the executive director of the limited liability company having no board of directors to bring a lawsuit before the people's court. If the supervisory board or the supervisors of the limited liability company having no supervisory board, or the board of directors or the executive director of the limited liability company having no board of directors, upon its receipt of the shareholders' written request as stipulated in the preceding Paragraph, refuses to raise a lawsuit, or fails to raise a lawsuit within 30 days upon its receipt of such request, or in case of emergency, the company's interests will suffer irreparable damage if no lawsuit is raised immediately, then, the shareholders as stipulated in the preceding Paragraph may, for the benefits of the company, directly bring a lawsuit before the people's court in their own name. Where others infringe the lawful rights and interests of a company and cause loss to the company, the shareholders as stipulated in the Paragraph 1 of this Article may raise a lawsuit in accordance with the preceding two Paragraphs." Article 150 states that "If the directors, supervisors and senior executive of a company violate the laws, administrative regulations or the articles of association of the company in performance of their functions and thus cause loss to the company, they shall be liable for compensation."

169   *See* a brief discussion in Introduction of Chapter 6 "Civil Litigation Arising from False Statements on the Securities Market".

170   Chapter 11 "Legal Responsibilities" consists of thirty-six articles, most of which were concerned with administrative and criminal penalties and only three articles (Articles 192, 202 and 207) were concerned with civil liability and civil compensation; throughout the 1998 Securities Law there was no more than six articles that were concerned with civil liability and civil compensation.

171   No provisions in the 1998 Securities Law gave rise to civil compensatory consequences for insider trading and market manipulation.

172   For example, there was no provision in the 1998 Securities Law concerning civil liability and civil compensation with respect to the activities of securities investment

The 2005 Securities Law has now enlarged the scope of application of civil liability and civil compensation. Companies or individuals who commit insider trading or market manipulation are now subject not only to administrative and criminal penalties but also to civil liability and civil compensation where losses are caused to investors.[173] Securities companies and their staff shall be held liable for compensation if they commit fraud on their clients and losses are caused to them.[174] Where a securities company buys or sells securities or handles other transaction matters in violation of instructions from a client, or handles matters other than transactions in violation of the true expression of intent of a client, which cause losses to the client, the securities company shall be liable for compensation.[175] Securities investment consultancy organizations and their staff shall be held liable for compensation if they engage in a range of activities prescribed in Article 171 of the 2005 Securities Law and cause losses to investors.[176] Apart from these amendments, there are some other amendments which have enlarged the scope of application of civil liability and civil compensation.[177] For those scholars who consider that civil liability and civil compensatory remedy do most, among the forms of legal liabilities, to bring investors into play in the protection of their rights, these amendments are significant amendments for the protection of investors in China's securities market.[178]

Protection of Investors

In addition to the improvement of the law on civil liability and civil compensation, there are important amendments to the 1998 Securities Law that have enhanced the protection of the rights and interests of investors, especially medium and small investors. For the first time, the 2005 Securities Law provides for the establishment of a statutory securities investor protection fund that shall be composed of the funds paid in by securities companies and other funds raised according to law.[179] In June 2005 before the promulgation of the 2005 Securities Law, the CSRC issued the

---

consultancy organizations.

173 Articles 76 and 77 of the 2005 Securities Law.

174 *Id.* art. 79, which prescribes a list of fraudulent activities of securities companies, such as purchasing or selling securities for a client without authorization from the clients, or purchasing or selling securities under the name of a client.

175 *Id.* art. 210.

176 *Id.* art. 171 which prescribes a list of activities that securities investment consultancy organizations may not engage in, such as to trade shares of a listed company which the securities investment consultancy organization provides services.

177 Including Articles 190, 191 and 214 of the 2005 Securities Law, which give rise to civil liability and civil compensation under certain circumstances of underwriting or takeover activities. In accordance with Article 190, for example, where a securities company underwrites or acts as an agent in the trading of securities offered publicly without being examined and approved, and has caused losses to the investors, the securities company shall be liable jointly and severally with the issuers.

178 *See* Junhai Liu, "Innovation of Securities Legal System", *supra* note 160 at pp. 48–49.

179 Article 134 of the 2005 Securities Law.

Administrative Measures on the Securities Investor Protection Fund, which set out specific measures for raising, managing and using the securities investor protection fund.[180] On 29 September 2005, the China Securities Investor Protection Fund Co. Ltd. was launched, which marked an important step in the improvement of investor protection in China's securities market.[181]

Protection of transaction clearing funds (*jiaoyi jiesuan zijin*) of clients of a securities company is another focus of the 2005 Securities Law to address the widespread problem of misuse of clients' money by securities companies. Article 139 of the 2005 Securities Law requires that such transaction clearing funds be deposited with a commercial bank under separate accounts in the names of each client; no securities company may take the clients' transaction clearing funds and securities as their own property; where a securities company is bankrupt or liquidated, the transaction clearing funds and securities of its clients shall not belong to its bankrupt property or liquidated property; no transaction clearing fund and securities of the clients may be sealed up, frozen up, transferred or enforced, other than due to the debts of the clients themselves or other circumstances as stipulated by the law.[182] Compared with Article 132 of the 1998 Securities Law,[183] Article 139 of the 2005 Securities Law has more specific and comprehensive provisions on the transaction clearing funds of clients of a securities company.

Between 1998 and 2005, the CSRC issued a series of regulatory documents setting out regulatory requirements for the management of transaction clearing funds of clients of a securities company.[184] In November 2004, the Supreme People's Court, in consultation with the CSRC, issued the Circular on Relevant Issues Concerning Freeze and Transfer of Securities Transaction Clearing Funds, which clarified certain issues concerning freeze and transfer of securities transaction clearing funds by the people's court in enforcement proceedings.[185] It is made clear, among other

---

180   The Administrative Measures on the Securities Investor Protection Fund (Zhengquan Touzizhe Baohu Jijin Guanli Banfa), issued by the CSRC on June 2005, effective as of 1 July 2005.

181   *See* newspaper interview: "An Important Component Part of Securities Investor Protection System – Answers to the Questions of Correspondence by Senior Member of the China Securities Investor Protection Fund Co. Ltd." ("Touzizhe Baohu Tixi de Zhongyao Zucheng Bufen – Zhongguo Zhengquan Touzizhe Baohu Jijin Youxian Zeren Gongsi Fuzeren Da Jizhe Wen"), *China Securities Journal* (*Zhongguo Zhengquan Bao*), 29 September 2005.

182   Article 139 of the 2005 Securities Law.

183   Article 132 requires that transaction clearing funds of clients be deposited to designated commercial banks under a separate account.

184   The Measures on the Administration of Client Transaction Clearing Funds (Kehu Jiaoyi Jiesuan Zijin Guanli Banfa), issued by the CSRC on 16 May 2001, effective as of 1 January 2002; the Circular of Several Opinions of the CSRC on Implementation of "The Measures on the Administration of Client Transaction Clearing Funds" (Guanyu Zhixing "Kehu Jiaoyi Jiesuan Zijin Guanli Banfa" Ruogan Yijian de Tongzhi), issued on 8 October 2001; the Circular of the CSRC on Further Strengthening Supervision and Regulation of Client Transaction Clearing Funds of Securities Company (Guanyu Jinyibu Jiaqiang Zhengquan Gongsi Kehu Jiaoyi Jiesuan Zijin Jianguan de Tongzhi), issued on 12 October 2004.

185   Circular on Relevant Issues Concerning Freeze and Transfer of Securities Transaction Clearing Funds (Guanyu Dongjie, Kouhua Zhengquan Jiaoyi Jiesuan Zijin Youguan Wenti

clarifications, that the people's court may not freeze and transfer the securities or funds that have entered into the clearing and delivery procedures following completion of a securities transaction.[186] The 2005 Securities Law has confirmed this position, giving priority and protection to the fulfillment of contractual obligation in securities clearing and delivery.[187]

Another important aspect of investor protection that has been enhanced by the 2005 Securities Law and 2005 Company Law is the shareholders' right to protect their rights and interests through civil litigation. The 2002 Code of Corporate Governance for Listed Companies in China[188] states that under the circumstances that the resolutions of shareholders' meetings or the resolutions of the board of directors are in breach of laws and administrative regulations or they infringe on shareholders' legal rights and interests, the shareholders shall have the right to initiate litigation to stop such breach or infringement.[189] The directors, supervisors and mangers of the company shall bear the liability of compensation in cases where they violate laws, administrative regulations or articles of association and cause damages to the company in the course of performance of their duties; shareholders shall have the right to request the company to sue for such compensation in accordance with law.[190]

These standards of corporate governance have now been codified in the 2005 Securities Law and 2005 Company Law. Shareholders have the right to bring an action in the people's court to request court to cancel a resolution;[191] to request

---

de Tongzhi), issued on 9 November 2004. It superseded a similar circular of the Supreme People's Court issued on 2 December 1997: Circular of the Supreme People's Court on the Issues Concerning Freeze and Transfer Clearing Account Funds of Securities or Futures Exchanges, Securities Registration and Settlement Organization, Securities Companies or Futures Firms (Zuigao Renmin Fayuan Guanyu Dongjie, Huabo Zhengquan Huo Qihuo Jiaoyisuo, Zhengquan Dengji Jiesuan Jigou, Zhengquan Jingying Huo Qihuo Jingji Jigou Qingsuan Zhanghu Zijin Deng Wenti de Tongzhi).

186 *Id.* Point 4 of the 2004 Circular on Relevant Issues Concerning Freeze and Transfer of Securities Transaction Clearing Funds.

187 Article 167 stipulates that no one may, before the deliver is completed, use the securities, funds and security used for delivery. Article 168 stipulates that the clearing funds and securities of various kinds collected by securities registration and settlement organization according to their business rules must be deposited in designated clearing and delivery accounts, and may only be used for the clearing and delivery following completion of a securities transaction according to the business rules, and shall not be subject to any enforcement.

188 The Code of Corporate Governance for Listed Companies in China (Shangshi Gongsi Zhili Zhunze), issued jointly by the CSRC and the State Economic and Trade Commission on, and effective as of, 7 January 2002.

189 *Id.* art. 4.

190 *Id.*

191 Article 22 of the 2005 Company Law provides that shareholders have the right to bring an action in the people's court to request court to cancel a resolution if the resolution is reached in violation of law, administrative regulations or articles of association, or the content of the resolution is in violation of the articles of association.

court to order the company allow inspection of the accounts of the company;[192] to request court to dissolve the company;[193] to initiate litigation if the shareholder and the company cannot reach an agreement upon purchase of shareholding of the shareholder;[194] to request the company to sue for compensation where the directors, supervisors and managers of the company violate laws, administrative regulations or articles of association and cause damages to the company in the course of performance of their duties, or to sue directly in their own name for the interests of the company;[195] to sue for compensation where the directors and managers of the company violate laws, administrative regulations or articles of association and the interests of the shareholders are harmed;[196] and to sue in their own name for the interests of the company where the board of directors of a listed company fails to reclaim the profits gained through trading of the company share in violation of six month restriction by the directors, supervisors, managers and the shareholders who hold over 5% of shareholding.[197] The combined effect of the 2005 Securities Law and the 2005 Company Law means that shareholders of listed companies have much improved protection in terms of their right to take a legal action in the people's court.[198]

Future Development of the Securities Market

The 1998 Securities Law, the first securities law adopted in the PRC, made important contributions to the legal and regulatory framework of China's securities market. But on the other hand, as China's securities market was moving forward, the 1998 Securities Law became incompatible with a need of further market development, and in some aspects, the restrictive provisions of the law became a restraint of the market development.[199] In response to the call for changes, the 2005 Securities Law has made

---

192   Article 34 of the 2005 Company Law provides that shareholder have the right to request court to order the company all inspection of the accounts of the company if the company refuses the inspection request of the shareholder without reason.

193   Article 183 of the 2005 Company Law provides that shareholders have the right to request court to dissolve a company where the company has serious difficulties and continuous existence of the company will cause major loss to the shareholders.

194   Article 75 of the 2005 Company Law provides that shareholders have the right to initiate litigation if a shareholder and the company cannot reach an agreement upon purchase of shareholding of the shareholder who votes against the resolution of the company to, for example, merge, divide or transfer its substantial assets.

195   Article 152 of the 2005 Company Law, *supra* note 168.

196   *Id.* art. 153.

197   Article 47 of the 2005 Securities Law.

198   For a brief assessment of the 2005 Securities Law and the 2005 Company Law, *see* Yang Tiecheng et al., "Steady as She Goes – China's New Securities Law", *China Law and Practice*, December 2005/January 2006, pp. 16–17; Craig Anderson and Bingna Guo, "Corporate Governance under the New Company Law (Part 1): Fiduciary Duties and Minority Shareholder Protection", *China Law and Practice*, April 2006, pp. 17–24 and "(Part 2): Shareholder Lawsuits and Enforcement", *China Law and Practice*, May 2006, pp. 15–22.

199   *See* Legal Department of the CSRC, "Landmark of the Development of Chinese Securities Legal System – Background, Process and Significance of Securities Law

important breakthroughs in five areas. First, securities business may be blended with banking business, trust business, and insurance business and securities companies with banks, trust companies and insurance companies.[200] Second, securities trading will include not only spot trading but also trading of derivative products.[201] Third, the funds allowed to enter into the stock market shall be broadened, which may include funds from banks which has been banned since June 1997.[202] Fourth, restrictions are lifted to allow state-owned enterprises to engage in securities trading.[203] Fifth, restrictions are lifted to allow securities companies to provide finance to their clients in securities trading.[204] It is expected that these changes will have profound impacts on the future development of China's securities market. In relation to these changes, new types of civil securities disputes or new issues may emerge in the process of future development of China's securities market.

The 2005 Securities Law has also changed the way the listing of securities is regulated. In the past, applications for the listing and trading of securities had to go to the CSRC for examination and approval. The 2005 Securities Law has now conferred the approval power to stock exchanges.[205] Applicant companies shall submit their applications directly to the stock exchanges for examination and approval, and the two parties shall sign a listing agreement after the stock exchange has examined and approved the application.[206] One of the implications of this change is that the application for the listing and trading of securities has been changed from an administrative relationship between the applicant and the CSRC, as a government regulator, to a civil relationship between the stock exchange and the applicant. Where an applicant company challenges the decision of the stock exchange who disapproves

---

Amendments", *supra* note 161.

200　Article 6 of the 2005 Securities Law states that "except otherwise provided by the State, securities business shall be engaged in and administered as a business separate from banking business, trust business and insurance business, and securities companies shall be established separately from banks, trust companies and insurance companies."

201　*Id.* art. 42, which states that "securities trading shall take the form of spot transaction or other forms stipulated by the State Council."

202　*Id.* art. 81, which states that "the channels for the funds entering into the stock market shall be broadened according to law, and the flow of funds into the stock market against regulations shall be prohibited." *See* also Circular of the PBOC on Prohibition of Banking Funds from Flowing into Stock Market in Violation of Regulation (Zhongguo Renmin Yinhang Guanyu Jinzhi Yinhang Zijin Weigui Liuru Gupiao Shichang de Tongzhi), issued by the PBOC on 6 June 1997.

203　*Id.* art. 83, which states that "state-owned enterprises and enterprises where state-owned assets constitute a controlling interest, when purchasing or selling shares listed for trading, must abide by the relevant provisions of the State."

204　*Id.* art. 142, which states that "provision of funds or securities by a securities company to their clients for purchasing or selling of securities shall follow the provisions of the State Council and subject to approval by the securities regulatory authority under the State Council."

205　Article 48 of the 2005 Securities Law.

206　*Id.*

of the company's application for listing and trading of its shares, the matter should be dealt with as a civil relationship, rather than an administrative relationship.[207]

In amending Article 168 of the 1998 Securities Law,[208] the 2005 Securities Law has strengthened the investigative responsibility of the CSRC with a wide range of quasi-judicial powers in the enforcement of securities law.[209] The CSRC has power, among others, to conduct an on-site inspection on securities issuers, listed companies, securities companies and other securities institutions;[210] to enter the site where an illegal act is committed to investigate and collect evidence;[211] to inspect and make copies of the materials, such as registration of property right and communication records connected with the event under investigation;[212] to freeze or seal up related property, such as illegal capital or securities that is evidenced to have been or likely to be transferred or concealed, or when the key evidence has been or is likely to be concealed, forged or destroyed;[213] to restrict the trading of securities of the parties connected with the event in the investigation of major securities violations, such as the manipulation of securities market and insider dealing.[214] From judges' point of view, the number of securities administrative litigation is likely to increase in connection with the exercise of investigation powers by regulators.[215]

Financial Futures Market and Futures Law

Following the promulgation of the 2005 Securities Law which lay down the statutory basis for the development of financial futures market in China,[216] China Financial Futures Exchange (CFFEX) was formally established in Shanghai on 8 September 2006.[217] It is a significant development given the fact that the experiment of commodity and financial futures markets in China since late 1980s went through

---

207 *See* Shouye Cao, "Major Contents of Revision of Securities Law and Impact on Litigation", *supra* note 165 at p. 25.

208 Article 168 prescribed a list of measures that could be taken by the CRSC in the investigation and collection of evidence relating to violation of securities law and regulations.

209 Article 180 of the 2005 Securities Law, which has added and changed the list of measures prescribed by Article 168 of the 1998 Securities Law. An important change, for example, has been made to the effect that the CRSC can freeze or seal up capital, securities or evidence with an approval from heads of the CSRC instead of an approval from court, as previously required by Article 168 of the 1998 Securities Law.

210 Article 180 (1) of the 2005 Securities Law.

211 *Id.* art. 180 (2).

212 *Id.* art. 180 (4).

213 *Id.* art. 180 (6).

214 *Id.* art. 180 (7).

215 *See* Shouye Cao, "Major Contents of Revision of Securities Law and Impact on Litigation", *supra* note 165 at pp. 24–25.

216 *Supra* note 201.

217 China Financial Futures Exchange (Zhongguo Jinrong Qihuo Jiaoyisuo) is launched jointly by five exchanges, namely, Shanghai Futures Exchange, Zhengzhou Commodity Exchange, Dalian Commodity Exchange, Shanghai Stock Exchange and Shenzhen Stock Exchange. *See* www.cffex.com.cn.

a tortuous passage and the crackdown campaign embarked upon by the government from 1993 to 1999 led to a substantial reduction of number of futures exchanges, cancellation of certain futures products, suspension of offshore futures trading and closure of government bond futures market.[218] With the introduction of financial futures products[219] and the development of financial futures trading, CFFEX could become an important and integrated marketplace alongside with Shanghai and Shenzhen stock exchanges and three commodity futures exchanges.[220]

An issue which needs to be considered in this context is whether there should be a separate Futures Law alongside the 2005 Securities Law and the 2003 Securities Investment Fund Law or if the regulation of the financial futures market should be left to the 2005 Securities Law and relevant administrative regulations. In the early 1990s, the work of drafting the Futures Law was suspended in the midst of the government's crackdown campaign.[221] Later, in 1999, the State Council promulgated the Provisional Regulations on the Administration of Futures Trading,[222] which was supplemented by four implementing rules issued by the CSRC.[223] To guide the people's courts in their dealing with futures dispute cases, the Supreme People's Court twice issued guidelines, in 1995 and 2003 respectively.[224] All these regulatory and judicial rules have contributed to the establishment of the regulation of futures trading. As an important judicial guideline for the resolution of futures disputes, the 2003 SPC Futures Judicial Provisions represents a unified understanding and approach among the people's courts, the regulators and the futures business on major civil law issued concerning futures market and disputes.[225] Some judges, scholars and regulators advocate that a comprehensive Futures Law must be promulgated if China develops a market in financial futures products, such as foreign exchange futures and share index futures.[226] Given that the financial futures market in China is expected to develop substantially in future, the promulgation of the Futures Law seems a sensible step to provide for uniform principles and rules for the regulation and development of China's financial futures market and for the resolution of the disputes in the financial futures market.

---

218   *See* Chapter 5, "Commodity and Financial Futures Markets", especially the sections "Introduction", "Financial Futures Market" and "Summary".

219   Consultation has been conducted by the CFFEX regarding introduction of Shanghai and Shenzhen 300 index futures contracts, *see* www.cffex.com.cn. *See* also www.csindex. com.cn, the website of China Securities Index Co. Ltd., a company established in August 2005 to develop index products and provide related services.

220   Zhengzhou Commodity Exchange, Dalian Commodity Exchange and Shanghai Futures Exchange. *See* Chapter 5.

221   *See* footnote 4 of Chapter 5 and accompanying text.

222   *See* footnote 19 of Chapter 5 and accompanying text.

223   *See* footnotes 20, 21, 22, 23 and 24 of Chapter 5 and accompanying text.

224   *See* footnotes 30 and 35 of Chapter 5 and accompanying text.

225   *See* footnote 36 of Chapter 5 and accompanying text.

226   *See* Wu Qingbao and Jiang Xiangyang (eds), *Civil Liabilities of Futures Trading* (*Qihuo Jiaoyi Minshi Zeren*) (Beijing: China Legal System Publishing House, 2003), Preface, p. 2.

Summary

The resolution by the people's courts or through mediation and arbitration of the securities disputes of various kinds in share issuing and trading market, government and enterprise bond market, securities repurchase market, and commodity and financial futures markets has led to the development of legal, regulatory and judicial rules and procedures for securities dispute resolution in China. In light of the examination and discussion in the previous chapters of the different types of securities disputes in each securities market and their resolution, this chapter attempts to offer an overall assessment of the development of securities dispute resolution in the past two decades in China.

In contrast to the early stages of development in the late 1980s and early 1990s, when there were rather limited legal, regulatory and judicial rules and procedures available for the people's courts to apply to the securities disputes that had begun to come before them, a system of law, regulations and judicial interpretations and guidelines for securities dispute resolution has been built up and has been gradually improved. Securities Law, Securities Investment Fund Law and Company Law on one hand and a group of judicial interpretations and guidelines on the other hand have been developed on the basis of China's general legal, regulatory and judicial framework. The judicial interpretations and guidelines from the Supreme People's Court that have direct application to the resolution of securities disputes have facilitated the process of securities dispute resolution by the people's courts. Further reform and improvement arc necessary in areas such as joint action procedures and the role played by the judicial committee of the people's court.[227]

Arbitration was employed as a means to resolve securities disputes in the early years of China's securities market. CIETAC was designated in 1994 as the arbitration tribunal for the disputes between securities firms or between securities firms and stock exchanges.[228] In 2003, CIETACT adopted Financial Dispute Arbitration Rules, which specifically apply to financial disputes, including securities disputes.[229] The 2004 Securities and Futures Disputes Arbitration Circular, issued jointly by the Legal Affairs Office of the State Council and the CSRC, set out provisions for the resolution of securities and futures contractual disputes through arbitration.[230] Similar development occurred in mediation. One task highlighted by the fourth general meeting of the SAC, for example, is to work on the mediation procedures of the SAC.[231] Judicial mediation by the people's court during a civil proceeding, an integrated part of civil procedural rules, has the benefit of efficiency in that a full litigation process has been replaced by a mediation process, and thus the people's courts close a securities dispute case in a relatively efficient and time-saving manner. But a key issue is to ensure that the voluntary principle set out in the 1991 Civil

---

227   *See* above sections "Reform on Joint Action and its Limitation" and "Judicial Committee of the People's Court".

228   *Supra* note 137.

229   *Supra* note 132.

230   *Supra* notes 154, 155, 156, 157, 158, 159 and accompanying text.

231   *Supra* note 116.

Procedure Law is adhered to by the people's courts. Recent developments suggest that a future trend in securities dispute resolution in China is to encourage and facilitate more securities disputes to be resolved through mediation and arbitration.

The year 2005, described by some scholars as a "legal construction year for China's securities market",[232] witnessed major and important amendments to the 1998 Securities Law and the 1993 Company Law at the same time. The amendments, which covered a substantial portion of the provisions in both old securities law and company law, have brought about many important changes. The civil liability and civil compensation has been improved;[233] the protection of investors has been enhanced;[234] some important changes have been made for the future development of China's securities market;[235] and the amendments have paved way for the development of a financial futures market in China.[236] In general, the combined effect of the 2005 Securities Law and the 2005 Company Law will have a positive impact on the future development of securities disputes resolution in China. Much work on further implementing administrative regulations and detailed judicial interpretations and guidelines need to be done in order to bring these changes brought about by the amendments into practice.

The future development of securities dispute resolution in China is, to a certain extent, inevitably going to be influenced by and dependant upon the evolution of China's overall administrative, economic, legal, social and political system. In the past, the involvement and intervention of administrative authorities and securities regulators in resolving civil securities disputes,[237] the sensitivity and emphasis on the social stability and financial security,[238] and the questionable role played by the judicial committee of the people's court in adjudication of major and complicated securities dispute cases[239] all show that the process of resolution of securities disputes reflects the particular contexts of China's administrative, economic, legal, social and political system. As China's securities market is a new and transitional market that has emerged in the process of China's transformation from a socialist and planned economy to a capitalist market economy, it is not surprising to see that, time and again, the government has started clearing-up campaigns in the securities market, and the process of resolution of securities disputes by the people's court during such campaign periods became predominantly a process in which the people's courts were implementing the government clearing-up policy.[240] In the environment of China's

---

232 *Supra* note 160.

233 *See* above section "Civil Liability and Civil Compensation".

234 *See* above section "Protection of Investors".

235 *See* above section "Future Development of Securities Market".

236 *See* above section "Financial Futures Market and Futures Law".

237 *See* above section "Securities Dispute Resolution in China's Administrative, Economic, Social and Political Contexts".

238 *Id.*

239 *See* above section "Judicial Committee of the People's Court".

240 For example, the people's courts stopped accepting, hearing and enforcing the cases of securities repurchase disputes listed on the national chain of debt clearance, which lasted about eighteen months between 1998 and 2000, *supra* note 46.

WTO membership, the current and future legal and judicial reform programmes [241] are expected to bring about continuous improvements in the system of securities dispute resolution, especially the resolution of disputes involving foreign parties or cross-border issues.

---

241   For example, the judicial reform programs under "The People's Court Second Five-Year Reform Outlines (2004–2008)", *supra* note 43.

Conclusion

The development of China's securities market since the 1980s has been accompanied by an increase in securities disputes of various kinds in share issuing and trading markets, government and enterprise bond markets, the securities repurchase market, and commodity and financial futures markets. This book examines different types of securities disputes in each of these securities and futures markets and the way in which these disputes are dealt with. In conclusion, the following summarizes the examination and discussion in previous chapters.

China's securities market is a new market, one which has recently emerged in the process of China's transformation from a socialist and planned economy to a capitalist market economy. Securities dispute resolution by the people's courts or through mediation and arbitration is taking place within China's overall administrative, economic, social, legal and political contexts. Understanding of the process of securities dispute resolution in China has to take into account both the relevant factors of the general system in China and the process of transformation which China is undertaking towards a capitalist market economy without making fundamental changes to the political system.

Resolution by the people's courts or through mediation and arbitration of securities disputes has led to the development of legal, regulatory and judicial rules and procedures which are applicable to the resolution of securities disputes in different securities and futures markets. In contrast to the early stage of the development, in late 1980s and early 1990s, when there were rather limited legal, regulatory and judicial rules and procedures available for the resolution of securities disputes, a system of law, regulations and judicial interpretations and guidelines has been built up in the past two decades for the resolution of securities and futures disputes. The four stages of the development, as outlined in Chapter 7, show that the law, regulations and judicial rules and procedures applicable to securities and futures disputes are becoming more and more comprehensive and specific.

The majority of the cases examined in this study are the cases dealt with by the people's courts of all levels, which covers a wide range of securities disputes, including disputes in sale and purchase of securities, disputes between securities agents and investor clients, disputes involving securities repurchase contracts, disputes in share and bond issuing and trading, disputes involving trading of commodity and financial futures, and disputes arising from false statements made on the securities market. In general, they are either disputes involving securities contracts in one form or another or disputes arising from civil tort of false statements made on the securities market. These disputes are examined in their respective securities and futures market and they reflect special features of that particular securities and futures market.

The securities and futures cases are new types of civil and commercial cases not dealt with before by the people's courts. With the emergence of China's securities market, the people's courts – for the first time in their history since 1949 – are faced with the challenges presented by the cases involving securities and futures transactions. While the people's courts endeavored to resolve the disputes fairly and correctly, the efforts of the people's courts were limited in the early years of China's securities market by a lack of experiences of the people's courts in dealing with these new types of disputes and a lack of detailed and operational securities law and regulations and judicial guidelines. Inappropriate, inconsistent, unfair, confusing or wrong judgments of the people's courts were not rare.

Along with the establishment of the Shanghai and Shenzhen stock exchanges in 1990 and 1991 and the creation of the CSRC in 1992, a body of detailed regulatory rules and trading rules were gradually established, which helped the people's courts in their dealing with technical and specific issues involved in securities disputes. Guided by the general principles of the 1986 GPCL and other basic civil and commercial laws, the people's courts have developed approaches to deal with special issues involved in securities disputes, such as dealing with the issue of market risk in securities and futures market in relation to the losses suffered by investors and the way in which these losses are calculated by taking into account of normal market risks; dealing with the issue of obligation of investor principals and taking necessary and appropriate actions to stop further losses under circumstances where their securities investments were affected by acts of securities company agents while the market was falling.

Throughout the years, the Supreme People's Court has established a distinctive body of judicial interpretations and guidelines especially for dealing with different types of securities disputes. These judicial interpretations and guidelines have filled the gap between general principles of civil and commercial law and securities market transactions and between general civil litigation procedural rules and specific civil securities litigation procedural rules. For example, the 2003 SPC Futures Judicial Provisions, an improved set of rules from the Supreme People's Court formulated on the basis of the 1995 SPC Futures Judicial Guidelines and in consultation with government regulators and business circles, represents a unified understanding and approach among the people's courts, the regulators and the futures businesses on major civil law issues concerning the futures market and disputes.

The discussion on the disputes in share issuing and trading market focuses on the disputes between investor principals and securities company agents. The disputes in most of the cases discussed are caused by acts of securities company agents, such as the mistakes made by securities companies and the failure of securities companies to fulfill their duties under certain circumstances. A primary task of the people's courts is to look at the parties' agreements and the circumstances of the case to see whether the agreements are lawful according to the law and regulations, whether the parties have fulfilled their respective contractual obligations, whether there is any breach of contract by the parties and if so, where the fault lies and who is the at-fault party. A line is drawn by the people's courts between losses occurring as a result of normal market risks and losses occurring as a consequence of fault or fraud of securities companies; losses occurring as a result of normal market risks are not recoverable from securities companies. Opportunity to make profits in share trading is recognized by the people's courts, and if such an opportunity is lost because of securities companies, investor principals should be compensated depending upon the circumstances of the case.

A main cause of government and enterprise bond disputes is default by defendants in one way or another. A widespread violation of restrictive and compulsory regulations of government and enterprise bonds, particularly in the early years, coincided with the default problem. Loan transactions were disguised by transfer of government bonds or by issue of enterprise bonds; parties entered into government bond agreements or enterprise bond agreements without license; agreements for issue of enterprise bonds were not approved by government regulators. An agreement would be invalided by the people's courts if the agreement violated the law and regulations. The people's courts would examine whether the agreement in question was valid, whether the parties had license or qualification to engage in the agreement, whether the agreement was a genuine transaction or a sham transaction, and whether the transaction was carried out in the market designated by the government. In this way, the people's courts play a role in enforcing the law and regulations governing government and enterprise bonds.

In the first few years after the emergence of the securities repurchase market in 1991, a vast increase in the volume and amount of market activity was witnessed, accompanied by widespread irregularities and violation of regulations. A main cause of securities repurchase disputes was the default by sellers on their contractual obligation to repurchase securities and repay the buyers at the end of securities repurchase agreements. Lack of proper regulation in the early years of the securities repurchase market contributed to the occurrence of irregularities and violation of regulations, which in turn contributed to an increase of securities repurchase disputes. Examination of the validity of securities repurchase contracts by the people's courts was a first and important stage in the resolution of securities repurchase agreement disputes. The people's courts would examine, among other things, whether there was a real and full amount of collateral securities pledged and whether the term of the contract was within the limit set out by the regulations. Determination of the validity of a repurchase contract forms an important basis on which the people's court decides the liability of the parties.

The experiment in the 1990s of commodity and financial futures trading in China proved to be problematic and the futures market became a "big litigation family" generating a high rate of dispute and litigation. The market was dominated by market manipulation, unauthorized trading by numerous futures firms, irregularities of various kinds and excessive speculation. The people's courts were faced with an increasing number of the disputes arising from commodity and financial futures trading soon after the emergence of the futures market. It took time for the people's courts to understand the nature of the futures market and the issues arising from futures disputes. Wrong judgments and misunderstanding of certain issues were inevitable when there was a lack of regulations and judicial guidelines in early years. With the promulgation of the 1995 SPC Futures Judicial Guidelines, the resolution of futures disputes was improved. The people's courts deal with a range of issues of futures disputes, such as the issue of responsibility of futures exchanges, with an aim of resolving the disputes fairly and correctly and protecting lawful rights and interests of the parties. The 2003 SPC Futures Judicial Provisions provide the people's courts with a more mature and settled guideline for the handling of futures disputes.

Between September 2001 and January 2003, the Supreme People's Court issued three circulars instructing local people's courts on how to deal with civil compensation claims arising from securities market fraud. From January 2002, the designated people's courts formally began to accept and hear civil compensation cases arising from false statements made on the securities market, marking the beginning of civil litigation in the people's courts in relation to these claims. The Rules of the SPC, welcomed by lawyers, academics and investors at large, are a first and important step towards the establishment of a civil litigation and compensation system to address securities fraud cases by the people's court. However, the Rules of the SPC fail to surpass its predecessors and transcend their limitations. The scope of the cases that are accepted and heard by the people's court is limited; the eligibility of shareholder investors for compensation of losses suffered as a result of false statements is limited; shareholder investors are not provided with a helpful and effective procedure by which they may access the court and judicial remedies. Further changes to improve the procedures are still necessary.

Looking at the path of securities dispute resolution experienced in the past years by the people's courts in the wake of emergence of securities market in China, it is clear that the people's courts could not operate beyond the limitation of China's legal, regulatory and judicial system. The procedural barriers existed in the civil litigation arising from the false statements made on the securities market and questionable interpretation power of the Supreme People's Court in this context, as an example, show that the Court's role is limited by China's current legal, regulatory and judicial system. Continuous legal, regulatory and judicial reform, such as the reform projects proposed in the People's Court Second Five-Year Reform Outlines (2004–2008), are necessary to bring about further changes and improvement in the way the law, regulations and judicial interpretations are applied by the people's courts in resolving securities disputes, the way the people's courts approach the issues presented by the cases involving securities transactions, and the way in which securities disputes are resolved by the people's courts.

In a wider social and economic context, the people's courts have to maintain a balance between upholding the legal rights and interests prescribed by the law and regulations and responding to the changing government policies about the development of securities market; between upholding the legitimate demand and means of individuals, companies and organizations to raise capital and punishing illegal financing activities in the securities market; between upholding the principle of freedom of contract to respect legal agreements of parties and supporting the government policy of strict control and scale-down of the securities market in certain periods of time; and between protecting lawful rights and interests of investors and maintaining social and financial stability. The procedural rules for the civil litigation arising from false statements, for example, show a balance being made between the Court, the government, social stability, the protection and development of state-owned listed companies, and the need to protect and compensate all investors who suffer losses as a result of securities fraud.

In the 1980s and 1990s, the share issuing and trading market saw a frenetic involvement of countless individuals, described as "share frenzy" or "stock fever". Investors took to the streets on several occasions and rioted against police for a mere opportunity to obtain subscription forms and engage in the securities market. In late 1990s and 2000s, cases arising from false statements made by public listed companies have a potential involvement in litigation of a large number of shareholders and investors, which could have a significant social impact. Of paramount concern to the government has been the impact of securities disputes on social stability. This concern has been reflected in the thinking of the people's courts and judges and in the handling of securities disputes. The people's courts assumed a dual role of protecting lawful rights and interests of investors while maintaining social stability. The reason for the reluctance of the Supreme People's Court to make local people's courts fully open and available for cases arising from securities false statements was mixed. Apart from the obvious pressure on the resources of the people's courts and other similar reasons, concern about the adverse impact on social stability was argued by critics as an important reason for this reluctance.

In the 1990s, the securities and futures market in China was dominated by speculative activities. After the regulations were relaxed in the late 1980s to allow transfer of government bonds, short selling government bonds became a serious problem, and one which prompted the government to take measures to curb such activities. In the securities repurchase market and commodity and financial futures markets, millions of yuan were involved in disputes, which became a threat to the stability of the securities market and financial system; in the enterprise bond market, funds raised from issues of enterprise bonds were speculated in the stock market or in the property market, which contributed to the cause of default problem. For the government, short selling government bonds and excessive speculation in commodity and financial futures market posed a threat to market stability and the implementation of government economic policies. The government's priority was to maintain stability of financial market and public confidence. In implementing the government's priority and related measures in the resolution of securities disputes, the people's courts played a judicial role in stabilizing the securities market and the financial system.

The crackdown campaign embarked upon by the government from 1993 to 1999 to stop chaotic situations and a blind development of the futures market led to a substantial reduction of number of futures exchanges, cancellation of certain futures products, suspension of offshore futures trading and closure of the government bond futures market. From the point of view of the government, the conditions were not ready for China to go beyond an experiment of a selected number of futures products in a limited number of futures exchanges. A similar clearing-up campaign was launched in securities repurchase market. The 1996 Circular of the State Council, a key government policy document on the clearing-up of debt disputes of securities repurchase agreements, made no distinction between valid and invalid securities repurchase agreements, but the 1996 SPC Securities Repurchase Judicial Guidelines, which facilitated government clearing-up policy, distinguished between a valid and invalid securities repurchase agreement, and thus respected the integrity of the contract lawful made and gave judicial protection to the interests of parties who abide by the law and regulations. This shows that the people's courts balanced between respecting the legal agreements made lawfully by the parties and providing a judicial support for the government clearing-up policy.

In the process of securities dispute resolution, administrative authorities and government regulators may be involved under certain circumstances. The involvement of administrative authorities and regulators, as in the case of securities repurchase agreement disputes, could speed up the process of dispute resolution, and thus save the resources of the people's courts and reduce the adverse impact of the disputes on the securities market and on economy as a whole. But investors who suffer loss may not be able to get remedies through civil litigation because of involvement of administrative authorities and regulators, as in the case of procedures for false statement cases, where an alleged false statement might not be investigated or punished by securities regulators or other administrative authorities, and consequently the case could not be brought up to the people's court. Given that China is in an economic and social transformation, the changing government policies formulated on economic, financial, social or political grounds may prevail at the cost of the legal rights and interests prescribed by law and regulations that should be upheld by the people's courts through judicial process rather than through administrative resolution.

Efficient securities dispute resolution is important in China's securities market. The pattern of securities dispute resolution through mediation and arbitration fit China's situation in that mediation and arbitration are generally and traditionally encouraged in the resolution of civil and commercial disputes. The resolution of securities dispute through mediation and arbitration reduces costs, saves time and has some other advantages over civil securities litigation, and so is beneficial to the development of China's securities market. Mediation and arbitration could also reduce pressures of the people's courts, which is desirable given that people's courts are facing an-ever increasing caseload of civil and commercial disputes. As far as the voluntary principle is adhered to by the people's courts, judicial mediation has a benefit of efficiency as it helps people's courts close securities disputes case in a relatively efficient and time-saving manner. The recent development of securities mediation and arbitration in China, discussed in Chapter 7, suggests that a future trend in securities dispute resolution in China is to encourage more securities and futures disputes to be resolved through mediation and arbitration.

The year 2005 witnessed major and important amendments to the 1998 Securities Law and the 1993 Company Law, which have brought about many important changes, as outlined in Chapter 7, covering, among others, the areas of civil liability and civil compensation, protection of investors, and the future development of China's stock market and financial futures market. The combined effect of the 2005 Securities Law and the 2005 Company Law will have a positive impact on the future development of securities and futures dispute resolution in China. It remains to see how successful these changes are implemented in practice through further detailed implementing administrative regulations and judicial interpretations and guidelines. In post-WTO China, it is expected that more and more foreign securities investments will come into China as China's securities and financial markets further open up to foreign investment. Continuous legal and judicial reform of China's legal system in general and the procedures of securities dispute resolution in particular would help build a better and efficient system of securities dispute resolution in China so that it may face future challenges.

Bibliography

References in English

Anderson, Craig and Guo Bingna, "Corporate Governance under the New Company Law (Part 1): Fiduciary Duties and Minority Shareholder Protection", *China Law & Practice*, April 2006, pp. 17–24 and "(Part 2): Shareholder Lawsuits and Enforcement", *China Law & Practice*, May 2006, pp. 15–22.

Anderson, Daniel M., "Taking Stock in China: Company Disclosure and Information in China's Stock Markets", *Georgetown Law Journal*, Vol. 88, 1999–2000, pp. 1919–1952.

Auspitz, Jack C., Charles C. Comey and Paul W. Boltz, "Asian Issuers Face Rising Class Action Threat", *International Financial Law Review*, Vol. 23, Issue 7, 2004, pp. 23–25.

Chen Alber Hung-yee, *An Introduction to the Legal System of the People's Republic of China* (3rd edition) (Singapore, Malaysia, Hong Kong: Butterworths Asia, 2004).

Epstein, Edward J., "The Evolution of China's General Principles of Civil Law", *American Journal of Comparative Law*, Vol. 34, 1986, pp. 705–713.

Epstein, Edward J., "Codification of Civil Law in the People's Republic of China: Form and Substance in the Reception of Concepts and Elements of Western Private Law", *University of British Columbia Law Review*, Vol. 32, 1998, pp. 153–198.

Fitzgerald, Darren, "CIETAC's New Arbitration Rules: Do the Reforms Go Far Enough?", *Asian Dispute Review*, 2005, pp. 51–53.

Friedman, William I., "One Country, Two Systems: The Inherent Conflict Between China's Communist Politics and Capitalist Securities Market", *Brooklyn Journal of International Law*, Vol. 27, 2001–2002, p. 477.

Fu Tingmei, "Legal Person in China: Essence and Limits", *American Journal of Comparative Law*, Vol. 41, 1993, pp. 261–297.

Green, Stephen, *The Development of China's Stock Market, 1984–2002: Equity Politics and Market Institutions* (London: Routledge, 2004).

Hutchens, Walter, "Private Securities Litigation in China: Material Disclosure about China's Legal System?", *University of Pennsylvania Journal of International Economic Law*, Vol. 24, 2003, p. 599.

Jiang Ping, "Drafting the Uniform Contract Law in China", *Columbia Journal of Asian Law*, Vol. 10, 1996, pp. 245–258.

Jones, William C. (ed.), *Basic Principles of Civil Law in China* (Armonk, New York; London: M.E. Sharpe, 1989).

Lawrence, Susan V., "Shareholder Lawsuits: Ally of the People", *Far Eastern Economic Review*, May 9, 2002, p. 27.

Ling Bing, *Contract Law in China* (Hong Kong: Sweet and Maxwell Asia, 2002).

Lu Guiping, "Private Enforcement of Securities Fraud Law in China: A Critique of the Supreme People's Court 2003 Provisions Concerning Private Securities Litigation", *Pacific Rim Law and Policy Journal*, 2003, p. 781.

Lubman, Stanley (ed.), *China's Legal Reform* (Oxford: Oxford University Press, 1996).

Lubman, Stanley, *Bird in a Cage: Legal Reform in China after Mao* (Stanford: Stanford University Press, 1999).

Moore, John and Nick-Anthony Buford, "In the Ascendancy", *International Financial Law Review*, Vol. 25, Issue 9, 2006, pp. 26–30.

Note, "Class Action Litigation in China", *Harvard Law Review*, Vol. 111, 1997–1998, p. 1523.

Otto, Jan Michiel et al. (eds), *Law-Making in the People's Republic of China* (The Hague, London & Boston: Kluwer Law International, 2000).

Palmer, Michael, "The Revival of Mediation in the People's Republic of China: (2) Judicial Mediation", *Yearbook on Socialist Legal System* 145 (William. E. Butler ed. 1989).

Wang Liming and Xu Chuanxi, "Fundamental Principles of China's Contract Law", *Columbia Journal of Asian Law*, Vol. 13, 1999, pp. 1–34.

Xia Mei, Philip D. Grub and Jian Hai Lin, *The Re-emerging Securities Market in China* (Westport: Ouorum Books, 1992).

Yang Tiecheng et al., "Steady as She Goes – China's New Securities Law", *China Law & Practice*, December 2005/January 2006, pp. 16–17.

Zhu Sanzhu, *Securities Regulation in China* (Ardsley, NY: Transnational Publishers, 2000).

Zhu Sanzhu, "Reforming State Institutions: Privatizing the Lawyers' System", in *Governance in China*, edited by Jude Howell, Chapter 4, pp. 58–76 (New York: Rowman & Littlefield, 2004).

Zhu Sanzhu, "Civil Litigation Arising from False Statements on China's Securities Market," *North Carolina Journal of International Law and Commercial Regulation*, Vol. 31, No. 2, Winter 2005, pp. 377–429.

Zhu Sanzhu, "Implementing China's WTO Commitments in Chinese Financial Services Law", *The China Review*, Vol. 6, No. 2, Fall 2006, pp. 3–33.

Zimmerman, James M. and Diarmuid O'Brien, "CIETAC Financial Dispute Arbitration Rules: Practice and Problems", *Asian Dispute Review*, 2004, pp. 69–70.

References in Chinese

Adjudicated Cases of Guangdong (*Guangdong Shenpan Anli*), edited by the research department of the Guangdong High People's Court (Guangdong: Guangdong People's Publishing House, 1997).

Bai Yan, Fu Jun, "Compensation Liability for the Tort of False Statement" (Xujia Chenshu Qinquan de Peichang Zheren), *Zhongguo Faxue* (2 *China Legal Science*), 2003, at p. 104.

Bin Jiancheng, "Current Status and Development of Government Bond Repurchase Market of Our Country" (Woguo Guozhai Huigou Shichang de Xianzhuang yu Fazhan), *Study on Finance and Business* (*Caimao Yanjiu*), Issue 4, 2002, pp. 81–84.

Cai Xin et al. (eds), *Commentary on Typical Cases and Complement to Legal Deficiency* (*Dianxing Anli Pingshu Ji Falü Loudong Buchong*) (Beijing: The People's Court Publishing House, 2002).

Cao Shouye, "Major Contents of Revision of Securities Law and Impact on Litigation" (Zhengquan Fa Xiuding de Zhuyao Neirong Yiji Dui Susong de Yingxiang), *China Law* (*Zhongguo Falü*), Issue 2, 2006, pp. 23–25, (English translation of the article at pp. 81–84).

Carefully Selected Cases of the People's Courts (*Renmin Fayuan Anli Xuan Jingbianben*), Vol. 1, 2001, edited by China Law Application Research Institute of the Supreme People's Court (Beijing: Xinhua Publishing Press, 2001).

Chu Hongjun and Chen Jingyu, "Study on Several Problems of the System of Judicial Committee – Also on the Reform and Improvement of the System of Judicial Committee" (Shenpan Weiyuanhui Zhidu Ruogan Wenti Yanjiu – Jian Lun Shenpan Weiyuanhui Zhidu de Gaige He Wanshan), pp. 50–54, *Falü Shiyong* (*Application of Law*), No. 10, 2005.

Chu Hongjun and Wang Zhuan, "Adjudication of Cases of Securities Repurchase Contract Disputes" (Zhengquan Huigou Hetong Jiufeng Anjian de Shenli), *People's Judicature* (*Renmin Sifa*), Issue 11, 1996, pp. 9–11.

Cui Zhennan, Ma Mingsheng, "Study on Liabilities of Directors to Shareholders for False Statements" (Xujia Chenshu Zhong Dongshi Dui Gudong Zheren Yanjiu), *Zhongguo Faxue* (2 *China Legal Science*), 2003, at p. 96.

Du Erli and You Jun, "On Several Issues to Which Attention Should Paid in Hearing Securities Repurchase Dispute Cases" (Tan Shenli Zhengquan Huigou Jiufen Anjian Ying Zhuyi de Jige Wenti), *Journal of Liaoning Administrators College of Police and Justice*, Issue 3, 1999, pp. 24–27.

Essential Selection of Adjudicated Cases in China (*Zhongguo Shenpan Anli Yaolan*) (*Civil Adjudicated Case Vol. 2001*), edited by National Judges College and School of Law of the People's University of China (Beijing: China People's University Press, 2002).

Essential Selection of Adjudicated Cases in China (*Zhongguo Shenpan Anli Yaolan*) (*Commercial and Administrative Cases Vol. 2001*), edited by National Judges College and School of Law of the People's University of China (Beijing: China People's University Press, 2002).

First Securities Civil Compensation Case Concluded by Settlement with 800 Yuan Compensation to the Plaintiff (Zhengquan Minshi Peichang Shouqi Jiean Hejie Yuangao Huopei 800 yuan), *Xinhua News Agency*, 15 November 2002, http://www.chinacourt.org.

Fu Weiwei and Zhang Xuliang, "On the Problem and Reform of Current Judicial Mediation System" (Lun Xianxing Fayuan Tiaojie Zhidu de Biduan he Gaige), *Falŭ Shiyong* (*Application of Law*), No. 4, 2000, at p. 12.

Gao Xiqing and Cheng Dagang (eds), *Textbook on Cases of Securities Law* (*Zhengquan Faxue Anli Jiaocheng*) (Beijing: Intellectual Property Publishing House, 2004).

Gao Yan and Yi Pingjun (eds), *Understanding and Application of Securities Law and Case Commentary and Analysis* (*Zhengquan Fa Lijie Shiyong Yu Anli Pingxi*) (Beijing: The People's Court Publishing House, 1996).

Gazette of the Supreme People's Court of the People's Republic of China (*Zhonghua Renmin Gongheguo Zuigao Renmin Fayuan Gongbao*), an official publication of the Supreme People's Court since January 1985.

Guan Shengyin, "Exploration and Improvement on Working Mechanism of the Judicial Committee" (Shenpan Weiyuanhui Gongzuo Jizhi Tansuo Ji Wanshan) *Renmin Sifa* (*People's Judiciary*), No. 10, 2004, pp. 27–30.

Guo Feng, "Determination of Tort of False Statement and Compensation" (Xujia Chenshu Qingquan de Rending ji Peichang), *Zhongguo Faxue* (*China Legal Science*), No. 2, 2003, at p. 96.

Huan Xiding and Xu Qinzhong, "On False Statements in the Securities Law" (Shilun Zhengquanfa Zhong de Xujia Chenshu), *Zhengfa Xuekan* (*Journal of Political Science and Law*), No. 4, 2001, at pp. 22–25.

Interview: "An Important Component Part of Securities Investor Protection System – Answers to the Questions of Correspondence by Senior Member of the China Securities Investor Protection Fund Co. Ltd" (Touzizhe Baohu Tixi de Zhongyao Zucheng Bufen – Zhongguo Zhengquan Touzizhe Baohu Jijin Youxian Zeren Gongsi Fuzeren Da Jizhe Wen), *China Securities Journal* (*Zhongguo Zhengquan Bao*), 29 September 2005.

Jia Wei, "The Commencement of Civil Liability for the Tort on the Securities Market – Explanation and Analysis of 'Several Provisions of the Supreme People's Court on Hearing Civil Compensation Cases Arising from False Statements on the Securities Market'" (Zhengquan Shichang Qinquan Minshi Zeren zhi Faren – Jiexi "Guanyu Shenli Zhengquan Shichang Yin Xujia Chenshu Yinfa de Minshi Peichang Anjian de Ruogan Guiding"), *Falŭ Shiyong* (*Application of Law*), No. 3, 2003, at p. 9.

Jiang Bixin (ed.), *Understanding and Application of "the 2003 Provisions of the Supreme People's Court on Several Issues Concerning Adjudication of Cases of Futures Disputes"* (*"Zuigao Renmin Fayuan Guanyu Shenli Qihuo Jiufen Anjian Ruogan Wenti de Guiding" de Lijie Yu Shiyong*), compiled by the Second Division Court of the Supreme People's Court (Beijing: The People's Court Publishing House, 2003).

Jiao Jinhong, "On 'the Fraud on the Market Theory'" ("Qizha Shichang Lilun" Yanjiu) *Zhongguo Faxue* (*China Legal Science*), Vol. 2, 2003, at p. 114.

Jinan Shareholders Sue Dongfang Dianzi, Claiming Figure Reaches Over 3 Million Yuan (*Jinan Gumin Zhuanggao Dongfang Dianzi, Suopei Jin E Da 300 Yu Wanyuan*), 10 July 2003, http://www.chinacourt.org.

Kang Ming, *A Study of Commercial Arbitration Service* (*Shangshi Zhongcai Fuwu Yanjiu*) (Beijing: Law Publishing House, 2005).

Kong Lin and Ye Jun, Conditions for Acceptance of Civil Compensation Cases Arising from False Statements on the Securities Market (Zhengquan Shichang Yin Xujia Chenshu Yinfa de Minshi Peichang Anjian de Shouli Tiaojian), *Falǔ Shiyong* (4 *Application of Law*), 2003, at pp. 21, 22.

Legal Department of the CSRC, "Landmark of the Development of Chinese Securities Legal System – Background, Process and Significance of Securities Law Amendments" (Zhongguo Zhengquan Fazhi Fazhan de Lichengbei – "Zhengquanfa" Xiuding de Beijing, Licheng He Yiyi), *China Securities Journal* (*Zhongguo Zhengquan Bao*), 17 November 2005.

Li Guoguang, "Deputy President of the Supreme People's Court Li Guoguang Talks in Detail about Judicial Protection for the State Financial Safety" (Gaofa Fuyuanzhang Li Guoguang Xishuo Guojia Jinrong Anquan de Sifa Baozhang), *News Weekly*, 23 July 2002, http://www.ccmt.org.cn (Zhongguo Shewai Sangshi Haishi Shenpan Wang) (China Foreign-Related Commercial and Maritime Trial Website).

Li Guoguang et al. (eds), *A Complete Book of the PRC of Leading Adjudicated Cases – Economic Volume* (*Zhonhua Renmin Gongheguo Dianxing Shenpan Anli Quanshu – Jingjijuan*) (Beijing: China Democracy and Law Publishing House, 1998).

Li Shiping et al., *A Study on Cases Involving Cutting – edge Issues of Securities Law* (*Zhengquanfa Qianyan Wenti Anli Yanjiu*) (Beijing: China Economic Publishing House, 2001).

Liang Tingting et al., *Securities Law Cases and Commentary* (*Zhengquanfa Anli Yu Pingxi*) (Guangzhou: Sun Yet-Sen University Press, 2005).

Liu Jiaxing, *Minshi Susong Jiaocheng* (*Textbook on Civil Litigation*), Beijing Daxue Chubanshe (Beijing University Press, 1982).

Liu Junhai, "Innovation of New Company Law System" (Xin Gongsi Fa de Zhidu Chuangxin), *Legal Daily* (*Fazhi Ribao*), 1 November 2005.

Liu Junhai, "Innovation of Securities Legal System" (Zhengquan Falǔ de Zhidu Chuangxin), *China Finance* (*Zhongguo Jinrong*), Issue 22, 2005, pp. 48–50.

Liu Ping and Yi Shuren, "Securities Repurchase: An Important Trading Tool" (Zhengquan Huigou: Juzu Qingzhong de Jiaoyi Shouduan), *China Lawyer* (*Zhongguo Lǔshi*), Issue 4, 1996, pp. 27–29.

Ma Shiling, *The First Joint Action Case Was Filed, Daqing Lianyi Case Compensation Over Ten Million Yuan* (*Gongtong Susong Diyi An Jian, Daqing Lianyi An Suopei Yu Qianwan*), 11 February 2003, http://www.chinacourt.org.

Ouyang Mingcheng and Zhang Min, "Improving Legal Mechanism for Securities Repurchase Trading" (Zhengquan Huigou Jiaoyi de Falǔ Guizhi Zhi Wanshan), *Modern Legal Science* (*Xiandai Faxue*), Issue 1, 1996, pp. 63–64.

Selection of Analysis of Adjudicated Cases (*Shenpan Anli Xuanxi*), edited by Beijing Haidian District People's Court (Beijing: China Political and Law University Press, 1997).

Selection of China International Economic and Trade Arbitration Awards (1995–2002) (*Financial, Real Estate and Other Disputes Volume*) (*Zhongguo Guoji Jingji Maoyi Zhongcai Caijueshu Xuanbian (1995–2002)* (*Jinrong, Fangdichan Ji Qita Zhengyi Juan*), compiled by the China International Economic and Trade Arbitration Commission (Beijing: Law Publishing House, 2003).

Selection of Financial Dispute Cases Heard by the Supreme People's Court (1996–1998) (Zuigao Renmin Fayuan Shenli de Jinrong Jiufen Anli Xuanbian), compiled by the Economic Division Court of the Supreme People's Court (Beijing: China University of Politics and Law Press, 1999).

Series of Adjudicated Cases of the Supreme People's Court of the People's Republic of China (*Zhonghua Renmin Gongheguo Zuigao Renmin Fayuan Pan'an Daxi*) (*Civil and Commercial Vol. 2001*), Chief Editor Xiao Yang, compiled by the Second Division Court of Civil Court of the Supreme People's Court (Beijing: The People's Court Publishing House, 2003).

Shao Tingjie et al. (eds), *Securities Law* (*Zhengquan Fa*) (Beijing: Law Publishing House, 1999).

Shenyang Intermediate People's Court Hear Jinggang B Share Case, KPMG Branch Office Becomes Defendant (*Shenyang Zhongyuan Shenli Jinggang B Gu An, Bimawei Fenzhi Jigou Cheng Beigao*), 11 February 2003, http://www.chinacourt.org.

Sheng Huanwei and Zhu Chuan, "On Causal Link of Civil Compensation Cases Arising from Securities-related False Statements" (Zhengquan Xujia Chenshu Minshi Peichang Yinguo Guanxi Lun) *Faxue* (*Legal Science*), Vol. 6, 2003, at p. 102.

Song Yixing, "Thoughts on Several Issues of the Litigation System for Civil Compensation Arising from False Statements" (Xujia Chenshu Minshi Peichang Susong Zhidu Ruogan Wenti de Sikao), *Falü Shiyong* (*Application of Law*), Vol. 4, 2003, at p. 9.

ST Hongguang Claim Case Successfully Mediated (ST Hongguang Suopeian Tiaojie Chenggong), *Zhongguo Zhengquan Bao* (*China Securities Daily*), 26 November 2002, p. 1.

ST Jiabao False Statement Case Concluded – 16 Plaintiffs Got Economic Compensation 61,773.66 Yuan (ST Jiabao Xujia Chenshu An Jiean – 16 Wei Yuangao Huode Jingji Peichang Renminbi 61773.66 Yuan) *Zhengquan Ribao* (*Securities Daily*), 28 January 2003, http://www.zqrb.com.cn.

Studies of Judicial Decisions Related to Financial Disputes (*Jinrong Shenpan Anli Yanjiu*) (Vol. 2001), edited by Economic Division Court of Beijing High People's Court (Beijing: Law Publishing House, 2001).

Tu Binhua, "On the Mechanism for Civil Compensation Liabilities for Securities-related False Statements" (Zhengquan Xujia Chenshu Minshi Peichang Zheren Jizhi Lun), *Faxue* (*Legal Science*), Vol. 6, 2003, at p. 96.

Wang Dan, "On the Method for the Calculation of Compensation from Securities-related False Statements" (Zhengquan Xujia Chenshu Peichang Jishuan Fangfa Lun), *Faxue* (*Legal Science*), Vol. 6, 2003, at pp. 103–108.

Weng Xiaobin, "On Reform of Judicial Mediation System" (Lun Fayuan Tiaojie Zhidu Gaige), *Xiandai Faxue* (*Modern Law Science*), Vol. 5, 2000, at p. 66.

Wu Qingbao, *Essential Explanation of Difficult Issues in the Practice of Commercial Adjudication* (*Shangshi Shenpan Shiwu Nandian Jingjie*) (Beijing: The People's Court Publishing House, 2003).

Wu Qingbao and Jiang Xiangyang (eds), *Civil Liabilities of Futures Trading* (*Qihuo Jiaoyi Minshi Zeren*) (Beijing: China Legal System Publishing House, 2003).

Wu Qingbao et al. (eds), *Principles and Precedents of Futures Litigation* (*Qihuo Susong Yuanli Yu Panli*) (Beijing: The People's Court Publishing House, 2005).

Wu Zhipan and Tang Jiemang (eds), *Explanation and Analysis of Typical Cases of Financial Law, 1st Issue* (*Jinrong Fa Dianxing Anli Jiexi, Diyi Ji*) (Beijing: China Finance Publishing House, 2000).

Xi Xiaoming and Jia Wei, "Understanding and Application of 'Several Provisions of the Supreme People's Court on Hearing Civil Compensation Cases Arising from False Statements on the Securities Market'" (Guanyu Shenli Zhengquan Shichang Yin Xujia Chenshu Yinfa de Minshi Peichang Anjian de Ruogan Guiding de Lijie yu Shiyong), *Renmin Sifa* (*People's Judiciary*), No. 2, 2003, at p. 11.

Xiao Yu, *China Government Bond Market* (*Zhongguo Guozhai Shichang*) (Beijing: Social Science Document Publishing House, 1999).

Yang Limao and Chen Chaoyang, "Discussion on Prerequisite Procedure in Securities Tort Litigation" (Zhengquan Qinquan Susong Qianzhi Chengxu de Tantao), http://www.chinacourt.org (*Zhongguo Fayuan Wang*), 25 November 2002.

Yang Wei and Pan Jing, "Li Guoguang: To Work on Adjudication and to Protect Social Stability is the First and Important Task of the People's Court" (Li Guoguang: Zhua Shenpan Bao Wending Shi Fayuan Shouyao Renwu), http://www.chinacourt.org (*Zhongguo Fayuan Wang*), 15 September 2002.

Yin Jie, "On the System of Civil Liability of Securities-related False Statements" (Zhengquan Xujia Chenshu Minshi Zheren Zhidu Lun), *Faxue, Legal Science*, Vol. 6, 2003, at pp. 110–11.

Yinchuan City Intermediate People's Court Formally Accepted Yinguangxia Civil Tort Compensation Case (*Yinchuanshi Zhongyuan Zhengshi Shouli Yinguangxia Minshi Qinquan Peichang An*), 1 August 2002, http://www.chinacourt.org.

Zhang Jinhan (ed.), *Application of Law and Ajudication in Commercial Cases* (Shangshi Anjian Falu Shiyong Yu Shenpan) (Beijing: The People's Publishing House, 2003).

Zhao Xudong (interview), a member of the company law revision team: "Talk by Company Law Revision Expert" (Gongsi Fa Xiugai Zhuanjia Tan), *Legal Daily* (*Fazhi Ribao*), 30 October 2005.

Zhang Yongjian, "On Several Dates Concerning the Tort of False Statement" (Lun Xujia Chenshu Qinquan Xingwei de Jige Shijiandian), *Falü Shiyong* (*Application of Law*), Vol. 4, 2003, at pp. 13–16.

Zhong Futang et al. (eds), *Commentary and Analysis on Futures Trading Dispute Cases* (*Qihuo Jiaoyi Jiufen Anli Pingxi*) (Shanghai: Xuelin Publishing House, 1998).

Laws, Regulations and Judicial Interpretations and Provisions Index

List of Cases Index

Subject Index